HOMICIDE AT ROUGH POINT

HOMICIDE AT ROUGH POINT

Peter Lance

TENACITY MEDIA BOOKS

FIRST EDITION

Library of Congress Cataloging-in-Publication Data has been applied for.

ISBN 978-0-9962855-9-9

Tenacity Media Books
244 Fifth Avenue Suite 2454
New York, NY 10001
212-203-6123
212-591-6029 (fax)
peterlance.com
email: pl@peterlance.com
Book design and cover by
Tom Morine
tommorine@gmail.com
and
Walton Mendelson
walton@12on14.us
Map design by Carlos Cuellar
ccuellarte@aol.com

Cover photograph by Jerry Taylor

Mario Puzo famously began *The Godfather* with Balzac's observation that "Behind every great fortune there is a crime." Few concentrations of American wealth are associated with as many crimes as the tobacco, aluminum and energy fortune inherited by Doris Duke. This is the full, unexpurgated story of one of them.

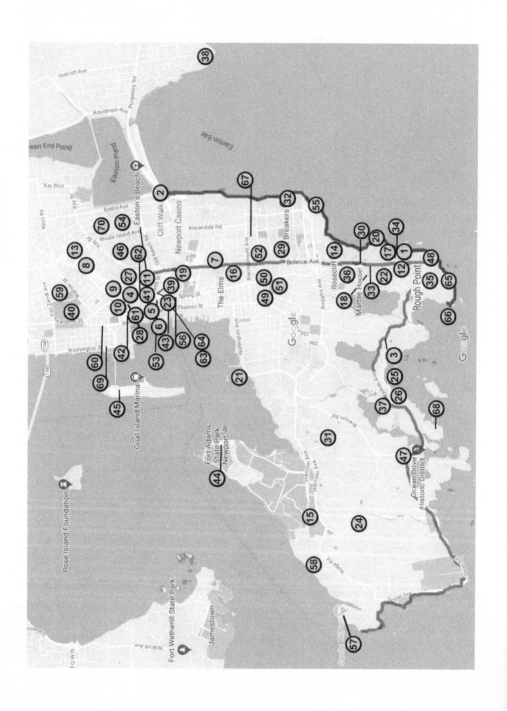

Newport Map: Locations cited in Homicide At Rough Point.

1   **Rough Point:** 680 Bellevue Avenue

2   **Cliff Walk:** Memorial Boulevard to Ledge Road

3   **Ocean Drive:** Ocean Avenue to Castle Hill

4   **Touro Synagogue:** 85 Touro Street

5   **Newport Daily News:** 140 Thames Street (1967-1968)

6   **The Black Pearl:** 10 ½ Bannister's Wharf

7   **De La Salle Academy:** 364 Bellevue Avenue

8   **Cranston-Calvert School:** 15 Cranston Avenue

9   **The Quality Lunch:** 25 Broadway

10   **Newport Police Headquarters (1967-68)**

11   **Newport Reading Room:** 29 Bellevue Avenue

12   **Quatrel/Lorillard Estate:** 673 Bellevue Avenue

13   **Newport Hospital:** 20 Powell Avenue

14   **Rosecliff:** 548 Bellevue Avenue

15   **Hammersmith Farm:** 225 Harrison Avenue

16   **The Elms/Berwind Estate:** 367 Bellevue Avenue

17   **Miramar/Rice Estate:** 646 Bellevue Avenue

18   **The Holmwoods:** 161 Coggeshall Avenue

19   **Newport Casino:** 190 Bellevue Avenue

20   **Clarendon Court:** 626 Bellevue Avenue

21   **Ida Lewis Yacht Club:** 170 Wellington Avenue

22   **Belcourt/Tinney Estate:** 657 Bellevue Avenue

23   **Touro Park:** Bellevue Avenue & Mill Street

24   **Newport Country Club:** 280 Harrison Avenue

25   **Baileys Beach:** 34 Ocean Avenue

26   **The Ledges/Cushing Estate:** 66 Ocean Avenue

27   **Tubley's Spa:** 58 Spring Street (1967)

28   **Superior Courthouse:** 45 Washington Square

29   **Chateau-Sur-Mer:** 474 Bellevue Avenue

30   **Marble House:** 596 Bellevue Avenue

31   **Beacon Hill/Swiss Village:** 152 Harrison Avenue

32   **The Breakers:** 44 Ochre Point Avenue

33   **Beaulieu:** 615 Bellevue Avenue

CONTENTS

INTRODUCTION

Cielo Drive cuts like a beautiful scar along the bottom of a V-shaped canyon in the hills of Bel Air, off of Benedict. In the winter, when the rains come, it's lush and green and that's the way Sharon Tate saw it from 10050 Cielo, the red farmhouse she'd rented with her husband Roman Polanski. As she unpacked the moving boxes on Valentine's Day in 1969, she had no way of knowing that she only had another six months to live.

On the night of August 9th, four hyper-violent members of "The Manson Family" would invade that red house and murder Sharon, along with three of her closest friends. But strangely, half a year earlier, Sharon had a short brush with a *different* killer.

It happened in late February after her younger sister Patti, looked across the canyon at the ominous Spanish-Moorish estate Sharon called "The Haunted House." In their remarkable memoir, *Restless Souls,*[1] Alisa Statmen and Brie Tate wrote that Patti, then eleven years old and curious for a look at the place, hiked down the cul-de-sac and across Cielo Drive. She walked up Bella Drive to number 1436. There she encountered an open gate where two white pillars topped with carriage lamps bore the name of the estate: Falcon Lair.

In 1925 it had been purchased by Rodolfo Alonso Raffaello Pierre Filbert Guglielmi di Valentina d'Antonguolla, otherwise known as Rudolf Valentino. [2] Worshiped by silent film fans as "the great lover," Rudy, as friends knew him, once observed that, "I am merely the canvas on which women paint their dreams." Still, at that time he was Hollywood's reigning king and the 16-room villa that sprawled across eight acres equipped with stables, kennels and servants' quarters, sat atop the hill like a white stucco castle.

In 1953, that estate was bought by Doris Duke, the fabulously wealthy heiress to a fortune amassed by her father from the profits of American Tobacco Company, Alcoa Aluminum, and Duke Power. She was the reigning female scion of the family that endowed Duke University.

TEA & COOKIES

The big black wrought iron gates were open when young Patti wandered inside that day. Suddenly, she heard the caretaker yell out in a loud British accent, "This is private property. What are you *doing* here?" Startled, Patti turned and lost her balance in the gravel driveway, falling and skinning her knee. Just then, as if on cue, a black limousine pulled in. A tinted window rolled down and a tall woman in back lowered her sunglasses and asked who she was.

Once Patti identified herself as the sister of "Sharon," who lived "across the way in the red barn," Doris Duke knew that this wasn't just *any* eleven year old. She was the sister of the hottest young star in Hollywood who was married to one of the hottest young directors. So, in her imperial style, Doris snapped to the caretaker, "Stop being such an *ogre* and bring Patti in so we can clean those scrapes. And get me the Polanskis' phone number."

Later, as Patti recounted in the book, the Duke staff had bandaged her knee and served her tea and cookies when Sharon walked in, "nervously chewing her lower lip" and apologizing to the blond billionairess who, at that moment, was the third richest woman in the world behind Queen Elizabeth II & Queen Juliana of The Netherlands. [3] But Sharon Tate, whose motion picture career was taking off like an Atlas rocket, was royalty herself. Her husband Roman, just coming off the hit film *Rosemary's Baby,* was a kind of cinematic Polish prince. So why was she nervous? What would make her bite her lip in the face of a woman whose caretaker's aggressive warning had caused her little sister to draw blood?

Because Sharon was killed so mercilessly that summer, we'll never know. But one thing is sure. That wasn't the *first* time Sharon Tate had been drawn into Doris Duke's orbit. Nearly two and a half years earlier, one of Sharon's closest friends, designer Eduardo Tirella, had been violently killed after Miss Duke crushed him under a two-ton station wagon and many of his friends suspected that it was murder.

There have been dozens of books chronicling what infamously became known as the "Tate-LaBianca murders;" [4] from Vincent Bugliosi's groundbreaking *Helter Skelter* to Ed Sanders' terrifying Manson bio, *The Family.* The brutal stabbing of Sharon Tate, then eight and a half months pregnant with her son Paul, is a tragic cautionary tale of a young woman of great promise cut down in the prime of life. But the same can be said for Eduardo, whose career as a Hollywood set designer was just beginning to catch fire, when he told the possessive, often violent heiress that he was leaving her, just minutes before she ran him down outside the gates of her Newport, Rhode Island estate. Because Doris Duke had the money and the power, she succeeded in effectively erasing his death from the narrative of her controversial life. For more than fifty years, the full truth behind what happened at Rough Point on the late afternoon of October 7th, 1966 has been hidden.

Until now.

PREFACE

I grew up in Newport, Rhode Island, where I learned to write my first five-point lead. After college I went away and came back 50 years later to try and crack a homicide case. It had sat unsolved, like a stone in my shoe, ever since I'd left town. In the beginning, I thought that there were two principal characters in the story: the billionairess and her victim, but I soon came to realize that there was a third protagonist: Newport itself.

Two legendary men of American letters, the social critic Cleveland Amory and the novelist/playwright Thornton Wilder, who twice won the Pulitzer Prize, each saw the former Rhode Island colonial capital as a series of cities. In his 1953 study of the country's great playgrounds for the rich, *The Last Resorts*, [5] Amory described "three separate Newports." But Wilder was far more discerning. Twenty years later, in his novel *Theophilus North* he understood Newport in the context of German archaeologist Heinrich Schliemann, who had discovered ancient Troy as "nine cities, one on top of the other." [6]

That took me back to my first trip to Rome where one can find evidence of multiple eras within a few city blocks. From the balcony above the Piazza Venizia, where Il Duce delivered his frightening Fascist rants in the 1930's, to the Forum Boarium, site of the first gladiatorial combat in 264 BC, and not far away, The Palantine Hill where mythology tells us that Romulus and Remus were birthed from a she-wolf 500 years before that. All I had to do was "roll focus" and I could time travel without changing hotels.

So it was and still is with Newport, a city of layers where the history of the American experiment in liberty has been manifested in all of its glory, heroism, ambition, accomplishment, treachery and grace.

This is a story about a brilliant life cut short too soon by one of the luckiest beneficiaries of unbridled capitalism who ever lived. But it's also a tale of generations of every class and color who endeavored -- and for the most part succeeded -- in making that experiment work. I loved this town as a kid and going back now, as I sought to examine it in hindsight, I love it even more.

So let's take a walk from the Newport waterfront, up Historic Hill past the old Stone Tower and down Bellevue Avenue to the Ocean Drive and let's see how many layers we can find as we unravel the homicide at Rough Point.

Peter Lance
Newport, Rhode Island
February, 2021

PART ONE

CHAPTER ONE

MURDER AT
THE GATES

On the last full day of his life -- October 6th, 1966 -- Eduardo Tirella flew into Newport, RI, the storied summer colony of The New York 400.[7] Doris Duke, the wealthiest woman in America[8] picked him up at the airport and they drove to Rough Point, her English-manor estate on Bellevue Avenue, known to Newporters as "Millionaire's Row."[9] Tirella, whose close friends called him "Eddie," was about to declare that he was leaving Doris[10] after seven years as her constant companion,[11] artistic curator and designer at her estates in New Jersey, Bel Air, Honolulu, and Newport. It was now time to let his patron know, face to face, that he was severing his professional ties with her, for good.

The handsome Tirella, a war hero and Renaissance man with movie star looks, had just finished the set design for *Don't Make Waves,* a new film starring Tony Curtis and his close friend Sharon Tate.[12] With his Hollywood career amping up, he was anxious to get back to the West Coast, so he'd asked Doris to rent a station wagon.[13]

His plan was to load up his paintings and effects and drive to his mother's house in New Jersey, where he'd drop them off and fly home. [14] At 42 he was on the edge of an important new career. But nobody left Doris Duke without consequences. A notoriously jealous Scorpio, she was known for her violent temper. [15] A few years back, in a drunken rage, she'd stabbed her common-law husband with a butcher knife when *he'd* angered her, [16] and Eduardo, who was gay, had been warned by his partner and friends not to test her. [17] He assured them that he could handle Doris and agreed to come back to Newport for one last curating job.

Still, by late the next afternoon, October 7th, servants at Rough Point remember them getting into a heated argument. [18] Doris, then 53, had rented the Dodge Polara wagon from the local AVIS dealership and they were about to head out to pick up an artifact Eddie had deemed worthy. [19]

Moments later, as they exited the estate with Tirella behind the wheel, he got out to open the massive wrought iron gates. Suddenly, Duke slid into the driver's seat and seemed to snap.

She released the parking brake, shifted into drive and slammed down on the accelerator. The rear tires of the two-ton wagon spun, leaving gouges in the gravel driveway. From a dead stop the wagon roared forward, hit Tirella, burst through the gates and dragged him halfway across Bellevue before smashing through a fence and crashing into a tree.[20] As Doris sat stunned behind the wheel, Eduardo's body lay beneath.[21] With massive injuries to his lungs, spinal cord and brain, death was instantaneous. [22]

Ninety-six hours later, with no inquest – basing the brief probe of Tirella's homicide *entirely* on the word of Miss Duke – police chief Joseph A. Radice declared the death accidental. [23] Doris later signed a transcript of an interview prepared by the police [24] and the case was closed. [25] Seven months after that, Radice retired and later bought the first of two condominium units in Hollywood, Florida. [26] The Lieutenant Inspector who had first questioned her, leap-frogged over the Captain of Detectives to become chief. [27] Another cop at that interview was promoted to Sergeant. [28]

Eight days after the homicide, following years of haranguing with Newport after she blocked off Cliff Walk, [29] the pedestrian path surrounding her estate, Doris donated $25,000 to restore it. [30] It was the equivalent of $200,000 today. [31] Next, she gave $10,000 ($80,000 in 2021 dollars) to Newport Hospital, where she'd been hidden away from authorities on the night of the crash while her lawyers traveled from New York to create a cover story. [32] In the months that followed, she began to set up The Newport Restoration Foundation which eventually renovated 70 original colonial buildings. [33] Her sudden burst of philanthropy led one cynical Newporter to muse, "The death of one man was well worth the long-term benefit to this City." [34]

Tirella's closest surviving niece sees it another way: "She killed him twice," said Donna Lohmeyer, 74, who's been searching for decades for the truth behind his death. "She destroyed his body and then she eviscerated his memory." [35] That came four and a half years later after Doris steadfastly refused to settle with Tirella's five sisters and three brothers who were willing to accept as little as $200,000 [36] at a time when she was making $1 million a week in *interest* on her money. [37]

Instead, she forced them to file a wrongful death civil suit which led to a 10-day trial in the summer of 1971 [38] in the same Providence Superior Courthouse where the second trial of Duke's Bellevue Avenue neighbor, Claus von Bulow, had taken place. [39] In that action the Tirella family was asking for $1.25 million. [40] After all, Eddie was at the top of his game professionally. He had more than two decades of earning capacity ahead of him and the year before his death he'd made more than $43,000 [41] – the equivalent of $355,000 today. [42]

At that trial Doris testified that she "always asked Eduardo's advice before buying or planning anything for her estates." [43] Over the past decade he'd counseled her on the purchase of art worth tens of millions -- pieces they'd acquired together on more than 100 occasions. [44] He traveled with her to London, Paris and Italy to scout paintings, tapestries and rare furniture and he'd transformed Duke Gardens, a series of abandoned greenhouses on her New Jersey estate, into a spectacular series of themed botanical displays considered one of the most significant glass-house collections in America. [45] Eddie had his own living quarters in each of Doris's five estates [46] so she clearly wanted to keep him close.

"But even more," said Pola Zanay, a longtime friend, "She hated the idea of *him* leaving her." [47]

Eduardo Tirella and Doris Duke. Mid 1960's

Doris Duke was actually found "negligent" in Tirella's homicide, [48] but during the damage phase, her lawyer portrayed him as a spendthrift, ne'er-do-well and "financial fiasco." [49] The shocking result: after legal fees and disbursements were deducted, each of his siblings was awarded a grand total of $5,620. [50] "Considering what he had done for her and meant to her, it was shameful," said Zanay who was also close to Eddie's partner, sculptor Edmund Kara. "It was the worst kind of character assassination, considering the sort of nationally-known designer that he was." [51]

As a gay man in the mid-Sixties Tirella had a diverse and complex resumé that ran deep. He'd been a performer at New Jersey nightclubs in the early 1940s, falling in with Frank Sinatra. His niece Donna told me that her mother "Remembered them coming home to eat Italian after some of Frank's dates at the Meadowbrook, where the big bands played. But the war changed all that." [52]

In 1943, Eduardo enlisted in the Army and shipped off to Europe, earning a Bronze Star for his service at the Battle of the Bulge. [53] In the early Fifties he ran the millinery department at Saks in Beverly Hills [54] where he designed hats for gossip columnists Hedda Hopper and Louella Parsons. [55]

As he further developed his design skills, he transformed Peggy Lee's Los Angeles hilltop home, showcased on CBS's interview program *Person to Person* in 1960. [56] Ironically, in a piece published three weeks after his death, *Vogue* cited his design [57] for the "vast" new kitchen in Falcon Lair. [58]

Eduardo's partner Edmund Kara was the most prominent natural wood sculptor of his day [59] and apart from Miss Lee, Tirella counted among his personal friends Richard Burton, David Niven, Alan Ladd, Kim Novak and James Coburn. [60] He'd recently created Elizabeth Taylor's beach house for the 1965 Vincent Minnelli-directed Hollywood production, *The Sandpiper* [61] as well as sets for *Don't Make Waves,* [62] in which Sharon Tate co-starred with Curtis and Claudia Cardinale.

Eddie played cameos in both films. [63]

But after Doris Duke finished with him in court, he was relegated in the eyes of the jury to the status of celebrity sycophant. [64] By then, she had gone to great lengths to erase him from her own life as well as the public record.

CHAPTER TWO

LITIGIOUS & VINDICTIVE

Rough Point was built in 1892 for Frederick William Vanderbilt, [65] the grandson of "The Commodore" Cornelius, progenitor of the family responsible for six spectacular Newport estates. [66] The gardens were designed by Frederick Law Olmsted who gave Manhattan Central Park. Yet when James Buchanan "Buck" Duke bought it in 1922 he found the red sandstone and granite estate so inadequate that he added a new ballroom. Back then, he considered its "Great Room" too small to accommodate the coming-out party he envisioned one day for his beloved 10 year-old daughter, Doris. [67]

After his death, when she was presented to Society at the age of 17, some 600 guests celebrated on the final evening of Tennis Week at The Newport Casino, site of the first U.S. Open [68] On that night in 1930, two orchestras played at Rough Point as the tall blonde debutante sat next to her mother Nanaline. Five years earlier, her future had been cemented by a $50,000,000 inheritance. [69] But as she sat under colored lights on a specially-constructed cliffside marquee amid the top shelf of Newport Society, Doris couldn't have imagined that 36 years later, outside the gates of that very same estate, she'd be willing to kill the handsome younger man she'd been so close to.

In 1993 when she died in Los Angeles, leaving a fortune of $1.3 billion and generating years of lawsuits involving her butler, Bernard Lafferty, accused of hastening her death, [70] Doris Duke's 2,900-word obituary was sprawled across ¾'s of a page in *The New York Times*. But Eduardo Tirella, her trusted friend and advisor, earned only a single sentence of 34 words. [71]

Rough Point 52 years to the day after Eduardo Tirella's Death.
(Adam Fithers photo)

In her *L.A. Times* obit, which was more than twice that long, he got two sentences; the second of which reported that "an inquest cleared Duke;" though there never was one:

> Interior designer Eduardo Tirella was helping refurbish Duke's home in 1966 when he jumped from the driver's seat of her car to open the gates of her Newport mansion -- and the vehicle slammed into him. Although an inquest cleared Duke, who was in the passenger's seat, she turned more reclusive. [72]

"Doris Duke was bent on controlling the narrative of her mangled legacy," said her one-time business manager, Patrick Mahn, the former NYU professor she put in charge of her finances in 1984. [73] "Litigation was her favorite foreplay." [74]

Starting at age 13 when she sued her own mother, [75] Duke was involved in more than 40 lawsuits over the next seven decades. [76] "She could be incredibly vindictive," says Mahn, who co-authored *Daddy's Duchess*, a scathing Duke biography. [77] "After I left, she went bonkers and sicced the legal dogs on me."

Her godson, Pony Duke, who co-wrote another bio entitled *Too Rich*, put it this way: "Doris gave no second chances. She collected people and then she threw them away." [78]

Buck Duke, who made his first fortune with American Tobacco Company, creating the modern cigarette as we know it, [79] warned his daughter on his deathbed to, "Trust no one," [80] and she'd been famously paranoid ever since. Dee Dee, as her few close friends called her, [81] was infamous for hiring ex-FBI agents to intimidate disgruntled friends and lovers who might be sources for reporters or biographers. [82] Columnists were harassed to print retractions. [83] Ex-staffers were threatened and bullied. Thirty-nine months before Tirella's death, she slashed the arm of her common-law husband Joe Castro in that jealous rage. [84] Then, after Castro sued her for assault, he was effectively kidnapped in Hawaii by private investigators hired by her lawyers and induced to drop the suit.[85]

THE MISSING PHOTO

The only known photograph of Doris and Eduardo, published on page 6, is strangely unaccounted for in the archives of Getty Images, owner of the Bettmann Archives which had previously licensed the photo. [86] The entire file of the Tirella wrongful death case is gone from R.I. Judicial Archives. [87] The file on the police "investigation" was reported missing from the Newport Police Department in 1990. [88] Even the negative of the photograph of the crashed 1966 Dodge Polara station wagon which made the front page of *The Newport Daily News* the next day, was selectively removed from archives at The Newport Historical Society. [89]

Daily News October 8th 1966 Headline + Missing Photo

Fifty-three years after Tirella's death in April, 2020, a laudatory 316-page biography, *The Silver Swan: In Search of Doris Duke,* [90] was published by Farrar, Straus and Giroux. Authored by heiress Sallie Bingham, whose own papers are archived at Duke University, the book covers Tirella's brutal homicide in a scant 15 paragraphs and continues to perpetuate the "accident" theory -- demonstrating that even in death, the late billionairess maintains a firm grip on her troubled legend.

THE CASE THAT GOT AWAY

The truth of what happened at Rough Point has gnawed at me for decades, ever since I started working as a cub reporter for *The Newport Daily News* eight months later. [91] I went on to report for ABC News as a correspondent on *20/20, Nightline* and *World News Tonight* [92] and over 13 years post-9/11, I wrote four investigative books on counter-terrorism and organized crime for HarperCollins. [93]

But when Donald Trump declared, "I could stand in the middle of Fifth Avenue and shoot somebody and I wouldn't lose any votes," [94] a light bulb went off. The notion of a self-professed billionaire openly bragging that he could get away with murder sent me back home to the story I should have covered in the summer of '67, when life and my career got in the way.

In 2010, during my investigation into the FBI's pursuit of al Qaeda, I'd worked with veteran NYPD Detective James Moss, of Brooklyn South Homicide. At that time, with the help of ex-FBI undercover operative Emad Salem, we cleared the 19-year-old unsolved murder of imam Mustafa Shalabi, who'd been shot and stabbed on Coney Island in 1991. [95]

If *that* trail of evidence had been cold, getting the truth behind Tirella's death would be an even bigger challenge, given Doris Duke's efforts at hagiography. But when I started to kick over rocks, I was surprised at the number of current Newporters who still had passionate opinions on the homicide. Dozens of members of the dedicated Facebook group, "If You Grew Up In Newport, RI Share Some Memories," regularly posted comments like, "I never believed it was an accident" and "If you have enough money, you can kill someone."

Another wrote, "I don't think we will ever know the real story." [96]

Taking that as a challenge, I began reaching out to people in that group who claimed to have personal knowledge of the incident. One identified the first cop on the scene who gave me a groundbreaking interview. I tracked down the first surviving civilian witness, then a young Navy nurse, who got there minutes after the crash and found Doris wandering back into Rough Point. I spoke at length with the investigator for the Registry of Motor Vehicles, now 87, who told me that he'd been prevented by the police from interviewing Miss Duke. I had a revealing conversation with a retired Newport Police detective who talked to Duke before she was locked away from that same State investigator in a private room at Newport Hospital.

I found a Newport Fire Captain who remembered visiting the scene as a 9-year-old. He was so taken by the prospect of re-examining the death, that he went up into the attic at Fire Headquarters and unearthed the original logbook from that fatal night, which helped me rewrite the timeline.

I even located the blacksmith hired to repair the two massive wrought-iron gates forced outward by the impact of the two-ton wagon.

Now 89, he told me that the damage to the seven-by-fifteen-foot gates was so severe that they were twisted and bent. Five of the gates' inch-thick iron baluster rungs were knocked out.

A crucial find turned out to be the stepson of the news photographer who arrived at the scene within minutes of the crash and took a series of heretofore unpublished photos that opened a new line of investigation. They show a Newport Police sergeant, who was the department's chief accident investigator at the time, working the scene shortly after the death. Ironically, 14 months later, I'd written a story in *The Daily News* about how he'd trained the Police Department's rookies. [97]

That sergeant's take on the death was a shocking scenario in which Eduardo had gone up onto the hood of the station wagon after Duke hit the gas and roared forward from a dead stop 15 feet from the gates. Still alive at that point, he might well have looked her in the eyes as the Dodge Polara burst out onto Bellevue Avenue. But then, as the sergeant saw it, Doris hesitated for a millisecond, causing Tirella to roll off. At that point, the sergeant believed, she made a decision to *commit*, hitting the accelerator one more time and dragging him under the vehicle to his death. This previously undisclosed copy of Eduardo's Death Certificate contains important clues (we'll discuss later) that support the sergeant's "up on the hood" analysis.

COPY OF CERTIFICATE OF DEATH
STATE OF RHODE ISLAND

Back in 1966 I had no idea that this police sergeant had done an investigation of the case and effectively concluded that Doris had killed Eduardo Tirella with intent. When I finally I got the missing report I learned that those specific findings had been excised -- editing necessary at the time to justify Chief Radice's accident theory. But elsewhere in that document there is prima facie evidence of a cover-up at the highest level of The Newport Police Department.

One of the most important breakthroughs for me came when I located Donna Lohmeyer, Eduardo's niece, who had eight pages of trial transcript documenting how her father, a former Marine captain and engineer, had visited the crash site within hours after Eddie was declared DOA at Newport Hospital. He'd photographed what he described as parallel "gouges" an inch-and-a-half to two-inches deep, inside the gates. Those gouges were the width of tire tracks, suggesting that Miss Duke had gunned the station wagon's engine before it roared forward.

Donna also helped me find the undisclosed autopsy report from the County Assistant Medical Examiner, who signed on as Dee Dee's personal physician moments after pronouncing the death. He'd protected her within the walls of the hospital until her lawyers took over. When I learned that this official was Dr. Phillip C. McAllister, I was stunned, because he'd been *my own family doctor* growing up and I'd never had even a hint of his blatant conflict of interest.

In this case, the man legally charged with determining the cause of death had allowed himself to be paid to protect the killer. As we'll see later in this book, Dr. McAllister, a prominent member of the Newport medical community, would see his own personal life and career unravel in the years after he made the decision to protect Doris Duke.

A BARGAIN MADE IN BLOOD

All of this reporting, which I'll go into in depth, leads to the unambiguous conclusion that on the eve of his departure, after Eduardo Tirella had declared that he was leaving her for good, the heir to one of America's greatest fortunes, exploded in a jealous rage, turned a vehicle into a murder weapon and crossed into the perilous territory of intentional homicide.

That's what I found after a two year investigation involving interviews with dozens of surviving witnesses and the accumulation of more than 10,000 pages of documentary evidence which underscore not just Doris Duke's *motive* for the murder, but the lengths that she, her attorneys, private investigators and press flacks went to in covering it up.

Keep in mind as you read this that a jury of seven women and five men found her civilly *negligent* in the homicide, the same way a civil jury later found O.J. Simpson liable after he was acquitted of criminal charges. The difference was that Simpson still owes some $70 million in damages [98] for the wrongful death of his ex-wife Nicole Brown Simpson and her friend Ronald Goldman, but in this instance, after shamelessly denigrating the decedent, the total award Doris Duke was on the hook for was only $75,000, plus interest.

Another eye-opening discovery for me was that the five lawyers for Tirella's family shaved 42% of that damage award off the top. One of them included J. Joseph Nugent, the retired Attorney General of Rhode Island, who had initially pledged to get to the bottom of the anemic police investigation but later acquiesced to it. [99] He then sat in court during trial and charged the Tirella family the equivalent (today) of $11,549. [100]

"In lieu of the proper damages," said his niece Donna, "all we have is Eddie's memory which I'm working to restore – to let people know the kind of man he was."

And what kind of woman was Doris Duke? One Newporter I found on that Facebook Group had a very pointed opinion. Denise Clement's late mother, Rosemarie, had been Chief Radice's secretary at the time of Tirella's death. In a lengthy interview in which she seemed happy to unburden herself after so many years, she told me this:

"Doris Duke *bought* the City of Newport and got away with murder. My mother read the full police report and knew that there was a cover-up, but there was nothing she could do. After she retired and we drove past those houses Doris had restored that helped Newport become a tourist destination, she'd say, 'It was blood money that paid for all this.'" [101]

CHAPTER THREE

LEARNING THE RULES
OF "THE GAME"

N ewport is known by many names: "The Queen of Resorts," "The
Sailing Capital of The World," and "The City By The Sea." A
good candidate for the creator of that last moniker was none other than
Charles Henry Dow, the American journalist who co-founded Dow-
Jones & Company, publisher of *The Wall Street Journal*. In 1880 he authored a laudatory 130 page ode to the island community with this
rather eponymous and intriguing title:

> Newport: the City by the Sea: Four Epochs in Her History.
> An Age of Shadowy Tradition. An Era of Commercial
> Success and Social Splendor. A Generation of Decadence.
> A Half Century of Unparalleled Development. [102]

Indeed, Newport first grew rich on the highly lucrative, but morally
reprehensible Triangle Trade of slaves, molasses and rum between Africa, the Caribbean and Rhode Island. At that time, the city was known
as "the rum capital of the world," [103] The wealth from those ventures

helped finance the American Revolution, and a century later, Gilded Age families like the Vanderbilts, Astors, and Belmonts built a necklace of "summer cottages" around Newport's famed 10-mile Ocean Drive. Beginning in 1723 when 26 sailors were hung as pirates on a warm summer day before what historians later called "a jubilant crowd," [104] Newport has spawned enough moral ambiguity to program five seasons of "Breaking Bad."

Newport Harbor and Historic Hill (Duncan G. Todd photo)

Built on a slave economy, but a bastion of early religious tolerance, President Kennedy had planned to make Newport the site of the official Summer White house when his life was cut short. [105] But his wife, Jackie who spent summers at her mother's estate, Hammersmith Farm, continued to visit and later signed on as Doris Duke's Number Two on The Newport Restoration Foundation. [106] Given the good that was eventually done for tourism, few on "The Avenue" or the commercial streets along Newport's waterfront, felt compelled to ask too many questions about that "accident" up at Rough Point back in 1966.

The city was founded in 1639 by a group of religious refugees led by a Puritan woman, Ann Hutchinson, who had been tried, convicted and banished from The Massachusetts Bay colony for espousing a more tolerant interpretation of scripture. [107] From the Narragansett Indian tribe Hutchinson and a group of eight men purchased Aquidneck island, which dominates the Bay south of Providence. They settled in Portsmouth on the northern end of the island which ran vertically north to south for 15 miles, eventually expanding the community to include Newport at the southern end.

By 1658 Newport's first Jewish émigrés arrived from Barbados. Largely of Sephardic Spanish and Portuguese ancestry, they prospered to the point where, 100 years later, they built a synagogue named for Cantor Isaac Touro that is now the oldest surviving Jewish house of worship in America.[108] The financial support of Newport's Jewish community during the first war against the British, led George Washington himself to send them a letter of thanks. [109]

Newport is also a landmark community when it comes to journalism, *The Newport Daily News* was established in 1846, but its sister paper, *The Newport Mercury* was first published in 1759 by the widow of Ben Franklin's brother, James, making it one of the oldest continuously-published papers in America.[110]

More than two centuries after Franklin, it was owned and operated by the Shermans, an old Yankee family led by two brothers. Ned was editor-in-chief and Albert ran the business side.

In 1966 *The Daily News* was located in an ancient building on Thames, the waterfront street in Newport. My Irish grandmother pronounced it "Temms," as the Brits did.

The Newport Daily News

When I was a kid, Thames St. was swarming with sailors on weekends. It was a dingy, almost dangerous, part of town with tattoo parlors -- even an old burlesque house called The Blue Moon. In those days "when the ships were in," Newport had a bustling population of just over 47,000. [111]

My father Joe, who served most of World War II in the cruel Atlantic as a Chief aboard the Battleship Arkansas, worked days as a mechanic at The Newport Navy Base. He'd come home each afternoon at 4:30 pm, take a half hour nap and then, after an early dinner with my mother, sister and me, he'd go off to his second job working five nights a week and all-day Saturdays pressing Naval officers' jackets and sewing hash marks onto sailors' uniforms in a tailor shop on Thames Street. It was run by a kindly old Sicilian with white hair and a bushy mustache named Nick Merlo. As we'll see, like so many curious aspects of this story, Nick too, had a distant connection to Doris Duke.

By the time 1968 rolled around, Newport was beginning its transition from Navy town to tourist destination. The change came because of two principal factors: the death of Eduardo Tirella which ignited Miss Duke's sudden payback to the city, and Richard Nixon's election results.

That year Nixon won the presidential popular vote over Hubert Humphrey by only 812,415, but like Donald Trump in 2016, he captured the Electoral College: 301 to 191.[112] Still, in solidly blue Rhode Island, Humphrey crushed Nixon by more than two to one and in 1972 when the only state Nixon *didn't* win was Massachusetts (Kennedy country) "Little Rhody," gave George McGovern his second-highest state win in the nation.[113]

Nixon retaliated with a vengeance.

A year later he announced plans to move the entire Cruiser Destroyer Force Atlantic Fleet (CRUDESLANT) from Newport to *three* different bases in the South.[114] He shut down Quonset Naval Air Station across Narragansett Bay and slashed 21,000 jobs in the state. It was a blow that would have bankrupted Newport if tourism couldn't become its salvation and, in this story, with its murderous quid pro quo, that's when Doris Duke stepped in. By the time she'd finished most of her restoration project, the number of tourists visiting Newport jumped from a reported 890,000 a year in 1974 to 3 million by 1977.[115]

ONE HELL OF A LIFE

The man who first got me interested in journalism was Gardner Dunton (Harvard Class of 1918) a Brahmin if there ever was one. The Bureau Chief for *The Providence Journal* in Newport, he lived near me and used to walk home from work each night past my house. He would see me on my front step folding *The Journal* and *Daily News* into a bag for delivery. I guess you could say I began my career in news as a paperboy at the age of ten.

Anyway, Gardner was a handsome man who looked like Christopher Plummer does today. He had silver hair and a mustache, and he'd talk to me in the Patrician manner of Franklin Roosevelt, telling me, "Petah boy, if you decide to write for a newspapah, you'll never make a dime at the game, but I promise that you'll have fun and one hell of a life." And he was right.

I graduated from De La Salle, Newport's Catholic boys' high school, in 1966 and got a full scholarship to Northeastern University in Boston, which had a unique program called "Co-Op." It took five years to earn a B.A. degree, but by the time you graduated, you could get a year of on-the-job experience. I was a philosophy major but had wanted to be a reporter since my days throwing folded copies of *The Daily News* and *Journal* onto porches across Newport.

The "homicide at Rough Point" had occurred barely a month into my freshman year at N.U. but the next summer, 1967, when I started a six-month run as a cub reporter (at $50.00 a week) the town was buzzing with rumors that Doris Duke had bought her way out of murder charges.

My desk was in the middle of the newsroom. I had an old Royal Upright that I bought when I left. I owned it until my Dad died in 2004. Sadly, it was lost to a yard sale when we cleaned out the house. But knowing that I was hungry to cover the news, my mother Albina, a former Deputy Clerk in the Superior Court, who everyone called "Bina," sent me to Milgram Secretarial School one summer in high school, so by June of '67 I was good for 60 words a minute.

The City Room at *The Daily News* was a Spartan place with wainscoting on the walls and huge windows with counterweights. They wouldn't open in summer and were hard to close in winter. The ropes had long since broken. The radiators banged like hell, especially when you were on deadline. The fellow behind me in that photo was T. Curtis Forbes (known as Tom) a handsome ex-Jesuit with Wellesley lockjaw who had bought an old Jag Daimler Sovereign and rented a little guesthouse on the edge of one of the estates. He affected the air of one "to the manor born," but he was the son of a legendary *Providence Journal* reporter and he soon took me under his wing, teaching me how to write a punchy five-point lead and read upside-down when the cops withheld the accident reports.

Tom was also a lady's man; making up for lost time once he'd put down the Roman collar. After work I got to observe his technique as he romanced women at The Black Pearl, [116] a popular bar/restaurant in an old sail loft on Bannister's Wharf named for a 72-foot square-rigged brigantine moored alongside. [117] During the summer of '67 that vessel, which resembled a tiny pirate ship, would play a role in a spectacular Newport Society party; the details of which we'll recount in Chapter Nine.

The table behind me in that photo was our "research section" of old city directories, which would get overloaded with yellowed papers. *The Daily News,* published Monday through Saturday, had a one o'clock deadline each day. I'd clock in at 7:00 am and go to Police Headquarters, then on Marlborough Street, where a Sergeant would stand behind a bullet-proof window like you'd see in a bank. He'd hand me and a reporter for *The Journal* the accident reports from the night before. We'd copy down the details, then visit The Court House to cover the arraignments if any of the drivers in those crashes had been cited for DUIs or other crimes.

Back then, *The Journal* tended to hire Ivy League boys from Harvard, Yale and Brown. I often beat them to crime scenes because I knew the back roads in town, but they were formidable adversaries. Tim Phelps of *The Journal*, who competed with me for stories, later broke the Anita Hill scandal for *Newsday* in 1991. [118] He went on to a celebrated career as a reporter and editor at *The Baltimore Sun* and *The New York Times* before retiring from *The LA Times* Washington Bureau in 2015. [119] With competitors like that, Newport proved to be an aggressive playing field when it came to learning the rules of "the game," so each morning after court, I'd rush back to the paper to write it all up. Often at night I'd have a City Council meeting or other event to cover and there were assorted obituaries and small pieces to write. I could have left at 1:00 pm every day and gone to the beach where most of my friends were hanging out, but I was driven.

DE FACTO SEGREGATION

For years, the shameful little secret in Newport was "West Broadway," a distressed neighborhood tucked behind the blocks across from City Hall. Some of its residents were the descendants of Africans imprisoned by Portuguese slave traders. The little house that my parents bought for $5,000, with a loan from my grandmother, Julia Harrington, was on Ashurst Place, a long block up from Broadway, the main street in town. West Broadway was on the other side of that.

Cranston Calvert, the grammar school that my sister Mary and I went to, was right between our house and Broadway. Most of the Black kids who were our classmates had only to walk a few blocks to what was then the best public grammar school in Newport. We all got along. In fact, that house I grew up in on Ashurst Place was purchased from the Hickes, a distinguished Black family that had made it across Broadway decades earlier. After school I'd play baseball or basketball with my classmates Ralph Jackson and Girard Williams.

Then one day in September, 1959, when I'd just started the sixth grade, almost all of the Black kids at Cranston Calvert were gone. City officials blamed it on overcrowding, but my mother discovered that some conservatives on The School Committee had gerrymandered the district so that Black children just across Broadway would now have to go to the far-inferior Mumford School downtown, while well-to-do white kids from blocks away -- the sons and daughters of doctors and lawyers and the slumlords who owned West Broadway — got to go to Cranston Calvert. I could still play ball with Ralph and Girard after school, but it wasn't the same. In fact, it was de facto segregation in a northern city five years after <u>Brown vs. The Board of Education</u> had outlawed the concept of "separate but equal."

That latter day hijacking of the Black students from Cranston Calvert school stayed with me for years until I had a chance to do something about it. In my second summer on *The Daily News* I began researching my first investigative series: an exposé of slum housing conditions in the West Broadway neighborhood called "Newport's Back Yard." Back then it shook up the town. The story of how it was written and almost never published will be told in Chapter Fifteen.

But before I get there, it's fair to say that I wouldn't have had the chops to write it if I hadn't already sunk my teeth into a genuine murder story involving a brutal double slaying. It happened in the fall of 1967 almost a year to the day after Doris Duke ran down Eduardo Tirella and it not only took place in a cafe co-owned by close family friends, but the young man who pulled the trigger was a classmate of mine from De La Salle.

CHAPTER FOUR

RIFLEMAN SLAYS
TWO SAILORS

In 1967, during my first six-month run at the paper, I got to cover the Jazz and Folk Festivals and work as a stringer for *Agence France-Press* filing international stories on the 20th race for The America's Cup. [120] In that series, Intrepid, skippered by Emil "Bus" Mosbacher, defeated Dame Patti, helmed by Jock Sturrock of Australia, four to none.

Intrepid off Fort Adams
(Photo by Duncan G. Todd)

Then, that October, nearly a year after Eduardo's death, I was assigned to cover the murder of two sailors in a coffee shop on Broadway. It was a Friday. I usually got to police headquarters by seven for the daily pile of accident reports, but that morning the phone at my house rang around six. Jim Edward, *The Daily News'* Managing Editor, was on the line.

"There's been a double murder at The Quality Lunch."

After a late night at The Black Pearl trading G&T's with Tom Forbes, I was still shaking off sleep and I wasn't sure I'd heard him correctly.

"What?"

"John and Koula Sarras's place. They run it with the Gianiotises, right?"

"Yeah. Gianiotis. They live half a block up from me on Calvert."

One of my best friends growing up was Paulie Gianiotis, the red-headed son of Gus, a Greek immigrant and his feisty wife Julia. Gus worked nights at the diner on Broadway. It was a late-night hangout for drinkers after the bars emptied out.

"Some guy killed two sailors just after one am," said Jim. "The police are mum. Get up to the Gianiotis house and see what you can learn. Forbes may take the lead on it, unless you can do better."

He hung up. I didn't bother to shower. I got dressed, grabbed a Reporter's Notebook and ran up a block east of Ashurst Place to 21 Calvert Street.

It was around 6:15 am so I knocked on the back-porch door gently. Julia pulled a curtain away, nodded and let me into the small kitchen. Gus, who was heavy-set and about a decade older than his wife, was at the table with his head in his hands. There was a half empty bottle of red wine in front of him. Julia was pacing back and forth shaking her head. I asked her, "What the hell happened?" [121]

"It was Robertson," she said.

"Who?"

"You know, Steve. The one they call Magoo."

"Goo Robertson? From the Boys Club?"

He was a year ahead of me at De La Salle. We were in the chess club together.

"No... It can't be. He's at West Point."

"He dropped out," she said. "He's been comin' in late nights."

"Really?"

"Yeah. Last night he sits down at the counter around one. Says he's had a couple of Gansetts. Asks Gus to cook him a steak sandwich." She looked over at her husband for confirmation and he nodded.

"Keep going..." I was scribbling notes.

"There were these three sailors, down the counter. Southern boys. They were botherin' Willie Amato."

"That little guy? Janitor who works down at Lenthal School?"

"Yeah. He was half in the bag." She shot a look toward her husband who'd just downed another glass; clearly traumatized. "Next thing Gus hears Steve shoutin' at them sailors... Tellin' 'em to leave Willie alone. One of 'em leans over and pushes Steve so hard he almost falls off his stool. So he gets up and looks like he's gonna punch the guy, when the other two sailors come up on him."

"Then what?"

"He runs out."

"What did the sailors do?"

Julia spoke to Gus in Greek.

"He says they just laughed and sat back down."

I turned another page in the notebook and she stopped.

"So that was it?

"No. One of 'em looks like he's gonna be sick so John comes over and tells him to leave. He opens the door on Broadway and says to get out. Willie starts mouthin' off, so John 86's him too."

"O.K. So Willie and this third sailor are outside... I forgot to ask, were they in uniform?"

"No. Gus hears one of 'em say they'd been up gettin' loaded at the Tavern all night. Anyway, he goes back to cookin.' Next thing he knows, the back door opens and Steve walks in with this big gun. So my husband ducks down behind the counter."

"Anybody say anything?"

Julia turned to Gus and spoke to him in Greek again. "Eípane kati kanenas?"

He shook his head, "Den thimáme."

I waited for the translation.

"If they did, he doesn't remember. But all of a sudden, he hears BOOM! BOOM! BOOM! Then another shot."

Gus, who spoke perfect English, looked at me and nodded, sadly. There was a moment when Julia crossed the kitchen and put her arm on his shoulder. He nodded for her to go on.

"Some girl in one of the booths screams, 'Get the cops' So he gets up and looks around. Everybody's scared outa their minds..."

"Where was Steve?"

"By then he was gone. So Gus looked over the counter... down at the floor."

At that point I nodded to him.

"What did you see?" Gus stared at the kitchen floor and covered his face.

"So much blood."

Julia put her hand over her mouth and began to weep.

FINDING WILLIE

I asked to use the phone, called Jim Edward and gave him the account. He told me to get down to Lenthal School and find Amato, so I ran back to Ashurst Place where my '64 Volkswagen was parked. I broke a few traffic laws getting to the old school on Spring Street, which runs parallel to Thames. It was now about quarter to seven am. I parked and went around to the basement entrance.

Willie was down inside near the boiler. He was on a bench with a half pint of Old Grandad next to him, barely coherent. But I managed to get a confirmation of Gus's story. Willie said that one of the sailors had called him "a little Portagee piece of shit." [122]

"That really set him off," said Willie, "Goo."

"What happened next?"

"Those swabbies said they were gonna beat the shit out of me and after that they were gonna start on him."

"So what'd he do?"

"He took off out the back. Those fuckin' swabbies started pushin' me so John Sarras told me to go. One of them sailors looked like he was gonna throw up, so he pushed *him* out too and locked the front door."

"And then, what? Steve came back?"

"Oh yeah. He come back alright. From the back door on Spring. He's carryin' this big long rifle. I can't believe it. I'm lookin' through the front window. Next thing you know, the swabies yell somethin' at him and fuck, if he doesn't start firin'"

Willie took a swig of the whiskey and rubbed his head.

"How many shots did you hear?"

"Too many. One of 'em went through the corner of the front window. That's when I hit the sidewalk. When I got the nerve to look in, the two sailors are on the floor and Steve's gone".

"Out the back way onto Spring?"

"Must have. He didn't come by me on Broadway."

I made a few more notes and eyed him. "You know what kind of car Goo drives?"

"Mustang. Dark blue; maybe black. Christ I never had nothin' like this happen to me in my life."

"Yeah, well, neither has Goo."

I told him that if any reporter from *The Journal* came by, to keep quiet. There was no way I was going to get beaten on this story, so I played the Azorean card.

"You know who my grandfather was, right?"

"Silvia?"

"Yeah. John – Nunes Motors."

I was half Italian, one quarter Irish and one-quarter Portuguese. My ancestors from the Azores had jumped off a boat from that volcanic archipelago in the Atlantic in the late 1800's and by the 1920's they were connected to the first Ford dealership in Newport. Willie was a full-blooded son of Ponta Delgada, so out of respect for the Silvias he'd keep his mouth shut.

I raced back to the paper. Jim Edward was already at his desk. When I told him what I had, he gave me the lead on the story and said that Tom Forbes, who was on his way in, would back me up.

"He can work the cops," said Jim. "Type up your notes and see if you can get through to Robertson's mother. At this point there's nothing on the wire about the suspect, so we've got an exclusive."

I nodded and crossed to my desk ten feet away, when he turned to me.

"Listen, You deserve a byline on this. But you're connected through the Gianiotises and Steve."

"It's O.K. Mr. Edward. No problem."

My piece ran that night on page one. Ed Quigley, one of the *Daily News'* staff photographers, had driven over to The Quality Lunch

after I gave him that detail about the bullet hole and got a great shot.
A waitresses was pointing to it in the photo.

After the murders, Steve had fled the scene and driven all the way to
New York City, despite a multi-state All-Points-Bulletin for his arrest.
Then, beset by guilt, he'd doubled back. This was long before a bridge
was built across Narragansett Bay, so he'd actually had to take a ferry from
the island of Jamestown to get to Newport. But despite the "dragnet,"
nobody saw him or stopped him.

He drove a half dozen blocks to Marlborough Street, parked his car
and walked up the steps of Headquarters, greeting the startled sergeant
behind the window with these words:

"I hear you're looking for me."

Later that night I was outside in the middle of my first media gang
bang. Film crews from all three network affiliates in Providence were
huddling. Brian Jones, a prep school grad in horn-rims who'd succeeded
Gardner Dunton as Bureau Chief for *The Journal* was there with a photographer. Quigley arrived from *The Daily News* and winked at me. He
asked me if this was my first stakeout. [123]

"Is *that* what this is?"

Ed grinned.

"It's like what they say about flying -- The news business -- 'It's hour
after hour of boredom punctuated by moments of sheer terror.'" He set
fire to a short cigar. "At least for the camera guys. For us it's all about

the *shot*...You know? Grabbing it."

Just then, he looked up at the front door to Headquarters which was opening and bounded up the steps. Ed was fearless. There wasn't a police line he was afraid to cross.

FLASH! He was using a Nikon with a handheld electric flash. Another blast, then another. The TV crews with their 16 mm mag stripe Auricon film cameras were jockeying for position.

Magoo came out in cuffs. The County Sheriff was on one side of him, a Deputy on the other. I had to confront my old friend as he was led down the station's steps in the "perp walk." Brian Jones from *The Journal* was firing questions, so I yelled, "*Steve,* do you have anything to say?"

Just then, he stopped and stared at me blankly.

Strangely, the two of us had a lot in common. Post-War we had each lived at Park Holm, the public housing project near the Naval Base. That was where Steve got his nickname. His stepfather was a former Navy Chief Petty Officer, as was my own Dad. I'd worked side-by-side with Steve clearing brush as a counselor at the Boys Club Camp in Saunderstown. We'd played chess together at De La Salle and, ironically, we'd both learned to shoot .22s there in The Rifle Club. He'd graduated a year before me in 1965. We were all really proud of him when he got admitted to The Point. Now it felt wrong. Me exploiting whatever it was that brought him here. But when I looked over at Quigley banging off shots, doing his job, I realized that I had one too.

I went back to the paper and wrote up the story above. My initial piece on the shooting itself ran that afternoon and made *The Associated Press*. Robertson's name was withheld by the editors in Boston because the story went out to newspapers and broadcasters before his surrender.

> **Newport, R.I. AP** – A man armed with a high-powered hunting rifle shot and killed two sailors today as they sat at a lunch counter. Police were alerted in an 18-state area for the killer who reportedly had argued with the victims earlier. Eyewitnesses said the man walked into The Quality Luncheonette on Broadway shortly after 1am and shot the two victims with a .30 caliber rifle. One of the victims died at the scene while the other suffered wounds in the chest and abdomen and died en route to Newport hospital. Officials at the Newport Naval Base said that one of the victims has been identified, but his name is being withheld pending notification of kin. The second victim reportedly carried no identification and efforts are being made to determine his identity through fingerprints. Newport Police were tightlipped regarding details of the double slaying. Roadblocks were set up in the neighboring communities and Fall River Mass. Patrolman Manual Raposa said he spotted a car fitting the description of the getaway vehicle about 3am. Raposa said the car was heading toward Westport Mass. [124]

The second piece hit *The A.P.'s* New England wire that night.

> **Newport, R.I. AP** – A former Boy's Club "boy of the year" was held without bail tonight for the murder of two sailors as they sat in an all-night restaurant. Stephen Robertson, 21 of Middletown, surrendered Friday to Newport police. He is charged with shooting to death early Friday morning Commissaryman 3rd Class Russell A. Schilling of Newport, Washington and James D. Cook of Port Arthur

Texas, a boiler-tender-stoker-fireman. Robertson was arraigned in the police station before Judge Arthur J Sullivan. Pleas of innocent were entered for him and he faces a preliminary hearing October 13th. William Amato, who was in the restaurant said a man came in with a rifle, pointed it at Schilling and Cook and started firing. The Medical examiner said three shots hit the men and a fourth was found in the wall of a building across the street." [125]

Having to cover someone I knew, accused in a double homicide had a real impact. It taught me that journalism at the local level can be very personal. The ideal was to step outside yourself and cover the news with dispassion and that was the work ethic I lived by the rest of my career.

But every reporter is human. I hadn't forgotten what had happened to my classmates from Cranston Calvert and my next summer on *The Daily News* I decided to do something about it.

CHAPTER FIVE

OLD MONEY &
BLUE BLOOD

As a "townie" and son of a former Navy Chief, I understood early on the strange reverse noblesse-oblige with which local officials treated members of "The Summer Colony." Starting in the summer of 1962, at the age of 14, I worked as "Third Boy," at The Newport Reading Room, one of the oldest private men's club in America. [126] Back then I served drinks to the Members, even though the state liquor authority would have pulled the license of any other bar in town for the same offense. But the rules never applied to "Those People," as we knew them.

My Irish grandmother had been a maid in one of the mansions. She remembered how, on the day Franklin Roosevelt got elected, the dowager she worked for put up "black mourning crêpe," because until The New Deal (which introduced Social Security) the wealthy paid income tax at a far lower rate. [127] We'd sit around at family dinners and she'd remind us, in her brogue, that, "They could never spend all their money. Nor could their *children* or their *children's* children."

It was against that backdrop that I started this new investigation of the incident at Rough Point – trail very cold – fifty-two years on, but with so many of my fellow Newporters hungry to help me get at the truth. It's a story of class privilege and the concentration of wealth that resonates now more than ever since Donald Trump took the White House.

"THAT HORRIBLE NIGHT"

The dedicated Facebook Group, "If You Grew Up in Newport, RI," has more than 10,500 members: [128] current and former residents who share old pictures and memories. In the late summer of 2018 as I data-mined that list, one comment jumped out at me: "The memory of that night and the days after, have stayed with me even until today."

The Facebook Friend who left that post was Linda McFarlane, whose father Howard had been Doris Duke's principal caretaker at Rough Point on what Linda would go on to call, "That horrible night." Writing of Eduardo's death, she posted, "The help that night were all in shock. When I came into the kitchen they were crying and holding each other. My mom told me what had happened. I believe they all thought it was an accident. I know others believe differently."

It took me months to track her down.

Linda McFarlane (now Knierim) was so impacted by Eduardo's death that she devoted 11 pages to him in a 134-page memoir she self-published in 2016. [129]

"Who was the man who was killed on that Friday night?" she wrote. "To me he was a gentle, kind man who would be missed... No more hearing him whistle as he arranged the flowers, see his big smile or hear his soft voice or see him wave as he walked by the kitchen."

Linda herself was an eyewitness to the aftermath of the crash. This is how she described it in her book: "My mom came over and said that Dad was down at the front gate. I walked down (there) and heard noises. What a sight to see, the car across the street, the gate open, blood on the road, tire marks and so many people looking, shaking their heads and asking questions."

In another section of her book, describing Eduardo's death she wondered, "What was the public really thinking? Did they think it was not an accident? How could anyone mistake a gas pedal for the brake and step so hard that it knocked down a fifteen-foot iron gate and went straight across the street straight into a tree? Did they really think she got off without a punishment?"

Linda even speculated as to whether Doris Duke's restoration work following the crash, might have been somehow linked to it. "Was anyone offered a payoff?" she wrote. "Did (Miss Duke) start a new project in town? To some it was yes. Each of us will have our own thoughts of what happened that night." [130]

Linda also painted a stark portrait of Rough Point itself in the weeks following Eduardo's death.

"The house was closed," she wrote, "with sheets covering everything. Little was said of Mr. Tirella after that fall. His room, the beautiful red velvet room (the same room Miss Duke had as a little girl) with the gorgeous canopy bed was never slept in after that horrible night." [131]

Rocky Cleffi, a family friend of Eduardo from Dover, New Jersey, agreed with Linda's sentiment when it came to his devotion to the staff at Rough Point.

"Eddie was always sticking up for the help in all of Doris Duke's residences where he lived," he said. "She would treat them like chattel, and it was always a point of conflict between them." [132]

Perhaps, but what level of conflict on the night of October 7th could have ended in his death? That was the question gnawing at me in the summer of 2018 as I started to dig in.

THE ONLY LIVING WITNESS

In the ensuing hours of what soon became a cover-up, the only surviving witness to the homicide was the killer herself. The morning after the death, the headline over the page-one story in my old paper, *The Newport Daily News* was, "Doris Duke Kills Friend in Crash." But the lead below that reinforced just how little was known of the homicide that soon made international news:

> Newport police this morning refused to indicate when they would question Doris Duke, who was at the wheel of a station wagon that killed her 42-year-old male friend yesterday afternoon. The accident occurred about 5:00 pm The only witness was Miss Duke who was admitted to Newport Hospital suffering from facial cuts and severe shock.

The piece quoted, "Dr. Phillip C. McAllister, acting state medical examiner (who) said Tirella died instantly of brain injuries." But it gave no hint (because local reporters didn't know it) that moments *after* Doris entered the hospital, McAllister had hired on as her personal doctor. He then proceeded to wall her off in a private room, protecting Duke from state investigators who would be on their way to question her.

The two-ton Dodge Polara wagon after it crossed Bellevue Avenue, dragging Eduardo Tirella underneath, then knocked down 20 feet of post and rail fence (Newport Police Dept. Photo)

Most of the coverage over the next few days from *The AP, UPI* and *The New York Times* was cobbled together from wire stories, but *the New York Daily News* sent Alton Slagle, a veteran police reporter, to Newport. He soon learned of McAllister's conflicted status and got statements from him that not only exaggerated Doris's condition but ran counter to what we now know to be the facts.

"Dr. McAllister," Slagle wrote, "county medical examiner and Miss Duke's acting physician, said that 'On the ordinary grounds of humanity, anyone would be left alone under these circumstances until she has had a chance to compose herself.' He said he doubted that Miss Duke knew what had happened and said he believed it was a 'freak' accident." [133]

Already making a legal judgement that he was not in the position to make, McAllister went on to give Slagle this account of his new patient's injuries:

"The heiress suffered two facial lacerations requiring 30 stitches, one three inches long below the lip; another on the lip."

In a Slagle piece the next day, the doctor insisted that, "There was absolutely no evidence of alcohol in the blood of either Miss Duke or Tirella. Everything was completely normal."

With respect to Doris that was also untrue. While Tirella's blood was tested, hers wasn't. Finally, defending his hospital sequestration of "the heiress," McAllister opined, "It would have been inhuman to make her recall the tragedy so soon." Slagle then asked him if it could have been anything but an accident. "'Unthinkable,' McAllister said flatly. I think they were devoted.'" [134]

Hospital Assistant Director William H. Wood Jr. was quoted as saying, "No one except hospital personnel (would) be allowed in Miss Duke's private room for at least 24 hours," adding that her doctor (McAllister) "Had asked police not to interrogate the heiress until she had sufficient opportunity to recuperate from shock and face cuts." [135]

Indeed, until now, the narrative of this story has been that the first time the Newport PD got to question Doris was on Sunday, October 9th, *two days* after the crash. It was a brief four question interview conducted in her bedroom at Rough Point in the presence of her New York attorney, Wesley Fach and her business manager, Pete Cooley. Doris sat in bed, flanked by her German Shepherds, [136] as Lieutenant Frank H. Walsh asked the questions while Detective George Watts took notes.

Doris Duke's bedroom where the interview by Newport police was conducted on October 9ᵗʰ, 1966, two days after the crash. (Adam Fithers Photo)

That bedside encounter was chronicled by *The Associated Press* the next day, October 10th

> Police Chief Joseph Radice said Miss Duke told police she had been sitting on the passenger side of a late model station wagon operated by Tirella as the car was leaving the grounds of the estate. Miss Duke said that when they reached the heavy gates, Tirella jumped out to open them and she shifted into the driver's seat to pull the car out into the street. 'It was something we'd done a hundred times before,' she told police. 'Suddenly the car leaped forward, and I was on top of him,' Miss Duke told Walsh. 'Tirella… was crushed against the irons gates and then dragged across Bellevue Avenue and pinned under the car when it struck a tree.'[137]

As we'll see when we compare Radice's account with the official transcript of that bedroom interview, the Chief left out crucial details about the distance of the station wagon from the gate and Eduardo's position at the time he was struck. [138] He also added lurid details that never made it into Lt. Walsh's typewritten report of the interview which became a part of the official file.

FINAL   DAILY ☆ NEWS   7¢
NEW YORK'S PICTURE NEWSPAPER ®

COPS CLAM UP ON DORIS QUIZ

Where Tragedy Struck.

See Birds Fly in Series Fotos—Centerfold

Within hours of that published story and on the basis of that account alone, Radice pronounced Tirella's death the result of "an "unfortunate accident" and closed the case. But he quickly walked that back, insisting that the probe was still open, after he was criticized in *The New York Daily News* by Rhode Island Attorney General Nugent, who announced that he was "dissatisfied with the slow progress of the investigation over the weekend." He then asked the Newport police for a full report. "This is an extraordinary case," said Nugent, who was empowered to investigate any potential crime mishandled by local authorities. [139]

Chief Radice also came under fire personally for releasing so little news to the press. In that same piece, Slagle revealed that Radice had taken off for "the two-day weekend in the midst of the investigation which was conducted in his absence by Walsh and Watts." But the 67-year-old chief who had run the Newport PD for 41 years at that point, defended himself by saying, "I can't be involved in every fatal accident." [140] Given the gravity of the case and the worldwide celebrity status of the heiress still in hiding, that ham-handed response was reflected in a full-page *New York Daily News* headline over an aerial of Rough Point.

CHAPTER SIX

"A TALL WOMAN GOT OUT"

I was in my first semester at college in Boston when the crash occurred, but my mother sent me copies of *The Newport Mercury*, a weekly compilation of *Daily News* stories. Distracted by my course of studies at the time I somehow missed the fact that my own family doctor, Phillip McAllister, was so entwined in the story, and to a lesser extent, William Wood, the hospital administrator who appeared to endorse the conflicted Medical Examiner-turned-Duke-private-physician's decision to lock her away from state officials.

That discovery really surprised me. Not only did Bill Wood and his family live next door to me growing up, but his oldest son Michael had been one of my best friends. Knowing Mr. Wood as a man of integrity and based on a recent interview with a surviving hospital staff member, I'm now convinced that he never had any personal knowledge of the cover-up. According to the source, who asked not to be identified, Bill Wood was following the dictates of senior hospital administrators at the time. [141]

We don't know what, if anything, Doris or her lawyers may have promised *those* officials for the special treatment no other homicide suspect would have received. But later on, she *did* write that check to the Hospital for the equivalent of eighty thousand dollars. And with the press and State authorities closing in, that kind of money could have bought her the privacy she needed while her minions worked to craft a cover story.

Like so many of the Newport police officers who were in no position to challenge the chief or knew only fragments of the truth, I believe that Bill Wood was personally out of the loop.

Dr. McAllister's betrayal of his oath was another matter. It was particularly painful for me to learn about it since my family and I had so much respect for him in the twenty years he cared for us. I was a classmate of his eldest son Phil and knew his younger son Brendan, both of whom later died from drug overdoses. In the end, after falling on his sword for Doris Duke, Dr. Phillip C. McAllister's professional and personal life seemed to unravel; a story we'll examine in Chapter Twenty-Seven, "The Duke Curse."

The Dodge Polara wagon was so heavy that a tow truck had to be summoned to lift it so that Eduardo Tirella's body could be extracted. At lower left in the shot, two of the baluster rungs, knocked out of the heavy wrought-iron gates, can be seen. (Ed Quigley Photo)

Half a century later, looking at the case in hindsight, I found glaring inconsistences, including the timing of Doris's account. An examination of the news coverage revealed that the day after the "accident" on *Saturday* October 8th, the press published *precisely* the same statement that Doris had supposedly given to police for the first time on *Sunday*, October 9th.

> "Police said Miss Duke had remained in her car while Tirella got out to open the heavy iron entrance gate on Bellevue Ave. The car leaped forward and crushed Tirella against the gate." [142]

But how could the authorities have *known* that if she'd been held incommunicado in the hospital? Linda McFarlane Knierim, the caretaker's daughter, told me that "Miss Duke came quickly back home the next day (Saturday) when her lawyers had come up from New York." At the civil trial in 1971 Chief of Detectives Paul Sullivan testified that he'd gone to Rough Point that day to question Doris, "but she was in bed under care and (her) attorney let it be known that she would not answer questions at that time." [143] So where did Chief Radice get that initial account, if not from Doris Duke, and when did he get it?

The truth emerged after an exhaustive search for the records in <u>Alice Tirella Romano et. al vs. Duke</u> came up empty. The file in that wrongful death case against Doris personally, had mysteriously disappeared from state archives. But as it turned out, Tirella's siblings had also sued AVIS Rent-A-Car Systems, Inc., the owner of the Dodge Polara wagon.

After State Registry of Motor Vehicle investigators found both the brake and accelerator in perfect working order, that parallel case never went to trial. But because it was filed in Federal Court and Duke's involvement gave it historical significance, I found 173 pages of pleadings, depositions and interrogatories in The National Archives. This is what they revealed:

On June 30th 1968 under oath and in answer to a series of questions, AVIS Regional Claims Manager Donald W. Bechtler stated, "Miss Duke informs us that on October 7, 1966 at the hospital she discussed the accident with police officers whose names she does not know." [144]

I later found out that, in fact, Doris *had* exchanged a few words, not with *officers* plural, but with a young patrolman who had been dispatched to meet her in the hospital's Emergency Room.

When he got there, he found her on the phone in the hospital lobby, but he was able to ask her a few questions as she held a piece of cloth up to a cut on her lip. [145] What he learned found its way into Chief Radice's account to the press the next day. But in that same interrogatory from the AVIS case, Doris was asked to give a concise statement of facts on how the "accident" occurred. Her response, which added new details, was revealing:

"Edward Tirella drove the automobile up to 12 or 15 feet from the north gate. I was sitting in the passenger's seat. He got out to open the gate which was locked. I moved over to the driver's seat. I put my left foot on the brake and moved the gear shift lever from "park" to "drive." The car immediately moved forward through the gates and across Bellevue Avenue where it struck a fence and stopped. I was injured and dazed. I looked around for Mr. Tirella. I did not see him. I went back into the house to see if he was there. A man and a woman helped me." [146]

Indeed, the first civilians on the scene that late afternoon were Lewis Thom, a Milwaukee policeman and his daughter Judith, who had graduated the day before as an Ensign from the Officer Candidate School at The Newport Naval Station.

Mr. Thom and his wife Elda were about to leave for Wisconsin the next day but decided to take a sightseeing trip down Bellevue Avenue with their daughter, a newly commissioned officer. Now known as Judith Wartgo and retired after 30 years as an EMS worker, I tracked her down and she gave me this account:

"It was very beautiful that Fall afternoon. Leaves were falling. We were just looking at the houses and we came upon this accident. The car was against a tree across the road from this open gate. I didn't know who lived there. My Dad got out first and went to the vehicle. I stayed with my Mom in our car for a moment then got out and went over to the car. A policeman arrived, and he was looking around the station wagon to see if anyone else was hurt and not responding, At that point a tall woman got out of the driver's seat. She was in the street, walking back and forth, hysterical, hollering something like, 'I can't find him... I can't find him...' As I approached her, she took off for the house running. [147] I decided to go after her because I didn't know if she was going for help. We didn't have cell phones back then, and no one could hear us if we called out, since the houses were so far apart. Also, I wasn't sure if she was going to pass out. She was acting really hysterically. I assumed she was in some kind of shock."

Once she followed Doris into the 30-room mansion, Judith said that "the house was eerily quiet. She ran up this big huge staircase and I thought, 'I've got to keep up with this woman or I'm going to get lost and not be able to find her.'"

Now on the second-floor, Judith said that Doris was yelling for someone whose name she couldn't make out, but she soon circled back and ran outside.

"I was trying to get her to stop," she said. "But she was a very fast runner. When she finally got outside, she blurted out that she'd run him over; someone named Ed." [148]

That admission ran counter to Doris's sworn claim in the AVIS case that she'd run into the house to *look* for Tirella. After all, why search for him if she already *knew* that she'd hit him?

At that point, Judith moved closer to the station wagon which was parallel to Bellevue Avenue with its front end smashed against a tree. A large section of post and rail fence had been knocked down at Quatrel, the estate across from Rough Point. Judith told me that she finally got a look under the vehicle.

"It was still quite light outside, but it was difficult to see under the station wagon. If I recall the victim had a dark jacket or shirt on and he was rolled up under the wheel on the driver's side. My father was calling to this person and there was no response. The policeman was there, and they were trying to figure out how to get to the victim when other police vehicles arrived."

At that point the young Ensign got a good look at Doris's face.

I read her Alton Slagle's *New York Daily News* story with Dr. McAllister's account that Doris needed 30 stitches. Slagle also reported that Judith and her father had found Duke "bleeding from head cuts." [149] Right away she stopped me.

"No," she said. "She had a few bruises and scratches. But nothing where blood was running down her face or an obvious blow to the head." [150]

Judith seemed surprised by that detail since she'd left Newport the next day and had never seen the press accounts. In fact, the first time anyone had contacted her about the incident was around 1990 when she heard from Stephanie Mansfield, a former *Washington Post* reporter who was writing a Duke biography. [151]

BRIEF WITNESS INTERVIEWS

As we'll see in the official police report, Judith and her father are quoted briefly, but the accounts they gave, with important admissions by Doris regarding Eduardo Tirella, never made it into any of the public pronouncements by Chief Radice or his surrogates.

Further, the Thoms weren't the only key witnesses to the crash aftermath with important evidence the police seemed bent on suppressing. Tirella's brother-in-law Robert Aughey, a former Marine Captain, drove to Newport with his son Robert Jr. the night of the crash. He got to Rough Point at 6:30 am and photographed those tire-width "gouges" in the Rough Point gravel. "I remember those gouges clearly," Robert Jr. told me. It was like someone was sitting in the car, stomped on the gas and made deep impressions in the gravel. [152] Lieutenant Walsh questioned us briefly that morning about my uncle's relationship with Doris Duke, but he didn't seem to want to hear anything about what we found."

"It's highly unprofessional that you would be investigating a vehicular homicide and not get detailed statements from the first eyewitnesses on the scene," said retired NYPD Detective James Moss, who worked hundreds of murder cases over the years for Brooklyn South Homicide. [153] "Jimmy," a big gregarious Irish-American, was the cop with whom I'd worked that al Qaeda cold case murder in 2010. He agreed to visit Newport with me in early October 2018, fifty-two years after Tirella's death.

"On this Duke case," he said, "if you had family members there in town that you could question about the relationship between the killer and the decedent, you would absolutely want to talk to them in detail on the issue of a possible motive -- to determine if the death involved intent. Also when it came to Dr. McAllister, the M.E., *his* behavior was highly unethical. He was the highest medical law enforcement official in Newport that night and yet he decided to take on Miss Duke as his private patient. She was the primary person-of-interest and the only witness to the crash. How was he able to separate his official responsibility to the county from the apparent decision of Doris Duke's lawyers to lock her into a private room where the State Investigators from the Registry of Motor Vehicles couldn't get to her?"

I shared some of my investigative work product with Det. Moss and he came to this conclusion: "Very little about the way the Newport police handled this case had anything to do with responsible homicide investigation; particularly the fact that they wrapped it up in ninety-six hours principally on the basis of a Question and Answer interview which was requested by the person-of-interest's own lawyers. Keep in mind that Doris Duke admitted driving the vehicle that violently killed Mr. Tirella. She had given a paper-thin account of it two days after his death and on that basis, Chief Radice was ready close out the case. Only *after* he was pressured by the State Attorney General for more, did he supposedly interview Miss Duke a second time." [154]

CHAPTER SEVEN

THE FABRICATED
TRANSCRIPT

It was that <u>second</u> official statement that ended any criminal liability for Doris Duke. I learned the genesis of it from Newport attorney William O'Connell, who'd been in practice with Joe Houlihan, a well-respected local lawyer, now deceased. Houlihan had sat for a time as "second seat" to Aram Arabian, the Roy Cohn-like attorney who defended Doris in the 1971 wrongful death case. "Arabian's tactics were win at all cost," said O'Connell. [155] "Joe told me that Radice had been pulling his hair out because he didn't think Doris' initial statement would be enough to close out the case -- particularly after the Attorney General started making waves. So Radice talked to Arabian and said, 'You've got to give me *something more* to put in this report,' and Aram said, "You write something up and if I go along with it, she'll sign.'" According to Doris's account in the AVIS case, it happened like this:

> "On October 11, 1966 (Miss Duke) signed a statement consisting of questions and answers prepared for her signature by members of the Newport Police Department. Chief Joseph Radice, Captain Paul Sullivan and Policewoman Alda Brito were present when she signed the statement." [156]

That second statement, sprawled over three legal-sized pages in the official police report, became the justification Radice needed to close out the case. But we can now see that on its face, it was a fraud – little more than a "script" concocted by the police at Arabian's request, to create *the appearance* of an "interrogation" conducted in real time.

How do we know that? Because the Q&A was so contrived that in the answer to the very first question the police got Duke's birth date wrong -- an error that she had to correct on the transcript and initial by hand.

In the pages that follow, that transcript is published exactly as it was contained in the official police report, which had been missing for decades. But before we get to it, it's important to consider what prompted it: the half-page transcript of the first and only interview of Doris Duke in the ninety-six hour investigation of Eduardo Tirella's death. As noted, it was conducted in her bedroom at Rough Point on October 9th, less than two days after the crash.

As she sat in bed surrounded by two of her dogs, the heiress was questioned by Lieutenant Frank H. Walsh and Det. George Watts of the Newport Police Department. The interview was witnessed by her principal attorney Wesley Fach, and her business manager Pete Cooley who was based at 30 Rockefeller Center in New York. In Lt. Walsh's typed transcript of that interview above, Cooley is identified as "Mr. Conley" and the victim is identified as "Mr. Tirello."

Newport Police Department
October 9, 1966
About 12-30 P.M.

In the presence of Attorney Wesley Fach personal Attorney to Miss Doris Duke, Mr. Conley her personal business Manager, Detective George Watts and myself (Inspector Frank Walsh) we spoke to Miss Doris Duke at her residence, Rough Point, Bellevue Avenue this date, this was shortly after receiving a call from her physician Doctor Philip C. McAllister that she would talk to us.

I informed Miss Doris Duke of her rights and asked her after reading the attached form if she would sign same before making any statement.
Miss Doris Duke read same and signed

Q. Where you operating the car involved.
A. Yes

Q. Will you tell me in your own words just what happened.
A. Yes

A. We were going out of the estate Mr. Tirello was the operator we did what we have done a hundred times before, the gate was locked, Mr. Tirello got out of the car to open the gate, it was locked he was at the lock, the car was about fifteen feet from the gate, I was getting ready to drive thru the gate, the car just leaped forward and I was on top of him, He was in the middle of the gates at the lock at the time.

Q. Do you have an operators license
A. Yes, I have a Rhode Island operators license

Q. He had not opened the gates.
A. No

On the basis of that brief interview Chief Joseph Radice closed out the case, declaring it "an unfortunate accident." This was the story published the next afternoon in *The Newport Daily News*:

Death Of Miss Duke's Friend Ruled 'Unfortunate Accident'

But within hours, Rhode Island Attorney General J. Joseph Nugent told *The New York Daily News* that Radice had moved too quickly. So Radice walked back his initial finding. He called the wire services and within minutes, United Press International sent this new bulletin.

DORIS DUKE FACES MORE QUESTIONS

DOVER, NJ (UPI) – Services were held for Eduardo Tirella today while police in Newport, R.I. disclosed they planned to question multimillionaires Doris Duke further about the death of the movie set designer. "There are some unanswered questions we seek answers to," Newport Police Chief Joseph Radice said.

The Associated Press then ran with the story at right in which the Chief backtracked further. At that point he appealed to Aram Arabian, Duke's Providence-based attorney, who came up with the scheme to prepare a more detailed Q&A of a purported second *interview* of Doris Duke.

In the hours that followed, a three page "transcript" was typed up to look like a stenographer's record of an actual live "interrogation" conducted at Rough Point, the next day, Tuesday, October 11th. What follows is the actual "transcript" I found in the missing police report.

Doris Duke Accident Probe Open

NEWPORT, R.I. (AP) — Police Chief Joseph A. Radice said Tuesday the investigation of the fatal accident involving tobacco heiress Doris Duke and movie-set designer Eduardo Tirella "is not yet completed."

Radice said he intended to question Miss Duke, again about the accident that crushed Tirella against the front iron juri s. Miss Duke's estate Friday night. Tirella, 42, died of brain injuries.

Radice said he was disturbed that his statement Monday, when he called the death "an unfortunate accident," had been misinterpreted. Radice said it was an unfortunate accident but his statement did not mean the investigation was over.

"We've not ruled out anything," said Radice. "The investigation is not yet completed."

The following statement was given in the presence of the
following named individuals at Rough Point, Bellevue Avenue,
Newport, Rhode Island at 12:30 p.m. on Tuesday, October 11,
1966:

Aram Arabian, Esquire; Wesley Fach, Esquire, attorneys for
Miss Doris Duke; and Chief Joseph A. Radice and Captain Paul
J. Sullivan of the Newport Police Department.

The interrogation is being done by Captain Sullivan.

Q. Miss Duke, what is your full name, age, date of birth
   and residence?
A. Doris Duke, fifty-three (53), November 22, 1928/2
   Rough Point, Bellevue Avenue, Newport, Rhode Island.

Q. What city were you born in Miss Duke?
A. New York City.

Q. Miss Duke, you have been informed that you do not have
   to make a statement. You have signed a waiver dated
   October 9, 1966 which has just been observed by your
   attorney, Mr. Aram Arabian, will you now make a statement?
A. Yes

Q. On October 7, 1966 at about 5:00 p.m. were you in
   a motor vehicle, Rhode Island registration ▓▓▓▓▓
   an Avis rental car?
A. Yes, it was an Avis car but I am not sure of the registration.

Q. Where was this?
A. On my property.

Q. Who was with you?
A. Mr. Eduardo Tirella.

Q. Who was the operator of the vehicle?
A. Mr. Tirella.

Q. Can you describe the area in which this car was operated?
A. From the house to the north gate on Bellevue Avenue.

Q. Was Mr. Tirella operating at this time?
A. Yes

Q. Was the vehicle stopped for any reason?
A. Yes

Q. For what reason?
A. To open the north gate.

Q. How far from the gate was the vehicle stopped?
A. About twelve to fifteen feet.

Q. Who opened the gate?   went to
A. Mr. Tirella left the vehicle and/open the gate.

Q. Was this gate locked?
A. Yes

Q. Where were you sitting in the vehicle?
A. In the front seat, passenger side.

Statement of Doris Duke   October 11, 1966
Page Two

Q. Can you describe what happened?
A. When he went to the gate I slid over to the driver's seat
   and I placed my left foot on the brake and I disengaged
   the gear with my right hand. The car shot ahead.

Q. Did you shift the gear from parked position?
A. Yes

Q. What gear did you shift into?
A. Drive.

Q. You placed your foot on the brake also?
A. Yes.

Q. The car then moved forward?
A. Yes

Q. Can you estimate the speed the car went forward?
A. No

Q. Is there any possibility, Miss Duke, that your foot could
   have engaged the accelerator pedal?
A. Not to my knowledge.

Q. Was the hand brake on when the car was left in parked
   position?
A. No

Q. When the car started forward, did you think to pull the
   hand brake?
A. No, I had no time to do this.

Q. Is there a possibility that your foot slipped off the
   brake pedal onto the accelerator pedal?
A. That could have happened, *but I have no recollection of it*

Q. Do you have an recollection as to how fast the car was going?
A. It was fast.

Q. Would you say very fast?
A. From an absolutely dead stop, and it was fast.

Q. When Mr. Tirella got out of the car was the car ideling
   fast?
A. I don't know.

Q. What happened when the car was set in motion?
A. It went ahead through the gate, across Bellevue Avenue to
   a fence on Bellevue Avenue.

Q. Did you see Mr. Tirella?
A. Yes, I saw him at the gate.

Q. Do you recall what happened after the car went into motion?
A. I got out of the car. I could not see him. I looked
   around. This was not when the car was in motion but when
   it had stopped against the railing. I ran to the house.
   I thought he was in the house. I was in a state of shock.
   I looked around.

Q. Did you speak to anyone in the house when you came in?
A. No, I didn't open the pantry door. I went back to the
   street . I saw a woman on the street and she came and was
       trying to quiet me down. I said not to worry about me.
       I asked about my friend.

Doris Duke

Statement of Doris Duke   October 11, 1966
Page Three

Q. What happened after that?
A. I was taken to the Newport Hospital in a police wagon.

Q. Do you recall who you spoke to on the street?
A. A man and a lady came up to me and the girl was trying
   to quiet me down.

Q. When you went to the Newport Hospital, did a police officer
   speak with you?
A. Yes

Q. Do you regall who he was?
A. No.

Q. Did you rent this car yourself?
A. No, one of my employees, Mr. MacFarland, rented the car.

Q. Had there been any difficulty with this car?
A. No, I drove it twice previously. I went to meet Mr.
   Tirella at the airport and I had driven it on Friday
   morning.

Q. Was it a practice for you to slide over in the front seat
   of the car when Mr. Tirella would open the gate?
A. Yes, I had done so that morning.

Q. It was actuall the third time you drove the car. Is that
   correct?
A. Yes

Q. Would you consider yourself totatally familiar with this
   car after driving it three times?
A. No

Q. Had you had anything to drinking of an intoxicating nature
   on that day?
A. No

Q. How long had you known Mr. Tirella?
A. At least six to eight years.

Q. How long had he been here visiting?
A. About three weeks.

Q. Did you have any arguments or misunderstandings with him
   on that day?
A. No.

Q. Is there anything else you would like to say about this
   incident, Miss Duke?
A. No, I have told you every thing.

Q. Will you please read the questions and answers contained
   on these three pages of your statement, and after making
   any corrections you deem necessary, will you please sign
   your name on all pages and on all carbon copies of your
   own free will without any promises of reward or immunity
   having been offered to you.

WITNESSES:

_____   _____
                                      Doris Duke

"We can see that this is a clear fabrication," said former NYPD Det. Moss, "If a stenographer had been typing a record of the interview as it happened and Captain Sullivan, who purportedly questioned her, had mistaken her date of birth, she would have corrected him on the spot. But Doris Duke had to cross out the erroneous DOB, write-in the correct one and initial it, because the Newport police presented her with that document *after* they had created it. In more than twenty years of murder investigation in New York City I have never seen anything like this." [157]

There is further evidence that this "transcript" represented an affirmative cover-up by Chief Radice and Capt. Sullivan. Lewis A. Perrotti and his partner Al Massarone were the two state investigators for the Registry of Motor Vehicles assigned to the case. After Doris Duke was cleared, Perrotti issued a detailed eight-page report, which I uncovered. Along with the official police report, it had been missing for decades. Now, in that report, we can see how Perrotti, who was told that a second Duke interview had taken place, was clearly misled by the Chief. He writes:

> On October 11, 1966, Miss Duke made a formal statement at her estate to Chief Radice and Captain Sullivan. Inspector Massarone and myself were again refused the right to question Miss Duke. When we asked for a copy of this statement, Chief Radice stated this statement was similar to the first one taken (October 9th 1966) and that he felt the initial statement was enough for our Department. [158]

"In other words," said ex-NYPD Det. Moss, "Radice didn't want any other officials, outside of the upper ranks of the Newport PD, to see that three page statement, with its handwritten corrections by Doris; because if they had, they would have immediately known that the document was a fraud."

But Chief Radice took the deception to another level, telling *The New York Daily News* that the "interview," conducted by "Inspector Paul Sullivan" took place on October 11th in "the drawing room of the 30 room mansion." [159]

Still, after she fixed her signature to the Q&A which the cops had drafted for her, it was over. The next day, October 12th, 1966, *The New York Times* reported that, "The police termed today as 'Definitely an accident' the death of Eduardo Tirella… killed by a car driven by Doris Duke, the tobacco heiress. [160] Chief Joseph A. Radice said: 'As far as we're concerned, the case is closed.'"

That same day, Capt. Sullivan, who purportedly conducted the interrogation told *The Providence Journal* that "there was no evidence of foul play in the death." [161]

Doris was cleared. But the way the Newport PD had handled it left Det. Moss shaking his head.

"The idea that the finders-of-fact in a homicide probe would do little or no forensic investigation, ignore eyewitness accounts and base their conclusion exclusively on the word of the woman who caused the death – then add insult to injury by cobbling together what her attorneys *wanted* her to say into a statement that looked like the transcript of an actual interrogation? That is beyond belief."

Doris Duke escaped any criminal liability for the death of her "constant companion" and the damages she paid to Eddie's family after being found civilly negligent in 1971 didn't even equal the cost of the Goddard Chippendale mahogany highboy she bought a month before trial at Parke-Bernet for $102,000. It was a record price at the time for a piece of furniture. [162]

On July 1st, 1971 the case went to the jury in Providence, the state Capital, which had a large minority population. As to Duke's skill at manipulating the media, the day before, stories ran on *UPI's* national wire and in *The New York Times* reporting that she'd recently appeared in the choir of a predominately Black church in Nutley, New Jersey near her 2,700-acre Duke Farms. [163]

When a reporter happened to show up at The First Baptist Church to hear Doris sing soprano, she was quoted as saying, "I don't want any publicity." [164] But coming on the eve of the jury's decision on how much she'd have to pay Tirella's family, the timing was suspect.

Bill O'Connell told me that as a law school grad, during the class he took to prep for the Rhode Island bar exam, the instructor actually used <u>Romano et. al. vs. Duke</u> as an example of the principal that before a lawyer agrees to represent a client in a wrongful death case, he or she should ensure that the victim had a strong earning capacity post-mortem.

Still, as flawed as the Tirella family's lawyers may have been, *they actually proved just that.* The Appeal brief established Eduardo's ability to earn many thousands of dollars a year for the next several decades. But those same attorneys made *the fatal mistake* of deposing Mrs. Lee Bunker who had worked as an occasional secretary and bookkeeper for Eduardo.

One of the bedrock rules of civil practice is that before you put somebody under oath, make sure that they're going to advance *your* case and not your adversary's. But once she was sworn in a deposition, Bunker, turned into the best possible damage witness for Doris Duke. Despite the overwhelming evidence that Eduardo had been the designer, architect, and general contractor for Duke Gardens, the sprawling New Jersey glasshouse display, and that he had curated virtually every piece of art Doris had acquired for years, Aram Arabian used Bunker -- who testified at trial for *the defense* – to portray Tirella as a "financial fiasco" who couldn't hold onto a dime.

It was all smoke and mirrors.

The fact that Eduardo may not have been good at keeping financial records or saving money had nothing to do with his capacity to earn hundreds of thousands of dollars for years to come. But the impression left with the jury was that he was a loser.

Arabian may have even played "the gay card," reinforcing a sexist trope to the urban jury that Tirella was "something less than a man." If that had happened in 1971, years before the gay rights movement shattered that myth, it might, on its own, have *insured* the paltry $75,000 damage award.

Did Aram Arabian do that? Did he play that card? We don't know, because the trial transcript is missing. But one thing is clear: when it came to *the liability phase*, during which the billionairess was found *culpable* for Tirella's death, Edward I. Friedman, the lawyer for Eddie's survivors, added crucial details in his opening statement, reported by *UPI*, that were never challenged by Arabian:

> Friedman said Tirella was opening the massive iron gates at Miss Duke's Rough Point estate when the accident occurred. Tirella stopped the car about 15 feet from the gates, put the brake on and left the car in "park" as he went to open the gates. Miss Duke slid into the driver's seat, released the brake and put the car into gear. The car shot forward and hit Tirella, went through the partially open gates, crossed Bellevue Avenue, knocked down 20 feet of iron fence and then struck a tree in a neighbor's property. Tirella was dragged about 40 feet and was pinned beneath the car when it stopped. [165]

Decades later, as I sought to deconstruct the official police account of the death - sourced largely from the killer herself - those details of Eddie engaging the parking brake and Doris releasing it, along with the account of just how far across Millionaire's Row she'd dragged his body, made the case that this was no "accident." It was intent-to-kill murder.

CHAPTER EIGHT

COMING OF AGE
IN NEWPORT

In the summer of 1973 the Navy's shocking announcement that it was pulling out of Rhode Island [166] was temporarily eclipsed in The City By The Sea by the start of production on a new adaptation of F. Scott Fitzgerald's Jazz Age classic, *The Great Gatsby,* starring Robert Redford in the title role and Mia Farrow as his obsession, Daisy Buchanan. Rosecliff, the Bellevue Avenue mansion designed by Stanford White and built in 1902 for silver-heiress Theresa Alice Fair Oelrichs, [167] doubled for Gatsby's lavish West Egg mansion and Hammersmith Farm stood in for Daisy's East Egg estate. [168]

While Fitzgerald's plot demanded "cottages" within driving distance of Manhattan, his description of the Buchanans themselves perfectly suited the idle rich of Newport: "They had spent a year in France," he wrote, "then drifted here and there unrestfully wherever people played polo and were rich together." [169]

Apart from my two year stint at The Reading Room, my own perspective on "those people," came from two "members of service," Albert and Dorothy Holmwood. My mother had sworn them in as U.S. citizens in her capacity of Deputy Clerk in The Superior Court and they soon grew so close that my sister and I thought of them as "Uncle Bert" and "Aunt Dorothy."

Bert was born in 1900 in Buxton, Derbyshire, England, Dorothy, a year younger, was a delicate blue-eyed Scottish lady from The Isle of Skye. Even as a young man Bert was an imposing figure: six foot three, and a former member of the Coldstream Guards, he made his first crossing to America in 1926 on the RMS Celtic. [170] After securing employment, he returned to the U.K., booking passage in September of 1927 aboard the RMS Mauretania, this time with his bride-to-be. [171] They were married July 23rd, 1928 in Oyster Bay, Long Island. [172] In those days Bert went into service as a valet and Dorothy as a housemaid.

By 1931 Bert had risen to become the butler at Miramar, the estate three doors down Bellevue Avenue from Rough Point. There he presided over a staff of twenty. Over time, Dorothy became a much-in-demand lady's maid who worked for legendary socialites like Perle Mesta, the inspiration for Irving Berlin's *Call Me Madam*. She also attended Celeste Holm, Bette Davis's co-star in *All About Eve*.

Bert and Dorothy knew the history of every "summer cottage" in Newport and at holiday gatherings they would hold forth as I took in every word. Until I started serving them myself at the age of 14, my own view of the Summer Colony was largely positive; shaped by Dorothy and Bert who became the trusted majordomo for one of the wealthiest and most storied millionaires in America: surgeon, geographer and explorer Dr. Alexander Hamilton Rice Jr.

A REAL LIFE INDIANA JONES

Known at Harvard as "Ham Rice," [173] he was the grandson of a Boston mayor who went on to become Massachusetts governor and a Member of Congress. [174] After earning his A.B. from Harvard College and M.D. from Harvard Medical School in 1904, Ham volunteered to work on the surgical staff of Ambulance Américain, a cadre of civilian doctors serving Europe under the leadership of Dr. George Crile, who later co-founded the renowned Cleveland Clinic. [175] Starting in 1907, Dr. Rice made the first of seven expeditions to the Amazon Basin, ultimately exploring and surveying 500,000 square miles aboard the steamer yacht Alberta. [176] For his service during WW I he was awarded the French Légion of Honor, [177] but the sinking of the RMS Titanic had a fateful impact on the next 25 years of his life.

In 1912, Eleanor Elkins Widener, the daughter of a Philadelphia streetcar magnate, her husband George and their son Harry traveled to Paris in search of a chef for their new hotel, The Philadelphia Ritz Carlton. On April 10th they boarded the Titanic in Cherbourg, hosting the ship's captain, Edward Smith himself, on the very night of the disaster. [178] After the "unsinkable ship" hit the iceberg, George and Harry were lost, but Eleanor took the oars of a lifeboat with her maid and survived. [179]

Soon after she returned to the States, she donated the 2021 equivalent of $70 million to found the Harry Elkins Widener Memorial Library at Harvard. [180] It was at the library's dedication in 1915 that she met Professor Ham Rice, a dashing explorer and certified Boston Brahmin, [181] of whom it was said, "He knew head *waters* the way other society folk knew head *waiters*." [182]

At the time of her first husband's death, famed Gilded-age architect Horace Trumbauer had completed drawings for a 30,000 square foot French neo-classical style mansion on 7.8 acres overlooking Cliff Walk in Newport. Earlier, for coal baron Edward Julius Berwind, he'd designed another spectacular Newport French Chateau called The Elms. [183]

Miramar, the summer cottage of Dr. Alexander Hamilton Rice Jr. and Eleanor Elkins Widener Rice. (Library of Congress photo)

Eleanor decided to go ahead with construction on Miramar, the 27 bedroom "cottage" which included a 6,000 square foot carriage house and a 10,000 bottle wine cellar with a 20 foot stone basin capable of icing up to 200 bottles of champagne at once. [184]

The mansion opened on August 20th, 1915 with a costume ball, described by *The New York Times* as "the largest social event of the summer." [185]

That October, Eleanor and Dr. Rice were married in a quiet Boston ceremony in order to avoid the publicity of their previously announced wedding at Boston's Trinity Church. The nuptials before 12 friends required a judge to sign a special court order, [186] and soon the intrepid Mrs. Rice was accompanying her husband on expeditions deep into the South American jungle. [187]

In 1922 Trumbauer designed a lavish four-story townhouse for the Rices at 901 Fifth Avenue [188] and they later purchased an oceanfront winter estate in Palm Beach. [189] Throughout his adventures, Dr. Rice held a professor's chair in geography at Harvard and founded the University's Institute of Geographical Exploration, though he later became embroiled in a bitter dispute with the University over the custody of his 10,000 volume collection of books and maps, which he ultimately left to The Naval War College in Newport. [190]

PARTIES UNTIL DAWN

In his well received 1952 book, *The Last Resorts,* Cleveland Amory described Dr. Rice as "the country's first ranking clubman," listing "43 societies and 26 clubs in his Who's Who autobiography." [191] Covering "The annual Tennis Week Balls at Miramar," which Amory described as among "the particular bright spots" of the Summer Season, he went into detail on how Mrs. Rice handled the events, which "lasted all night in the great Newport tradition."

> Shortly after midnight she would disappear and take a nap. Early in the morning she would reappear fresh as a daisy and cheerfully breakfast with the late stayers. Equally exemplary was the 55th birthday party of Dr. Rice held at Miramar in 1931, as at this affair 55 people were seated at two tables and the dinner had such dignity that (an) Ambassador rose and made a short speech. "I wish a representative of the press might be with us tonight," he said, "to see for himself that Newport is not all 'Monkey Dinners.'"

The latter reference was to an infamous turn-of-the-century soiree thrown by Mrs. Marion "Mamie" Stuyvesant Fish, then Newport's reigning eminence gris, in which invitees were summoned to meet a certain "Prince del Drago," from Corsica, only to encounter a simian in full formal dress.[192] It was a true low point in the history of The Summer Colony's forays into wretched excess.

But Eleanor Elkins Widener Rice always held her head high and conducted herself with grace. Then, in 1937, Dr. Rice was accompanying her and their daughter to Paris when Mrs. Rice died suddenly of a heart attack while shopping on the eve of Bastille Day. She was 60.[193]

Twelve years later, also in Paris, Dr. Rice married Dorothy Farrington Upham, then 59, who had been presented in 1933 at The Court of St. James in London. [194] Her first husband, a member of The New York Stock Exchange, had committed suicide 15 years earlier. [195]

One of the highlights of Bert Holmwood's career came in 1955 when he presided over a gala birthday celebration which the second Mrs. Rice, known as "The Madam," gave for her husband at Miramar on the occasion of his 80th birthday. It was attended by 700. [196]

On that night the 200 bottle champagne basin was put to good use.

A REAL LIFE JOHN GIELGUD

In 2012, *The New York Times* did a profile of James Silvia, whose grandfather had been an ornamental gardener, at Miramar. After hiring on for a low-level position there in 1952, Silvia described Albert Holmwood as "a charming man in the front of the house," but "a beast in the pantry," He noted, however that "If you searched for the classic butler, Holmwood would be it; on the telephone he sounded like John Gielgud." [197]

In 1976, 20 years after Dr. Rice's death, Bert was interviewed by Terry H. Schwadron, a reporter for *The Providence Journal*. [198] Then in semi-retirement, the veteran butler was asked to assess the accuracy of the highly popular British television import *Upstairs Downstairs* and an American network pretender called *Beacon Hill*; both precursors to *Downton Abbey*.

"The houses (the actors) were working in were too small," said Bert. "A gentlemen would never have had his kitchen and his pantry together like that. It was too crowded to be real." He also opined on a recent party he'd been asked to supervise. "They sent some help in from Providence. One of the men was actually wearing *brown* shoes. Well, I absolutely could not use him in the front of the house. I had to put him in back behind the counter."

Reading that piece made me recall an incident in New York City in March of 1969 that was "vintage Uncle Bert." It occurred in what was known as my "Middler Year" at Northeastern when I was halfway through the five years necessary to earn a B.A.

AUDACITY VS. DIPLOMACY

From my first summer at *The Daily News*, two years earlier, I had my sights set on Columbia J-School's graduate program and I'd already made one trip to The City in August, of '67 armed with some of my clips from that summer. I didn't have an appointment, but I took the train down from Kingston, RI. The fact that I wouldn't be able to formally apply until the fall before my graduation in 1971 didn't seem to impede my exuberance. When I got off the subway at Morningside Heights and gazed up at The Joseph Pulitzer building, I stopped. Seeing the word JOURNALISM carved into the stone on the side of the building gave me the kind of jolt a young seminarian might have received on approaching St. Peter's Square.

The lobby Directory listed the Admissions Office on the top floor. After getting off the elevator, I found myself lucky on three counts: first that Dean Christopher Trump (a handsome Canadian unrelated to "45") was lunching alone in his office; second that his Assistant wasn't there; and third, that he greeted me kindly when I knocked on his door, then barged in.

He sat with me and examined three or four of my pieces on The Cup races and the Folk Festival. He then handed me an application and said, "Make sure you get it in early this fall," at which point I confessed that I wouldn't be able to send it for three more years."

I gritted my teeth and waited to see how that disclosure would fall.

The Dean, paused, then smiled.

"You know Peter, if you were applying to the Georgetown School of Foreign Service, I'd say what you did just now wasn't particularly *diplomatic*. But as far as this game goes, audacity is considered a strength."

I exhaled, thinking to myself, "He even used the same term Gardner Dunton of *The Journal* had used to describe the marvelous profession I was bent on entering.

At that point the phone rang, and as I got up to leave, he said, "Keep in touch."

Naturally I took him literally, so in March of 1969, after I'd written that exposé on slum housing and with infinitely more clips in my folder, I called ahead to schedule another meeting.

The night before I got to The City, Manhattan had been hit with what Newporters would call "a wicked snowstorm," but I couldn't wait to get down there and show Dean Trump the four-part series. After that, Uncle Bert and Aunt Dorothy, who were house sitting at "The Madam's" two floor maisonette at 960 Fifth Avenue, invited me over for an early dinner.

THE BUTLER'S BUTLER

The snow had let up that morning, but the streets were still slushy. Uncle Bert instructed me to come up to the 5th floor via the separate service entrance, which I did. When he opened the door to the kitchen, I could smell a nice leg of lamb that Dorothy had just prepared. I rushed in and hugged her and was about to shake the ex-Coldstream Guard's hand when suddenly, he looked down at my shoes, which were covered with grime and salt.

He eyed me in a way that was more fatherly then judgmental.

"Now what's this, I see?"

"What? My shoes? Uncle Bert I've been out---"

He held up an index finger, signaling silence. Then he smiled.

"A young man with his eye on the Ivy League can't be walking the city with shoes that look like that..."

"Alright, I'll tell you what? Tomorrow, when I hit Penn Station for the trip back, I promise to visit one of those shoeshine stands."

But he wouldn't have it.

"Sit down boy and unlace them."

I complied. Then, before I could protest, he went to a cupboard and pulled out an elaborate box with multiple polishes in tins and bottles, along with assorted brushes and buffing rags.

Within minutes, a man who had served one of the greatest archeologists and explorers in the world, brought my shoes to a spit and polish shine.

When he finished, he handed them back and gave them his imprimatur.

"Now that's a pair of brogues a young man on his way up can be proud of." As Dorothy leaned in and hugged him, he said, "Now let's have a proper meal."

THE COTTAGE ON COGGESHALL

After Dr. Rice's death in the mid 1950's his heirs left the sprawling estate to the Episcopal Diocese of Rhode Island [199] and the second Mrs. Rice moved to an upscale converted Firehouse on Coggeshall Avenue, the street parallel to Bellevue. [200] It was connected to a property that included the extensive greenhouses that had, for decades, supplied flowers and fresh vegetables to Miramar. Next to the firehouse, into which Mrs. Rice had installed an elevator, were a pair of identical cottages separated by a covered walk. In one of them lived James Murdoch, the Scottish gardener for Miramar, his wife and their adult son. Bert and Dorothy had the mirror image cottage across the walkway.

It was there in summer that my mother, father, and sister Mary would visit them. After tea we would spend time in the greenhouses where a red talking parrot (from Dr. Rice's expeditions) would entertain us with salty language.

During the first twenty-five years of his service to Ham Rice, Bert and Dorothy would winter with him and his first wife in Palm Beach. Later, they attended the Rices when they were in residence at 901 Fifth, [201] but they always summered on Coggeshall Avenue.

In 1965, the Madam's health began to decline. That spring her jewelry was auctioned off by Park-Bernet Galleries for $1,342,560, a world record at the time for a sale by a single owner. [202]

One of the Holmwoods' closest friends was William Brown, known as Wiggie, who visited them on Coggeshall with his daughter Eileen nearly every afternoon after he retired. [203]

"The history of what happened in so many of those estates was handed down, generation to generation in story form," Eileen told me in an interview for this book. "Almost every estate had a caretaker who lived with his family on the property: like John Almeida who took care of The Ledges for Howard Cushing or Dan Mello whose father and his before him, took care of Harbor Court, John Nicholas Brown's estate which is now The New York Yacht Club."

On my own family's visits to Coggeshall, the Holmwoods would tell those stories of other summer colonists; always protecting the privacy of The Rices. Between what we heard from them at their "summer place" and at the annual Christmas celebrations at our house, we got an inside view of what went on behind those massive irons gates. Most of the tales were amusing, but one, which was downright bizarre, will be chronicled in the Chapters ahead.

All of it prepared me well for my first real paying job at one of America's oldest private men's clubs—a sanctuary that predated The Union League in Philadelphia and The Oglethorpe Club in Savannah: the venerable Newport Reading Room. [204]

CHAPTER NINE

BOCCE, BILLIARDS & PONY DAIQUIRIS

A number of my friends were ball boys at the Newport Casino for "Tennis Week," [205] cabana boys at Bailey's Beach, or boat boys at the Summer Colony's Ida Lewis Yacht Club. Assessing that roster today, I'm mindful that back then, reflective of the inequities of the times, there weren't a lot of service jobs in Newport for young women. But for teenage boys, one of the coveted positions for after-school employment was at The Reading Room, the men's club at the opposite end of Bellevue Avenue from Rough Point. In 1962 my mother, active in local politics, helped get me a job there through William D. Doyle, the county Democratic chairman, who was the club's devoted superintendent.

The Reading Room was founded in 1854 by William Shephard Wetmore, who'd made a fortune in the China Trade. He'd built Chateau Sur Mer, one of the first "cottages," two years earlier. [206] Established "to promote literary and social intercourse among its members," [207] the club had an unflinching set of bylaws. While traditional card games were allowed, "Faro, Rouge-et-Noir, Roulette and round games of cards and dice" were forbidden. [208]

The Newport Reading Room on Bellevue Avenue

In fact, the rules, which awarded Honorary Memberships to current and former U.S. Presidents, were otherwise so inflexible that they were rumored to have inspired the founding of The Newport Casino, further south on Bellevue in 1880. That occurred, according to legend, after one Reading Room Member, James Gordon Bennett Jr., publisher of *The New York Herald*, [209] challenged British Cavalry Officer Captain Henry Augustus "Sugar" Candy, to ride his horse up onto the Reading Room's porch which he did. That resulted in Candy's expulsion as a guest Member and a reprimand to Bennett, who promptly withdrew to start his own exclusive enclave down the block. [210]

Over time, the Reading Room membership included Vincent Astor and Washington Irving, not to mention every one of the Vanderbilts from Cornelius, the patriarch, forward.

As servants at the club, our livery consisted of turn-of-the-century bell hop uniforms -- thankfully, without the hats. We wore long black pants with gold stripes that ran from hem to pocket along the outer legs. The trousers came up to mid-chest and were held in place with black braces. The short white cotton jackets extended to waist-level just far enough to cover the tops of the pants. They had holes for three gold buttons in front that we fastened with cotter pins when the jackets came back from the laundry.

The three "Boys," sat on a red tuck and roll leather bench in a corner of The Office which contained a walk-in safe where Members stored pre-Castro Cuban cigars worth a fortune. There was a barber's chair behind that. If one of the Members wanted a shave or a trim, his preferred hair cutter would be summoned. There was a little box on The Office wall with numbers corresponding to the various rooms in the club. Reading Room No. 1 stocked the latest newspapers and periodicals. The magazines were kept in hard blue covers with the titles engraved in gold. Reading Room No. 2 had a fireplace and card tables.

The Bar was flanked by a series of sterling silver trophies. The walls were lined with framed *Vanity Fair* covers dating from the 1920s. While some of the Members wore slacks and sweaters, the standard dress was a dark blue blazer over trousers—typically red in summer—over boat shoes - typically Sperry Topsiders.

The porch outside the bar, where the members played backgammon on inlaid boards, led down to the backyard, which featured a manicured lawn and a sundial adjacent to a clay-rolled bocce court with green and yellow striped cushions covering benches at each end.

The Reading Room's bar. (Jerry Taylor Photo)

When one of the Members wanted a drink, they'd push a button and a number would drop in the little box by our sitting area in The Office, signaling their location, and we'd be off to serve them. Another part of our job was acting as referees during bocce games, where the scores of each round were recorded on a mounted wooden abacus with round red corks and cylindrical blue corks corresponding to the colors of the balls.

We also officiated in The Billiard Room which contained one pocketed table and three billiard tables under a ceiling two stories high. The favorite game back then was "Cowboy Pool" in which Members made points by sinking balls and making caroms or billiards. In order to win, you had to sink the cue ball off the No. 5 ball in a pocket of your calling.

The Reading Room was an all-male redoubt. Women were admitted only twice a year, on "President's Day" in February and in the summer during a party known as "Bocce Night."

In the two years I worked there, Dan Konchar was "Second Boy." He went on to a distinguished career on the faculty of Rogers High School. As a former math teacher, when we reminisced about the club, he reminded me about the hours we worked and what we got paid.

"We typically worked, six or seven hour days in the summers and three to four hours a night after school during the week," he recalled. [211] "Over a four week stretch that meant 168 hours and at the end of the month we got a pay envelope which contained $40.00 in cash. In short, we were working for less than 23 cents an hour."

That led to a discussion between us regarding the only Member who ever tipped regularly: Gustave J.S. White. He had been President of The Club in the early 1950's and ran a highly successful real estate company specializing in "the cottage" trade.

Every year, Gus, as we called him, got a new navy blue luxury automobile. He would have a six inch yellow stripe painted below each window on the two front doors and his initials G.J.S.W. emblazoned in a half-inch navy blue typeface over the yellow.

Once a week around lunch time he would drive into the Club's parking lot with an attractive woman with whom he was apparently having an affair. He'd beep his horn and whoever was on the bench would know to run to the bar and order a pair of champagne cocktails, which, we would take care not to spill as we rushed out to the lot and served them.

"Every time we'd bring him those drinks," said Dan, "he'd tip us a buck. The only other Member who tipped in the four years I worked there was John Rovensky, who donated Rovensky Park on Bellevue in honor of his wife."

In 1956 at the time of her death in Newport at the age of 73, Mrs. Rovensky, the Gilded age beauty Sarah Mae "Maisie" Caldwell, was one of the wealthiest women in America. She'd inherited $50 million from her second husband Morton Plant, a steamship and railroad magnate who was Commodore of The New York Yacht Club at the time. They traded their Fifth Avenue mansion worth $950,000 back then, for two strands of pearls designed by Pierre Cartier worth $1 million. [212] That beautiful Neo Renaissance building on the corner of 52nd Street and Fifth Avenue in Manhattan is Cartier's New York flagship to this day.[213]

John Rovensky was Maisie's fourth husband and until her death, they held forth at Clarendon Court, another Horace Trumbauer-designed English-style mansion. [214] Located at 626 Bellevue Avenue, two doors down from Doris Duke, it will forever live in infamy as the place where Sunny von Bulow lapsed into a coma in 1980, purportedly at the hands of her husband Claus, who was later convicted of attempted murder, and then saw the verdict overturned in a second trial. [215] That saga was memorialized in *Reversal of Fortune,* the feature film, staring Glen Close and Jeremy Irons, based on the best seller written by lawyer Alan Dershowitz. [216]

THE NEWPORT RABBIT HOLE

By the way, *that* little aside is typical of the "down-the-rabbit-hole" journey you'll find yourself on if you pull any significant thread in the intricately woven tapestry of Newport Society.

In 2008 *The New York Times* covered the death of 92 year-old Eileen Slocum, described as "a doyenne of Newport, R.I. society... whose family history is dotted with connections to the most moneyed and powerful of the American aristocracy." [217]

The obit cited a *Providence Journal* interview she gave in 2000 in which she was asked how Newport's closely held circle of private clubs like the Reading Room and The Clambake Club were able to stave off invasions from Hollywood and Wall Street; remaining such "bastions of old money."

"By being rather fastidious about the people in the clubs," she said; choosing a word that was a dog whistle for Eileen's darker side. When Deborah Davis, author of the splendid book *Gilded,* arrived to interview Mrs. Slocum during a research trip to Newport, she brought along a first edition of her 2006 best seller, *Party of The Century,* which chronicled Truman Capote's Black and White Ball. [218] Thinking she might offer it to Mrs. Slocum as a gift, Ms. Davis later recounted how the Society matron stared at Capote's picture on the cover, then handed it back to her and snapped, "He was a nasty homosexual." [219]

Such was the way certain members of "The Avenue Crowd" could bluntly express their sense of entitlement and their bigotry. Happily, I saw none of that at The Reading Room. In fact, two of the Members were particularly kind to me.

THE PAPAL CHAMBERLAIN

Herman C. Huffer Jr. was born in Paris in 1883. [220] His family history could be traced back to Count Armand Marc de Montmorin, the former ambassador to Madrid under Louis XVI, who perished during the French Revolution in 1792, [221]

After driving an ambulance in World War I, Mr. Huffer donated five of the rescue vehicles to The British Army, to which he was attached. Making his fortune in banking and railroads, he was an avid yachtsman and former Commodore at Ida Lewis on Wellington Avenue.

There, over the decades, he raced a series of boats named for his mother. In 1957 his 37 foot Herreshoff sloop Estelle Dunbar VII won the Newport to Point Judith Race. [222] Three months later it was lost in a fire that ravaged Wharton's Shipyard on the island of Jamestown where it was being stored for the winter. [223] Undaunted, Mr. Huffer launched Estelle Dunbar VIII, a 5.5 meter-class yacht that competed in the Olympic trials held off Brenton Point in 1964.[224]

Known for his philanthropy, Mr. Huffer was named one of 400 Papal Chamberlains by Pope John XXIII. That office required him to serve 10 days every two years at The Vatican in uniform, designed after the formal court dress of The Spanish Renaissance. It included a white ruff collar, sword and chain of office.

Mr. Huffer was not quite so formally dressed, but always impeccable, when he entered the Reading Room, typically in a custom tailored jacket, slacks and suede Oxfords. When I came to know him, he was in his late seventies. Blind in one eye, he wore glasses with one lens grayed out and he walked with a cane. Tall, and bone thin, he'd come into the club each afternoon and read for a while before taking a short nap on the sofa in Reading Room No. 1.

When he woke up, he always coughed heavily, then lit an unfiltered Chesterfield and ordered a "pony daiquiri;" a smaller portion of the conventional cocktail.

Even at his advanced age he was known to have an eye for beautiful young women and on Bocce Night that summer, when he walked in, he shoved a ten dollar bill in my hand, winked and instructed me to let him know when Marguerite Slocum had arrived.

"I want to make sure she doesn't leave without me," he said.

Just days before that, Eileen's beautiful 18-year-old daughter had made her debut at a ball attended by 700 at The Harold Brown Villa, her mother's mansion at 459 Bellevue. [225]

When Mr. Huffer passed me and entered the club, I stared at that portrait of Hamilton and shook my head, thinking to myself, "Does he *actually* think I can accomplish this mission or even *try?*" I shrugged it off but made sure he got home safely that night by calling him a taxi.

Later that winter, Mr. Huffer treated me to the first of two acts of generosity. I'd come down with the flu in February around my birthday and after he inquired as to my absence, he ordered five quarts of ice cream delivered to my house from The Newport Creamery.

In the Fall, it came time for me to try and raise money for "The Saint La Salle Auxiliary," one of the many drives at my Catholic high school. Any student who brought in more than a $100 got a blazer with the school crest. I'd never raised more than $50. But after his gift of the ice cream I pushed audacity to a new level.

The next afternoon, after he came in, took his nap, had his cigarette and pony daiq, I shifted from one foot to the other nervously, looming over him with the drink tray. He looked up and said sternly, "Come, come boy what do you want? I cleared my throat and handed him a St. La Salle donation form. He looked at it through his one good eye, smiled and pulled a small checkbook from his jacket pocket, gesturing me forward with the empty tray which he motioned for me to turn over so he could balance on it to write the check.

He then pulled out a Mont Blanc Meisterstück fountain pen and with a flourish of handwriting one might expect see at the bottom of a Papal Bull, wrote $500. He ripped off the check and handed it to me, saying

"God bless you boy."

I got a blazer that year.

Thinking back, I remembered hearing how, just months before his death, Mr. Huffer, half blind, was still going out on the water at the tiller of his 5.5. So I reached out to Richard Tracy, his boat boy at the time, who told me another remarkable story about The Papal Chamberlain.

NAVIGATING BY INSTINCT

Back then, it was the fashion of many Members to drive American cars and Herman C. Huffer, who could have afforded a Rolls or a Bentley, owned a coal black Mercury Comet.

"Two or three times a week," recalled Tracy, "I'd go up to The Reading Room and we'd head down to Ida Lewis. [226] It was a daunting experience, since Mr. Huffer insisted on driving and he was seeing with only one good eye. But he had driven the route so many times before that, he had it memorized. So, as if navigating by instinct, we'd go south on Bellevue, and take a right on Dixon Street. He had the windows open and he seemed to be sensing our direction by the sound the car made off the parallel walls of the estates we passed.

"He'd make a right on Spring and a sharp left on Lee Avenue down to Thames, then a left and a right on Wellington past King Park to the club. We'd take the launch out to the boat which was on a mooring. He never changed his clothes. He was always dressed smartly in a white shirt, Navy Blue blazer and an old yachting cap with the club insignia. It was encrusted with salt from his many voyages.

"Anyway, as I trimmed the sails, he took the tiller and we'd go out for an hour and a half, with Mr. Huffer demonstrating a remarkable sense of direction inside the harbor where sailing without power could be dangerous because of the passing ferries. But he did it with joy and style. The wind was all he seemed to need for a sense of direction. His sensitivity was amazing. I was sad to hear that just a few months after our last sail he'd passed away at the age of 80. But on those afternoons, he skippered that Olympic-class yacht like a man in his 30's who'd lived a full life. I met many amazing people in Newport, but he was in a class by himself."

THE GOOD DOCTOR

My second patron at The Club actually helped to advance my career as a writer. When it came to The Reading Room, the Board seemed to have an admission policy based partly on social standing and partly on the skill of a given prospective Member. If an applicant might serve as a worthy opponent at the billiard, card or backgammon table he'd have a leg up, even if he didn't have a great fortune behind him.

Case in point: Dr. Charles S. Dotterer, a former Navy Lieutenant Commander and ophthalmologist who was admitted to this enclave of tycoons, in part, because he was a world-class pool player. He was also a scratch golfer and member of The Newport Country Club where he repeatedly won The President's Cup. [227] A former President of the staff at Newport Hospital, [228] Doctor Dotterer lived in a modest Victorian house next to The Redwood Library, within walking distance of The Club where he used a custom-made cue to run the tables. He and his wife had three daughters named Nina, Nancy and Norey (Cullen), who went on to become the co-owner of The Black Pearl restaurant and her own successful namesake cafe on Broadway. [229]

Though many of the Members looked down their noses at the Reading Room staff, Dr. Dotterer was a true egalitarian. He overheard me one day going on to one of the other boys about the superiority of the U.S. Navy which, unlike the other major service branches, could compete in the air, on and under the sea and, with the Marine Corps, on land. He asked me about that, and I told him that I'd recently quit the Boy Scouts and joined the Naval Sea Cadets. We drilled every Friday night at the Base, and I was lucky enough, that past summer, to take a cruise to Annapolis on a destroyer. Doctor Dotterer suggested that I enter an essay contest, sponsored by The Newport Navy League. One of the advantages of taking first prize was that the winner would get the essay published in *The Newport Daily News.*

The subject that year was: "Which of the Perry brothers of Newport had more impact on the history of this country, Commodore Oliver Hazard Perry (hero of The War of 1812) or his younger brother Matthew Calbraith Perry (who opened the ports of Japan to U.S. trading)."

Each of those naval heroes had earned a statue in a different part of town. Oliver Hazard presided over the park in front of the Superior Courthouse on Washington Square, which was later named for President Dwight D. Eisenhower, a regular Newport visitor. Matthew C's statue was in Touro Park, just a block south of The Reading Room.

I chose the younger brother and The Navy League judges kindly awarded me first place. I won a $50.00 Savings Bond which Dr. Dotterer handed to me in front of Matthew's statue. But the real thrill of the assignment was getting my first ink in the paper I once delivered. [230] After the brief ceremony attended by my parents and Rear Admiral Leslie J. O'Brien, Chief of Staff of Cruiser-Destroyer Force Atlantic Fleet, the good doctor and I walked back to the Reading Room.

THE CAT'S CRADLE THAT IS NEWPORT

In one connection to this story, Matthew C. Perry's daughter Caroline married August Belmont, the Hessian Jewish immigrant who had worked for The Rothschilds of Europe and later founded The Belmont Stakes – third leg of The Triple Crown. In 1890 his son Oliver commissioned architect Richard Morris Hunt to design Belcourt, the French chateau-inspired mansion down the street from Rough Point, which ironically, played a significant role in my Duke investigation.

Proof of the few degrees of separation in the cat's cradle of Newport, Rhode Island. The reader will encounter a dozen more instances in the course of this book.

The Park where Perry's statue stood was named for Judah, the son of Isaac, who founded Touro Synagogue. Judah was seriously wounded while carrying ammunition in The War of 1812, but after he survived, he became a prominent New Orleans merchant and philanthropist, endowing a series of Jewish and Christian religious sites in the Northeast as well as the New York City hospital that became Mt. Sinai.[231]

In 1854 he bought 2.25 acres of land at the highest point on the island, on Bellevue Avenue south of the Synagogue, and donated it to the City as a park. [232] Its central focus at that time was an ancient round Stone Tower, believed to have been built by the Vikings.

The Tower played such a central role in Newport's history that it merits a chapter of its own in the book ahead. Further proof of the many interwoven threads within The City By Sea, and with respect to The Reading Room, there's one more.

Another Member of the club who was a fierce competitor of Dr. Dotterer's in The Billiard Room and on the links of The Country Club, was Howard Gardiner Cushing. Tall, grey-haired and handsome, his four adult children were gifted with movie star looks: Howard III, Freddy, Tom, and Mary, whom they called Minnie. Howard Senior was a character cut from the Hemingway cloth. A big game hunter, sportsman and heir to a great railroad fortune, he presided over The Ledges, a sprawling white Victorian-era estate built in 1850 that overlooked Bailey's Beach, a quarter mile from Rough Point.

The Ledges, home of the Cushing Family

In August, 1967 it was the dazzling scene of Minnie's storybook marriage to famed African wildlife photographer, adventurer and Nairobi-based preservationist Peter Beard, whom she'd met on Safari. Minnie had made her debut at The Ledges in 1961 and worked, until her marriage, as an assistant in New York to Oscar de la Renta, who, naturally, designed her wedding gown.

Outdoing any Newport summer colony marriage in memory, the "rehearsal dinner" was actually a torchlit black-tie party at Bailey's Beach, the night before the nuptials, featuring drum playing African dancers in native dress. [233]

They entertained the guests with songs and indigenous dances before jumping into canoes and staging a mock sea battle with The Black Pearl, the square-rigged brigantine from Bannister's wharf, that rounded a peninsula and sailed toward the beach, firing its cannon under a crescent moon as the couple held sparklers. [234]

The next day, they were married at Newport's historic Trinity Church by the reverend Canon Lockett Ford Ballard, who would clash with Doris Duke in a different kind of battle a decade later. The Cushing-Beard wedding party of twenty-six, celebrated along with 416 guests under a green and white tent on the lawn of The Ledges before the couple was whisked away in a helicopter with the groom filming the lift off. [235]

As I later learned when I pulled on another thread in this story, Howard Senior had another ironic connection. Through his philanthropic work he was the Vice President of The Newport County Boys Club and in 1964 he handed the award to Stephen Robertson as Boy Of The Year.

CHAPTER TEN

THE CHIEF,
THE CONDOS
& THE MOB

Seven months after summarily wrapping up the Eduardo Tirella homicide case, Chief Joseph A. Radice retired. By then he'd spent 42 years on the job. The rumors of how he may have profited by allowing Doris Duke to walk, still rebound on the dedicated Newport Facebook Group: "We all know she did it," wrote one Newporter, "The chief retired to Key Biscayne right next to Bebe Rebozo, Nixon's buddy." [236] Another speculated that he "bought an island off the Florida keys." [237] None of that is how it happened. But like so many aspects of this story, the many half-truths may contain the full truth.

Joseph Augustus Radice was a complicated figure. Born in 1899, with only an 8th grade education, [238] he put on a badge in 1925. By 1938 when he made Sergeant, he was already well schooled in the upstairs-downstairs rules that protected the wealthy and defined the working-class officials in Newport who catered to them. Back then, a single uniform was responsible for patrolling the entire ten-mile Ocean Drive.

Chief Joseph A. Radice as a young motorcycle cop (left) and on his last day in uniform 7 months after closing the Duke-Tirella homicide case.

"In the winter," Radice recalled, "patrolmen had to walk in the snow and the ice. You couldn't get a cup a coffee (or) a ride. No cars. But you could get warm if you knew somebody" on one of the estates. [239]

"Radice was a real bulldog and an outlier," said retired Newport Fire Capt. Paul Faerber. "An Italian who hung on for more than four decades in a department dominated by the Irish." [240] It took him 20 years to make chief, but long before the "unfortunate accident," Radice was well acquainted with the reclusive heiress at Rough Point.

Ever since her father's deathbed warning to "Trust no one," Doris had been famously paranoid, allowing vicious German Shepherds and Akitas to roam the grounds of her estates in Newport, New Jersey, Beverly Hills and Hawaii, causing passersby to repeated get attacked and bitten. [241]

In May of 1964 after two tourists on Cliff Walk were victimized in a single week, Radice ordered "the destruction or removal" of two of her dogs. [242] Counter-puncher that she was, Doris made front page news a month later, after she cut off the Cliff Walk with chain link fences. She'd been in a pitched battle with the City since 1958 when she put up "heavy wire fencing and thorny bushes" along the Walk, one of the top tourist attractions in Rhode Island. [243]

Doris was the only estate owner to block the 3 ½ mile stretch; erecting fences as recently as four months before October 7[th,] 1966. [244] But all of that ended eight days after Tirella's death when The Duke Foundation made what was described as "the first substantial pledge" to The Cliff Walk Foundation then trying to raise $493,000 toward a goal of $1.2 million for the pathway's restoration. It was a clear message to the City. "Newport was reminded," wrote her godson Pony Duke," that "Doris was its only hope for refurbishment." [245]

Rough Point as seen today from Cliff Walk. The dogs are long gone, but there is still a sense of foreboding about the estate. Despite dropping her lawsuit with Newport after Tirella's death and contributing to The Walk's restoration, the stretch surrounding the Duke estate remains the least passable section of the 3 ½ mile public walkway (Adam Fithers photos)

With respect to Tirella's homicide, if there *had* been a quid pro quo, nobody was in a position to benefit more than Joseph Radice. "Oh boy, the word was, 'Radice's gonna make out on this one,'" recalled Woody Ring, one of the first young police officers on the scene the night of the incident. [246] But did the Chief make out? And if so, for how much?

At the time he left the Newport PD in 1967, Radice's annual salary was a mere $7,000. Four years later he bought the first of two units at The Warrenton House, a new condominium complex in Hollywood Florida. [247] He also owned a pair of lots near the beach in Middletown, the city adjacent to Newport. [248] In order to get some sense of whether any of the funds in his Florida property buys came from Doris Duke, one has to consider his tangled family connections.

MARRIED INTO THE MOB

Radice's first wife was a waitress named Ada Pollack. In 1919 they had a daughter Mary, but eight years later, Radice abandoned both of them. "He walked out," recalls his granddaughter Elayne Paranzino, a former Roman Catholic nun. [249] "Ada was able to get a divorce on grounds of desertion. He paid nothing to her, and she would bring my mom every day to an orphanage, then walk to her waitressing job to support the two of them."

By 1935, still a patrolman, Radice was married to Agnes O'Loughlin, a typist at The Naval Training Station. [250] Nine years after that, they separated. [251] The date of their divorce is unclear, but in 1970 Radice married into a Mafia-related family when he exchanged vows in Miami with the former Mary Capochiano Flynn. [252] Her brother Dominic was a bookie for Raymond Patriarca, the Cosa Nostra boss of New England, based in Providence. That's according to her grandson, Andrew Flynn who loved Radice and considered him his surrogate grandfather.

"My blood grandfather David Flynn was a real violent guy and a nasty drunk," he said in an interview for this book. [253] "Somebody told him he needed to get out of town, and he was leaving when he got hit by a train."

The details of the accident in 1955 were highly suspicious.

At the time of the crash, Flynn's car was parked on a railroad crossing with gates down and lights flashing on either side of it. After impact with the New Haven Railroad's Merchant Limited, the vehicle was hurled 150 feet (with Flynn pinned inside). [254]

Andrew told me that he's sure it was murder.

"He'd been tied to the steering wheel at the time. Word in the family was that the Capochianos killed him." [255]

At that point, Joe Radice had made Captain, but this was one "accident" he didn't have to investigate, since it took place in Richmond, RI., some 25 miles away from Newport.

Radice died at the age of 98 in 1997. [256] By then, though he and his third wife wintered in Florida, his principal home was at 22 Rhode Island Avenue in Newport. Andrew said that Mary, his grandmother, got the chief's pension, and property records show that she inherited the last of Joe's Hollywood condominiums. [257]

Radice's granddaughter, Elayne, who long ago reconciled with him after she left The Sisters of Saint Joseph, told me that for years, she's had to live with the rumors that he'd been bought off by Doris Duke. "I was in the convent when the Tirella tragedy happened," she said. "But I confronted my grandfather one day. I said, 'Don't you lie to me.' He said 'None of these rumors are true, Elayne. I didn't get *any* money from her.' Then, when I pressed him, he chuckled. 'You think I was paid off? You can *have* it if we can find it." [258]

Still, a conflict remains within the Radice/Flynn/Paranzino family over where his money went. "My grandmother Mary, Joe's wife, got his pension, the condo and their house on Rhode Island Avenue," said Andrew. [259] It's unclear who in the family received the proceeds from the two lots in Middletown near Easton's Beach and Elayne insists that *she* got Radice's $25,000 life insurance policy and nothing else. [260]

Meanwhile, property records in Broward County, Florida show that in 1971, while still maintaining his principal residence in Newport, Radice bought Unit 432 at the Warrenton House, a new four-story complex in Hollywood. The price was $13,900 – the equivalent of $88,588.00 today. He financed it with a down payment of $4,780 which was 68% of his last year's salary as Chief. In 1976 he bought another apartment, Unit 433, in the same complex for $19,000 and sold the first unit in 1977. [261]

Another Warrenton condo, Unit 428 on the same floor, was owned by Mary Radice's brother Dom (aka Donald) the mob bookie. [262] His widow Betty later sold that apartment to Elayne Paranzino's parents Albert and Mary. Radice's granddaughter contends that she had no knowledge of her parent's connection to the Warrenton complex, but she acknowledges that her father Al was Dominic Capochiano's partner in Ann's Kitchen, a popular Middletown restaurant, and that he too, ran numbers for Mafia boss Patriarca.

The mob ties to the Capochianos date to 1951 when the RI State Police raided two variety stores in Newport where bets were being placed. [263] One was co-owned by Dominic, whose sister Mary later became Radice's wife. After the raid she and her then husband David posted bail of $1,500 for two of the arrestees - equivalent to $14,790.00 today. It was an era before credit cards were in wide use, [264] so it's likely that the bond was posted in cash.

David Flynn was the same man who, four years later, was apparently murdered on the railroad tracks by his in-laws in the Capochiano family. Joseph Radice was a Lieutenant at the time of the raids, which State Police conducted in secret without informing the Newport PD. [265]

"That tells you something," says retired NYPD Detective James Moss.

OTHER BENEFICIARIES

With his property acquisitions in The Sunshine State and his complicated family connections, the rumors continue as to whether Chief Radice's rush-to-judgement on the Duke-Tirella homicide financed his retirement. But one thing is clear: two other Newport cops directly connected to the case, benefited. Det. George Watts who took Dee Dee's brief bedroom statement on Sunday the 9th was promoted to Sergeant within months [266] and Lt. Frank Walsh succeeded Radice as chief, [267] though the clear heir-apparent was Capt. Paul Sullivan, then the Chief of Detectives.

Capt. Paul Sullivan (left) the heir apparent for the Newport Police Chief's job and former Lt. Frank H. Walsh who got it, at a press conferences in October 1967 following the arrest of Stephen Robertson. (Peter Lance photo)

One of the biggest unanswered questions in my investigation was why *he* didn't get the Chief's job? Paul Sullivan was the effective Number Two in the department. An alumnus of USC and graduate of the FBI's National Police Academy, he was also a civic leader. He'd been chairman of the annual March of Dimes drive and served on the Newport School Committee; a larger than life law man, who might have even contemplated a run for Congress one day after serving as head of the Department. [268]

"No one was more qualified to succeed Radice," says Tim, one of the late Sullivan's sons. [269] "He was never quite right with the way the Duke case was handled."

Still, Captain Paul ended up ratifying that contrived Q&A and he testified at the civil trial that there had been "no foul play." [270] So, if he *had* acquiesced to Radice, I was curious as to why Lt. Walsh had beat him out for the Chief's job. After pulling my old *Daily News* files out of storage, I found a dog-eared Reporter's Notebook, where I'd written three cryptic lines in the fall of 1967, during my first stint on *The Daily News*:

-Robertson

-Tubley's – Sullivan

-Doris

Those lines brought me back to an encounter I'd had with Captain Sullivan a year after they closed the Duke-Tirella case. It happened on the day of the preliminary hearing in the Stephen Robertson murder at the same Superior Court house where my mother worked as a Deputy Clerk.

On the night after the two sailors were killed, when Steve had surrendered, he'd been arraigned at Police Headquarters and ordered held without bail pending trial. Moments later, he was led out in that perp walk and driven in a State Police unit to the Adult Correctional Institution, Rhode Island's ominous maximum-security prison in Cranston, known as the ACI.

A week later they brought him back for the prelim and when it was over, Capt. Paul went to lunch at Tubley's Spa, a coffee shop on the corner of Spring and Touro Streets near The Superior Courthouse. I still had a number of unanswered questions, so I tracked him down there and waited until he got up from the counter to pay his bill, catching him as he was about to exit.

"Captain Sullivan," I said.

"Yeah?" He'd stepped onto the sidewalk and was about to cross Spring Street toward where his unmarked unit was parked.

"I wanted to ask you about the night Magoo walked into Headquarters."

"What about it?" He was moving into the street now, so I stayed with him.

"I understand that after he walked into the lobby, nobody bothered searching him for a weapon."

At that point he stopped. We were right in the middle of Spring, just a block up from the back door of The Quality Lunch.

"Who the hell told you that?"

"I've got my sources."

"Yeah, well, charges have been filed against Steve and you know I can't comment."

He started moving, so I called out over his shoulder, "The way I heard it, you took Goo outside where he showed you the murder weapon in his car."

That made him stop. He turned around. The light changed on Touro Street and traffic was now approaching us, but he held up his hand, like the street cop he'd once been and stopped the line of cars.

"So what's the question?"

"At what point did you read him his rights?"

The Chief of Detectives gritted his teeth for a moment. He looked me up and down. I was standing in the middle of the street, holding up traffic along with him in my Madras jacket, skinny tie and chinos. Finally he smiled.

"Peter, you're a De La Salle boy. You went to school with Steve..." He nodded toward the Court House. "Your mother Albina's a wonderful woman, so I'll do you a favor and say only this: Someday I'll answer *that* question, just like someday you'll find out what *really* happened in the Duke case."

Before I could get off another question, he walked away.

I've only now gotten a chance to learn what he might have been hinting at. The truth behind Tirella's death was actually uncovered *within hours* of his DOA at Newport Hospital and the Police Department, at the highest levels, had conspired with Doris's lawyers to cover it up.

But if Captain Paul Sullivan had fallen on his sword for Doris Duke, it didn't help him. When he retired in 1976 after 30 years, his last assignment was as Night Watch Commander of The Patrol Division. In law enforcement terms, he ended up in Siberia.

PART TWO

CHAPTER ELEVEN

IF YOU BUILD IT, THEY WILL COME

There are cities where a single street acquires legendary status over time: Broadway in Manhattan, North Michigan Avenue, known in Chicago as "The Magnificent Mile," or Brickell Avenue, that two mile north-south stretch of U.S. 1 in Miami they call Biscayne Boulevard. When it came to the Gilded Age and the dominance of Newport Rhode Island as the summer playground of the New York 400, it was Bellevue Avenue.

Deborah Davis reported in *Gilded,* that what later became known as "Millionaire's Row," was the creation of two land speculators Alfred Smith and Joseph Bailey, who had acquired an undeveloped beach and some sandy fields at the extreme southern end of Aquidneck Island. In 1851, through deft engineering and landscaping, they turned Bellevue Street, little more than a wide dirt lane at the time, into The Avenue, a thoroughfare connecting "the busier part of town to (the) remote beach property" that, as Ms. Davis so eloquently wrote, "evoked the scenic boulevards of Paris." Soon, in the tradition of "if you build it, they will come," the wealthiest New York industrialists and the southerners who sought to emulate them, came to Newport. This is a brief excerpt from *Gilded*:

In 1852, Daniel Parrish, a rich southern planter, built Beechwood, a Florentine palazzo. Two years later, William Wetmore…built an Italian style villa he called Chateau-Sur-Mer. A few years after (it) was completed, Wetmore hosted a party that set a new record for extravagance in Newport — and everywhere else in the country. He invited more than twenty four hundred guests to join him for a fête champêtre, a garden party held on the spectacular grounds of his estate. [271]

Mr. Wetmore, you may recall, had founded the Newport Reading Room, which became the nexus of an exercise in one-upmanship unlike any in America's history. Over the next 60 years, one tycoon after another erected grand mansions of every architectural style that rose up like marble pieces on a Monopoly board.

One palace -- literally called Marble House – was built in 1892 at the cost of $11 million. It featured a freestanding Chinese Tea House overlooking Cliff Walk. [272] At Beacon Hill House, the estate of railroad magnate Arthur Curtiss James, a replica of an entire "Swiss Village" was installed. It was a fully functioning hamlet within his sprawling property that housed and employed more than 100 people.[273]

By 1907, writing in *The American Scene,* Henry James, who summered on the island in the 1860's, observed that Newport had become "a breeding ground for white elephants." [274] But just as the castles and keeps of Europe defined the power and reach of nobility on The Continent, Newport's cottages marked a new hierarchy of American social climbers.

One might call it the tyranny of the pecking order.

In 1930 James Watson Gerard, the U.S. Ambassador to Germany prior to World War I [275] was in Newport when he compiled a list of what he termed, "The Sixty Four Men Who Run America." [276] At the time he was visiting General Cornelius Vanderbilt III, [277] great grandson of the "The Commodore," the family's patriarch who had built one of America's greatest fortunes in an empire of steamboats, ocean-going steamships and railroads. [278]

It was the General's father, Cornelius II, who had commissioned The Breakers, crown jewel of Newport summer cottages, an extraordinary Renaissance-style palazzo located on Ochre Point along Cliff Walk just east of Bellevue. Raised largely of marble without a single timber, [279] the 70 room, five floor mansion with 62,482 square feet of living space [280] was designed by Gilded Age Architect Richard Morris Hunt who also designed the 250 room Biltmore Estate in Asheville, North Carolina for Cornelius II's nephew George Washington Vanderbilt II. [281]

The Breakers at Ochre Point as seen from The Cliff Walk

The front doors of The Breakers weighed 70 tons. Its chandeliers were initially wired for electricity and piped for gas. Both salt and fresh water flowed through the bathroom faucets. The great hall rose 45 feet over two floors. A fresco entitled *Aurora At Dawn* was painted over the dining room. [282]

In 1948 Cornelius II's youngest daughter, Countess Gladys Széchenyi, leased the mansion for $1.00 a year to The Newport Preservation Society which bought it outright in 1972 for a mere $395,000; the equivalent today of just under $2.3 million. The visionary who made that great deal was Katherine Urquhart Warren who founded The Society and went on to follow Jacqueline Kennedy Onassis as Vice President of Doris Duke's Newport Restoration Foundation (NRF)

There were reports that Eduardo Tirella was driving Doris to a meeting with Mrs. Warren on the night he was killed, [283] and a decade later *The New York Times* described a rumored encounter between the two women who were said to be having tea one day after Tirella's death. It was in 1968 when Doris was gearing up the NRF to reshape Newport into a kind of real-life Colonial Williamsburg. Concerned that their two organizations might overlap after the Society had restored Hunter House, a 1754 Georgian Colonial, [284] Doris was said to have turned to Mrs. Warren and quipped, "All right, Katherine, you take the 19th Century and I'll take the 18th." [285]

Beyond The Breakers, the Vanderbilt family was responsible for six of the great "cottages," including Rough Point itself, originally built for the brother of Cornelius II. Other estates included Marble House, the summer home of William K. Vanderbilt; Beaulieu, purchased by Cornelius III in 1911; Reginald Claypoole Vanderbilt's Sandy Point Farm, in nearby Portsmouth; and Rock Cliff, the home of Harold Stirling Vanderbilt, William K's son, who successfully defended The America's Cup three times; first in 1930 in the magnificent J-Class yacht Enterprise, beating Sir Thomas Lipton in Shamrock V.

That victory put him on the cover of *TIME,* but as Commodore of The New York Yacht Club, he was at the helm again in 1934, defeating aviation pioneer Thomas Sopwith and doing it again three years later, winning four straight in Ranger, the last J-Boat to win "100 Guinea Cup."

In September of 1967, as part of *The Newport Daily News* coverage of the 20th Cup challenge, a chance to interview "Mike" Vanderbilt came up and I jumped at it. As we sat in a den off the main foyer at Rock Cliff, he was visited by Rod and Olin Stephens, who had crewed for him back in '37 and went on to design every Cup winner but one in the previous 30 years.

After they left, I asked Vanderbilt, then 83, his greatest memory of the series. He went on to describe a nail biter of a race against Sopwith in 1934.

"I was skippering Rainbow," he recalled. "We had lost two races of a best of seven series to Sopwith's Endeavor and we were 6 ½ minutes down at the final mark of the race. I never felt as unhappy. The breeze was light. We were on a leeward, windward 30 mile course. But after the last mark our luck changed. Endeavor made 4 tacks to fetch the finish line. We didn't tack at all and passed right through her lee to victory." [286] After that he went on to steer Rainbow to three more wins.

I asked him about Sr. Thomas Lipton, the Irish tea baron who had waged five unsuccessful challenges for the Cup in his Shamrocks I-V.

"I met him during the 1930 series," Vanderbilt remembered. "He couldn't have been a more congenial fellow, although he was quite a good advertiser for his tea company. I understand they still put a little picture of him on the boxes."

The legendary yachtsman delivered that last line with a twinkle in his eye.

Three years later, Harold Stirling Vanderbilt passed away peacefully, earning a front page obituary in *The New York Times*. [287] Also remembered as the innovator of contract bridge, he was one of the last male heirs of that remarkable American dynasty to summer in Newport. But not all members of the Vanderbilt line got such notable coverage. In fact, one who had married into the family briefly, became the object of some infamy.

ANOTHER MURDER?

George Washington Vanderbilt III, the Commodore's great-great-grandson inherited $40 million [288] but somehow seemed marked from birth. The youngest son of Arthur Gwynne Vanderbilt, he was only a year old when his father perished on the RMS Lusitania, sunk by a German U-Boat off the coast of Ireland in 1915.[289] Dying a hero, Arthur Gwynne, who couldn't swim, was said to have given his life belt to a valet with the instruction, "Save all the kiddies you can, boy!" [290]

Never attending college, George Washington started out as an earnest adventurer and naturalist, leading expeditions to Panama and Africa by the time he'd turned 21. [291] An avid yachtsman like his uncle "Mike," GW mounted his fifth major expedition aboard the schooner yacht Pioneer in 1941, exploring the Galapagos islands. [292] After one foray to the South Seas, he returned with 5,000 snakes, 15,000 insects and 10,000 birds, specimens he donated to The Philadelphia Academy of Natural Science.[293]

Between 1936 and 37 he sponsored the renewal of automobile races for the Vanderbilt Cup, founded by his uncle William K. II in 1904. He endowed the George Vanderbilt Foundation at Stanford and won The Legion of Merit for heroism in the Pacific Theater in World War II. [294] But at some point, George's life became troubled. He went to the altar four times -- first to Lucille Parsons in 1935. Divorced in '46, he married Anita C. Zabala Howard four years later. That marriage lasted until 1958 when George tied the knot with Joyce Branning, a tall blond beautician 13 years younger. [295] They separated after only six and a half months before splitting formally on March 22nd, 1961.

Then, just two days later, George married a fourth time to Louise Mitchell Paine in Scottsdale, Arizona and soon his life took a radical turn for the worse.

On June 26th, 1961, the couple drove down to San Francisco from his Shadow Valley ranch near Mount Shasta. They checked into The Mark Hopkins hotel, reportedly for a Saturday night at the theater. At some point as darkness fell, Louise told police that George had called out to her from the sitting room in their suite and when she'd gone to respond, she found a window open. Afraid to look down, she called the hotel desk and George's body was discovered 150 feet below. [296]

No note was found, but in Hawaii, GW's doctor E.F. Cushnie furnished a possible motive, reporting to the press that his patient had suffered from chronic pancreatitis and "lived in terror of being struck down at any time by a coma." [297] Louise was quoted in *The New York Times* as saying that he'd been despondent over business setbacks. [298]

Documents in Honolulu Probate court showed that he'd left an estate of $4,000,000 -- ten per cent of his initial inheritance. The assets included $3,200,000 in cash, stocks and bonds, and $800,000 in real estate between California and South Carolina. Louise, his wife of less than three months, soon became the beneficiary of his $700,000 ranch and one third of the estate's income. Lucille Vanderbilt Balding, GW's daughter from his first marriage, got another third.

But as it turned out, the suicide victim had drafted his last will and testament *the day before* he took his own life, so his daughter decided to contest it, prompting years of litigation. [299]

Represented by the fashionable New York law firm of Jackson, Nash, Brophy, Barringer and Brooks, Louise ultimately retained in excess of $2,091,000, but then refused to pay her legal bill, prompting the firm to sue her in 1967 for $53,352 in fees. [300] It wouldn't be the last time that Louise Mitchell Paine Vanderbilt resisted paying what she owed.

When I chased down that story it raised the prospect of another unsolved Society murder with an ironic second-hand connection to Doris Duke.

CHAPTER TWELVE

FIRST WITNESS
TO THE CRASH

The long missing official report of The Newport Police Department into Doris Duke's murder of Eduardo Tirella contains the statement of one James Hanley who was apparently the first person to notify the authorities about the crash across from Rough Point. [301] Hanley was the only original witness to the aftermath that I wasn't able to locate, but according to Officer Edward Angel, the first patrolman on the scene, who helped me solve the case, this is what Hanley told him:

> "I was driving south on Bellevue Avenue. I noticed a car that had crashed into a tree. I did not see the accident take place. I got out of my car to assist a woman whom I noticed was bleeding from the mouth. I then left to call the police. [302]

Hanley's address was listed as "The Mailands," an estate on Ledge Road, which was around the corner and less than 50 yards from the crash site. According to the timeline from that night, it was his call at 5:07 pm –placed first to the Newport Fire Department-- that had hastened the arrival of Officer Angel.

Located at the corner of Bellevue Avenue and Ledge Road, Mailands had been the former summer estate of Oliver Gould, a financier and heir to the Standard Oil fortune. [303] In 1952, Louis Chartier, a highly successful Newport contractor and developer who prospered by converting many of the "summer cottages" into apartment complexes, sought a zoning variance to do the same to The Mailands after a fire had badly damaged the residence. [304] He'd bought the old estate three years earlier when it was valued at just $70,000. [305] In yet another bit of irony, by 1966, Chartier's part-time residence was Roselawn, the estate next to Quatrel, across from Rough Point where Duke had crashed the two ton Dodge Polara wagon into that tree. More on that later. But 17 years after George Washington Vanderbilt's 10-story plunge to his death, his widow Louise was still balking at paying her bills.

She had been leasing two units in The Mailands for $950 a month and went public with a protest after Harry. B. Casey (who bought the property in 1978) tripled her rent to $2,850.[306] In response, Louise agreed to an increase of only $150 a month. After Casey filed an eviction notice on October 1st, Louise won the first round and succeeded in getting the action dismissed. [307] But Casey, who was also the High Sheriff of Newport County, proved to be an effective adversary. After he served her with an enforceable eviction notice, she barricaded herself behind the doors of the twin Mailands flats, declaring that she was "Holding The Fort."

The New York Times weighed in on the incident in a short piece on New Year's Eve, observing that, "If you have to ask how much it costs to live in Newport, RI, you can't afford it." [308]

By the following April when Casey pulled a moving van up to the premises, Louise agreed to vacate one of the flats, but only *after* officers had to smash a first floor window to unlock the front door and gain entry. The possessions of one of her units were then taken into storage as Louise declared, "They push you around in your own house. This is a terrible way to treat me…The worst day in my life." [309]

It wasn't the last time that Louise Mitchell Paine Vanderbilt would dodge her creditors.

After the turmoil on Ledge Road she moved to new quarters in Sherwood, another Bellevue Avenue estate with huge white columns that resembled The White House in Washington, D.C. It had been the summer residence of socialites Pembroke and Sarah Jones of Wilmington, North Carolina whose lavish lifestyle reportedly inspired the phrase, "Keeping Up With The Joneses." [310]

In 1986, after Sherwood was converted to 13 apartments, Louise, then 74, leased one for $3,000 a month. After she got two months behind in her rent, her new landlord filed suit, claiming that she'd rented the unit for all of 1986, then failed to pay the rent for August and September.

A Superior Court Judge agreed and ordered Louise to ante up the $6,000. But by then she'd departed Newport for Hawaii where she wouldn't face the same threat from collection agents she had from Sheriff Casey. After *UPI* broke the story of her latest unpaid bill, it ran in newspapers across the country. Such was the Vanderbilt name when it came to generating headlines.

This time, Louise had no comment.

SUICIDE OR HOMICIDE?

She passed away nine years later at the age of 83, earning only six lines in a list of death notices in *The Honolulu Advertiser*. [311] Sheriff Harry B. Casey, long retired, is alive, well and living in Portsmouth at the other end of Aquidneck Island. In late September of 2020 as I closed in on finishing this book, I called to get his take on the struggle with the woman whose claim to the Vanderbilt name had been so short-lived. After I refreshed his recollection of the events surrounding the dispute, citing the newspaper coverage, he paused, then chose his words carefully.

"I will say this: her husband that died, did *not* commit suicide." [312]

That put me a bit back on my heels.

"Really?"

"That's right," he said. "Louie Chartier, who I worked with in real estate, told me, 'You're going to have trouble with that woman.' At the time, I said, 'Louie, whatever it is, I'll deal with it.' That's when he said, "She pushed her husband out of a hotel window and killed him. He did not jump.'"

That response got me to thinking. "You know Harry, I have to tell you. When I first heard the facts about GW's death in San Francisco, there were several aspects of the story that didn't feel right and now you're beginning to confirm my suspicions."

"I'm listening."

"First, there was the fact that she was only married to Vanderbilt for three months. Second, they changed the will the day before his death. Third, there was no other witness to what happened. Fourth, no suicide note, and she later described her eviction by you as 'The worst day of her life.'"

"That's right."

"You would have thought that the night her husband went out a window would've been worse."

"Unless it wasn't," said the retired Sheriff.

"Then there were her ties to Hawaii," I said. "That doctor Cushnie, quoted in the papers, offered the most plausible explanation for GW's suicide. I wonder what her relationship with *him* was?"

"Guess you'll have to find out when you write *that* book," he said. "The fact is, she ended up with her husband's fortune, went on with her life and cheated everybody."

"So if she *did* kill him, how do you think Chartier knew?"

"I never asked him, but Louie Charter was a very honorable man and Louise Vanderbilt was..."

He stopped himself and I didn't press him. But when the interview ended, I couldn't help but think that he'd opened the door to another Newport heiress who might have gotten away with murder.

Strangely, for one who had exploited the family name for decades, Louise generated more national publicity than a true Vanderbilt who got embroiled in a Newport scandal just days before Eduardo's death in 1966. It's a story that's never been told outside the local press until now and it had a real impact on police Chief Joseph Radice's handling of the Tirella death investigation.

THE BLACKMAIL OF MURIEL VANDERBILT

The onetime "Golden Girl" of East Coast Society, Muriel Vanderbilt Adams' pedigree far outshone Doris Duke's. An international horsewoman, she was the daughter of William K. Vanderbilt, President of The New York Central Railroad and Virginia Graham Fair whose father made his fortune in The Comstock Lode. Her aunt, Consuelo became the Duchess of Marlborough. [313] Her uncle was Harold Stirling Vanderbilt, the America's Cup defender we met earlier in this chapter.

In July, 1925, *The New York Times* devoted four columns on its society page to her first marriage to Frederick Cameron Church. The article described a party that weekend thrown by Mr. and Mrs. James H. Van Alen, to honor Muriel's great aunt, Mrs. Frederick W. Vanderbilt whose husband had built Rough Point. [314]

Muriel's second husband, Henry Delafield Phelps, was a dapper member of The Newport Reading room, and uncle to Tim Phelps, the *Providence Journal* reporter who covered Newport in the mid-1960's. She lived with her third husband, Dr. John Payson Adams, at Idle Hour, an estate on Hazard Road off Newport's Ocean Drive. Each season, she supplied the sandwiches for police officers working extra duty during the Jazz Festival. Chief Radice thanked her for that himself in the summer of 1966. [315]

Then, for reasons still shrouded in mystery, on October 4th, 1966, three days before Doris crushed Eduardo to death, Muriel became the target of an extortion plot in which the

Dr. John Payson Adams and Muriel Vanderbilt at Hialeah Racetrack 1958

blackmailer demanded $600,000 or he would reveal some secret. [316] In a letter dropped into her mailbox at Idle Hour, he instructed that the payoff take place at The Clambake Club, a summer colony shooting venue located on Tuckerman Avenue near Middletown's Second Beach.[317]

Without informing Donald Homen, Chief of Police in the adjacent community, Radice concocted a harebrained "sting" operation in which a heavyset Newport patrolman in a wig would pose as Mrs. Adams, then, as the blackmailer approached her car outside the club after dark, he'd be arrested.

But on the night of the set-up, when the extortionist moved toward her vehicle, a second cop hiding in the back seat popped up his head. The suspect saw him and ran off, whereupon the decoy cop jumped out and started firing wildly into the night. [318]

The suspect was never found and Radice was lambasted by Chief Homen. [319] He was also criticized by the press, who would soon be at odds with him for revealing so little information about Tirella's death. [320] Radice never disclosed Mrs. Adams's identity, though it became widely known that she was the blackmail target.

Retired Newport Detective Al Conti, who helped me immensely on the Duke investigation, told me that the Chief was so obsessed with breaking the Vanderbilt Adams case, that he ordered junior patrolmen, including Conti, *to hide up in a tree* overlooking Mrs. Adams' mailbox in nightly stakeouts, on the off-chance the blackmailer would reappear. [321]

He never did.

Just a week after closing the Duke case, *The Boston Globe* reported that Radice and Capt. Sullivan had "gone to Massachusetts" to pursue what they called "a lead" in the plot surrounding the 64-year-old horse-woman. [322] On Dec. 28th Radice claimed that he had "a prime suspect," adding, "He is in Newport right now, to the best of our knowledge." [323]

The case was never solved.

MRS. ADAMS EXITS NEWPORT

Five months later, Muriel Vanderbilt Adams, who'd been a Newport summer resident and philanthropist for decades, announced that she was leaving Idle Hour and moving all of her horses to Florida. [324] The 52-acre estate was later sold for a mere $200,000 and broken up into parcels for development, ending an era. [325] Nothing of that or the unsolved extortion plot was mentioned when Radice himself retired *five days later:* ultimately ending up in The Sunshine State himself, but for other reasons. [326]

There's an irony in all of this that's inescapable: Joseph Radice's incompetence caused a member of Newport's royalty, who was an actual *crime victim,* to flee town, but his corruption permitted Doris Duke, whose money was far newer, to get away with murder.

CHAPTER THIRTEEN

THE SLASHED ARM &
THE BROKEN JAW

Doris Duke's first two husbands disappointed her in different ways. First, there was Palm Beach socialite James Cromwell, 16 years older, whose check bounced when he tried to pay for their 1935 honeymoon. [327] Next came notorious Dominican playboy Porfirio Rubirosa, whose male endowment was legendary. In Paris restaurants, when diners asked for their steaks to be seasoned, rather than calling for a peppermill, waiters would yell, "Bring me the Rubirosa!" [328] Eartha Kitt, one of many legendary women who succumbed to his charms, was said to have compared him to Cary Grant, Errol Flynn and Burt Lancaster, rolled into one. [329]

On their wedding day in 1947, Rubirosa insisted on smoking through the entire ceremony and after his appointment as the Dominican ambassador to Argentina, he embarrassed Doris with a series of notorious affairs in Buenos Aires, with rumors that he had even conquered Eva "Evita" Peron herself. [330] Little more than a year after the marriage, when he and Duke split, Rubi was gifted with $25,000 a year until he remarried, along with a 17th century house in Paris and a converted B-25 bomber. [331]

He then proceeded to devastate Doris by marrying her arch rival, Woolworth heiress Barbara Hutton. [332] When they divorced in 1954 his settlement included $2.5 million and a coffee plantation in the Dominican Republic. [333]

Doris Duke was infamous for her taste in exotic men and the lover who took her on the longest sexual roller coaster

Doris at her wedding to Porfirio Rubirosa Sept. 1st, 1947 (A.P. Images)

ride of her life was the brilliant young Mexican-American jazz pianist and band leader Joseph Armand Castro. [334] The story of their decade-long drug and booze-fueled trajectory offers the best insight I could find into why she stepped on the gas that night at Rough Point. Unlike Eddie Tirella, Castro survived, but Doris's attempt on his life and the ensuing cover-up, offer a textbook case in how her crisis-managing henchmen bullied even the closest people in her life into submission. Fifteen years younger than Doris, Castro was a piano prodigy who played the top jazz clubs from Basin Street East and Birdland in New York to international venues like Bricktops in Rome; jamming with every great from Louis Armstrong to Zoot Simms. [335]

Duke and Castro (far right) serenaded at Birdland by Big Jay McNeeley (Getty Images)

After recording for Atlantic Records, he finished out his career as musical director of The Tropicana in Las Vegas where he died in 2009. According to author Stephanie Mansfield, Joe first met Doris, who had frequented his sets at The Mocambo in L.A., at a concert in Honolulu, after which she invited his trio back to her Islamic-themed Diamond Head estate, Shangri-La.[336]

By 1953 they were living together at The Bel Air Hotel and he later claimed in a legal complaint that she bought the Valentino estate, Falcon Lair, for the two of them. [337] For the next decade they lived off and on as common-law husband and wife. Pony Duke writes, "She believed Castro to be a musical genius, perhaps the greatest jazz pianist in the world." [338]

But over time, jealous at the attention Joe got on stage, Doris swung into frequent bouts of depression. Fueled by booze, barbiturates and Castro's temper, their fights got more frequent and more violent, culminating the night of June 15[th,] 1963 at Shangri-La. Doris was playing a jazz piece on piano and when Joe reportedly made a crack, she grabbed a butcher knife and slashed his arm. [339]

On New Year's Day, 1964, she threw him out of Falcon Lair and 10 days later, Joe filed the first of three lawsuits in Los Angeles, including one for assault and battery, alleging that she'd "attempted to kill him," causing "a large permanent scar on his left arm" that prevented him from working. [340] He asked for $150,000 in damages.

Two other actions, filed by his L.A. attorney R. Edward Brown, demanded that Castro's alleged common-law marriage to Doris be formally ratified, that he get $5000 a month in alimony [341] and a declaration that they were co-owners of the Valentino estate. [342] Castro, who claimed that he and Doris had been married twice, once in Rhode Island in 1956 and later in 1960 in Philadelphia, also succeeded in getting a restraining order forbidding Doris from disposing of any property she had acquired after those purported nuptials. [343]

But within weeks, through a series of attorneys in Los Angeles and Hawaii, including former-FBI agent J. Harold Hughes in Honolulu, Doris responded with what Hughes later called "Fabian Tactics," a kind of guerrilla warfare strategy designed to wear Castro down in "a war of attrition." [344] The full details of those strong-arm methods used against Castro, reveal just how far the vindictive billionairess was willing to go to crush an opponent – even one who had shared her bed for more than a decade.

THE BATTLE PLAN FOR ATTACK

On February 4[th,] 1964, nearly a month after Castro's attorney Brown had filed the three suits in Los Angeles, Doris was staying at The Mandarin Hotel in Hong Kong. Ten days earlier, the L.A. law firm of Hill, Farrer & Burrill had succeeded in getting Castro's alimony petition quashed for lack of proper service.[345] Now, in a revealing 15 page letter to the billionairess, Morton B. "Tony" Jackson of that firm, laid out what he described as "A Counter-Offensive Action." [346]

Jackson wrote that the time gained in achieving the initial legal victory would give Doris's team the chance to determine "whether Joe might quit if he didn't make a fast killing or get his hooks in for alimony." [347]

Later, Jackson went on to write that, "Castro and his attorney have made no bones of the fact that their battle plan is one of subjugation through harassment."[348] Jackson then suggested that Duke's "counter-offensive" against Joe could include, "criminal proceedings which might be instigated," with a "range of possible charges" including "prosecution for possession or use of narcotics (which is a state and a Federal offense)." [349]

While *that* didn't happen, Doris Duke was certainly open to using her considerable resources to get her adversaries charged with crimes. As we'll see in the Chapters ahead, she went to great lengths in 1966 to encourage State Prosecutors in New Jersey to file criminal charges against her own chef at Duke Farms whom she alleged had stolen two valuable plates.[350] Then, a decade later, after she testified before a grand jury, Somerset, NJ prosecutors indicted an ex-FBI agent she had hired to investigate a jewel theft at the 2,700 acre estate. [351] In both instances, convictions of the men could have sent them to jail.

Two weeks after Jackson's letter to Doris, her Hawaii attorney, Hughes -- another Bureau alumnus -- suggested that a legal "counter-attack" should be mounted in Hawaii. [352] In a three page memo pointing out the dangers of "Litigation in California," Hughes suggested that if a court found that Doris was "a resident of California (she) would be stuck with" a state income tax bill of $70,000 for every million dollars of her net income.

Characterizing Castro as "a fortune hunter," and noting that his first thought was to "bleed him to death" in L.A., Hughes now suggested that Honolulu would be a better venue for litigation, particularly if "the California court allowed the issue of mental cruelty to be proved."

Within weeks, Joe was literally picked up in Honolulu and held incommunicado at Shangri-La, where Hughes and his armed operatives worked on him to renounce his litigation and betray his L.A. lawyer Brown. In his book, *Daddy's Duchess*, Doris's former business manager, Patrick Mahn, described it as a kidnapping in which John Pease, a friend of Castro's was falsely labeled a racketeer who would "chop off (Joe's) fingers or kill him" if he got the chance. [353]

On March 31[st,] Tony Jackson filed an action against Castro in Hawaii Circuit Court seeking to enjoin his L.A. suits. [354] Hughes followed that with a Notice of Substitution of Attorney after inducing Castro to fire Brown. But Hughes was so audacious (or sloppy, depending on one's point of view), that he actually typed Castro's letter to Brown *himself* on the same typewriter he'd used to draft his legal pleadings. It was proof that he was manipulating Castro, and a clear violation of the canon of ethics, wherein lawyers are barred from contacting clients they know to be represented.

As to other "Fabian tactics" used by Hughes, Peter Brooke, a freelance writer, was hired [355] and flown to Hawaii, [356] where he sought to tie-up Castro in a life-rights deal for what amounted to a phony biography. [357] Designed to prevent Joe from going public with the butcher knife story, it was an early version of the "catch and kill" scheme that Donald Trump reportedly perfected in conjunction with *The National Enquirer*. Later, private investigators were engaged to literally bug, not just the phone lines of Falcon Lair, but the estate itself, after Doris coaxed Joe into coming home. [358]

She set up a recording company for him (Clover Records) [359] and placated him by promising to include him in her will. She had already bought him a Mercedes SL 300 Gullwing roadster worth the equivalent of $100,000 [360] and for the next year, things between them seem to stabilize.

ALLEGED SUICIDE ATTEMPTS

After his dismissal by Castro, Brown filed suit against Hill, Farrer & Burrill as well as Weber, Schwartz, & Altshuler, another L.A. firm that represented Doris against Joe. In a sworn deposition in support of that action, Brown painted a lurid portrait of Doris Duke's, multi-year relationship with his former client that was shocking in its allegations. [361]

Quoting Castro, Brown testified that, "he told me he was frightened of her and of (her) private detectives. He told me that he saved her life twice (when) she attempted to commit suicide. He told me that at the time she stabbed him with the knife, she begged him not to go to the hospital or call a doctor because she was afraid the police might be called in." [362]

Another surprise allegation by Brown involved blackmail. "He related a story to me that she told him about a voodoo man who was blackmailing her in the late Forties."

That appears to relate to another lawsuit filed by Doris against *Confidential Magazine;* the reigning tabloid of the 1950's that some critics suggest was the prototype for James Ellroy's "Hush Hush" gossip sheet in his novel *L.A. Confidential.* [363]

In its May, 1955 issue, one of the three *Confidential* cover stories was headlined, "Doris Duke And Her African Prince." [364] Inside, the piece alleged that Doris had hired one "Prince David Madupe Mudge Paris, a 54 year-old, five-foot, brown skinned royalist, who claims his right to his title because his father was King of a tribe on Africa's Gold Coast."

Asserting that Madupe had "entered the country illegally by jumping ship in New York," the magazine alleged that years later, Doris, suffering from insomnia after "a steady diet of sleeping pills" had invited him to Falcon Lair, whereupon he started her "on a course that involved breathing exercises broken up by sessions of African voodoo dancing."

After allegedly buying him a Buick Roadmaster, Doris reportedly soured on Madupe and when she refused to invest in his business venture, he allegedly threatened to go public with recordings and diaries he'd made of their "relationship." At that point, a private eye, reportedly hired by Doris, lured him to Tijuana where he was barred from re-entering the U.S. [365]

Apart from the stunningly racist nature of the *Confidential* story and the fact that Duke's suit against the tabloid was later dismissed, the "Fabian" tactic of manipulating a potential blackmailer had the same feel as the Machiavellian methods used by Hughes in his successful effort to induce Castro to sever ties with his first lawyer, Brown.

In that same 1965 depo Brown related details of Doris's smothering relationship with Castro that seemed chillingly similar to her possessive treatment of Eduardo Tirella.

"(Joe) told me that he had wrecked his career because of her; that every time he would start to promote himself as a jazz pianist, she would insist that he give it up; that she wanted to learn to play the piano; that he taught her for several years, that eventually they toured Europe with a group and that she played the piano with a wig on so no one recognized her." [366] Over time, as Brown quoted Castro in that deposition, he described a volatile, toxic relationship between Joe and Doris in which she used her wealth to control him.

"She told him he would never have to worry the rest of his life about money and that everything she acquired after their marriage would belong to the two of them... that she used alcohol to excess and used some type of drugs... that they had numerous and constant fights, both verbal and physical of a violent nature... that he left her on many, many, many occasions... that he had entered into contracts with various musicians and groups; and when he was away from her, she would, after several months, call him constantly and write him and talk him into giving up his employment and returning to her." [367]

CRISIS AT FALCON LAIR

Then on July 5th 1965, after an all-night drinking binge, Doris's ex-husband, Porfirio Rubirosa, was killed when he crashed his silver Ferrari 250 GT into a tree outside the Bois de Boulogne in Paris and she lapsed into another deep depression. [368]

With Castro unable to console her, she spent more and more time with Eduardo Tirella, taking extended trips with him to Paris. [369] She also traveled to Big Sur in California where she met Eddie's partner

Edmund Kara who shared a house with him. There Edmund carved the celebrated phoenix sculpture at Nepenthe, [370] a legendary restaurant and performance space high on the coast. One of Eduardo's dreams was for Doris to buy the nearby Post Ranch and preserve it as a public outdoor space. [371]

But by March of '66 Doris, then 53, was growing angrier at Castro after he'd begun seeing Loretta Haddad, a beautiful young singer who performed at Honolulu's Outrigger Club. [372] Things got so petty between them that the heiress balked at paying a bill for less than $150 to repair his Mercedes. [373]

Then on May 20th, she abruptly pulled the plug on Clover Records where Peter Brooke had become an executive. [374] Not long after that, in author Mansfield's account, Brooke was awakened at 3:00 am by a desperate Doris who begged him to come right away to Falcon Lair.

When he got there, a maid reportedly led him into the kitchen where, as Mansfield told it, "The room had been ransacked, broken dishes thrown on the floor. Standing in the open frame of a French window, wearing a T-shirt, though naked from the waist down, was Castro, urinating over the railing into the garden below." Brook reportedly found Doris in her bedroom with a broken jaw, barely able to speak. She pleaded with him to "…get him away from here."

Coaxing Joe into his car with a bottle of champagne, Brooke told Mansfield that near the Beverly Hills Hotel, Castro threw the bottle out onto the street where it exploded.

"The next morning," she wrote, "Doris fled Hollywood for Newport, accompanied by Eduardo Tirella." [375]

CHAPTER FOURTEEN

THE MYSTERIOUS STONE TOWER

Not all architectural marvels in Newport were built during the Gilded Age, and not all the landmarks dated back to when the City was founded in 1639. One structure located in Touro Park is at least half a century older, and it's been the object of fascination and study by archeologists and historians for hundreds of years: the strange three story cylindrical structure built of native stone and variously called, The Newport Tower, The Viking Tower and The Old Stone Mill. I've been fixated on it since my teens when I wrote a pair of essays about it at De La Salle.

Back then, the school's curriculum was limited to a choice between studying Latin or Biology. So as a Junior while many of my classmates were contemplating science fair projects, I produced a 24 page research paper titled "Who Really Discovered America?" [376] preceded in my Sophomore year with a more focused 12 page essay captioned "Who Really Erected The Newport Round Stone Tower?" [377]

In the first assignment, relying on the work of historians Paul Du Chaillu, [378] C.F. Keary, [379] Edward G. Bourne & Julius Olson, [380] Sofus Larson, [381] and Helge Ingstad [382] I credited the discovery of "the New World" to Leif Ericson, the Viking son of Eric Thorvaldsson, aka "Eric The Red," who sailed from Greenland to what was Newfoundland, Canada nearly 500 years before Columbus; establishing a settlement he called Vineland.

The Stone Tower in Touro Park

Norse artifacts dating back to 1,000 A.D. were unearthed there in an area known as L'Anse aux Meadows. [383] While that discovery answered the broader question, the prospect that Leif's progeny had somehow made it South to Narragansett Bay and erected the round tower on Newport's highest point, was undercut first in the late 1940's.

In 1948, an analysis of the "shell, lime, sand and gravel" mortar used to build the Tower, found that it was similar to mortar used in the construction of several Newport houses between 1640 and 1643. [384] Carbon-14 dating of Tower mortar by a Danish team in 1993 estimated that the structure was probably built between Columbus's first voyage to America in 1492 and the Pilgrims' landing in Plymouth in 1620. [385] Another mortar-dating study in 2003 put the construction date between 1635 and 1680. [386]

Amid those conflicting results, a credible new theory, which we'll explore in depth, assigns the Tower's origin to a British expedition circa 1582, twenty-five years before the establishment of the first English settlement in Jamestown Virginia in 1607. If correct, that theory would make Newport, Rhode Island the first British outpost in The New World. [387]

WHO DIDN'T BUILD THE TOWER?

In the centuries since The Tower has been studied there have been multiple theories put forth as to its origin, most of them simply grounded in legend. The most popular story in Newport when I was growing up was that The Vikings were responsible. In fact, so many people believed it, including the City fathers, that the largest hotel in town, opened in 1926, was named The Hotel Viking. Later when Bell Telephone (the precursor to AT&T) set up the modern dialing system, the first three digits of every phone number in town were either 846 or 847 representing Viking 6 or 7. Even Rogers, the public high school, which dominated Rhode Island sports in football and basketball for decades, adopted "The Vikings" as its mascot. [388]

In 1976 when Queen Elizabeth II visited Newport to dedicate Queen Anne Square -- a signature project of Doris Duke's Restoration Foundation -- the mayor at the time, Humphrey "Harp" Donnelly, presented her with the official Newport flag featuring the Tower surrounded by a wreath with the slogan AMOR VINCET OMNIA -- Love Conquers All. At the time, the mayor identified the structure for Her Majesty as "The Viking Tower." [389]

We'll explore that irony in depth, since the most intriguing theory for the Tower's origins to date suggests that the current reigning monarch's namesake: Elizabeth I underwrote the 16th century expedition that actually built it. In any case, in his 1942 ground-breaking study of the Tower, historian Phillip Ainsworth Means, who had previously studied Andean civilizations, called it

Newport Mayor "Harp" Donnelly presenting the flag to Queen Elizabeth II, as The Duke of Edinburgh looks on.

"The most enigmatic and puzzling single building in the United States." [390]

The Viking theory was first proffered in 1837 by Carl Christian Rafn, a Danish archeologist, who based his research largely on the series of strange markings on Dighton Rock, a 40 ton boulder found in a river bed in nearby Taunton, Mass. [391] The Rock, with its collection of abstract figures and hieroglyphs, also became the foundation of several other theories about the origin of The Tower: that it was built by the ancient Phoenicians who had succeeded in colonizing the Canary Islands off Africa in 400 B.C.; [392] that the Chinese constructed it as a lighthouse in 1421; [393] that The Knights Templars built it in 1398 as a church; [394] and that it was erected by a Portuguese explorer as a watchtower in 1502.

That theory, largely propounded by Edmund B. Delabarre, a Brown University Professor in 1919, [395] was also heavily linked to Dighton Rock. It involved a pair of explorer brothers: Miguel and Gaspar Corte-Real, who made three separate expeditions between 1500 and 1502 to what became Canada and later America. Initially intrigued by the adventure behind it, I devoted most of my 1964 high school essay to that theory; only to learn that the two central figures were slave traffickers. This is how I explained it back then:

THE BROTHERS CORTE-REAL

In 1501, Gaspar Corte-Real, a Portuguese nobleman born in the Azores and his brother Miguel led a three ship fleet in the service of King Henry VII of England. They reached Newfoundland where they captured 57 indigenous people with the intent of selling them as slaves. With these captives in chains, Gaspar returned to Portugal in a separate ship, but on the way back, unknown to Miguel, the ship was lost. [396]

By 1502 when his older brother didn't return, Miguel led an expedition to find him. But the younger Corte-Real brother too, never made it back to Portugal. Prof. Delabarre theorized that after sailing into Narragansett Bay, Miguel built The Tower on the highest part of Aquidneck island as a beacon light to signal his brother in the event he sailed by.

In 1820 the skeleton of a Native American who died circa 1750 was found in nearby Fall River Massachusetts wearing Portuguese armor. Prof. Delabarre theorized that the second brother remained with his men near Newport and, following his own death, from unknown causes, his armor was considered an artifact worthy of burial with the remains of a high-ranking tribe member. The American poet Henry Wadsworth Longfellow, in fact, immortalized that legend in his poem "Skeleton in Armor," writing:

> There for my lady's bower
> Built I, the lofty tower
> Which, to this very hour,
> Stands, looking seaward.

A more recent rendering of the Corte-Real story by the Native Heritage Project, appropriately asked the fate of those 57 "Native slaves." [397] At the time I wrote the essay, Prof. Delabarre's thesis, which was embraced by Newport's large Azorean community, seemed the most plausible explanation for the creation of what was then commonly known as, "The Old Stone Mill."

That title was a consequence of the first written identification of the structure as "my stone built Wind Mill," in the last will and testament of Rhode Island's first colonial Governor Benedict Arnold, the great great-grandfather of the infamous Revolutionary War traitor. [398]

Gov. Arnold had moved to Newport in 1651. He soon became the wealthy owner of considerable property including the land which is now Touro Park. But *owning* the Tower didn't mean the Governor *built* it and several factors mitigate against it. First that the three story circle of stone was laid out according to True North, when structures built after 1600 utilized compass bearings reflecting Magnetic North. Second, the Tower contained a fireplace literally built into the walls that would have made its use as a working grist mill unlikely due to the highly combustible nature of freshly ground flour.

So if it wasn't the Vikings, The Azoreans, or Governor Arnold, who *was* responsible for erecting this fascinating ancient structure, used during the American Revolution by the Continental Army as a lookout and later by British occupiers as a magazine to

The Tower, covered with ivy as it looked in 1867

store munitions? Further, and more importantly, given its curious design, what was its original purpose?

THE NEWPORT TOWER MUSEUM

Beginning his research in the 1990's James Alan Egan, a former commercial photographer, turned polymathic historian, believes that he has found the answer and today, just yards away from the Tower at 152 Mill Street, he operates a storefront museum dedicated to proving it.

"My father had spent his career selling watches," he told me when I visited his Museum in the fall of 2018. [399] "So my first fascination with the Tower began when I met Professor William Penhallow, an astronomer and physicist from the University of Rhode Island who believed that it was essentially a horologium -- a grand time keeping device -- constructed so that certain astronomical alignments would be visible through the windows of the Tower on certain days of the year."

In a paper published in The New England Antiquities Research Association Journal in 1994, [400] Prof. Penhallow wrote of the Tower's design that, "Numerous alignments involving the Sun and Moon indicate an emphasis on determining the location of the nodes of the Moon's orbit. Accurate determination of True North by observing Polaris at upper culmination is evident. Possible observations of Sirius are indicated. These results provide strong evidence that astronomy was involved in the design and use of this intriguing structure, first mentioned in Governor Arnold's Will in 1677. Further study is clearly warranted."

On that last suggestion Egan took the professor seriously and he's spent the past 25 years developing what he calls "The Renaissance Thesis" of the Tower's origins, arguing that it was designed by Anglo-Welsh mathematician and cartographer John Dee as an enormous "camera obscura" for telling time and creating a more precise calendar. [401]

The Tower has three main windows: facing northeast, south and west. The photos below taken by Egan are stark pictorial evidence that support his thesis. Every year on the Winter Solstice the Sun shines directly into the south window, through the Tower and out the west window and every 18.6 years, during an event called Lunar Minor, the moon follows a similar trajectory through the northeast and west windows.

The Tower on the Winter Solstice when the sun shines through two windows every year. The moon shining through two windows on Lunar Minor, an event that takes place every 18.6 years. (Photos by James Alan Egan)

"Dee was also an expert in navigation," Egan wrote. "He provided navigational advice to many of the explorers of the Elizabethan Era. A remarkable man with a library of 4,000 books, he lived in a time when science was separating from magic and astronomy was separating from astrology. Alchemy was becoming chemistry, botany and medicine. It was also a time of great strife in England between Protestants and Catholics, who, through the Spanish, Portuguese and French were staking multiple claims to The New World.

"When Elizabeth I came to the throne in 1559, she was so taken with Dee that she consulted him on the most propitious day for her coronation, which he selected as January 15[th.] Soon after that, highly regarded in Elizabeth's court, Dee convinced her that England held the best legal claim to North America."[402]

With exhaustive documentation Egan demonstrated that in the Spring of 1578 Dee presented Her Majesty and The Privy Counsel with "The Limits of the British Empire," a proposal that led her to gift explorer Sir Humphrey Gilbert "letters patent to all of North America." [403]

"All Gilbert had to do," wrote Egan in his book, *Elizabethan America*, "was to build a fort, settle a colony and remain there for a year. He was given 6 years to accomplish this after which the patent would expire. For his legal and cartographical assistance Gilbert granted Dee all of the lands north of the 50th parallel, which constitute much of modern-day Canada and Alaska." [404]

On my visit to the museum, Egan described what happened next:

"Dee had determined that the best site for colonization, which he called 'The Dee River' was Narragansett Bay, which Verrazzano had visited in 1524. [405] In June of 1582, a preliminary two-ship expedition of 80 men led by Anthony Brigham, left England. [406] They were gone for at least nine months. Though their destination was kept secret, I believe they reached the island of Aquidneck, and using Dee's plans, built the Tower as a horologium that was to be the focal point of an ever expanding city center. It would also serve as a temporary fort for a major colonizing expedition that left England 11 months later. In short, it was John Dee's intent that the Tower would become the center of what, in success, would have been Great Britain's principal capital in North America."

On July 11th 1583, Gilbert departed from Plymouth, England with a five ship fleet, the largest one of which, containing most of the expedition's supplies, was captained by his half brother Sir Walter Raleigh. [407] But just a day out, a contagious disease swept that ship and Raleigh turned back.

Gilbert reached St. John's Newfoundland, which he formally took possession of in the name of England, [408] but when more of his crew became ill, he sent another ship with them back home and headed south to "The Dee River" (Narragansett Bay) with the 3 remaining vessels.

"Then off the coast of Sable Island, east of Halifax Nova Scotia," said Egan, "The Delight, Gilbert's second largest ship, ran aground in a hurricane and broke up. Discouraged, he set sail for England with his remaining ships when, off of the Portuguese Azores, his ship, The Squirrel, was caught in another violent storm. It was swallowed by a gigantic wave and Gilbert drowned. At that point, the deed to North America, which was only in his name, became void. [409] The surviving ship, The Golden Hind, made it back to England, which is why we know the details of Gilbert's fate."

"Sadly," said Egan, "the Newport outpost was abandoned, and after Gilbert's death, the Queen charged Sir Walter Raleigh with colonizing the New World, which he did -- only in the Carolinas and not Rhode Island. Still, if I'm correct, The Tower was built in 1583 and it was only *after* Benedict Arnold claimed Newport as a trading post decades later -- taking control of the land it stood on -- that the Tower became his property. Let me emphasize that. Benedict Arnold, the man who became Rhode Island's first governor in 1663 *owned* it, but he didn't *build* it."

Over the last ten years Egan's storefront museum has attracted more than 10,000 visitors. He's written 20 books on "The Renaissance Thesis," and he's confident that he's found the one plausible explanation to solve the Tower mystery.

Support for his thesis keeps growing. In 2019 on the Winter Solstice, 150 people came to the Tower at dawn to witness the solar alignment as the sun passed through those two windows.

CHAPTER FIFTEEN

NEWPORT'S
BACK YARD

By the Summer of '68, as anti-Vietnam War protests erupted, followed by the assassinations of Martin Luther King and Robert F. Kennedy, when urban riots swept the country, I was ready to take on the first serious investigative reporting of my career: an exposé of slum housing in the same West Broadway neighborhood where my friends from Cranston Calvert School lived. It was a scandal that had somehow eluded the international media covering The America's Cup Races, the Jazz and Folk Festivals, the National Tennis Championships and the tony movements of America's aristocracy.

The previous fall, I'd learned that Newport was eligible to receive millions in Federal redevelopment money to clean up the waterfront and begin the transition to tourism. But there was a catch: tied to that package, the City's Minimum Housing Code had to be fully enforced. [410] That meant no slum housing, and on the other side of Broadway, just yards from City Hall, there was a devastated neighborhood over a hundred years old. For much of that time, West Broadway had been Newport's embarrassing little secret and it now threatened to stop the city's transformation from Naval economy to tourist Mecca.

The gerrymandering of the school district back in 1959 when my fellow classmates from West Broadway were excluded from Cranston Calvert was an incident that had stayed with me. So, starting in mid-July, I spent every afternoon going into the Housing Inspector's office, copying down the multiple code violations on each of the 50 or so dwellings in the ten block area west of Broadway and the surrounding neighborhoods of The Point and Upper Thames Street.

That part of town had a storied history.

By 1774, there were 147 free African Americans living in the area, but another 1,069 were still enslaved. [411] Then following The Revolution in 1784, Rhode Island's Gradual Emancipation Act decreed that any child born after April 1st that year would be free.

As James C. Garman writes in his detailed study of the area, for Salve Regina University, "Some owners, resigned to what they saw as an inevitable process, simply freed the enslaved members of their households. Others had disappeared earlier." But since the right to vote in Rhode Island was not based on race, but property ownership, "African Americans negotiating the complex world of post-Revolutionary War Rhode Island had a powerful incentive for purchasing real estate" [412] and by 1860 when the Irish emigration led to a relatively integrated neighborhood known as "Kerry Hill," a number of Black families from the Jim Crow South moved to town.

Among then was Armstead Hurley, who arrived in Newport at the age of 32 from Virginia as a skilled carpenter glazer. [413] He ran a painting company and co-founded the state's first Black-owned bank. [414] Joseph T. Ray, who bought a property at 30 Kingston Avenue, was Newport's last survivor of The Civil War. As a young Black man from Bristol, RI, he'd enlisted in the Union Army at the age of 18.[415]

But over the decades, the once thriving West Broadway neighborhood fell into decay and most of the badly deteriorated homes were owned by slumlords. So that summer of 1968 as I poured through the City's housing files, I found repeated violations of the Minimum Housing Code. Virtually all were serious, like frayed electrical wiring, broken windows, cracking lead paint, lack of proper toilet facilities and infestation by roaches and rats. Many of the violations had been on the books for years.

Some of the dwellings were in danger of collapse and in one of them, poor children were sleeping five to a tiny room. Most of the residents were African-American but about 20 percent were poor whites. These are two of the images taken when I visited some of those homes:

Helping me get access to them was a remarkable 47-year-old Black woman named Philippa "Phil" Almeida who worked for the county anti-poverty agency, New Visions For Newport. Back then, she was assisted by Pauline Perkins, a 27-year-old community organizer who was a tenant in one of the houses.

The children in this house, ranging in age from 2-5 years old, were sleeping in one 10 x 10 foot room. The bedroom window of the house where this little girl lived has been broken since Spring.

When I first approached Phil and said that I wanted to tell the truth about West Broadway, she smiled, put her hand on her hip and cocked her head, declaring, "There ain't no way they're *ever* gonna let you put that kind of story in The Daily *Snooze*."

She may have been right. In its 122-year history, the progeny of *The Newport Mercury,* Ben Franklin's brother's paper, had never printed *anything* controversial. But I was determined to win a Pulitzer before my 25th birthday, so I was off and running.

I completed the reporting and wrote it up as a four-part series called "Newport's Back Yard." It was fully documented by housing inspection records, photographs and transcribed interviews. These were the opening paragraphs to Part One:

Slum Homes Lack Bath, Stove

The travel pamphlets refer to Newport as a "City of summer pleasures with the largest concentration of magnificent houses produced by American art." But in the shadow of that elegance there are parts of this city not described on tourist maps, where native Newporters live out their days paying rent for decrepit hovels their landlords refuse to repair. These are the central neighborhoods of Newport's inner city.

According to the latest housing survey published by The Redevelopment Agency, 1,256 Newport families live in deficient housing -- nearly 14% of the families in the city.

Consider the case of Mrs. Rose Machado and her family at 28 Marsh Street. On December 21, 1966, housing code inspector Nathaniel Jenkins visited the house, listed to Maurice Ball and Alex Teitz, and declared it unfit for human habitation. The house, which was vacant and infested with rats and other vermin, was boarded up and labeled a fire hazard. Three months ago Mrs. Machado and her six children ages 6 to 24, moved into the building. Since then, Teitz has collected $50 a month rent.[1] The only major repair to the dwelling was the replacement of a faulty sink trap.

More than a quarter of the house's windows are still broken and there is no hot water or tub, nor is there a gas or electric stove on which to cook. Mrs. Machado cooks and heats water on electric hot plates. The toilet leaks and is frequently plugged. The ceilings in the kitchen and living room have partly caved in. The rats are gone but the roaches remain.

Then there is the case of Paula Butler, tenant of another flat owed by Teitz overlooking the cemetery on 93 Kingston Ave. The three floor apartment house, adjacent to a big Newport Electric transformer, was found to be substandard and referred to The City Solicitor's office for action (four years ago) on August 18, 1964. The violations have not been corrected. The windows over the bunks in the room where Paula's five children sleep have been broken since March.

---

1 The equivalent of $375 a month in 2021 dollars.

Paula pays $37 a month rent, but when utilities and heat are added, her monthly expenses run upwards of $60. She applied in July for public housing. At the time, she was told she was 14th on the list. Repeated attempts by this reporter to reach Teitz at his home and at his law office on Bellevue Avenue proved unsuccessful.

"People think the people in these houses are poor because they're dirty," said Philippa Almeida, neighborhood organizer for the local arm of the Office For Economic Opportunity. "The truth is their homes are dirty because they're poor and they're forced to live in conditions their landlords allow to exist. Most of them, contrary to belief, make an effort to fix up the places as best they can but there's only so much you can do."[416]

GETTING SPIKED

One day at the end of the month, I waited until around 3:00 pm to present the series to Jim Edward. He was the stern but kindly managing editor of *The Daily News* who'd allowed me to ride point on the Stephen Robertson murder coverage the year before. Jim was an old Yankee who knew so many people in town that he could dictate obituaries.

When I handed him the stories, I could see his eyes widen as he began to read the series of pages called "takes." They were taped together; each take with the word (MORE) on the bottom so the Linotype operators in the basement composing room would know that additional pages were coming. In the tradition of newsrooms everywhere, the last page at the bottom of each story bore the designation -30- a holdover from when three X's (the Roman numeral for thirty) were used to indicate when a story had ended.

As Mr. Edward examined my allegations, he'd stop and ask for proof and I would plunk down on his desk the record of a code violation or some other document. He kept reading and I could see his backbone straightening. He was becoming the idealistic young reporter he'd been thirty years before, when he'd walked into his first newsroom.

Jim made a few corrections with a red pencil and finally deemed the four pieces "newsworthy."

Then he cleared his throat, straightened his tie, slicked back his hair, tightened his belt and entered the back room where Ned Sherman, the owner, co-publisher and editor-in-chief was reading that day's paper, hot off the presses.

There was a glass wall with wainscoting at the bottom separating me from the two of them, but right away I could see that Ned was upset. As he looked at the series, his face got redder. At one point his brother Albert, from the money side of the paper, walked in and I could hear the word "advertisers." Some of the slumlords I named in the series had businesses and bought ad space in *The Daily News*. Many of them had owned those decrepit buildings for years, always blaming their condition on the tenants, "Who didn't know how to live."

Anyway, my gut was tightening as I saw their argument escalating and then, suddenly, and without warning, Ned took my entire series and SPIKED IT – meaning, he jammed the pages though a hook on the wall reserved for stories that had already run or were dead.

I couldn't believe it.

A few minutes passed. Albert left and Jim Edward, crestfallen and embarrassed, came back and looked at me. He didn't have to say he was sorry. I knew he wanted the series to run as much as I did.

"They'll be other stories," he said and walked out. I didn't have the heart to remind him that this was the last week of my second year at *The Daily News* and I wouldn't be back. Now, there I was, with almost a month's work on a hook because the publishers didn't seem to have the wherewithal to document the City's negligence in allowing that slum to exist.

But if *they* weren't going to run it, maybe the other paper I used to deliver would.

So I hitched up my pants, tightened my belt, slicked back my hair and stormed into that back office. Ned was still at his desk when I grabbed the stories off the hook. I rolled them up and turned to head down the three flights of stairs to *The Providence Journal* bureau on Thames Street.

Just then, Ned got up from his desk and stopped me. "Where the hell are *you* going?"

He was a big man, about six four, with curly blond hair and blue eyes. Until that afternoon I'd liked him a lot, but now he was standing over me like a lineman for The Patriots.

"Down to see Brian Jones," I said.

Some years back, Brian, who'd gone to The Lenox School For Boys, had taken over from my mentor Gardner Dunton as Bureau Chief at the state paper. I respected him and I had a hunch he'd fight to get the series in print.

Ned looked like he'd just been gut-punched. "What the hell did you just *say*?"

I turned to face him, gripping the rolled-up series like a small base-ball bat.

"Hey, I put a lot of work into this. It's an important story and some-body needs to run it."

"And you want to give this to the goddamn *Journal*? Work that you did for us and got *paid* for?"

I looked over at the wall.

"Yeah, and you just spiked it..."

I could hear my heart pounding.

"So now, all of a sudden, you're consorting with the *enemy*?"

The Providence Journal and *Evening Bulletin* had been eroding *The Daily News'* market share for years. But it wasn't just the competition. With the Shermans, an antipathy for the *Journal* and *Bulletin* had been forged into their DNA by their father and grandfather who'd run the paper before them.

I got closer to him and dropped my head.

"Look Mr. Sherman, if I'm wrong on some factual point, tell me and I'll correct it, but those pieces are bulletproof, and to see them spiked because of Albert and your advertise——"

"Careful son, you're about to accuse me of something a little above your pay grade."

I felt like saying, "At fifty bucks a week EVERYTHING's above my pay grade," but I bit my tongue.

"Look... I just want to see them run."

There was an awkward pause.

He eyed me, then cocked his head toward the rolled-up stories in my hand. I hesitated. What was he going to do now? Paper shredders hadn't even been invented back then.

"Come on kid, let me see them." He gestured with his fingers, motioning me forward. I handed him the roll. Ned walked back to his desk and started reading.

One take, then another and then he took out his own red pencil and made a couple of minor corrections. Pretty soon I could see that he was getting invested in the series, just as Jim had. His own backbone was straightening. At one point he even smiled.

"Jesus Christ... Jimmy O'Brien is gonna have a *shit fit* over this."

O'Brien was the darkly handsome, silver-tongued Irish-American City Solicitor. He was just below the City Manager in rank. It was his job to ensure that The Housing Code was being enforced and he'd been grossly delinquent. Suddenly I was hopeful. I leaned in toward Ned's desk.

"So you're gonna run it?

"Fuck, yeah," he said. "Something you've gotta know if you want to keep working here."

He waved me in closer and lowered his voice even though we were the only two people left in the building. "My love for the advertisers of this paper is exceeded *only* by my *hatred* of *The Providence Journal*. I'm gonna hold it and run it Wednesday through Saturday. Page one. You can call *The Journal* and tell them to kiss my ass."

And with that he walked out.

CHAPTER SIXTEEN

SHOCK, DENIAL, THEN ENFORCEMENT

Newport's Back Yard ran in four parts from August 28th to the 31st, 1968, Like the scene from *Casablanca* where Captain Renault, played by Claude Rains, tells Rick, played by Humphrey Bogart, "I'm shocked, *shocked* to discover that there is *gambling* going on here," only to have the croupier hand him his winnings, James S. O'Brien and the rest of the City Council expressed utter disbelief that a large Black ghetto existed 25 yards from the edge of City Hall.[417]

The collective guilt that swept the town – along with the potential loss of millions in Federal redevelopment money -- caused several civic and religious leaders to form the non-profit Church Community Housing Corporation which began building new houses that it sold to the West Broadway residents at affordable prices. [418]

One of them was Pauline Perkins, who had gone to work at New Visions and saved enough to buy a house at 24 Burnside Avenue in 1972. [419] It was just down the street from 54 Burnside, a three-story hovel with multiple code violations that I'd named in the series. [420]

Newport's Back Yard

Slum Homes Lack Bath, Stove

By PETER LANCE

Part One of the 4-part Series That ran August 28th-31st 1968

"I can't fully express what owning that new house meant to me," Pauline told me after I sought her out for an interview in 2020, [421] "The Church Community Housing Corp. gave the former tenants of those broken down houses a real stake in their homes. It gave us the pride of ownership. We were no longer the victims of these landlords."

Beyond The Church Community non-profit, Phil Almeida pressured the City to set up an escrow account at City Hall allowing tenants to deposit their rent money there until the slumlords corrected the code violations. It was passed as part of a Tenants' Rights ordinance on August 28th, the first night of the four-part series. [422] Before she had the wherewithal to buy her own house, Pauline paid *her* rent into that account, as did Paula Butler and other West Broadway tenants identified in the series. But one slumlord found a way to get around it.

EXPLOITING A LOOPHOLE

Alexander G. Teitz was a graduate of Yale University and Harvard Law School. He practiced law in Newport until 1973, when he became assistant general counsel to the Illinois Department of Public Aid and went on to become an administrative law judge on the appeals board of the Department of Health and Human Services in Washington, where he died in 1992. [423]

Thirty years earlier, in addition to the house at 93 Kingston Avenue, valued at $2,700, which he inherited from his father in 1962,[424] Teitz had a thriving law practice on Bellevue Avenue near Touro Park. Then, after the series ran, faced with the need to repair the dilapidated house while his tenants put their rent into escrow, Teitz chose to walk away.

He was exploiting a state law which provided that if the expense of repairing a property amounted to more than 50 per cent of the assessed value, a landlord was free to abandon it and avoid the cost of bringing it up to code. But before he could do that, he had to get his tenants out. So instead of repairing his substandard building, Teitz actually filed eviction proceedings against Paula Butler and two other tenants who lived in the Kingston Avenue property. [425]

LANDLORD'S HOME PICKETED — Members of Fair Welfare Rights Organization, some of them camera shy, picket in front of home of Alexander G. Teitz at 73 Cather- ine St. He owns property on Kingston Avenue, which does not meet minimum housing codes.

(Daily News Photo)

Repairs Costly, Owner Closes House

The notice said that she and her five children would have to vacate "immediately." That prompted more than two dozen West Broadway area residents to picket his home at 73 Catherine Street, in an upper middle-class neighborhood across Broadway and a few blocks east. [426] One sign carried by Pauline Perkins read, "Will Landlords House The People They Evict."

Another sign signaling a push back against Doris Duke's restoration project read, "Forget the Tourists. Think of The Residents."

At the time of the protest, Teitz had no comment. The picketers vowed to move to his law offices next. The photo on the previous page was part of the coverage in *The Daily News* on November 29th, 1968:

Property records show that the value of Teitz's 93 Kingston property had dropped by $1,000 to $1,700, which made the 50% abandonment threshold easier to achieve. But, seven months after the protest, despite that drop in valuation, Teitz was able to sell it to one Marguerite F. Chinn for $6,000. [427] In effect, he unloaded a property that had caused him much negative publicity in Newport for *a profit* of $4,300. Still, his tactics in divesting himself of the slum home and evicting Paula Butler brought her plight to the attention of State and City officials.

As a young mother on welfare she had applied for public housing in August of 1968 but was told that she was 14th on the waiting list. [428] With her back rent in the escrow fund, but served with an eviction notice by Teitz, Paula held out with her five children at 93 Kingston until December. The house was unheated. Although the Welfare Department had authorized funds for a space heater, the gas company refused to install it because of the poor condition of the building. [429]

Paula Butler was caught in the vicious catch-22 that afflicts so many of the poor. With the windows in her children's bedroom still broken, she was forced to vacate due to the freezing temperatures. It was two weeks before Christmas.

At that point, Leonard Scalzi, manager of The Hotel Viking, offered to shelter Paula and her five children in a room at the Viking's Motor Inn, where he frequently put up tenants displaced in emergencies. Scalzi, who managed the Viking for 22 years, was a civic leader in Newport. Past chairman of the Newport Red Cross, the Chamber of Commerce and The Rotary Club, he was also a war hero. As an Army colonel during World II he'd won the Bronze Star and the French Croix de Guerre. For two years following the Nazi occupation of Paris he actually ran the George V Hotel.[430]

When state and local officials of the Welfare Department got word of the Viking stay, they claimed publicly that they had not authorized the payment of Paula's bill [431] But Scalzi covered for the young mother.

Then after *The Daily News* ran a story under the headline, "Miss Butler, Children 'Guests' Of Hotel Despite Fuss Over Bill,"[432] the officials backed down and the next day Paula and her children were approved to move into the Tonomy Hill public housing project.

Once stabilized there, Paula got a job and began caring for the elderly. In 1974 she completed a course in gerontology sponsored by Salve Regina College and worked for years at Newport's Baptist Home.[433]

TEITZ RESPONDS TO PART ONE OF THE SERIES

When I'd first tried to reach him for comment while reporting the series, Alexander Teitz had been unavailable. But the day after Part One ran, he contacted me and took issue with my description of one of the tenants in his slum buildings. While ignoring the plight of Paula Butler, Teitz said that he had an agreement, signed June 7th with Mrs. Rose Machado at 28 Marsh Street, the mother of six. Teitz told me that she had not paid him "a cent" of the $50 a month rent on the property which the City had declared unfit for human habitation at the end of 1966.

He said that Mrs. Machado "had begged him to let her move into the house" although he didn't want a tenant there. He then produced a copy of a June 7th 1968 agreement he had drawn up. It amounted to a waiver of the welfare mother's right to rent a safe and habitable property:

> "It is understood that you have examined the premises and are aware of their condition. By renting the property to you, I assume no obligation whatsoever for the condition of the premises or their repair. It is understood further that you have done and will continue to have certain work and repairs done on the premises at your own expenses... I am renting the premises to you with the condition that you will see that they comply with any requirements of law such as the health statues and regulations and particularly the Minimum Housing Code of the City of Newport before you move in. Should there be any complaint concerning the condition of the premises, it is understood that it will be your responsibility to see that the premises are put in proper condition to comply with the law, at your expense." [434]

Setting aside whether Mrs. Machado with six children, including a crippled daughter, had the wherewithal to understand her rights, or whether this side deal crafted by Teitz had the legal authority to trump the City's housing laws, Teitz admitted that Mrs. Machado had already spent $61.90 for repairs, undercutting his claim that she had "never paid him a cent."

AN IRONY RECENTLY DISCOVERED

As I went back and examined the impact of "Newport's Back Yard" half a century later, I encountered another one of those distant but strange connections that occurred so often in a City where everyone seemed linked to everyone else. It turned out that one of the slum houses I named in the series, a colonial-era home at 47 Poplar Street, was scooped up many years later for restoration by Doris Duke.

Back in the 1920's it had been owned by the man who later became my father's boss, Nick Merlo, when he'd been a struggling young tailor. After Nick and his wife Mary sold it in 1929 for $2,648 [435] the subsequent owners let it fall into disrepair, resulting in multiple code violations. Then, in 1992, twenty-four years after my series ran, Doris's Newport Restoration Foundation (NRF) bought it for $130,000. [436]

As we'll see in Chapter Twenty Four, after the NRF acquired dozens of houses, displacing tenants, Doris was met by fierce protests, first from the African-American community and later from middle-class Newporters enraged after she demolished parts of the Mary Street YMCA where many of the city's children of all races had learned to swim.

Eventually the upper-middle class tenants of her restored houses were so outraged over her strong-arm tactics that they created a tenants' association to fight back. One of them was none other than the Rev. Canon Lockett F. Ballard, the rector of Trinity Church, who had married Minnie Cushing and Peter Beard in 1967 and had, for decades, been Doris's own pastor.

THE HOUSING CODE ENFORCED

Despite the efforts of slumlords like Alex Teitz to avoid responsibility or Doris Duke's exploitation of the evictions to pick up houses, "Newport's Back Yard" had a real impact. Eight months after it ran, the series won The Sevellon Brown Award given annually by the New England A.P. Managing Editor's Association. [437] *The Boston Globe* had won it the year before and placed third this time. [438] No paper under 100,000 circulation had ever won that prize. *The Daily News* sold 15,000 papers a day. The Shermans got a plaque [439] and I got a $50.00 bonus. But for me the payoff was far greater.

Daily News Winner
Of Top N.E. Award

Peter Lance

The Daily News was named winner today of the 11th annual Sevellon Brown Memorial Award, which goes to a New England newspaper for "disinterested and meritorious public service."

The winning entry was a series of articles on sub-standard housing here, published Aug. 28, 29 and 30. They were written by Peter Lance 21 a journalism student at Northeastern University who had worked on this paper in 1967 and 1968 as an intern under a cooperative work program He is the son of Mr. and Mrs. Joseph Lance of 2 Ashurst Place and a graduate of De La Salle Academy.

Managing Editor Ves Sprague of The Pawtucket Times, contest chairman made the announcement. He said that The Caledonian- Record of St. Johnsbury, Vt., and The Boston Globe received honorable mentions.

Citations will be presented to

the winners Monday in Boston at the spring meeting of the New England Associated Press News Executives Association. NEAPNEA sponsors the contest which is named for the late editor and publisher of The Providence Journal and Evening Bulletin.

Robert J. Boyle' editor of the Pottstown (Pa.) Mercury, judged the competition. He said the winning "series was selected because of the reporter's ability to construct an in-depth series; because he named names of slum landlords; and because of the courage it took to reveal conditions in the community in which the newspaper published."

Boyle said the author "was stepping on the toes of community officials by putting the responsibilities of journalism ahead of the facade of a perfect

(Continued on Page 4)

News Award

(Continued from Page 1)

community. Both he and. The Newport Daily News followed the finest tradition of journalism by exposing without fear conditions which should be rectified."

The newspaper, which has a circulation of 14,500 daily, is by far the smallest to win the award. The Boston Globe won last year and on two other occasions. The Boston Traveler won twice. Other winners have been the Boston Herald-Traveler, The Hartford Times, The Providence Journal, The Bangor Daily News and The New Bedford Standard-Times.

Entries for the competition came from Maine, New Hampshire, Vermont, Massachusetts, Rhode Island and Connecticut newspapers holding membership in The Associated Press.

Managing Editor James G. Edward of the Newport newspaper credited Lance "with coming up with idea for the series and with doing all of the digging. It was real tough at times because there was quite a bit of opposition from some of the people who had the records."

In a follow-up piece four months after the series ran, headlined, "Housing Code Enforced," *Daily News* reporter Peggy Elgin wrote, "For the first time since the city minimum housing code was approved in 1952, real strides have been made to eliminate conditions which make dwellings unsafe, unsanitary and unfit for human habitation." [440]

Today, West Broadway is a far better neighborhood. A number of the families from 1968 still live there. Phil Almeida passed away in 2008, but Pauline, now Perkins-Moyé, went on to become Director of Resident Services for The Newport Housing Authority.

At the age of 45 she got her college degree. In 2015, when she received *The Daily News* Community Service Award for a lifetime of civic improvement, she generously recalled working on "Newport's Back Yard." [441]

Once the Housing Code was fully enforced, Newport received tens of millions of dollars in federal redevelopment funds, and by 1976, the Bicentennial year, it had begun to develop what *New York Times* architectural critic Paul Goldberger called, "the city's growing identity as a center for tourism."[442]

For me, the series underscored the importance of local newspapers and good old American competition. Half a century later, what that series accomplished, with the help of women like Phil and Pauline, gave me the confidence that I could uncover the truth behind Eduardo Tirella's death.

CHAPTER SEVENTEEN

THE NIGHT BEFORE THE REST OF HIS LIFE

In the cruel reality that is *life* one moment and *death* the next, forty-nine minutes after he'd stepped out of the Dodge wagon to open the gates at Rough Point, the man born Eduardo Giuseppe Tirella was now Autopsy Number A66-27 [443] pronounced dead on arrival at Newport Hospital. [444] The newly uncovered Fire Department logbook indicates that the first alarm came in at 5:07 pm.

"Received a call for auto accident," the entry said. "Woman was hurt, and car went (out) of control. Man under car." [445] At that time, because Newport's ambulance (Rescue #1) was tied up on a call across town, Middletown's rescue wagon was dispatched.

A photo of the crash scene shot by Ed Quigley. The man at extreme left is Brian Jones, Bureau Chief of *The Providence Journal*. The tow truck is from Pelham Garage where Rough Point caretaker Howard McFarlane rented the Dodge Polara station wagon.

Nine minutes later, Newport's truck, then free, responded. [446]

Deputy Fire Chief John Blythe told reporters that the 4,000-pound Dodge was so heavy that the power jacks on the rescue truck were unable to raise it so they could get to Tirella's body. [447] A tow truck from Pelham Garage, the AVIS dealership where the wagon was rented, was then summoned. [448]

By 5:45 pm, the decedent's remains were loaded into a body bag and transported by Rescue #1. Doris was taken to the hospital in the Middletown wagon. [449] The final entry in the NFD's logbook reads: "Emergency call to auto accident at the end of Bellevue Avenue for Edwardo Gusippe (sic) Tirella 42, D.O.A. Rescue #1 out 33 min." [450]

I was puzzled at first as to how the victim's name and age would have been known within minutes of the crash, particularly since Miss Duke, reportedly in shock and quickly incommunicado, would have been unlikely to offer those details.

Part of the answer came when I spoke to the daughter of the couple who owned Roselawn, the estate next door to the crash site. As it turned out, Tirella's body had been dragged under the vehicle with such force that after it hit the tree, his wallet was thrown onto Roselawn's property. It was found the next morning by the owner, Ella Chartier.

As reported in Chapter Twelve, it was Ella's husband, developer Louis Chartier, who would later tell Sheriff Harry Casey that Louise Vanderbilt had murdered her husband George in San Francisco. In 2018 while researching Eduardo's death, I reached out to Ella's daughter Janet who remembered how her mother had recovered the wallet.

"She had a rose garden about ten feet from the edge of the grounds," she said. "It was next door to Quatrel, the estate where Doris had crashed through the fence. My mother noticed the wallet among the rose bushes on Saturday and gave it to the police." [451]

The billfold held Eddie's driver's license, but since the cops didn't get it until the day *after* his death, I was still confused about how the first responders had learned his full name. That part of the mystery was solved when I interviewed retired Newport Police Department Detective William Watterson, who arrived at the crash scene just after Eduardo's body was removed from under the station wagon's rear axle.

"At that point it was a mangled mess," he said. "Doris had crashed through a fence across Bellevue made of cement posts and iron rails. But when I searched the body, I found his passport." [452]

As to why that piece of identification had been separated from Eduardo's wallet, his niece, Donna Lohmeyer, told me that when the Tirella family traveled, "they typically wore money belts around their waists that held passports and other travel documents." [453]

I found Eduardo's passport application amid dozens of files from The Doris Duke Papers, a collection of more than 81,600 pages at Duke University's Rubenstein Library, made public 25 years after her death. [454] As a measure of just how close he was to Doris, Eddie had his U.S. passport sent to *her* offices at 30 Rockefeller Center in NY

MEMORANDUM

DATE October 11, 1966 .

TO   MR. ROBERT M. AUGHEY
            108 ELIZABETH ST.
SUBJECT   Dover, New Jersey

Enclosed please find the passport of Edward Tirella and some papers inside said passport. These were the only personal effects that were at the hospital.

Joseph A. Radice
Chief of Police

addressed in care of Pete Cooley, her business manager. Given the trauma his body sustained, that passport was the only piece of I.D. on his remains when they were transported to Newport Hospital. And, as it turned out, other than his body, the passport and some papers inside it were the only personal effects sent back to his family in New Jersey via his brother-in-law Robert Aughey, Donna's father.

It was accompanied by a curt, typewritten memo over the stamped signature of Joseph A. Radice. Strangely, for an Italian-American, the chief had Anglicized Eduardo's name, calling him Edward. [455]

SINATRA AND THE WAR HERO

"Eddie's loss left a huge hole in our lives," Donna recalled. "Among his many talents, he played the piano and initially hoped to make it as a singer." After paling around with Frank Sinatra in the early 1940's, war broke out with the Japanese invasion of Pearl Harbor. On June 1st, 1943 "The Voice" from Hoboken signed with Columbia Records and chose to remain a civilian. [456] But Eduardo felt compelled to enlist.

He entered the army three weeks later on June 25th and shipped off to Europe as a Rifleman in Company K of the 428th Infantry. Serving in both Northern France and The Rhineland, he carried, serviced and fired the Browning .30 caliber machine gun, seeing his heaviest action from mid-December 1944 to late January 1945 in the fierce counter offensive across the Ardennes Forest known as The Battle of The Bulge. It was the second-deadliest mass casualty action in U.S. history. [457]

His mother, Etilia Falgione Tirella, shown pictured with him after his return, sent him this letter on June 6th 1944, when Allied Forces invaded Normandy:

> "Dear Son, Well, today is D-Day and I just came from church. All the churches had prayer hours between 2-3 p.m. There were hundreds of people there to pray for the end of the war. Love, Mother. P.S. Congratulation for the stripes. I hope you get more soon."

The letter Eddie's mother sent him. Pictured with her after the War.

Hospitalized later in Europe for frostbite, and nearly losing the toes on each foot, Eddie spent months in the 1st Indorsement Hospital Center in Butner, NC when he returned stateside.[458] Little did his mother know at the time, but eventually he would be awarded one of the nation's top combat awards, The Bronze Star Medal.

Honorably discharged in August 1945, he was so humble about his war service that his family wasn't aware that he'd won that honor until after his death when The Department of Defense delivered a grave marker with the designation BSM.

Donna, then a 20-year-old, found his dog tags which he'd hidden away. "Fixed to them," she said, "was a St. Christopher's Medal and a Miraculous Medal honoring Mary, to whom my grandmother prayed every night he was in uniform. Twenty-one years later, we had to face the reality of how quickly he'd been taken from us. And frankly, given what he'd told me about Doris and how possessive she was, it was something I had dreaded." [459]

Eddie's Dog Tags with Miraculous Medal. His grave marker and The Bronze Star.

In 1965, after toiling for Doris for years and routinely getting underpaid by Pete Cooley, [460] Eddie had finally broken out. In the opening frames of the big-budget MGM Taylor and Burton production *The Sandpiper,* he'd earned a rare credit from producer Martin Ransohoff: "Coordinator of the Big Sur Scene." In fact, he'd designed the interior of the "beach shack" where Elizabeth's character, a Bohemian painter, lived. Eddie's partner Edmund Kara had sculpted the nude redwood bust of Liz that was a plot point in the film and he was also cited in the up-front credits. MGM even produced *A Statue for The Sandpiper,* a short film featuring Eduardo and Edmund which chronicled Kara's creation of the piece.

In the film, Liz's sculptor/love interest was played by Charles Bronson with whom Eddie appeared in a scene shot at Nepenthe.

At left, Eduardo next to Charles Bronson in *The Sandpiper*. **At right Edmund Kara and Eduardo in the MGM short,** *A Statue for The Sandpiper*.

"Between Big Sur and the house they shared on Stanley Hills Place in Laurel Canyon, Eduardo and Edmund had a full life," said Kara's longtime friend Glen Cheda.[461] "By 1966 they'd arrived at the cultural epicenter of the West coast art and music scene."

In the book, "*Canyon of Dreams*," L.A. music critic Kirk Silsbee described how "Tirella's renowned home parties were gatherings for creative people in L.A." including actors like Alan Ladd and Dennis Hopper, jazz greats Junior Mance and Cannonball Adderley, and songwriters like Johnny Mandell who composed "The Shadow of Your Smile" for the Taylor-Burton film. "Tirella was an accomplished vegetarian chef and he cooked fabulous meals," wrote Silsbee. [462]

Eduardo Tirella with Kim Novak and Sharon Tate.

"Eduardo and I shared the same birthday," said Pola Zanay, another artist. [463] "He had a little Morgan sports car, and we'd drive up to Big Sur on Fridays. He and Edmund lived in a cabin in Mule Canyon near Nepenthe. Every weekend they'd throw musicales. Eduardo loved to sing, so he'd have Bobby Short playing the piano. Little trios would come up. Kim Novak lived up there. She and I would be lying in a loft above the living area sipping champagne. It was a fabulous time."

"But he was transitioning to studio work," said Silsbee, "and that didn't sit well with Doris Duke." After Ransohoff hired Eddie to work on the new film *Don't Make Waves* starring Sharon, with whom he'd grown very close, the tension with Doris escalated.

"Doris was panicked," said Pony Duke, "when Eddie told her that he was *considering* the job he had actually *accepted*. Her entire life revolved around his ability to make things for her look beautiful. She pleaded with him not to leave her. He'd been a calming influence for her, but he was tiring of her mood swings and worried that his motion picture design career was suffering because (she was) monopolizing all of his time" [464]

Events came to a head in the late summer of '66. "He was going back to Newport to tell her in person rather than on the phone or through a letter, that he was leaving her employ," said Kara's friend Glen Cheda. "He was happy at Big Sur and Edmund felt strongly that he shouldn't go back. He felt fearful, because of his past knowledge of Doris. What she was capable of." [465]

Pola Zanay agreed. "We all felt that way. Eduardo really wanted to extricate himself from her clutches. But at the time he needed major dental work that ran into the thousands of dollars and working for her was the only way he could get that kind of money. Everybody else in our circle of friends told him, 'Don't go back to her. You can get the money some other way.'" [466]

As a precaution, Eduardo agreed to consult with a clairvoyant named Dr. Jacques Honduras, nicknamed "the Psychic to the Stars."

"He had the reading done," said Zanay and Jacques advised him absolutely *not* to go back to Newport. He sensed danger there." But, in the end, Eduardo decided to make the trip. "He really felt that he could control Doris," said Donna. "Eddie was a trusting soul. He always saw the good in people and he figured it would be this one last curating job and he'd be out. He even promised that I could come to work for him in L.A. when I graduated with my degree in art and design. That was the reason he went back... One last job."

THE RELIQUARY OF ST. URSULA

Until now there have been multiple false accounts of where Eduardo and Doris were headed that Friday at 5:00 pm when his life ended. Chief Radice said, "She and Tirella were going out to dinner." [467] But Linda McFarlane, the caretaker's daughter said, "No. My mom told me that they were going to meet somebody. A brief meeting, because the cooks were preparing a meal for when they came back." [468]

Other reports claimed that they were going out see Virginia Warren, then the head of Newport's Preservation Society, to discuss "the Newport Restoration project." [469] But Doris's plan to restore colonial houses didn't formally begin until two years later, and it's clear from this investigation that her sudden turn toward philanthropy in Newport commenced *after* Tirella's death.

Harle Tinney, who lived at Belcourt Castle across from Doris, supplied the answer.

As noted, Belcourt was designed for Oliver Hazard Perry Belmont, grandson of the Naval Hero. In 1966 it was the only mansion-museum in Newport that wasn't under the control of The Preservation Society. The Tinney family had bought it a decade earlier. [470]

"One of our very best friends," said Harle, "was John Perkins Brown. He was a famed preservationist and antique dealer with a shop on Franklin Street in Newport. John was close to both our family and Doris Duke. Sometime in the fall of 1965 he came to us and said, 'I've acquired an extraordinary piece.

"He showed us a picture. The bust of a woman, 15th or 16th century. Carved Wood. Decorated in polychrome.

"It was a reliquary, one of a number of works of art created over the centuries to contain the bone of a saint -- in this case, St. Ursula -- whom history had it, was martyred in the third or fourth century A.D. along with 11,000 of her handmaidens – all virgins. [471]

"John Brown offered to sell it to us for $2,500 and we said, 'We'd love to have it, but that's a little too rich for our blood right now.' So, he said, 'Well if I don't sell it to you, I'll sell it to Doris.'"

The Reliquary of St. Ursula. Eduardo's last curating job for Doris Duke (Adam Fithers photo)

"Eventually she bought it," said Harle, "sometime in the fall of 1965. but it took nearly a year to restore. For that John reached out to Adé Bethune, renowned for her expertise in bringing religious artifacts back to life.

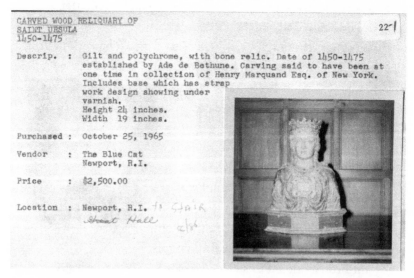

This card is from an inventory of art at Rough Point. It shows the purchase price, $2,500, the seller (The Blue Cat) John Perkin's Brow's shop on Franklin Street and the fact that Ms. Bethune, who restored it, also dated it.

"But before she took possession," Harle told me, "Doris wanted the finished piece appraised. She needed Eduardo's blessing. That's why she'd coaxed him back to Newport. They were literally on their way to John's shop on Franklin Street, late that afternoon, to pick it up when she killed him." [472]

"What makes this story a tragedy of Shakespearean dimensions," says Pola Zanay, "is that Eduardo was literally killed on the night before the rest of his life."

The Great Hall at Rough Point with photos of Doris Duke in the foreground and priceless works of art surrounding them. Many of the pieces in this room and throughout the home-museum were curated by Eduardo Tirella. (Adam Fithers photo).

CHAPTER EIGHTEEN

LITIGATION &
COVER-UPS

By the time she died at the age of 80, Doris Duke had been involved in more than 40 lawsuits.[473] She sued the non-profit Animal Medical Center that she'd invited to operate at Duke Farms. She sued Bob Guccione, publisher of *Penthouse Magazine* over the production of the film *Caligula*. She sued *Confidential Magazine* over that cover story alleging that she was intimate with an African prince. She sued the City of Newport seeking a reduction in the property taxes for Rough Point. She sued John Perkins Brown, whom she'd appointed the first head of The Restoration Foundation. She sued Citibank and Banque Continental. She sued multiple parties to whom she'd loaned money; many of them members of her staff and close friends. Further, as reported in detail, she forced the family of Eduardo Tirella to sue her after refusing to settle with them for his wrongful death.

Along with her lengthy civil litigation in California and Hawaii involving the stabbing of common law husband Joe Castro (recounted in Chapter Fourteen) Doris also defended herself against multiple suits filed by parties she'd damaged, including pedestrians mauled by her dogs in

Newport and Hawaii. [474] According to a source close to her Providence attorney, she settled for $50,000 out-of-court when one of her dogs attacked a young girl in Newport. [475]

Over the years Duke litigated a number of suits with employees or contractors she'd hired, then soured on, like the former FBI-agent she brought on to solve a theft at her New Jersey estate and, as recounted below, Daryl G. Ford, the initial contractor hired by The Newport Restoration Foundation.

Aram Arabian, her lawyer, and Doris Duke during the 1971 wrongful death trial (AP Images)

As we'll see in Chapter Twenty-One, one of the major unanswered questions surrounding the murder of Eduardo Tirella was whether, at the time she killed him, Doris Duke had a valid Rhode Island Driver's license. The one license I found was set to expire on September 30th, 1956.

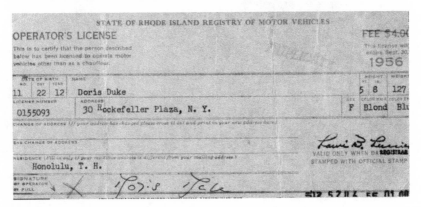

That RI license lists Doris's official Date of Birth, November 22nd, 1912, and though it puts her height at a more petite 5'8" when we know she was 6'2," it also contains two other pieces of information that demonstrate the extraordinary lengths she and her lawyers went to in order to reduce her tax debt by gaming the system on the precise location of her legal residence.

On that license Doris's ADDRESS is listed as 30 Rockefeller Plaza, NY, which was the location of her office and accountant Pete Cooley at the time. But under RESIDENCE it lists Honolulu T.H. (Territory of Hawaii) since the license's expiration date predated Hawaii's admission to the Union as the 50th State in 1959. [476]

In 1968 a list of Interrogatories was submitted to Duke's lawyers in the civil case against Avis Rent-A-Car surrounding Tirella's death. The second question asked how long she "was licensed to operate a motor vehicle in Rhode Island and/or any other state" at the time of the homicide. An Avis executive responded by testifying under oath that, "She informs us that she was licensed to operate for thirty-seven years, before the date of the accident." [477] Although that response didn't designate a state, the math would mean that she'd had a driver's license in one of the 48 U.S. States as early as 1931 when she was 19 years old.

LITIGATING TO CUT HER TAXES

Just where she lived officially became a major point of contention ten years later when officials in Hillsborough Township, New Jersey – the site of Duke Farms – sought to collect more than $13.8 million on $221 million in intangible assets from The Duke Endowment and Doris herself at a time when she was married to James Cromwell. The Board of Taxation of Somerset County tried to prove that she was an official New Jersey resident and, as evidence, they produced a copy of a 1941 application by Doris for a Garden State driver's license.

Signed and sworn to, she listed herself as "a resident of Duke Farms, Hillsborough Township, NJ." [478] But as was her practice, Doris went into U.S. court, claiming that the tax assessment was discriminatory and targeted her personally. Through her attorneys, she even argued that if the residency holding were to stand, "Every taxpayer in Somerset County might be called on to make a sworn statement listing all intangible assets." [479]

In that case, the tobacco heiress was demonstrating the same hardball tactics later perfected by Donald Trump: i.e., when sued, always counter-sue, pay as little to the government or creditors as possible and always seek the maximum advantage in any financial transaction.

While some might call that "good business," others might see it as unpatriotic – a strategy designed to avoid paying one's fair share.

A particularly egregious example of that occurred in 1942 about six months after the tax issue in New Jersey made headlines. It was reported by legendary columnist Drew Pearson, following the Japanese attack on Pearl Harbor. His column was headlined:

DORIS DUKE DICKERS ON PRICE OF YACHT BY NAVY

WASHINGTON: To help patrol Hawaiian waters after Pearl Harbor, the Navy ordered the requisitioning of many private craft, including yachts and cabin cruisers owned by wealthy Americans in Hawaii. Yacht owners were informed they would receive fair compensation to be fixed by the U.S. Maritime Commission. This was readily agreed to by most owners, some of whom patriotically offered to give their boats to the government outright. But there was one notable exception.

Among the craft ordered taken over was the sumptuous yacht Kailani, owned by Doris Duke Cromwell, the tobacco and utility heiress, famed before her marriage as "the richest girl in America." Naval officers were startled to receive a letter from R.W. Swearingen, Mrs. Cromwell's Honolulu agent, asking $35,000 for the Kailani. This price, Swearingen added, did not include Mrs. Cromwell's "sport fishing outfits and a few personal articles now on board."

"The original cost of this vessel," he wrote, "was in excess of $50,000 and approximately $15,000 has been expended in making alterations and improvements for her use in Hawaiian waters. Mrs. Cromwell offers to dock the vessel to permit your examination of the underwater structure and to conduct any trial operations considered necessary."

The "offer" was bluntly rejected. The lawyer was told to inform Mrs. Cromwell to hand over her yacht immediately and do her price-dickering later with the Maritime Commission. [480] Three months after that, it was reported that The Duke Power Company was one of nine large corporations moving their taxable locations within the state of New Jersey from Jersey City to counties more favorable in the assessment of intangible personal property. Records at the time showed that the power giant created by Doris's father had $101,288,523 worth of outstanding stock and had recently moved its corporate address to Flemington in Hunterdon County, where the tax rate was the lowest in the state, [481] The levy in Flemington, which funded schools and local municipal services, was 74 cents per $100 versus $5.37 per $100 in Jersey City. So the 1942 move resulted in a savings to Duke Power of more than $26 million a year.

The corporate offices of the company, which generated and sold electricity in North & South Carolina, and operated bus lines and gas and water plants in those states, *had* been located in Newark but when *that* city sought to add $15 million to the company's assessment in 1938, they moved to Hillsborough township, which in turn, levied the $13.8 million assessment which sent Doris to federal court. Initially the U.S. District Court reduced the number to $5.6 million but the company, controlled by Doris, moved to Jersey City before Hillsborough could bill it again.[482]

In effect, the Flemington move was the second for Duke Power in three years and the battle by county officials to make Doris pay her fair share of taxes wasn't over. After the reduction at the Circuit Court level, Hillsborough officials appealed to the Third District Court and they lost. In fact the court ruled that the entire $13.8 assessment was "null and void," [483]

Undaunted, Hillsborough appealed to The U.S. Supreme Court where Doris's attorney argued that she was an official resident of *Hawaii* at the time of the assessment. The High Court agreed, upholding the Third Circuit's decision in a 7-0 opinion written by Justice William O. Douglas.

That decision came down in 1945 and it begs the question: how did Doris Duke get a Rhode Island driver's license a decade later which listed her ADDRESS as New York City and RESIDENCE as Honolulu?

The matter is complicated even further when one considers that in her files at Duke University's Rubenstein Library, there's a copy of an affidavit that Doris signed on January 9th, 1968 in which she swore to her residency as "Duke Farms, Somerville, New Jersey 08876." [484] So was it legally possible to have a valid RI driver's license in 1966 if you lived in another state? As this book went to press, I couldn't find an authority to answer that question.

LITIGATION IN NEWPORT

In the years after Eduardo Tirella's death, one lawsuit Doris was drawn into was initiated by Newport contractor Daryl Ford who had renovated historic Prescott Farm in Portsmouth and restored multiple colonial era houses in Newport for her Restoration Foundation (NRF).

After working for the Foundation for months, when Ford submitted his bill, Doris took the position that he'd charged her for work not done and The NRF, which she controlled, refused to pay him. Ford then sued The NRF and Doris personally for $1.5 million, alleging, in part, that she'd initially paid him with tax deductible Foundation funds to do work at Rough Point, her personal home. [485] In Ford's complaint his lawyers charged that Miss Duke intended to gain a personal benefit for work done at the Bellevue Avenue estate. [486]

The charge that she misused Foundation funds for personal gain was similar to the allegation that would later get Manhattan hotelier Leona Helmsley, aka, "The Queen of Mean," convicted of criminal tax fraud. Back in 1983, she and her husband Harry had hired contractors to renovate Dunnellen Hall, a 21 room mansion in Greenwich Connecticut. After running up construction bills of $8 million, which they refused to pay, the Helmsleys were sued. The civil litigation then turned up evidence that Leona had repeatedly induced an engineer to make out false invoices billed to Helmsley-Spear, the couple's corporation.

In an epic example of irony, Rudolf Giuliani, then the U.S. Attorney for The Southern District of New York, indicted Leona in 1988 on a series of charges including tax evasion and extortion. [487] While acquitted on that latter charge, she was later found guilty of 33 tax-related counts that could have sent her to prison for life. [488] But in a double twist of irony considering all "the President's men" from the Trump era, she hired Alan Dershowitz, who appealed the convictions and achieved such a sentence reduction that Leona was out of prison in 19 months. [489] She then returned to that same Greenwich estate where she died at the age of 87. [490]

But when it came to similar allegations from Daryl Ford in Newport, criminal charges were never a real threat to Doris Duke. She hired Aram Arabian, the same lawyer who'd outmaneuvered the family of Eduardo

Tirella, and counter-sued Ford. In the end, the contractor reportedly settled for $55,000. But in return, Arabian insisted that Ford drop the $1.5 million fraud suit.[491]

SANITIZING THE RECORD

With respect to the death of Eduardo Tirella, Doris and her attorneys went to extravagant lengths to hide the truth behind what had happened. In a Nov. 11[th,] 1966 Memo to The File, Wesley Fach, her lead New York attorney, advised against filing a claim with Duke's principal insurer, Royal Globe, for the damage to Rough Point's gates because, "Any resistance to an insurance claim would result in a detailed investigation of the circumstances surrounding the accident." [492]

As recounted in Chapter Two, the file for Romano et. al. vs. Doris Duke, the case in which she was found negligent at that 10-day trial in July of 1971 is missing from RI Judicial Archives. The Rhode Island DMV, formerly the Registry of Motor Vehicles, is missing all files relating to the Tirella death and the investigation by Registry Inspectors Lewis Perrotti and Al Massarone. [493]

A key photo of the underside of the Dodge Polara Wagon, taken by Newport Daily News photographer Ed Quigley (seen in Chapter Two) was selectively removed from the newspaper's photo archives at The Newport Historical Society. The official Newport Police file on Tirella's homicide was reported missing from the PD as early as 1990. [494]

In October of 2018 retired Det. Al Conti went to the Department on my behalf seeking the file. He was told by Records Clerk Gwen George that she remembered seeing it "ten to fifteen years earlier" (which would have been 2008 or 2003) when she was copying files to Microfilm. But at that time, she told Det. Conti, a "detective," whose name she couldn't remember, took it from her.

A few weeks later, I learned that Donna Lohmeyer had filed a Public Records Request asking for the file. This was the formal response she got from the Newport PD:

> Dear Donna, I just wanted to let you know that we are in receipt of your request for public records involving your uncle Eduardo Tirella who was killed in a car accident in Newport on October 7, 1966. Unfortunately our records only date back to 1974 (sic) everything prior to that would have been turned over to the state archives. The following is information on contacting them: Rhode Island State Archives 337 Westminster St., Providence, RI 02903. If you have any questions or if we can be of further assistance, please feel free to contact this office. [495]

Believe it or not, that response was signed by none other than *Gwen George*, the same police records clerk who had told Det. Conti she'd seen the file on the Tirella homicide sometime within the last 10-15 years. Her response to Donna had been carefully worded.

She wasn't saying that the Newport PD *didn't* have the file, merely that prior to 1974 such files "would have been" turned over to the state. But I asked myself, if the file had gone to State Archives in 1974 how could Gwen George have seen it in 2003, some 29 years later?

I have no reason to believe that the files were intentionally misplaced by Ms. George or any current member of The Department or that they were complicit in any deal that Doris Duke may have made with their deceased predecessors in The Newport PD. But to me, that reply to Donna's public records request felt like what Carl Bernstein and Bob Woodward might have called "a non-denial denial." [496]

After I contacted Ms. George and left a detailed voice mail on her police department extension, I reached out to Newport City Manager Joe Nicholson, an earnest public servant whose own father had once represented mine. He contacted Ms. George who sent him a detailed response on January 9th, 2019. [497] It confirms Det. Conti's recollection of his meeting with her but doesn't explain the discrepancy between his account and her response to Donna Lohmeyer.

THE SEARCH FOR THE FILE

My hunt for that missing file turned into a year-long endeavor. After I received Ms. George's statement, I asked the City Manager if he would prevail upon Newport's current police chief, Gary Silva, to commence a thorough investigation for the file. After he did and that search reportedly came up empty, Joe arranged for me to meet with the Chief in person in June of 2019.

That encounter took place in Nicholson's office, during which the Chief appeared visibly angry; apparently insulted that I was questioning whether the file was being withheld within the confines of Police Headquarters now located across Broadway from the City Hall itself.

After I hit that dead end, retired Det. James Moss of Brooklyn South Homicide suggested that perhaps the Newport Police sergeant who had discovered the truth behind Tirella's death, might have kept a copy of the report as a kind of "insurance policy" in case the apparent deal that Chief Radice had made with Doris Duke ever became known.

That set me off on an investigation into where this sergeant, who later became the Department's Chief himself, had lived. Though he was long dead, I wondered if he might have stored the file in his house. Was it still intact in a basement or garage somewhere in Newport?

When I learned the identity of the deceased sergeant's step-grandson I tracked him down and he told me that his "grandfather" had kept his files on the third floor of his homestead located in The Fifth Ward on a street off Thames. [498] I was then disappointed to learn that the house had been twice sold and was being renovated into a duplex.

Still, while I was in Newport, I figured it was worth a visit and when I did a door knock at the address I ran into the contractor's mother. The next day, just hours before I was due to fly back home to California, her son contacted me, and we met at the house.

He told me that he hadn't yet reached the third floor in his makeover. In fact, he was intrigued by the prospect that the house might be hiding such an important document. So, for the next half hour, with flashlights in hand, the two of us crawled up into the third floor attic's eves which we found to be… empty. The place was dusty, but there was no hidden file.

I headed home without the missing report which might have proven to be the smoking gun of my entire investigation. But I hadn't given up, and throughout the summer of 2019 I continued to make inquiries – some official; some not -- in pursuit of the phantom document.

Then, more than a year after I'd first started looking into Tirella's death, a copy of that long lost file turned up in my email box after a confidential source decided that the truth should come out. It was the cyber equivalent of having a brown paper envelope shoved under my door. The contents turned out to be eye-opening. The report's arrival was well worth the wait and you'll learn what I learned when we drill down on it in Chapter Thirty-Three.

CHAPTER NINETEEN

"THE MIGHTY FIFTH"

To underscore the conflicts between the privileged members of the Summer Colony like Doris Duke, who lived "upstairs," and the Newporters from "downstairs," who served them, the legend of Timmy "The Woodhooker" Sullivan and his sister Julia must be told. Its populist roots are planted in the history of the Newport Irish, who for centuries, were the backbone of the city's working class, living primarily in a section of town between Bellevue Avenue and the waterfront known as "The Fifth Ward." Over the decades they prospered and eventually came to run City Hall, the police and fire departments and the courts; later giving way to immigrants from Italy and the Portuguese Azores. But it was the Irish – in particular, the Sullivan family – who made perhaps the most indelible mark on the cultural history of the local citizenry.

"In Newport, when it comes to the Irish – particularly in The Fifth Ward -- you can't go two blocks without running into a relative," said Patsy Gallagher (now Snyder) whose family stretches far and wide across The City By The Sea. [499] She and her cousin Pat were at St. Catherine's and De La Salle respectively. Between them they know half the town.

The Rhode Island Historical Preservation & Heritage Commission found that Newport was the state's first community to have a substantial

Irish population. "Although Irish settlers had come to Newport by the mid-eighteenth century, the first significant numbers of Irish immigrants arrived during the 1820s. (They) came to work on the construction of Fort Adams, and many settled in the Southern Thames area - the built-up portion of town closest to the construction site." [500] As a measure of what those Hibernians contributed to the City, consider Fort Adams's own history.

From 1776 to 1779, during The Revolutionary War, Newport was taken and forcefully occupied by the British. Half the town's population fled and the once thriving economy was in ruins. [501] The first Fort, built to defend against another attack, was a relatively small garrison commissioned on July 4th 1799 and named for President John Adams.

After the War of 1812, when Fort McHenry in Baltimore took the brunt of the British attack, Congress appropriated the equivalent of $1.33 million in today's dollars, and an Irish immigrant force of 300 laborers working six days a week for seven years [502] built what became "the largest coastal defense... of its kind in the United States." [503]

Fort Adams today, site of the annual Newport Jazz and Folk Festivals

Consisting of a central structure of irregular pentagonal design with a detached Redoubt, the massive walls of Maine granite and local shale, 900 feet long and three stories high, were initially designed to mount up to 500 pieces of artillery.[504] For the next century, through The Civil War and World Wars I and II, Fort Adams shielded Newport from land and sea assault. Many of the same Irish laborers who raised those walls did the stone work on St. Mary's Church, where John Fitzgerald Kennedy and Jacqueline Lee Bouvier were married in 1953.

Few cities of its size have celebrated the Feast of Saint Patrick like Newport and no ancestor of The Emerald Isle, beyond the 35th President himself, was more beloved locally in the first half of the 20th century than Timothy Sullivan,

"WHICH SULLIVAN WAS HE?"

"You couldn't throw a bottle of Guinness in this town without hitting a Sullivan," recalled Bill Dunn, one of my oldest friends, whose grandfather's first cousin, Big Eddie Sullivan, was Chief of Police long before Joseph Radice took the job.[505] After more than 30 years in uniform, he took control of the Department in the early 1940's to clean up corruption. [506] In those days Thames Street was rife with slot machines, betting parlors and prostitution as young sailors swarmed into town during the build-up to World War II. When Big Eddie died suddenly in 1952, more than 700 mourners showed up for his funeral at my old parish, St. Joseph's Church. [507] Chief Sullivan's first cousin had another nickname: "Con The Bender."

Some said it was because he'd lifted more than "a few jars" in his day. But Bill Dunn told me a story that touched me personally, since, in the 1950's, my father worked at The Naval Underwater Weapons Research and Engineering Station (NUWS) which Newporters always referred to as "The Torpedo Station."

During World War II, more than 13,000 employees labored around the clock at that facility to build eighty per cent of torpedoes used by the Navy against Germany and Japan. [508] Located on Goat Island, just off downtown Newport, it was accessible only by ferry until a causeway was built in 1962. According to Bill, "Con" worked there in the Forties and this is how he got his nickname:

"Cornelius Edward Sullivan was a machinist at the Torpedo Station. Every morning he'd walk from 13 Carroll Avenue in The Fifth Ward to Government Landing on Thames Street and catch the Goat Island ferry. In the winter, decades before Climate Change, he would go down to King Park and walk across the ice of the frozen harbor to the island. When people saw him, bent over with his head into the wind, they started calling him 'Con The Bender.'" [509]

Over the years there would be so many Sullivans – many of them residents of "The Mighty Fifth" --that they had to be distinguished by nicknames. "Which Sullivan was he?" was a phrase I heard almost weekly growing up.

So far in this story, we've met Capt. Paul Sullivan who declared "No foul play" in the Duke case and arrested Stephen Robertson. It was Superior Court Judge Arthur J. Sullivan who arraigned Magoo on the night of his surrender. Dr. Michael Sullivan, a pediatrician, brought so many Newport children into the world that a grammar school was named after him. [510]

In high school I had four Sullivans in my graduating class of 83. [511] I worked Saturday nights as a bar boy at Sully's Public House, a nightclub just off Bellevue run by Francis John Pershing Sullivan, a beloved local saloon owner and radio host. In the mid 1990's as I reconnected with my relatives in County Cork (where many in Newport hailed from) I discovered that my great grandmother was Johanna O'Sullivan. A compilation of more than 400 nicknames from a piece written by Cathy Callahan for *The Newport Daily News* is framed on the wall of The Irish Museum on Thames Street. [512] This is a sample:

Automobile Jack	Lightship Dick	Shieky Jim
Babe The Mourner	Little Tim	Silent Billy
Batty The Kid	Little Tom	Silver King
Biddy The Hen	Little Mag	Sis
Blind Eddie	Maggie The Bull	Skinny Biddy
Bridget The Snob	Marvelous Mary	Sleepy John
Bridget The Money	Mary Cup of Tea	Slippery Kate
Castle Hill Dan	Mexican Mike	Sneezy

Cod Fish Mary	Mike The Bear	Soda
Con The Bender	Moon	Soup
Dan The Bull	Neil The Nitpicker	Spider
Dan The Dog	Paddy The Kid	Stallion
Dan The Fox	Paddy The Bearer	Static
Dinny The Priest	Pat The Hang	Stoneface Jack
Dinny The Bitch	Noodles	Sweet William
Eddie The Brute	One-Arm Florrie	Texas Eddie
The Educated Sullivans	One-Arm Julia	Timmy The Ranty
Frisco Dan	Paddy The Fool	Tim The Cobbler

VAN RENSSELAER VS. SULLIVAN

From the century between the 1820's Irish diaspora through the 1950's, no Sullivan earned more national acclaim, legal standing and sheer affection from his peers than Timmy "The Woodhooker," who lived with his sister in a ramshackle wreck of a cottage on the corner of Howe Avenue and Bellevue that looked like the worst shanty in Appalachia.

It was the particular scourge of a prominent member of the summer colony, who, in later years would have given Downton Abbey's Maggie Smith a run for her money: Mrs. Peyton J. van Rensselaer. If there was ever a living embodiment of "Rich Uncle Pennybags," [513] the white mustached, top hatted, cane carrying tycoon who became the public face of the Monopoly game, it was Peyton Jaudon van Rensselaer.

He was a direct descendant of Killian van Rensselaer, the Amsterdam diamond and pearl merchant who co-founded the Dutch West India Company in 1621. [514] After establishing New Netherland, a colony along the Northeast coast, its third Director, Peter Minuit, acquired – some would say, "stole" -- the island of Manhattan from the Canarsie tribe of Lenape Native Americans for 60 guilders; the equivalent at the time of $24.00. [515] It soon became known as New Amsterdam and eventually New York City.

Peyton had the blood and looks of an aristocrat. Tall, handsome and gallant even in old age, the celebrated American painter John Singer Sargent, was said to have noticed him at the Ritz Hotel in Paris in 1921, introduced himself and asked if he could sketch him. [516] But van Rensselaer might not have *been* at the Ritz at that time, had it not been for his first marriage in 1909 to Mabel Gertrude Mason, a much sought-after Back Bay Boston heiress. [517] By then, at the age of 47, Peyton, a free spending bachelor, was effectively broke. So he cashed in on his name as many impoverished British aristocrats did, by "selling" their titles.

He and Mabel were joined in a gala wedding at her family's estate in Stockbridge, Mass., and on the strength of her husband's name, she soon became a prominent hostess in New York and Newport. [518] The couple summered at the former Daniel Swinburne House, an English Gothic Revival style cottage a few blocks off upper Bellevue Avenue [519] and wintered in Italy. [520]

By 1925, however, Peyton had succeeded in blowing through what was left of Mabel's fortune. Severely distressed and suffering from a "nervous disorder," her health began to fail. [521] As her condition worsened, she began making daily visits to her Manhattan physician, Dr. G. Reese Satterlee, at his office at 9 East 40th Street just off Fifth Avenue.

On the morning of July 2nd, she was scheduled to have an X-ray. According to an *Associated Press* report, "When she reached the offices, Mrs. van Rensselaer walked through the reception room and into the office of Dr. Satterlee, then unoccupied. She opened the window and, still holding her parasol and handbag, jumped out. She was killed almost instantly when she struck the sidewalk six stories below. Two pedestrians passing the building narrowly escaped being struck." [522]

Though Mabel had left him with what was described as "a comfortable trust," [523] Peyton soon found himself unable to sustain his lifestyle, so he began to seek out another woman of means.

By 1931 he had found one in Lillian Washburn Newlin, a career businesswoman who had made a modest fortune by buying and selling real estate to the well-heeled in Newport and Palm Beach.

Among her holdings at the time was "The Playhouse," [524] a small residence on the grounds of "Wildacre," the former Ocean Drive mansion of Albert H. Olmsted, brother of the aforementioned landscape architect Frederick Law Olmsted, who designed Central Park, the Boston Garden, and the campus of Stanford University, as well as the initial exterior blueprint for Rough Point. [525]

On April 9[th,] 1931 van Rensselaer and his second bride were married at St. David's Church in Radnor, Pennsylvania where Lillian's family lived. It was a small ceremony attended by 30 of her close friends. Peyton was 69 at the time. At the wedding, which rated two columns in *The New York Times*, [526] Miss Newlin, herself, 49, was dressed in an aquamarine gown of alençon lace. The *Times* notice ended by reporting that "Mr. van Rensselaer and his bride will leave tomorrow evening for Italy and will later go to London for the season. Upon their return to the country on August 1[st,] they will go to The Playhouse, their summer home in Newport."

That notice should have read, "her summer home," since she held the title. [527] Further, the prediction about the couple's post-honeymoon plans proved sadly optimistic.

Four months later, on August 13[th,] returning from Europe, Peyton was found dead in the couple's cabin on the luxury liner Homeric after it anchored off quarantine in New York Harbor. The official cause of death was described as "heart disease," although the ship's surgeon, Dr. J.B. Maguire, was quoted as saying, "there were no symptoms that he was seriously ill." [528]

At that point, the second Mrs. van Rensselaer asked that her husband's cousin Killian retrieve the body forthwith. A funeral was held the very next day at St. Bartholomew's Church on Park Avenue and he was promptly buried in the graveyard of Old St. David's in Radnor; apparently, without an autopsy. To quote Newport Chief of Detectives Paul Sullivan, speaking in the context of the Duke case, there was "no evidence of foul play."

At the time of his death, Peyton's estate left Lillian a mere $200,000. [529] But as a consequence of her brief marriage, she was now in possession of a platinum Society name that had an immense impact on her business, and she put it to good use

This ad later appeared in *The Palm Beach Post*:

PALM BEACH

MRS. VAN RENSSELAER OFFERS
TO TRADE
Palm Beach or Miami property
for
A beautiful 120-acre suburban
home near Chicago.

A beautiful home in Tuxedo Park.

A stone home in Larchmont, N. Y.,
and many other interesting properties.

Tenant paying $1,000 for season for
delightful home here, will sub-let
for $500.

Ocean frontage at Boynton Beach,
100 ft. by 1200 ft.
$4,500

VAN RENSSELAER REALTY, Inc.
335 Worth Ave. Opp. Everglades Club
Tel. 6663

Using her marriage name to earn a living was a practice no heiress worthy of ordering a Tom Collins at Bailey's Beach would ever *think* of doing. But it didn't seem to hurt Lillian's social standing, at least not in Palm Beach. Just 10 months after she ran that ad, a lengthy notice appeared in the society pages of *The New York Times,* headlined "Palm Beach Scene Of A Large Party." It described a lavish tea for 100 given by Mrs. van Rensselaer at Casa Rosada del Lago, her estate. [530] Another soirée at that address was thrown to honor "Lord And Lady Ashburton of London." [531]

While many of the attendees at these events were second-tier swells by Newport standards, the van Rensselaer name brought a luster to Lillian's reputation in the social columns that mattered most: those of "The paper of record," in New York City.

When it came to The City By The Sea, Lillian also seemed to be held in good standing. She acquired two major residences. One was Seaverge, a large 19th century timber-framed estate next to Rough Point on the southern end of Bellevue Avenue. [532]

Built in 1852, it had been the summer residence of Elbridge T. Gerry, the grandson of Elbridge Gerry, one of the original signers of the Declaration of Independence. [533] As Massachusetts governor in 1812, he was the first to manipulate a political district to his advantage; a practice, called "gerrymandering," that remains the scourge of free and fair elections to this day. [534]

Mrs. van Rensselaer's other estate was "The Hedges," an imposing mansion a mile north on Bellevue Avenue. That second "cottage" and the decade long legal war that ensued, damaged Lillian socially and cost her tens of thousands in legal bills.

But it was her plan to divide the first property into apartments that proved to be "a bridge too far," and led to her banishment by "The Avenue crowd." In each instance, the second Mrs. van Rensselaer, herself a late immigrant to Newport, had underestimated her adversaries at both ends of the social strata.

CHAPTER TWENTY

THE BATTLE OF
THE WOODPILE

The most complete account of her first struggle was written in 1970 by Jim Edward, Managing Editor of *The Newport Daily News*, who was my mentor. Under the headline, "Timmy The Woodhooker Wouldn't Like It, But House Finally Sold," Jim told of how "The Sullivan saga began in 1912 when Timothy F. and Julia Sullivan lived with their parents on Sharon Court," a short dead-end street near King Park in Newport's Fifth Ward. [535]

Timmy worked as a laborer and teamster before becoming a peddler of kerosene oil and fruit, moving across Newport in a horse-drawn wagon with a sign that read, "Yes Gertrude, we have fruit." Julia ran a small variety store around the corner from their house.

Later, after Bruen (Brown) Villa, one of the first Newport estates to be divided was sold, the Sullivans bid on one lot and got a tiny parcel of land which contained an old gardener's cottage. Their purchase was "much to the surprise and consternation of Summer Colonists," Jim wrote. "Bellevue was THE Avenue, which meant that townspeople were excluded as property owners, a condition in life reserved for the very rich."

Habitués of the surrounding estates just assumed that the siblings would sell if the price was right, but with Irish pluck, the Sullivans dug in, replacing the one floor cottage in the 1920's with a two story wooden building. "Meanwhile," wrote Jim, "Timmy, who had long since given up peddling, and Julia who had closed her store, lived almost as recluses on Bellevue Avenue. Timmy foraged about Newport and Middletown for lumber and junk of all kinds, sometimes using a pushcart, other times a wheelbarrow. The materials he salvaged were stuffed into the Sullivans' house or piled all over their yard, some of it used as fuel by Julia who seemed to have a smoldering fire burning on the Howe Avenue right of way at all times. The house had no electricity, no central heating or other conveniences." [536]

Timmy The Woodhooker's house amid the mansions. Junk he collected in his yard.

"SNOBBISHNESS AND SPITE"

By 1946, Mrs. van Rensselaer filed a petition with The Newport Board of Review, seeking to clean up what she described as "the trash heap" of wood, tin cans and mattresses that she passed each day when exiting her Howe Avenue estate. [537] Her pleadings were co-signed by 39 of her neighbors, including Mrs. Julia Berwind, the coal heiress who presided over The Elms, the nearby French Chateau, and Lord and Lady Camoys of Oxfordshire, England, whose daughter Noreen Drexel, a direct descendent of the founder of Brown University, would go on to become a pillar of Newport Society. [538] But despite that level of social weight on her side, Mrs. van Rensselaer lost out to Timmy, who called the petition an exercise in "snobbishness and spite."

Soon, he and his sister became favorites in the national media coverage that ensued.

The Associated Press sent out a story that began this way: "During the years that most of his neighbors were amassing millions, Timmy was assembling, in his front yard, a very impressive collection of old lumber and other discarded articles." [539]

Citing Lillian's petition, the piece noted that she had measured the volume of articles in the Sullivan's yard at "252 feet long and 15 feet high," with "the odor not pleasant."

Lillian's hometown paper, *The Philadelphia Inquirer* called the legal fight an "imbroglio." [540] *The Baltimore Sun* reported that "Timothy and his sister Julia are liked personally by their neighbors [541] and the lead in *The Boston Globe's* coverage seemed to be written with populist tongue-in-cheek:

NEWPORT ELITE RILED OVER JUNK
IN TIMMY'S BELLEVUE AVE. YARD

Newport, RI – July 30th. It has been alleged that the society people who come here every Summer hold their noses a little higher than usual. Today it was intimated that they hold them especially high when they pass the home of Timothy Sullivan on the way to ultra-swank Bailey's Beach.

Mrs. van Rensselaer said the 'trash pile breeds rats.' It's made up of objects Timmy has obtained over the years pushing a two-wheeled cart through Newport streets collecting old lumber and other discarded articles. Timmy is confident in the outcome of a hearing on August 15th, because he's faced such petitions before. [542]

A Sunday supplement to *The Philadelphia Inquirer* covered what soon became known as "The Battle of The Woodpile" from the Sullivans' point of view.

"'It's pure snobbishness on the part of our wealthier neighbors,' said Timmy, a bearded character in dungarees and two pairs of pants. Julia, whose equally eccentric garb was a red bathrobe fastened by seven safety pins, said, 'Mr. van Rensselaer was a man of profound common sense. He died on his honeymoon while his wife has harassed us until we are unable to do our work here.'" [543]

After the Sullivans removed some mattresses and other debris from the property, the Board of Review petition was set aside, so the increasingly frustrated widow sued the Sullivans in Rhode Island Superior Court. [544] They then counter-sued, asserting that she had taken unauthorized photos of their property and unfairly attacked Julia for the way that she wore her hair. [545]

Mrs. van Rensselaer upped the ante, calling the Sullivans' nearby property a "breeding ground for mosquitos." She passed another petition to her wealthy neighbors, but this time, only 15 signed. Among those who turned her down was Mrs. Cornelius Vanderbilt.

The conflict soon became a populist cause célèbre between the haves and have nots.

By 1949, Timmy and Julia seemed to take the legal high ground after engaging Matt Faerber, a legendary Newport lawyer and international expert on military justice. Matt was a larger-than-life Damon Runyon character with a steel trap mind and an impeccable string of victories that he achieved after prepping for trial at Billy Goode's, a saloon around the corner from The Courthouse.

Having done his research on Lillian, who, for years, had run ads offering not just houses and estates, but furniture and collectibles for sale, Matt filed pleadings charging that in her war on the Sullivans, she was effectively a pot calling the kettle black. He presented the court with a newspaper ad (run earlier in the month) in which Lillian had offered for sale, "beds, tables, stoves, iron rails, washtubs, windows, ice boxes, radios, screen doors, (a) lavatory toilet, couch, a wooden mantle (and) beautifully carved Gothic Caen fireplace etc." [546]

The lead in an *AP* story on June 27th, 1949 read, "Mrs. Peyton van Rensselaer, whose feud with junk-collectors Timmy and Julia Sullivan, has enlivened an otherwise dull Newport social season, indignantly denied tonight that she's in the junk business herself." [547]

Still, Lillian was forced to admit that she had run the ad, arguing that "it wasn't a regular thing with her," but that she'd recently cleaned out the basement at The Hedges. "I would have given them to Timmy," she said, "only he would have piled them up in his yard."

She then predicted disaster if "the woodpile" was allowed to remain. "It certainly endangers all of Newport," she speculated, "If a fire starts there, it will spread everywhere." [548]

The matter dragged on until 1950, when a détente was reached. The Sullivans agreed to stop stock-piling lumber and junk on their premises and Lillian agreed to build a wall around The Hedges with an alternate exit that allowed her to come and go without passing "the eyesore." One battle had come to an uneasy peace, but the one that erupted around her second estate would prove to be Mrs. van Rensselaer's undoing.

NEWPORT FIGHTS MILLIONAIRE'S HUT

Two years later, Mrs. van Rensselaer, then 70, enraged "the cliff dwellers of Society's most carefully guarded stronghold" -- as *The New York Daily News* called her neighbors -- when she sought to convert Seaverge, the estate next to Rough Point, into an apartment hotel. [549]

She'd recently purchased the 26-room, five acre mansion for $20,000 from A&P supermarket heir Huntington Hartford, whose mother, the Princess Pignatelli, had left it to him. *The News* quickly dubbed it, a "hut for middle-class millionaires" [550] and her plans to subdivide it prompted an attack from Newport's Old Guard who saw the conversion as crassly commercial.

By now Lillian had decamped from The Hedges and moved into Seaverge at the other end of Bellevue, which she'd started to renovate. [551] But the opposition from her neighbors was so fierce that her only play before the Zoning Board was to recast herself as Society's savior.

"I bought the property," she argued at the hearing, "to protect the social sanctity of ancient Newport." She'd done this, she declared, after meeting "a man named Stern whose expression and manner were obnoxious. He said he meant to run a hotel and bring in people I knew shouldn't be in Newport." [552]

It was a thinly veiled anti-Semitic threat in a town where Touro Synagogue was revered. She'd already alienated the Irish population. So with strong opposition from her neighbors, the Zoning Board turned her down and Lillian abandoned the scheme.

Three years later, her health had seriously deteriorated. The once formidable businesswoman, who had endured two legal losses at opposite ends of Bellevue Avenue, found herself a recluse on the top floor of Seaverge, attended only by a single servant named Billy.

That's the account I got from Harle Tinney; whose family agreed to take Seaverge off her hands for virtually the same price she'd paid for it. Part of the deal was that Lillian would continue to live there for the rest of her days. But at the age of 73, she still had a few moves left

"My father and mother-in-law took Seaverge," said Harle in an interview for this book, "with the understanding that it came with all furnishings included. Their initial goal was to open it as a museum. But in the week after the contract was signed, as they left to prepare for the move, Mrs. van Rensselaer arranged to sell off many of the contents of the house, worth tens of thousands of dollars, including an antique train set in the attic and more than 200 antique chairs. When they finally got back to the house, they found that it had been partially looted, but they felt sorry for the old woman who was then bedridden. She would call out at all hours of the day and night in a kind of mournful wail for 'Billy... Billy,' her one caretaker. Eventually Lillian's health failed to the point that she left Newport for Pennsylvania." [553]

The Tinneys persuaded the broker who'd sold them Seaverge to flip it and they were able to purchase Belcourt, a much more substantial estate, just north on Bellevue for the astonishing price of $25,000. The sellers were Louis and Elaine Lorillard who had founded The Newport Jazz Festival in 1954 and, lest the reader needs to be reminded, they later purchased an estate they called Quatrel, after the four "L's" in Louis' name. [554] Located on Bellevue, directly across from Rough Point, it was the site where Eduardo Tirella's life ended.

After her return to Pennsylvania in early February 1956, Lillian Newlin van Rensselaer died. Her death certificate listed multiple causes attendant to a heart attack, including Parkinson's Disease, and persistent hypertension. [555] She went to the grave next to her husband, still in possession of her Knickerbocker surname, but was remembered more for taking on Timmy and Julia. This was the lead in her *Associated Press* obituary which ran in *The New York Times:*

PITTSBURGH, A.P. Mrs. Peyton J. van Rensselaer, whose court fight with a Newport RI neighbor Timothy (Timmy The Woodhooker) Sullivan attracted nationwide attention five years ago, died here yesterday at the home of her sister. A member of the Newport summer colony for 25 years, her annual Bal Masques in Palm Beach in the 1930's were attended by European royalty. But she confronted formidable adversaries in the junk dealer and his sister. [556]

In 1968, State Representative George Newbury, a former political science professor at De La Salle, introduced a resolution in the Rhode Island General Assembly requesting that a small park on Bellevue be named for the Sullivans. The State never acted on the measure.

Today, like the site where Eduardo Tirella was killed further down Millionaire's Row, any evidence of "The Battle of The Woodpile" has long been erased. But there's another part of Newport history involving the class struggles of the Irish that's worthy of note. It also involves a property with a troubled history and an Irish-American immigrant to Newport; albeit one of a slightly different pedigree. That story's ahead.

PART THREE

CHAPTER TWENTY-ONE

"THE MURDERER'S HOUSE"

In *A Caretaker's Daughter*, Linda McFarlane's memoir of living as a teen-ager at Rough Point, she wrote, "One of the saddest memories was the autumn of 1966; the night of the terrible accident." [557] She was a sophomore at St. Catherine Academy, sister school to De La Salle, north on Bellevue Avenue, when she got a call from a friend that a man had been killed at the front gate.

"Right away," she said, "the fear struck me that it was my father" (the estate's caretaker). [558] "So, I ran outside and thank God, he was O.K. That's when I saw the blood and when I heard it was Mr. Tirella, I started crying."

The next day, after Doris got home from the hospital, Linda remembered, "Her lawyers came up from New York. I was going out to a football game and my Dad said, I shouldn't go. Some of Miss Duke's people suggested that there would be too many questions being asked, so I stayed home."

That Monday after school, Linda and some friends were walking past De La Salle on their way to The Newport Creamery, a local ice cream hangout in a shopping center further down Bellevue. As they passed the high school, one of the boys yelled, "There's the girl who lives at the murderer's house."

"I came home crying," she told me. "So my mother called Brother Bernard (the dean of students) at De La Salle. He asked me who the boys were, and I said I didn't want to give names. But he said that unless I *did*, he couldn't do anything about it. Still, I didn't want to say who it was, so he told me that maybe I should be a bigger person about it and just let it go."

In the meantime, Linda's parents told her never to speak of "the accident" again. [559] "After that," she said, "nobody said any more about it."

THE MAID WHO VANISHED

But Eduardo Tirella was apparently not the only Duke employee whose memory was erased after death. In her book, Linda writes of an incident involving one of Doris's maids. Like all of the junior female household staff at Rough Point she wore a white uniform and white shoes; identified only by the first letter of her last name: Miss C.

"One day," wrote Linda, "My mom took us aside and told us Miss C. had been sunbathing on the rocks, when a wave came over her and she drowned. Nothing else was ever said of her."

When I asked Linda if the police had been notified about the maid's drowning, she said, "No. Anything that happened at Rough Point, stayed at Rough Point." [560]

Knowing that, I was curious how the Rough Point staff had processed the details of Eduardo's sudden death. What Doris, via her lawyers, had told police was one thing, but how did those who worked "downstairs" at the sprawling 30 room estate understand it? Over the years, one theory of the crash stood out among the help. Some believed that because the estate's iron gates opened *inward*, Duke, unfamiliar with the rental car, had to put the vehicle *in reverse* to allow the gates to swing freely, but, in her confusion, she put it in *drive* and hit the gas. (More on that theory later.)

Johnny Nutt, who'd worked for years as a gardener at Rough Point, told me that other staffers had a different take on the crash. [561] His grandmother, Hulda Goudie, was Doris's beloved chef.

"She retired when she was 90 years old," he said. "Miss Duke loved her. Called her 'Grandma.' An incredible cook. She could

Hulda Goudie, Doris's chef, with caretaker Howard McFarlane. (Linda Knierim photo)

take a pair of work boots and turn them into a nine-course meal."

Though Johnny wasn't working in Newport at the time, this is what "Grandma" told him:

"Miss Duke and Mr. Tirella had a rented car from Pelham Garage. He wanted to go back to Hollywood to resume his career. But they had a big argument that night as they left the house. They got in the car. Mr. Tirella was driving. He got out to open the gate, but he left it in drive with the emergency brake on. He was going to come back and get in the car, drive it through and lock it behind him. But for some reason Miss Duke decided to drive. She was a big woman, a lot taller than him, and as she slid across the seat to drive it out, her knee hit the emergency brake release. It jerked forward. She went to slam on the brake, and she hit the gas by mistake. That's the way I heard it." [562]

Johnny Nutt's explanation puzzled me, first, because of his account that Eduardo intended to return to the vehicle after opening the gates and drive it out. In her first statement to police Doris had said that it was their regular practice for her to slide over behind the wheel -- something she'd done "a hundred times before" -- and drive out onto Bellevue Avenue as Eduardo closed the gates behind them. He would then get back into the driver's seat and they'd head off.

As to the parking brake, in many vehicles of that era the driver engaged it with their left foot and released it by pulling back on it –also by foot. Still, it was difficult to believe, knowing Doris as he did, that Eddie would have left the car in *drive* and turned his back on her, whether the parking brake was engaged or not – particularly after they'd argued.

I wanted to test Johnny's theory, so I got a copy of the 1966 Dodge Polara owner's manual and made a surprising discovery: the parking brake on that model could *only* be disengaged *by hand* - pulling a release lever located on the left side of *the dashboard*. Not only was it impossible to release the brake on the floor by foot, but in some Polara models (as an option) there was even A RED WARNING SIGNAL that flashed on and off when the brake was engaged. [563]

PARKING BRAKE WARNING SIGNAL (optional)
Red light in parking brake release lever blinks red when engine is running with parking brake on. Helps prevent unnecessary brake wear.

Keep in mind what Doris Duke had admitted to in sworn interrogatories in the AVIS case: that when "Edward Tirella... got out to open the gate...

Illustrations from the 1966 Dodge Polara's Owner's Manual

I moved over to the driver seat. I put my left foot on the brake and moved the gear shift lever from 'park' to 'drive.'" [564] In his unchallenged opening statement at trial, attorney Edward Friedman added that "Miss Duke released the brake." [565] In the fabricated Q&A which Doris's lawyer Aram Arabian asked the police to write up, she was quoted as saying that it was *possible* that her foot "could have" slipped off the brake to the gas pedal, [566] dovetailing the Rough Point staff's theory of the crash as told by Johnny Nutt.

Since the release of the parking brake would have taken an affirmative act by Doris Duke, was it somehow possible that she mistook the gas for the brake? "Not likely," said retired NYPD homicide detective James Moss. [567]

"When you consider the size of the brake and accelerator pedals in that model wagon. The brake was horizontal, and the gas pedal was vertical. They were perpendicular to each other. It defies belief that anyone would confuse them." That conclusion was later confirmed by Louis A. Perrotti, one of the two field investigators for the Rhode Island Registry of Motor Vehicles assigned to the case.

Now 87, and a distant relative of the Perrotti family of Newport, I tracked him down and he had a precise recollection of his own movements less than six hours after Eduardo's death. He arrived in Newport at 10:30 pm, after driving down from Providence and right away he went to the crash site.

"I was by myself," he said. "It was dark. Using a flashlight, I saw tire marks in the driveway gravel inside the gate. Later the next morning, which would have been Saturday, October 8th, I returned to Newport with my partner Al Massarone. By then the gates had been pulled back inside, but outside, on the Bellevue Avenue side we found the chain that had held them together. The padlock used to secure them was in a closed position inside one of the links, suggesting that the chain had merely been draped over the midpoint of the gates at the time the station wagon hit them. After Doris Duke got back from the hospital, we tried to question her, but a battery of lawyers had arrived, and they wouldn't let us see her." [568]

"THE FIX WAS ALREADY IN"

Perrotti told me later that day that he and Massarone inspected the Polara wagon after it was towed to Pelham Garage. At the civil wrongful death trial in 1971, he testified that their tests indicated the throttle moved freely and the accelerator and foot pedals appeared to move normally. [569]

At the time I first interviewed Perrotti in the fall of 2018, his official report, along with that of the Newport Police Department, was still missing. But once I obtained them, I refreshed his recollection by reading him his own findings from the report and he confirmed what he had testified to at trial: "When the gas pedal was manipulated in an attempt to cause it to stick, it did not stick." [570]

By law, the Registry investigators were supposed to question all drivers in vehicular homicides. "They put us off all day Saturday," he told me, "and then the police said we could be present when they interviewed her on Sunday."[571] But Perrotti said that when he and Massarone drove back to Newport that day they were told at the police station that the interview was already in progress.

"So, we rushed up to the estate," he said. "When we got there, they were just about finished. She was in bed with lawyers around her and two big dogs on either side. Lt. Walsh and the detective (George Watts) were wrapping it up. We were allowed to observe, but we didn't get to ask her any questions. It was almost like the fix was already in."

As noted in Chapter Seven, after being denied a chance to interrogate Doris themselves, Perrotti and Massarone asked to see the transcript of her second "interview" which the police claimed to have conducted two days later on October 11[th.] It was the fabricated Q&A of that "interrogation" which never took place that provided Chief Radice with the cover he needed to close out the case. But in a clear effort to mislead the state investigators and keep the phony transcript out of their hands, Radice told them that, "He felt the initial statement was enough" for the Registry. [572]

As to the truth of Doris's brief statement during that bedroom interview, Perrotti's official report, filed with the Registry on October 19[th,] contained details that directly contradicted Doris's bedroom account: that on leaving Rough Point, Eduardo would routinely get out to open the gates, she'd slide over to drive it out, then after he'd locked the gates, he'd return to the driver's seat and they'd be off. [573] The Newport Police had accepted that account. But when Registry investigator Perrotti questioned Rough Point caretaker Howard McFarlane, on October 10th, the day *after* that bedroom interview, his statement was in stark contrast to what Doris had told the police:

> Mr. Mcfarlane stated that whoever was chauffeuring Miss Duke when leaving the estate would drive up towards the gates and come to a stop approximately 15 to 20 feet before the gates. The chauffeur would then get out of the vehicle, open the gates, get back into the vehicle and drive the vehicle past the gates, stop the vehicle again and return to the gates, locking same and then return to the vehicle and drive away.

Mr. McFarlane stated that whenever he chauffeured Miss Duke, after bringing the vehicle to a stop, prior to reaching the gates, it was necessary to set the emergency brake or place the vehicle in a parked position because of a slight decline. Mr. McFarlane stated that to his knowledge Miss Duke never drove the vehicle beyond the gates once they were opened. [574]

THE MISSING DRIVER'S LICENSE

Another unanswered question in the Duke-Tirella cover-up by Newport Police was whether Doris was in possession of a valid driver's license when she got behind the wheel. Anyone who has ever driven a motor vehicle and been pulled over by police knows that the license and registration are the first documents the law enforcement officer who makes the stop asks them to produce.

As we'll see in Chapter Thirty-Three the one police officer who encountered Doris at Newport Hospital after the crash asked her if she had her license on her and she told him that she didn't. [575] That response was understandable, considering the shock she may have experienced. But in the hours and days that followed, if she *did* have a license that was up to date, was it produced? And if not, why not?

On Tuesday October 12[th,] *United Press International* reported that when "Miss Duke (was questioned) at her mansion, Chief Joseph A. Radice said, 'The only question that remained after the initial interrogation Sunday was whether Miss Duke had a valid driver's license.'" [576]

Apparently, Lt. Frank Walsh and Det. George Watts had failed to obtain the license during that bedroom interview even though the brief transcript contained in the Police Report indicates that they asked her about it:

Q: Do You have an operator's license?

A: Yes, I have a Rhode Island operator's license. [577]

If she did, why didn't Doris or her lawyer Wesley Fach, who was present, hand it over? According to Radice in that same *UPI* story, "She produced a valid license Tuesday," but the Police Report makes no mention of her giving it to police at that time.

Since Chief Radice cited the production of Duke's license as a key factor in closing out the case, it begs the question of whether it was valid at the time Doris killed Eduardo or whether, following the first bedroom Q&A when she was asked about it, her lawyers hastily sought to get the license renewed.

This much is clear: in 2018, after an extensive search of the database of the Rhode Island Department of Motor Vehicles (successor agency to the Registry) their chief legal counsel could find no record of any valid driver's license attributed to Doris Duke beyond the period when the license on page 145 would have expired. [578] So if she *did* have one on the evening of October 7th, 1966, that too is missing from the state's archives.

CHAPTER TWENTY-TWO

THEY THREW A PARTY & NOBODY CAME

James Jay Coogan was a turn-of-the-century Bowery upholsterer and furniture dealer, whose Irish political skills elevated him to the office of Manhattan Borough President in 1899. He soon struck it rich by marrying Harriet Gardiner Lynch, a descendant of the family that owned Gardiner's Island and vast real estate holdings in Manhattan which included The Polo Grounds, where the NY Giants played. [579] The promontory overlooking "Coogan's Hollow," site of the ball field, was called "Coogan's Bluff." [580] After summering in the lower-tier Rhode Island resort of Narragansett Pier and wanting their daughter to make a proper coming-out, Coogan and his wife Harriett set their sights on Newport. On June 30th 1903, they paid $42,100 for Whitehall, a spectacular McKim, Meade & White Colonial Revival estate on multiple acres where the Lorillards had summered. [581]

Whitehall as it looked before Jessie Coogan's aborted coming out party in 1910

But as the Coogans soon learned, having all the millions in the world meant nothing to "The Four Hundred;" the families in the New York Social Register, said to be the maximum number of "swells" who could fit into the Manhattan ballroom of Society's grand dame at the time, Caroline Schermerhorn Astor. [582] In fact, that number was chosen by social arbiter Ward McAllister who had compiled a list of old money families, like the van Rensselaers, dating back to "New Amsterdam" known as "the Knickerbocracy." [583]

Thus, in their quest to break into Newport Society, the Coogans had Jay's Irish blood working against them; not to mention his pedigree as a Democratic politician.

THE PARTY OF PARTIES

After spending the modern equivalent of $1.2 million to buy Whitehall and a comparable amount to refurbish it, the Coogan's reportedly lived their first seven years in Newport effectively shunned. As Deborah Davis writes in *Gilded*, "their names never appeared on any guest lists. There was a rumor that (Society doyenne) Mamie Fish disliked them. Sometimes hostesses banded together to exclude a 'Detrimental' and the Coogan's seemed to fall into that category. As one writer put it, 'Newporters continued to yank in the welcome mat when the Coogan's called.'" [584]

But by the summer of 1910, with daughter Jessie about to make her debut, Jay and Harriett planned one of the most extravagant coming-out parties in Newport history. No expense was spared. The Waldorf Astoria's sous chef was brought in to design the menu, ice sculptures were created, two dozen musicians from The NY Philharmonic were hired.

The Coogans sent out 300 engraved invitations. This account of what happened next was written by The Rev. Webb Garrison, a prominent Methodist Minister who occasionally commented on the excesses of the wealthy.

"On the evening of June 16, 1910, waiters stationed themselves at punch bowls while the orchestra tuned its instruments. The Coogans turned out in specially bought finery to await the arrival of Newport's finest. They waited and waited, until, by midnight, it was clear NO ONE WAS COMING. 'What are we going to do?' asked Mr. Coogan. 'Do?' retorted his enraged wife. 'We're going to leave and never come back. Whitehall can *rot* for all I care!'"

And they did. That very night. Brigands soon came in and stripped the place. The following year, the empty mansion burned and became an eyesore. [585] Getting her revenge on those who had spurned her, Mrs. Coogan left Whitehall to "rack and ruin," paying only its real estate taxes to keep the town from repossessing it. She became a recluse in New York City. Not until 1945 did her son convince her to heed the pleas of Newport socialites and have it razed. [586]

In 2005, the great-great nephew of Jay Coogan, a columnist for *The Cape Cod Times*, wrote, "In the last years of her life, Harriet rarely ventured from her hotel suite. Waiters delivered meals to her room, but they were never allowed to enter. Her unsuccessful quest for social acceptance in Newport probably contributed to her madness." [587]

But another account in the *People* column of *Time* magazine from the early 1940's, paints a portrait of Harriet, the Newport refugee, as a steely-eyed businesswoman. "For 25 years Mrs. Coogan, now well into her eighties, has seldom left her Manhattan hotel suite in the daytime, but each night at 9 o'clock she goes down in the freight elevator heavily veiled, drives to her cubby hole office in a loft building, and puts in five hours administering her real-estate fortune (which includes Coogan's

Bluff). She and her daughter, Jessie, do all the chores about their suite, which neither maid nor bellboy may enter. She never answers letters (and) for years has hardly glanced at a newspaper." [588]

However, that *Time* piece ended with a hint of Harriet's utter humiliation the night she vacated Whitehall with her husband and daughter. Found on the table next to her bed was a 1910 edition of *Burke's Peerage*, the definitive guide to the genealogy and heraldry of the United Kingdom.

A TALE OF TWO MANSIONS

The sad history of Whitehall got a much more benevolent telling on the website of The Newport Preservation Society.[589] In his account, Paul F. Miller, a former curator for the Society, called the snubbing story a "pervasive legend." [590] He included that same account in *Lost Newport,* his book on the many Newport mansions lost over the years to age, reversals of fortune, neglect and the encroachment of the middle class. [591]

Miller attributed the Coogan's abandonment of the Stanford White edifice to the fire that occurred nearly nine months *after* Jessie's aborted coming out party. That's the same story the Coogans' son Jay, 2d. told the press thirty-seven years after the 1910 soirée.[592]

Miller wrote, "In 1903, James Jay Coogan, a New York real-estate baron, purchased the estate. His family used it in season until seriously damaged by fire on March 10, 1911. Due to the remodeling of the family's Fifth Avenue residence, restoration work in Newport was postponed. With the 1915 death of Mr. Coogan, the house remained unoccupied. Although the family remained sentimentally attached to the estate, major repairs never advanced and led to the pervasive legend that the Coogans had been snubbed socially, having issued invitations for a dinner party to which no one came! In fact, the popular Mrs. Coogan was a great-grand daughter of John Lyon Gardiner and inherited from his estate a very large section of the upper end of Manhattan. The home was demolished in 1953 for a residential subdivision." [593]

Contributing to the controversy, Cleveland Amory recounted the story in *The Last Resorts*:

This legend, as Newporters tell it, began in 1910 when, they say, the Coogans gave a housewarming to their cottage and to it, invited all of Newport's best. A retinue of servants readied the grounds, and all manner of feasting & festivities were planned. On the night of the party, the Coogans descended into their drawing room and waited. Not one guest appeared. Mrs. Fish, the legend goes, disliked the Coogans and she'd sent out invitations for a party of her own... That very night the Coogan's paid off their servants took just one piece of luggage containing Mrs. Coogan's jewels and went back to New York.

Then the Coogans took revenge. For the next 35 years they allowed Whitehall to stand just the way it was that fateful night – in its first days, with dishes and even food still on the table. As time went by, windows were smashed, the cottage broken into and everything of value stolen including an enormous revolving statue of the son of William Tell complete with an arrow, apple and tree -- a statue which took five men to lift. Outside once velvety lawns... became hayfields. But each year the Coogans paid their taxes and not until 1945 did they decide that thirty-five years of revenge was enough to permit the town to tear down the dilapidated eyesore. [594]

After such an elegant setup Amory wrote, "Actually this legend is false." Like Miller, he based that conclusion on his assertion that, "The winter before the alleged party took place a severe fire had gutted Whitehall and the Coogans, believing that the cottage was totally destroyed, had not bothered to salvage what remained."

But the timing of the fire is undisputed. As reported in *The Newport Mercury*, on March 11th 1911, more than nine months *after* Jessie's aborted coming out party, "Whitehall, the handsome summer residence of Mr. J.J. Coogan, at the corner of Catherine Street and Rhode Island Avenue was completely gutted by fire early Friday morning; the flames presenting such a serious aspect that a second alarm was sounded as soon as the first apparatus arrived upon the scene." [595]

As a way of reconciling these conflicting narratives I spoke to Harle Tinney, who documented earlier for this investigation that Doris Duke and Eduardo Tirella had intended to set out from Rough Point so he could appraise The Reliquary of St. Ursula just moments before he was killed.

"On the Coogan legend, " she said, "I beg to differ with that fire story. Or that the Coogans were in good standing with the Newport establishment. Harriett's fortune cut little ice with them."

Disagreeing with Miller and Amory, Harle endorsed Reverend Garrison's account and she was in a unique position to assess the truth. [596] In 1960 she married Donald Tinney, son of the couple who purchased Belcourt in the mid Fifties. An historian in her own right, over the years Harle talked to a number of the surviving servants who worked the night of the Coogans' party for Jessie back in 1910. This is what she told me in an interview for this book:

"For the 300 invited guest that night, the Coogans had a staff of 50 and a number of them were very much alive in the 1950's. The one's I spoke to said that the Coogans were so traumatized that they'd been ignored, that they didn't even clean up that night. When nobody came, they left all the table settings, they left the food that was about to be served. They even left their night clothes on the beds. They went out of town and didn't come back. They were that hurt."

As to the truth, it should be noted that Mrs. Coogan's obituary, reported by *The Associated Press* recounted the snubbing story. [597] But whatever caused them to abandon Whitehall – social embarrassment or the ravages of fire, there's no doubt that by the mid 1950's a local legend had grown up that the grounds where the derelict mansion once stood were *haunted*.

In 1953 the 123,000 square foot site was finally sold. The two principal purchasers were C. Andrew Hambly Jr., the son of a future Newport Mayor and Albert K. Sherman, co-owner of *The Daily News*. [598] They initially discussed selling the land to the City for a park, but ultimately it was broken up into lots where single family houses stand today.

For some time after the sale and before "the lot" was cleared, it had overgrown into a small forest that attracted a number of boys from the surrounding area who would play there. By the mid 50's I'd heard the legend myself and we were warned by more than a few adults.

"Beware of Coogan's Lot," they'd say. "The place is bad luck. You'll be cursed if you go there." Naturally, as boys do, we took the warning as a challenge and repeatedly crossed the edge of "the lot" on our way to Easton's Beach.

THE BAREFOOT GENERAL

Another famous Newport legend is related directly to Doris Duke through her restoration work. As noted in Chapter Eighteen, she became embroiled in litigation filed by Daryl Ford, the contractor she'd hired through her Restoration Foundation to restore many of the colonial era homes in Newport as well as Prescott Farms in nearby Portsmouth. That happened to be the location of one of the most daring missions of the American Revolution told in brilliant detail by Leonard Falkner for *American Heritage* magazine.

The Abduction of General Richard Prescott

By July 1777, on what was the first anniversary of independence, the patriots of Washington's rag tag Continental Army were under siege. They were beset by Redcoats and Hessian Mercenaries in New Jersey. Fort Ticonderoga was about to fall to the north and after a massive seaborne British assault in December of '76, the Union Jack flew over Newport. Worse, Washington's Number Two in command, Maj. Gen. Charles Lee, had been captured. [599]

But Capt. William Barton, a one-time hat maker from Providence, hatched an audacious plan to grab a hostage for exchange. Rumor had it that British General Richard Prescott, notorious commander of The Newport garrison, spent his weekends consorting with the wife of John Overing, a wealthy Quaker, at her husband's farm north on Aquidneck Island, a mile from the shores of Narragansett Bay.

On the night of July 10th, 1777, with a team of 36 volunteers and five borrowed whaleboats, Barton led his convoy across the Bay from Warwick Neck with muffled oar, passing the British Frigate HMS Emerald, which was armed with three dozen cannon. They put ashore on Prudence, an uninhabited island just off Portsmouth. One of the volunteers was a Black man named Jack Sisson, aka Prince.

With a spyglass, the 29-year-old Barton observed a carriage and team arrive at the farmhouse, which was rumored to be heavily guarded. After making the short crossing to Aquidneck, the young captain's squad made its way up a gully to the Overing house where, as luck would have it, only one man stood sentry.

Barton crept up and put a sword to his throat, whispering, "Make noise and you are a dead man. Is Prescott in the house?" The terrified sentry nodded.

Sending men to breach each of the house's three doors, Barton burst in to find Mr. Overing seated, quietly reading before a fireplace. The old Quaker stayed silent, so Barton headed for the stairs, ordering his men to set the house on fire.

"If we can't have the General alive," he said, "we'll have him dead."

Just then, Sisson heard a noise behind a bedroom door and kicked it in, putting a pistol to the head of a man in a nightshirt on the bed. Barton came in and demanded, "Are you Prescott?"

"Yes, Sir," he replied.

"Then, Sir, you are my prisoner."

Barton ordered him to pull on breeches and a waistcoat, then dragged him down the hill and into a whaleboat. Apparently, there was no time for him to pull on his boots – hence the nickname that would forever follow him through history. [600]

A "MASTERLY" ABDUCTION

Surveying the scene at daybreak Lt. Frederick Mackenzie of The Royal Welch Fusiliers wrote: "It was most extraordinary that a general commanding 4000 men, encamped on an island surrounded by a squadron of ships of war, should be carried from his quarters in the night by a small party of the enemy without a shot being fired. They executed it in a masterly manner."

The former hat maker was celebrated in a resolution passed by the Continental Congress. Two days later, Gen. Lee was freed in New York. Prescott was released in Connecticut. Barton's daring raid was the first good news for the patriots in months and his legend became a story told among the Newport servant class for years. [601]

CHAPTER TWENTY-THREE

JACK & JACKIE

Jack Kennedy loved coming to Newport. The wide expanse of The Ocean Drive where he raced his beloved white 1961 Thunderbird convertible as The Secret Service sought to catch up, provided JFK with a much broader playing field than Hyannis Port, Massachusetts (the official Summer White House) where he was confined to the beach-bound Kennedy compound bracketed by tourist-crowded two-lane streets. [602] In Newport, the links of The County Club (home of the first U.S. Open in 1895) were literally across the street from his wife's mother's place. JFK could swim in the saltwater-fed heated pool at Fairholme, the estate of Mrs. Robert R. Young. Jackie was free to water ski in Narragansett Bay off the back of the Presidential Yacht, "Honey Fitz." They could watch majestic 12 meters competing for The America's Cup from the deck of the destroyer Joseph P. Kennedy. [603]

In fact, having access to Marine One around the corner at Fort Adams, Quonset Naval Air Station across The Bay and the home of CRUDESLANT minutes away gave the Commander-In-Chief the resources of the Presidency he could never access on Cape Cod. When the Kennedys were in Newport, in the early Sixties during his 400 day term, there was real excitement around town. [604]

JFK off Newport at the helm of the 62 foot sloop Manitou. (Robert Knudsen)

A tight network of locals always seemed to know where he would be. My family was among them and they had great sources. One day they'd get word that "Jack" might be seen on the 15th green of the Country Club at the corner of Harrison Avenue and Price's Neck Road. Another day, they'd hear that he was out for an early swim. My mother's sister Rita and her twin sister Julia proved to be particularly adept sleuths as was my cousin Mary Laverty, a tall redhead with an infectious laugh.

One morning in 1962, Julia, Rita, and Mary staked out Mrs. Young's estate on Ruggles Avenue along with Rita's son, my cousin Joe. The word was that Jack would be swimming that day. Another dozen Newporters were waiting on either side of the gate when it opened. A black Secret Service vehicle emerged slowly from the estate and the agents eyed the small crowd. One of them in the passenger seat nodded and radioed back to the "chase" car that the coast was clear and in seconds, the President drove out in the T-Bird with little Caroline on his lap.

As always, he stopped to chat with the locals who'd heard that he might be there. I remember my aunt Julia telling me how red his hair was and Mary Laverty commenting that he had freckles. "I trust that you're all Democrats and you are registered to vote," the President said, flashing the Kennedy smile and demonstrating the Irish wit that had helped propel him to The White House. "In another two years I'm counting on Rhode Island to send me back." [605] And with that, he drove off, with Caroline gripping the wheel as if she was driving herself.

Sundays it was easy to find the President and First Lady emerging from St. Mary's Church.

The photo below shows a throng of Newporters cheering the First Couple as they left Mass in the fall of 1961, Jackie resplendent in a white Chanel suit. The 14-year old with glasses in a striped shirt applauding is my cousin Joe and the woman in sunglasses waving behind him is his mother, my aunt, Rita Tremblay. [606]

My aunt Rita waving and my cousin Joe applauding the Kennedys

The President visited Newport twice in 1962, on August 26th when he took the helm of the 62-foot Sparkman & Stephens racing sloop Manitou, [607] and later in September at the Eighteenth challenge for The America's Cup. [608] During that series, the New York Yacht Club's 12-meter Weatherly, skippered by Emil "Bus" Mosbacher, defeated, Gretel, representing the Royal Sydney Yacht Squadron, helmed by Jock Sturrock. The U.S. took it four races to one.

One of my great memories from that year came when my father Joe, who worked at the Naval base, heard some scuttlebutt that if we got over to the Castle Hill lighthouse, just south of Hammersmith Farm, we might catch sight of a rare Naval event.

It was a Saturday afternoon, so we jumped into the family car and raced the back way around "the Drive" from Wellington Avenue. We parked in the lot of The Castle Hill Inn and hurried down to the lighthouse, just in time to catch The U.S.S. Joseph P. Kennedy (DD-850) named for the President's brother Joe, passing by. Its entire crew of 14 officers and 260 sailors was standing ramrod straight in their summer whites along the gunnel.

I asked my father what this was, and he said, "They're manning the rail." Then, as the destroyer approached Hammersmith Farm, the crew snapped to a full salute. Joe Lance, who had served as a Chief aboard "a Battlewagon" in World War II, put his hand over his heart and gritted his teeth to suppress the emotion he felt as the ship's band broke into "Hail To The Chief."

Aboard The Joseph P. Kennedy watching the 18th challenge for The America's Cup

I was fourteen at the time and I'd just starting working at The Reading Room. Five years later as a reporter for *The Daily News* I got to cover the 20th Cup race, a rematch between the U.S. and the Aussies with Mosbacher's Intrepid defeating Sturrock's Dame Patti four to none. Stringing for *Agence-Press,* the French wire service, I watched the races from The Coast Guard Cutter Vigilant, filing stories with some of the great sports reporters of the day. But for me, no single experience of growing up in The City By The Sea, equaled that moment with my family watching those sailors "man the rail."

THE MYSTERY OF ANNANDALE FARM

In researching this book I went into the online archives of *The Daily News* and found one piece that had a sad, ironic significance when it came to the Kennedys' love affair with Newport. In the fall of 1963, just three weeks before he was killed in Dallas, there was a front-page story authored by Emil Jamail, a senior editor, announcing that Jack and Jackie planned to rent Annandale Farm, the estate next to her mother's place, for the summer of 1964.

Kennedys To Occupy Estate Here In 1964

U.S. Demands Departure Of 3 Soviets In Spy Case

Dated October 30th, the piece quoted Press Secretary Pierre Salinger as confirming the rental, which was facilitated by Senator Claiborne Pell and brokered without a fee by Johnny Richmond, another Member of The Reading Room. Two years earlier, a group of Rhode Islanders had raised $250,000 to purchase the estate with the goal of making it the permanent Summer White House, but the President declined the offer, saying it would be "asking too much of Rhode Islanders."

Then, after three memorable summers in Newport, he was ready to rent for the '64 season. [609]

JFK's assassination derailed those plans and Annandale Farm sat empty for four more years. Finally, the Swiss bank that held the mortgage decided to auction it off along with Broadlawns, an adjoining parcel. On July 24[th,] 1968, Jim Edward sent me to cover the bidding at the estate.

It was a hot summer's day. The representative of the bank, Benson Scotch, was a tiny man in spectacles, dressed in a blue pin-striped suit under a straw boater. He was moving about amid the prospective bidders who were seated in wooden folding chairs lined in front of the estate's White House-like portico. At that time, Cosmos Bank of Zurich held the principal mortgage of $337,000; the equivalent of just over $2.5 million today.

Those present to bid on the estate resembled a series of wealthy archetypes straight out of central casting. There was a titled British woman, a Texas oilman (complete with Stetson) and one or two representatives of the Arab Emirates. State Senator Patrick O'Neill Hayes, a prominent Newport attorney, was representing unknown interests.

Francis G. Dwyer, the auctioneer, opened the bidding at $375,000. Hayes countered with $380,000 and then something surprising happened: Scotch, who represented the mortgage holder, began bidding for *the bank itself*. He went up another $5,000. Hayes upped his bid to $387,000, then said, "That's as high as I'll go." [610]

Scotch then topped him with $390,000 and Dwyer lowered his gavel. "Sold."

At that point, the other stunned bidders could only shake their heads as the bank that held the mortgage outbid itself and held onto the property. I approached Scotch for a brief interview.

"So, what's going to happen to the estate now?" I asked.

"I have no idea what plans my client may have."

"But I thought they already *owned* it."

He smiled at me enigmatically. "I have nothing further to say."

The auction had started an hour late and I had to rush back to *The Daily News* on Thames Street to write up the story before the 1:00 pm deadline.

When I got there and told Jim Edward what had occurred, his eyes narrowed. "So you're telling me that a Swiss Bank just bought up a mortgage it already held for the estate right next to Hammersmith Farm?"

I said, "Yeah." I'd never covered an estate auction before, but it seemed unusual.

"How long has Cosmos held the mortgage?"

I checked my Reporter's Notebook. "Since 1965."

"That was two years after the plans to make it "The Summer White House," said Jim. "So who the hell is Cosmos Bank?"

I eyed the clock on the wall. It was 12:30 pm. I had a half hour to make deadline. This was 1968. There was no internet. I glanced over at our "Research Table," full of old Newport Directories. As always, it was covered with a pile of yellowed newspapers. I didn't have any contacts back then on Wall Street, much less the international banking community.

"Why don't you give Pat Hayes a call," said Jim.

I rang the law offices of Corcoran, Peckham and Hayes, but the receptionist said that the Senator wouldn't be in for the rest of the day. I called his house and got his son Michael, another De La Salle boy, on the phone. He said he'd leave word for him to call me at the paper. So with nothing else to go on, I wrote up the piece with this lead:

> A 41-acre parcel of waterfront property on the Ocean Drive was auctioned today to a Swiss Bank that held the mortgage on the land. Annandale Farm, the former home of Barclay Douglas was sold for $390,000 to the Cosmos Bank of Zürich. The bank which held the principal mortgage of $337,000 on the property, was represented by Benson Scotch, a New York attorney who was high bidder after a brief bidding duel with a local lawyer, Sen. Patrick O'Neill Hayes. [611]

Given the deadline pressure, I had zero appreciation at the time of the story's significance. Jim was right. Who *was* Cosmos, this mysterious Swiss banking house that had bought up its own mortgage on an estate adjacent to the summer home of the fallen President's widow?

Later, that fall, after I'd returned to college where I was Managing Editor of The Northeastern News, I was as surprised as most Americans on October 20th when Mrs. Kennedy married Aristotle Onassis, the Greek airline and shipping tycoon. It had been a very private ceremony on the island of Scorpios in The Ionian Sea. When I heard that news, I thought to myself, "Onassis. Greek. Cosmos. Ari must be the one behind that bank in Zurich. My God. He's had that mortgage since 1965. That's how long he's been coveting Jackie."

At least that was my initial hunch.

Like the mystery behind the death of Eduardo Tirella, it was one of those elusive stories I wasn't able to chase at the time, given my class load and duties on the NU News. So I just filed it away under, "stories I should look into some day."

Cut to 2018, fifty years later.

In researching this book, when I went into *The Daily News* archives and retrieved my old stories, I found the auction piece under the headline, "Annandale Farm And Broadlawns Sold to Swiss Bank For $390,000." At the time, The *Daily News* copy editor on "the slot desk," who wrote that headline, didn't read deep enough into the piece to appreciate the *real* story: that a Swiss bank had staged an auction with the apparent intent of buying a property that it already owned. But in retrospect, that was *my* fault. Back in the summer of '68 I had buried my lead. And now that I've had time to explore who was *really* behind Cosmos Bank, I've stumbled onto a story of far greater significance.

THE MOBSTER, THE CASINO & THE BANK

I was wrong about Aristotle Onassis. As it turns out, Cosmos, which closed its doors in 1974, has since been linked by several investigative reporters to racketeer Meyer Lansky who invested in The Paradise Island Casino in The Bahamas after he was forced out of Cuba by Fidel Castro.

Initially, that casino was owned by none other than Huntington Hartford, former owner of Seaverge, heir to the A&P fortune, and the cousin of Nuala Pell, wife of Rhode Island's U.S. Senator, who had been instrumental in securing the rental of Annandale Farm for the Kennedys. But Hartford's sale of the casino is where the clean money ended and the dirty money began.

As reporter Don Bauder wrote in *The San Diego Reader*, "Hartford initially wanted (the casino) free of mob influence. But that was not to be, and (he) eventually sold most of his holdings." [612] At the time the Paradise Island resort, accessible *only by boat,* had been failing -- that is, until a causeway was built, financed by *Cosmos Bank.* After that, the casino flourished.

Enter Richard M. Nixon.

In the year 2000, investigative author Anthony Summers presented evidence that Nixon's friend and confidante Charles Bebe Rebozo, had a joint account with Nixon at Cosmos. Summers traced four deposits, totaling millions of dollars, that had allegedly gone into that account from October 1971 to April 1973, just months before Nixon resigned the presidency.[613]

Summers also found that Nixon made annual trips to Zurich, site of the bank's home office. Investigating further, I discovered that Cosmos had gone to strange lengths to hide its ownership of the Annandale mortgage. Six days after mortgaging the estate in 1965, Cosmos moved the loan to Chemical Bank, which moved it back to Cosmos on the same day as the auction. A curious bit of banking sleight-of-hand. Then, in that extraordinary move, Cosmos bought up its own interest in the property.

I'm still working the story, but at this point here's the question: Did Richard Nixon, who'd been obsessed with JFK ever since his loss of the presidency to him in 1960, use a mob-related Swiss Bank to gain an interest in an estate next to Jackie two and a half years after her husband's death and then get another major bank to hide his connection to the property? The investigation continues, but one thing is clear, when a reporter begins to disturb the firmament in Newport Rhode Island, any number of buried secrets may fall to earth.

CHAPTER TWENTY-FOUR

JACKIE & DORIS

The connection between Doris Duke and Jacqueline Bouvier Kennedy Onassis is well known. Two years after the homicide outside Rough Point, for reasons that had largely baffled the Newport public, Doris Duke became obsessed with restoring the town's rich collection of original 18th century colonial homes, most of which had fallen into serious disrepair. Perhaps sensing that she'd need to add some luster to the masthead, for what would otherwise appear to be a commendable exercise in preservation, Doris reached out to Mrs. Onassis, who agreed to become the first Vice President of The Newport Restoration Foundation (NRF). A year later they made headlines in a piece that ran in both *The Los Angeles Times* and *The Washington Post*. [614]

"Two of America's most glamorous, wealthiest women," the piece began, "are engaged in a scheme to turn a section of one of the nation's most glamorous, wealthiest resorts into a combination of Williamsburg and Georgetown." The story reported that "the former first lady may oversee collecting period antiques for the Newport museums, much as she did for the White House." It also noted that while the Navy was still Newport's principal economic resource, "proposed cutbacks in military budgets have convinced townspeople of the necessity of increasing tourism."

By April of 1973 those cuts went into full force and Rhode Island, the smallest state in the nation, took the brunt of Richard Nixon's revenge. Announcing the closure of 274 military bases nationwide, "Little Rhody" actually lost a staggering 49% of the 42,812 jobs cut across the country. [615] More than ever, Doris Duke became the key to Newport's economic survival.

But like so much of her philanthropy, the "giving" came with a heavy price, and from 1968 when she created The NRF to renovate and rent those 70 Colonial-era houses, she soon became the object of scorn from *three* distinct segments of Newport's population.

First, there were the West Broadway/Upper Thames Street residents who protested their evictions as Doris bought up houses at bargain-basement prices. In her memoir, Rough Point caretaker's daughter Linda McFarlane Knierim recounted how some of her displaced friends complained that "Members of my family have nowhere to live, thanks to your father's boss." [616]

Low-Rental Shortage Laid To Restorations

That was the headline in a *Newport Daily News* piece on August 12th 1969, nearly a year after my series ran. [617] Doris hadn't even formally announced the creation of The NRF, which came six weeks later, and already it was creating chaos in the town. Her rapid acquisition of the houses, many in low income neighborhoods, sparked multiple demonstrations, [618] forcing the removal of the NRF's first executive director [619] and prompting a rare public pledge on behalf of the billionairess herself: "It should be stated firmly that the Foundation has no desire or intention to force people into the street," she said, "nor to put rentals on restored houses at exorbitant prices that are out of line with existing rentals. Rather, we prefer to think that it will be a matter of considerable pride to be a tenant in a restored apartment or house for which only a normal rent will be charged." [620]

Miss Duke and the NRF soon broke that pledge, charging rents that no low income tenant could afford as the newly restored homes were leased to members of the middle and upper middle class. It was a classic case of gentrification, and eight years later, those higher-end tenants themselves were forced to adopt organizing tactics worthy of the poorest residents of West Broadway.

They get storm window bill

Doris Duke stirs wrath of tenants

By WILLIAM M. KUTIK

Doris Duke has asked the people living in Newport Restoration Foundation houses to pay for their own storm windows, and the tenants are hopping mad.

Some say they won't pay, others are unsure, but many are planning to attend a tenants meeting tonight to decide what to do collectively.

The wooden windows already are installed, and the tenants' complaint is that no prior arrangement was made about who would pay for them.

"This was just sprung on us," said one tenant, who refused to allow his name to be published. "We don't own the houses, she does. We just pay rent, and she should pay for the windows."

Saturday, many of the Foundation's 54 tenants received letters from Foundation officer Benjamin C. Reed Jr. asking a $35 payment for each storm window plus a yearly charge of $20 to $100 for in-

stallation and removal. Depending on the number of windows, the total payments range from $300 to $1,800, to be paid over five years.

Most of the tenants reached today refused to be quoted by name for fear of reprisals. Reed would not comment on the issue, but did say some tenants had agreed to pay.

Edwin P. Young, who lives in the largest Foundation house (37 windows) at 40 School St., said, "I was surprised at getting the letter. We had no prior notice and no suggestion that it would take place. My feelings haven't jelled yet, but I'm going to tonight's meeting."

Some of the tenants have been asking for the windows for years. "We all know the houses aren't insulated very well," one said, "but the lease specifically forbids us from putting up storm windows ourselves."

The Foundation started installing the wooden storm windows last winter, and some tenants got theirs last week. Those tenants didn't get a bill this year but are expecting one next year.

Reed said the Foundation would own the windows after the tenants finish paying for them. "They're being amortized," he said. "The windows go with the house."

Most tenants agree that Foundation rents are far below the market rate. A five-bedroom house rents for as little as $350. "But that's why we put up with all this stuff," one said.

But in the last year, rents have been increased from 25 to 60 per cent, and the heating bills have been enormous, as much as $300 a month. The Foundation houses are not the bargain they used to be, and one woman said, "If Doris pushes me out, I'll just go back to my house in Virginia."

They formed The Newport Restoration Association [621] after Doris retroactively billed them for storm windows, she installed without notifying them in advance. Depending on size, the cost of retrofitting could be as high as $7,700 per home in 2021 dollars. The Association included a retired general and the former Rector of Trinity Church, Doris's own parish, who had married Minnie Cushing and Peter Beard in August of 1967.

Those two uprisings by Newporters at different levels of society, and a third middle class protest after Doris unexpectedly demolished parts of the local YMCA, offer deep insights into the mindset and win-at-all-costs tactics of the billionairess.

There's another irony in a story full of it: as I looked back 50 years, I learned that my West Broadway exposé, "Newport Back Yard," became the initial flashpoint for much of the upheaval confronting Doris's Foundation. It was something I never knew about until I started looking into the truth behind Eduardo Tirella's death and reconnected with Pauline Perkins-Moyé.

The initial *sturm und drang* was the result of a 10-page report by Robert F. Cohen, a 22-year-old welfare rights organizer from Providence, who charged the NRF with "moving in and taking a large number of low income units off the market, creating greater scarcity and driving up rents." Informing the City Council that some tenants had already received eviction notices, Cohen wrote that "the Foundation was causing fear and resentment in the Point neighborhood… due to the mystery surrounding the high-handed way in which it operates."

It was a shot across the bow of the NRF's first executive director who happened to be none other than John Perkins Brown, the preservationist and antiques dealer who sold Doris Duke The Reliquary of St. Ursula.

In a story with more intersecting figures than the pieces on a chess board, it was John's shop, The Blue Cat on Franklin Street, that had been the destination of Eduardo Tirella and Doris Duke on October 7th, 1966 when she killed him. Brown had been one of the original incorporaters of The Newport Preservation Society and three years after Eddie's death, Doris asked John to lead the NRF [622]

In his report to the City, Cohen made three recommendations: first, "that the NRF fully explain what it has done and what it intends to do," second "that the NRF remove no more tenants until each has found adequate housing at equivalent cost to their current housing," and third, "that for each low income unit taken off the market, the NRF create another" to replace it. [623]

But soon, taking orders from his boss, Perkins Brown began to use tactics that were heavy-handed in the extreme. Pauline Perkins-Moyé, a former organizer with New Visions, the anti-poverty agency who had helped me examine slum conditions on West Broadway, described the action he took at one house the NRF had recently acquired.

"John was Doris's overseer," she told me in an interview for this book. "She'd bought a house at 55 Thames Street on the corner of Cozzens Court. My mother was living in that house. So was my sister who'd just had a baby. Do you know what John Perkins Brown did? He had the contractor come over there and start tearing the roof off. That happened, *while they were in it*. I called John up and said, 'Are you kidding me? This is going to kill my mother.' So he stopped it for a little while.

But then he said he was going to start buying houses on West Broadway. And why? Because Alex Teitz and others started selling their property and some of those houses had historical value." [624]

At a City Council meeting two days after Cohen's report, Perkins Brown (no relation to Pauline) tried to quell fears that the push-back by low-income Newporters would cause the NRF to stop its work. "It's nonsense," he said. "We have plans for the next ten years." At that same meeting Daryl Ford, the contractor (still on good terms with Doris) suggested that if the NRF shut down, about 100 workers with 95 dependents would be out of a job. [625]

The City Council took steps to stem the ongoing controversy which continued to threaten evictions. They added $2,000 to the escrow fund to pay for slum housing repairs. It had been set up after my investigative series ran a year earlier. [626] The Council then increased the number to $5,000 at the insistence of Councilman Paul F. Burke.[627] But the move came too late for John Perkins Brown, who was summarily dismissed by Doris after the NRF's aggressive tactics spilled into the public arena. [628]

When it came to terminations, it was Doris's custom to use her minions to deliver the bad news and, in this case, though Brown was her closest local advisor, she used a Foundation attorney to inform him of his sudden firing which he told the press was, "for reasons unknown."

"At least he exited Rough Point with his life intact," noted Tirella's niece Donna Lohmeyer. Until his dismissal, Brown, who had moved into Rough Point, after Eduardo's death, [629] had effectively "replaced" him as Duke's principal curator. But as the NRF's head, he'd also been forced to execute Doris's many edicts and Perkins Brown, who was gay, took the brunt of the local criticism.

"John was shocked at his dismissal," said Harle Tinney, whose family sheltered Perkins Brown at Belcourt long after Doris fired him. "He had trusted Doris Duke and fully expected that he would live at Rough Point and continue the Foundation's work for rest of his life." [630]

"But when it came to restoration," said Donna, "Doris's attitude seemed to be, 'I'm doing all this good for the City, so goddammit, get out of my way.' She had a singular transactional mindset. To Doris Duke, the ends *always* justified the means." [631]

Now in the early fall of 1969, the billionairess quickly sought to get ahead of the bad publicity by announcing the appointment of Francis A. Comstock as Brown's replacement. [632] He'd been the Associate Director of Princeton's School of Architecture, had summered in Newport for years and owned a home built in 1760. [633]

At that point Comstock assured the media that the NRF's aim was "to restore… the beautiful colonial architecture of Newport," and "appeal to the thousands of visitors to our City." While emphasizing the increased prospect of tourism, Comstock also pledged transparency. "The door of the main (NRF) office will always be open to concerned individuals," he said. [634]

Two days later, continuing the publicity blitz, he announced Jackie O's appointment as the NRF's first V.P. [635] Even activist Robert F. Cohen seemed to be won over. "It's very gratifying to hear that the Foundation intends to find housing for the people it is displacing," he said. [636]

But the upbeat news coverage in the wake of Comstock's appointment didn't last long.

On November 7th, Daryl Ford learned that his company was also being terminated by the NRF. [637] At that time he believed the Foundation's action was related to the ongoing protests of low-income tenants still feeling the brunt of evictions as Doris's hunt for historic buildings caused many slumlords to unload their derelict properties.

That same day, Phil Almeida, the New Visions activist who had been a principal source in my slum housing series, staged a sit-in with West Broadway residents at the offices of The Newport Housing Authority, creating more bad news for the NRF. [638]

The details of Daryl Ford's termination weren't known until late January, when his $1.5 million lawsuit against Doris went public. But in November, in the weeks prior to their falling out, Ford seemed to be telling tales out of school when *The L.A. Times* quoted him on Newport's new boom in housing prices spurred on by Duke's buying spree.

In the piece Ford recalled how "some small, run-down colonial(s) went for as little as $500 dollars six or seven years ago" but Duke's rapid acquisition of slum houses led to a huge hike in selling prices.

Pointing to a house in the path of Foundation development, he said, 'Three years ago the lady (owner) begged me to take it off her hands for $15,000. Last year the Foundation offered her $30,000. Now she's holding out for $65,000." [639]

By mid-November of '69 Francis Comstock proved as deft a politician as he was an architect, when he announced that Phil Almeida, the community activist, would henceforth act as a liaison between the NRF and neighborhood community groups. As a first step, he said, the Foundation would "release 13 apartments onto the market" in buildings the NRF had purchased. They would then lease them to low income families at affordable rents. He left it to Phil's agency to process the applications. [640]

The following October, Enid Nemy wrote a glowing piece in *The New York Times* headlined, "In A Way, Their Newport Landlord is Doris Duke." [641] It featured Charles O'Loughlin, the handsome young dean of Continuing Ed at Salve Regina College, who had recently moved into one of Doris's fully restored homes on Division Street with his pregnant wife. Their monthly rent was less than $300.

The O'Loughlins called the fully restored 250 year-old house "a dream come true." Comstock, who was also featured in the piece, noted that the NRF "had already restored six houses, has six more on the way and holds title to about 50 other properties in the area."

"The cost (of restorations) is outrageous if we do them right," Comstock said. Nemy cited an estimate that Doris's plan for creating a real-life Williamsburg could conservatively cost $10 million, reporting that "rentals range from $125 to $150 a month for a small one-bedroom house to $250 and $275 for a house with two bedrooms."

Comstock made it clear that none of the houses would be sold. "We'd lose control that way," he said, noting that, "Without permission in writing," the leases prohibited "washing machines, dryers, air conditioning, telephones and outside television antennas." Even clotheslines were banned.

According to Comstock, Doris herself would conduct an intense review of "every house we do from the plans on." [642] That iron grip by the heiress included mandates from the exterior colors of the restored homes to the colors of their internal appliances.

Her stringent rules would later erupt into the second major series of protests that besieged The Newport Restoration Foundation eight years later. In the meantime, Doris Duke, who began to look at Newport as her own personal redevelopment project, would leave many parties to her work stunned. One of them turned out to be no less than The Queen of England herself.

CHAPTER TWENTY-FIVE

MOVING HOUSES &
DEE DEE'S ROCK

By 1971 The Newport Restoration Foundation had purchased 70 colonial-era houses for renovation and Doris Duke had become a one-woman urban renewal force in Newport. [643] A year later the NRF's assets had risen from $3.5 million to more than $5.5. The newly restored houses were beginning to generate rents totaling $47,500. [644] But the tobacco heiress's master plan to remake much of historic Newport by moving the houses from one neighborhood to another before restoration, sparked a new controversy.

Veteran preservationists and anti-poverty activists questioned whether a home of historic value that the NRF wanted to move from a slum neighborhood to an increasingly gentrified one shouldn't be left in place as an anchor for renewal of the more impoverished area.

The flashpoint of that conflict became a single family building at 28 Kingston Avenue built in the mid 1770's. [645] Identified as "The Daniel Lyman House," the Foundation described it as "one among many small, two room Newport cottages with one-and-a-half stories and a gambrel roof. The NRF has five in its collection." [646] It had stood on its original foundation for nearly 200 years and now Doris Duke wanted to move it across town, near the Newport waterfront, to 11 West Third Street in what was becoming the increasingly more upscale Point Section.

Newport property records show that the house first appeared on the tax rolls in 1914. In 1971 its assessed value was set at $2,400, when it was purchased by a group called Afro American Business Leaders, aka ABLE, who hoped to keep the house in the West Broadway neighborhood. [647] By 1973, given Doris's shopping spree for historic buildings, the value had doubled. That's when the NRF bought it through an interim owner and decided to move it. [648]

But a group called the Citizens Advisory Committee for Community Development pushed back. [649] In January, 1974 after Benjamin C. Reed, Jr. the NRF's Assistant Director, petitioned the Zoning Board for a variance, a hearing was held in City Council chambers, where the fate of the historic home was discussed. The Point section was an area where the NRF had plans to restore at least a dozen historic homes, including four others that they intended to move there. [650]

The Citizens Advisory Committee, which included famed preservationist Adé Bethune, opposed the move, particularly because the NRF had no plan to replace the home. [651]

"Moving the house away from Kingston Avenue and leaving a vacant lot, would... contribute to the decline of the area," she wrote in a letter prepared for the hearing. She urged the NRF to reconsider the move and restore the Lyman house "on its original lot where it had been since before 1776." Restoring it there, she argued, would "contribute to the health, safety and renewal of (West Broadway) one of Newport's oldest Neighborhoods." [652]

The subtext was that it was also Newport's most historic concentration of African-Americans and The Point was fast becoming a largely all-white enclave.

But the NRF's Reed insisted that the house had been purchased with "the intent" to move it. "We want to save the house. We are willing to restore it on Third Street."

Ms. Bethune countered that moving the house, "might be considered a form of discrimination, as if Kingston Avenue were not considered good enough."

Reed replied, "She is right. That is not a good area."

Adé Bethune was a revered figure in Newport. A renowned artist known for her liturgical restoration work, she had emigrated to the U.S. from Belgium and trained at Cooper Union in New York City.

In another of the ironies that infect this story, she was sought out by John Perkins Brown to authenticate the Reliquary of St. Ursula' which played a pivotal role in Eduardo Tirella's death.

With deep roots in The Catholic Workers movement [653] Ms. Bethune had been a founding member of The Church Community Housing Corporation -- set up after my slum housing series ran in 1968 -- to build new houses for residents of West Broadway. [654] In fact, she designed several of the homes herself. [655]

But Adé Bethune was no match for the money, power and influence of Doris Duke. At that point, the positive impact her colonial restorations were having on tourism had earned the reclusive billionairess an almost obsequious level of praise from local politicians. Not long after that City Hall hearing, the Rhode Island State Senate unanimously passed a Resolution commending Doris and the NRF.

It read like a royal decree:

Resolved that "This Senate, with special thanks, turns to Miss Duke today and offers its highest commendations to her as a good citizen and benefactor of all who live in Rhode Island with a devout wish that the good Lord will speak to her many more years and that her generous and progressive deeds will long be remembered." [656]

In stark contrast to Adé Bethune's argument that plucking the Lyman House from 28 Kingston would diminish the neighborhood, the Resolution asserted that the NRF's work had "resulted in the neighboring property owners painting and beautifying their houses, tidying up what had been wasted plots and generally joining Miss Duke in making Newport a better place to live." [657]

Not unexpectedly, Doris prevailed. A month after the hearing, amid protests, The Lyman House was hoisted onto a large flatbed truck and moved. The lot at 28 Kingston stood empty until 1982 [658] and the Lyman House got a new address on a much tonier street.

Moving the Daniel Lyman House from 28 Kingston Avenue to its new address: 11 Third Street on The Point

DEMO THE YMCA BEFORE CHRISTMAS

Less than a year later, Doris Duke was stirring the wrath of a different group of Newporters. Months before she formally announced creation of the NRF, the Foundation had paid $150,000 for the YMCA. [659] At the time, John Perkins Brown, then the NRF's executive director, said that the purchase was "part of (the NRF's) philanthropic program." [660]

The beautiful Georgian Style Building at 41 Mary Street was built in 1908 after a $100,000 donation from Arthur Gwynne Vanderbilt in memory of his father Cornelius II who supported the Young Men's Christian Association in New York City. After the NRF's acquisition Doris pledged to leave the facility functioning for $1.00 a year until it could relocate to new quarters in Middletown, five years later. Then in early December of 1974 – nine months after the Lyman House conflict -- Ben Reed notified the Y by letter that the NRF intended to demolish its outside handball courts on December 26th and on that same date its contractors would start to knock down the gym. "This is necessary," Reed wrote, "in order to reduce a large tax assessment for the coming year." [661]

Doris had grown impatient when the opening in Middletown was delayed, so the day after Christmas, a wrecking crew from the NRF moved in and started to knock down the courts. It was an audacious move against a beloved Newport institution that only a transactional billionaire might contemplate, and the Y quickly sought a restraining order in Superior Court.

The Foundation responded by asking for a meeting the next day, agreeing that no further destruction would take place until then. But in its motion to halt the demo, the YMCA argued that, "Notwithstanding such assurances, the Foundation substantially destroyed the handball courts" and "it is believed they intend to destroy the gymnasium." To placate Doris until the new Middletown facility could open in May, the Director of the Mary Street Y even offered to pay any additional taxes the NRF might incur in the delay. Judge James Bullman granted their injunction, ordering the NRF to cease and desist the demolition until a hearing January 3rd.

A month later Doris Duke got her way again. This is how *The Daily News* covered it:

WHERE GENERATIONS EXERCISED
WRECKERS DEMOLISH YMCA GYM

The gymnasium at the Mary Street YMCA, which has served thousands of Newporters since it was built during the first decade of this century, soon will be just a pile of rubble. The Newport Restoration Foundation began demolishing the gym today, squeezing the last bit of athletic activity out of the facility. A space that formerly was the Y's swimming pool became a Foundation workshop last summer, and handball courts were destroyed early last month. The gym would have been torn down last month at the same time as the handball courts, had not the Y officials succeeded in obtaining a court order prohibiting the demolition. The order expired yesterday.

The realization that the gym would be torn down this week apparently stirred the emotions of many Newporters who have exercised and competed there all their lives. The Y's Director George Sarantos summed up local sentiments this way: "Many people in Newport have grown up in the YMCA and in this gymnasium. You feel like you're losing a part of yourself seeing that gym torn down. All I can say is the regulars have been coming in for the last week and reminiscing. Guys like Dr. Peter Integlia, Dick Wood and Sam Kusinitz. It's quite sad." [662]

DORIS AND THE NRF MAKE A KILLING

In examining Newport property records I made an interesting discovery. In the decade following Doris's initial restoration efforts, property values in the Historic Hill neighborhood of Newport had skyrocketed. By 1982, 13 years after the NRF's purchase of the Y for $150,000, its assessed value had grown to $428,000. Then on November 24th, 1986, for unknown reasons, the NRF transferred the historic Georgian building to Doris Duke *personally*, along with two additional lots, for $514,000, while at the time, the assessed value of all 3 properties was $726,000.[663]

Four years later, the heiress, who had become a one-woman development force in Newport, transferred the 3 parcels back to the NRF, which then proceeded to sell them in 1996 to Lancaster Associates, a Providence-based for-profit real estate company that also used the trade name Vanderbilt Hall. The price: $1,303,500, representing more than 8 times the original $150K purchase price by the NRF. But as some measure of what the complex was actually worth, less than 3 months later, Lancaster Associates transferred the original Y and those two lots to an entity called Vanderbilt Hall, LP for $5,700,000 or *38 times* what the NRF paid for it in 1969. [664] [2]

That raises the question of whether the Newport Restoration Foundation was dedicated solely to philanthropy and preservation or whether Doris's non-profit also saw a "profit" in its gentrification of Newport. Today, operating as "The Vanderbilt Grace," the old YMCA is a 33 room luxury hotel billed by The Five Star Alliance as one of "the world's best." [665]

FIGHTING THE CITY OVER TAXES

Back in 1975 when Doris Duke was running the NRF with little or no restraint, there seemed to be no limit to what Newport City officials would do to please her. Angry that she had received a bill increasing taxes for Rough Point, Doris went into Superior Court in May and filed yet another lawsuit charging that a recent three-year reassessment of the 10-acre estate had been "grossly excessive and illegal."

---

2   Records showed that in 1975 The NRF had a net worth in excess of $11 million and a profit from rentals of $120,604; the equivalent today of $583,714. Source: *Newport Daily News*, February 25th, 1977.

Earlier, The United Appraisal Company, used by the City, had raised Rough Point's valuation from $100,500 to $430,720. Even in 1975 it was difficult to argue that the vast cliffside estate where Bellevue Avenue met The Ocean Drive wasn't worth that much. But in the face of her lawsuit, the City caved, reducing the valuation by $100,000 and Doris got a $12,000 refund.[666]

Her iron will was soon on display again. Two years earlier, after fire destroyed Walsh Brothers Furniture store on the east side of Thames Street, an enormous gap was left in the block. Shortly thereafter, Doris became obsessed with creating a park between that gap and historic Trinity Church, further up what was known as Historic Hill.

Her idea was to restore a few existing colonial-era homes and move others to form a quadrangle of historic buildings around a grassy area west of the Church. The development of what ultimately became known as Queen Anne Square, soon became a tortuous process for the tobacco heiress. Below is a photo of how it looks today in relation to Trinity Church. There's a story behind the boulder in the foreground that begs to be told here.

The 16 ton boulder excavated from Rough Point as it rests today in Queen Anne Square near Trinity Church.

"Unaccustomed to spending time dealing with bureaucratic red tape, Doris Duke was on the verge of walking away from the project several times until it became clear that she wanted complete control of the project." That was the assessment in 2013 of famed architect Maya Lin, who was commissioned by the NRF to rescue the Square decades after Doris had finished it, then abandoned it. [667]

But early on in the design process when Doris was fully engaged, she decided that what the park simply *had* to have was a 16-ton boulder that she had noticed amid the rocks below Rough Point. The story of how she raised it from the waterline, hauled it up to her estate, then transported it down Bellevue Avenue and through the narrow streets of Historic Hill to the park is a tale that was best recounted by her one time business manager, former NYU economist Patrick Mahn and his co-author Tom Valentine in their Duke biography *Daddy's Duchess*.

Referring to it as "Dee Dee's Rock," their principal source was Tony Gessel, a German immigrant who'd served Doris for decades "from shrub trimmer to Director of Duke Gardens," the elaborate series of greenhouses Eduardo Tirella had created for her at Duke Farms in New Jersey. What follows is an excerpt from their book:

> She called faithful Tony and told him to meet her at water's edge immediately. By the time he arrived she had select-ed, by far, the largest boulder to be plucked from the tide pool and transported to the park. Tony knew better than to question a Dee Dee inspiration. He consulted a contractor who moved houses for the NRF. His verdict: "There isn't a crane in the state that could lift that rock." "Then go out of state to get one," was Dee Dee's solution as she walked away. Still, even if a crane could be brought in, the con-tractor doubted a tractor-trailer unit big enough to haul it could be found. It would've been cheaper to build a rock replica at the site than to bring in the largest crane and tractor-trailer rig in three states.

The crane came up from New York. Once in position, Dee Dee's workers wrapped a web of steel cable around the monster rock. The crane operator engaged the winches and the cables tightened.

The diesel engine roared. But before the rock budged, the mighty crane threatened to topple over into the sea. The operator hit the emergency release and the crane thundered back to the ground. Dee Dee suggested they tie the front of the rig to the trunk of the biggest tree on the property. Tony was sent to find a chain big enough to do the job.

In the Naval town of Newport, it didn't take long for Tony to procure a formidable piece of anchor chain. It required four men and a six wheel truck to move it and another two hours to secure the crane to the tree. Finally, black smoke belched from the crane, the cables tensed, the chain-to-tree anchor held and the giant rock broke free from its tide pool home.

It was placed on the flatbed trailer. However, the driver complained it was so much weight that the vehicle's brakes would burn up going down the Hill to the park. He feared he would end up rolling through half the buildings in downtown Newport before coming to a halt. Dee Dee, thrilled at so far accomplishing the impossible, suggested they "Clear all the roads surrounding the park." She punctuated her words by moving her right arm around and around. "Call Ben Reed at the NRF and tell him to arrange it." That afternoon the roads leading to the park were closed off temporarily, the truck careened through town and the park now has its own version of Plymouth Rock. [668]

CHAPTER TWENTY-SIX

SNUBBING
THE QUEEN

In 1976, during the 200th anniversary of America's declaration of independence from King George III, the "crown jewel" of Newport Restoration Foundation projects was Queen Anne Square, the park that stretched from the edge of Trinity Church to Thames Street. Designed by famed Newport architect Richard Munday and opened in 1726, the church, with its seven story spire, is one of the most important Anglican/Episcopal houses of worship in the New World. [669] Over the centuries, its parishioners included Gilbert Stuart, the artist famed for his portrait of our first President, the Perry brothers, Clement Clarke Moore, the poet who wrote "A Visit From St. Nicholas" in Newport, Gilded Age architect George Champlin Mason, and George Washington himself who worshiped there when the Continental Army recaptured Newport in 1799 following its seizure by the British.

In the days that followed, there were multiple attempts by loyalists on the winning side to bring down the gilded weather vane atop the spire, because from the ground, its bishop's miter resembled the

British crown. [670] But today it still holds sway over Newport Harbor as the church anchors Queen Anne Square.

Naturally, with the announcement that on July 10th, 1976, Queen Elizabeth II would visit Newport at a dedication of The Square, it was expected that Doris Duke would be in attendance. The ceremony capped off the visit to Newport of "The Tall Ships" on June 26th, a spectacular display of 19th and 20th century square rigged vessels from around the world, including Argentina's Libertad, The Gorch Fock of Germany, and The Winston Churchill from the U.K., which crossed the Atlantic with an all-female crew "dressing the yards." [671]

Her Majesty and Prince Philip arrived at Green Airport, across the Bay, late on the afternoon of July 10th and traveled to Newport by motorcade, where they drove past Doris's restored homes along Washington Street on The Point before arriving at the church. There a crowd of several thousand watched the Queen dedicate a plaque created by The John Stevens Shop.

Founded in 1705, for much of the last century and this one, it's been owned and operated by a family of stone carving masters beginning with John Howard Benson, a graduate of Rogers High School, trained at the Art Students League, who became a distinguished professor of sculpture and calligraphy at The Rhode Island School of Design. [672] His son John Everett, known as Fud, carved inscriptions for President Kennedy's Memorial at Arlington National Cemetery and designed the lettering for the date stones at the Vietnam Veterans Memorial in Washington. His son Nick, a third generation stone carver, was named a MacArthur Fellow in 2010 and runs the Stevens Shop to this day. [673] It was an association with the Benson family that brought Adé Bethune to Newport in 1938. [674]

Back in 1976 at the time of the Square's dedication, press coverage noted that "Miss Duke is the sole financial supporter of the NRF," but she was noticeably absent from the ceremony. [675]

It was expected however, that she would attend a black tie dinner that evening aboard the 451 foot Royal Yacht Brittania, anchored at Pier 1 on The Newport Naval Base. The Queen herself, the great-great-great-great granddaughter of George III [676] would host the affair, to be attended by President and Mrs. Gerald R. Ford, Vice President Nelson Rockefeller and his wife Happy as well as Henry Kissinger and a host of other dignitaries. [677]

But the seat reserved for Doris Duke stood empty.

"She decided she didn't want to go," Duke biographer Stephanie Mansfield later wrote, quoting one of Doris's friends. "After all, she was more important than the Queen anyway. She simply snubbed her." [678]

PROSECUTING AN EX–FBI AGENT

While Doris was known as a recluse whose aversion to publicity rivaled that of Howard Hughes, [679] the notion that she simply found the Queen beneath her gains more credence when you consider what she was doing just weeks before the Royal visit. She wasn't spending her time locked up on one of her estates. In fact, on June 21st she took the stand in a Somerset County, New Jersey courthouse testifying in the criminal trial of Arthur Whittaker, a former FBI agent-turned-private investigator whom she'd hired to look into the theft of jewelry and a jade figurine worth $10,000 [680] from her 2,700 acre Duke Farms estate in Hillsborough Township. [681]

After evidence showed that Whittaker had done an extensive investigation, including hiring a private company to give lie detector tests to all 114 Duke employees (at her insistence) and after he'd staffed the estate with additional security, he presented Doris with a bill for $21,000 which she promptly refused to pay. [682]

Though all of her workers passed the polygraphs, the jewels and jade were never found.

In what should have then been a civil matter reminiscent of the suit filed by NRF contractor Daryl Ford after she'd stiffed *him,* the Whittaker case soon turned into a *criminal* proceeding. In fact, the ex-FBI agent's attorney later suggested that Doris herself may have "informed" on his client to the State Police, who began an investigation after one of Duke's employees complained to the State Department of Labor about the polygraphs. [683]

Whoever the source was, a grand jury was empaneled, and Doris testified against Whittaker personally. He was then indicted for the crime of practicing investigative work in New Jersey without a license. It was a charge punishable by a $1,000 fine and up three years in prison. [684]

There was no doubt that the polygraphs had prompted the criminal probe which led to the charges and Whittaker testified that Doris was "adamant and determined" to give (the) tests to the employees, one of whom, she believed was behind the theft. [685] He also told the court that the heiress had suggested to him that additional security guards might "work undercover," to investigate the burglary. [686] It was an idea that raised privacy issues with the potential of blow back from the Duke Farms staff, so the ex-Special Agent rejected it.

In testimony before Superior Court Judge Arthur S. Meredith in the criminal case, Whittaker said that he'd filed *a civil suit* in New York to collect the $21K Doris owed him *before* the indictment against him in New Jersey had come down. [687] The implication was that Duke had instigated a *criminal* proceeding that could land him in prison just to avoid paying a civil debt.

Finally, after multiple days of trial, Judge Meredith ruled that Whitaker didn't need a New Jersey license for his short-term investigation of the jewelry theft and the charges against him were dismissed. [688]

Nine months later, a Federal jury in New York awarded him $20,000 of his $21,000 claim, but after Whittaker filed a civil action against Duke for malicious prosecution, she made a motion for summary judgement and prevailed. [689] That happened nearly three years after she had snubbed the Queen of England.

In the interim, Doris Duke had single-mindedly waged a battle in multiple courts across two states, costing tens of thousands of dollars in legal fees against a former Special Agent -- described at trial as "excellent" and "beyond reproach;" all in an apparent effort to avoid paying a bill for services he'd earned after a minor theft had ignited Doris's legendary paranoia. [690]

But the Whittaker case was just a warm-up for Doris's next major falling out, following her disappearing act before The Royals in 1976. This time she took on the beloved pastor of the very church that anchored the crown jewel of the Newport Restoration Foundation.

"BRUTAL AND CALLOUS"

On February 4[th,] 1977, when the temperature in Newport was averaging just below freezing, [691] Doris Duke sent letters to the 54 tenants of the NRF's houses notifying them of her intent to install storm windows in their rented homes. The charges of up to $1,800, in 1977 dollars, would be added to their monthly rents to be paid off over five years.[692] A piece in *The Newport Daily* News by William Kutik, reporting on the surcharge noted that "the tenants are hopping mad." [693]

"This was just sprung on us," said one tenant who wouldn't give his name. "We don't own the houses, she does. We just pay rent and she should pay for the windows." Kutik also reported that "in the last three years, rents have increased from 25 to 60 per cent."

Two weeks later, after 25 of the tenants refused to pay the disputed storm window charge, a steering committee was formed, headed by The Rev. Lockett F. Ballard, former Canon of Trinity Church, who had been Doris Duke's pastor for years and worked directly with her on Queen Ann Square. [694] The committee reached out to officials from The Duke Gardens Foundation in New Jersey, but after their request for a meeting was rebuffed by Doris, they formed a tenants association, employing the kind of tactics West Broadway tenants had used in the mid Sixties. [695]

"We've been met with a stone wall," the Association's temporary chairman said."A.D. Searles, a Duke Gardens official said he'd had a letter and phone call from Doris, then in Hawaii, and "The decision stands. The storm windows will be paid for or they will be removed." [696]

Two days later in a *Daily News* piece headlined "Doris Duke Tenants Strike Back,"The Newport Restoration Association announced its formal creation with Rev. Ballard as Vice Chairman and S.B. Griffith, a retired Marine Corps Brigadier General adding his name to the Executive Committee. The tenants voted to hire local attorney Patrick O'Neal Hayes, the prominent former State Senator who had bid on Annandale Farm, to assess their legal options. [697]

The NRF's upper middle-class residents were shocked by Duke's treatment, which one called "brutal and callous."A female member of the new Association was quoted as saying, "It's a tragedy. These nice people in nice houses are being treated like slum dwellers." [698]

Eleven days later, Doris escalated the fight by ordering the storm windows removed, despite a reported "gentlemen's agreement"between O'Neill and the NRF's lawyers to hold off.

Flabbergasted by the move, tenants charged that Duke had deceived them and was taking out her wrath on Association officials by "stripping *their* windows first." [699] Mrs. Byron Dexter, Association President, said she'd heard that four or five tenants were planning to vacate the restored homes rather than be forced to pay the window charge.

The conflict continued for another two weeks and then Doris crushed the Association by hiking rents by another 25 per cent, the third raise in three years. At that point, by early April, a quarter of the 54 residents were making plans to leave, including the Rev. Ballard at 44 Pelham Street after his rent went from $300 a month plus the cost of heat to $425. [700]

"We're just fed up and want to get out," the retired minister told Kutik. "It's all turning so sour." Canon Ballard, who had been the lion of Trinity Church for decades and had the initial idea for Queen Anne Square, passed away less than two years later after a series of strokes. In an interview for this book, his son Ford told me that the Association's struggles had taken a toll on him.

"As a clergyman of some standing in the community, he was used to standing up for things like this," said Ford. "Although he was retired and no longer formally associated with the church, he was acting as a private citizen and he had no compunction about doing what he did. It was quite courageous to stand up to Doris Duke and I'm proud of him." [701]

MOVING HOUSES

As I drilled down on Doris Duke's restoration work, I was reminded of the pledge made by Francis Comstock, John Perkins Brown's successor as executive director of NRF. Back in the fall of 1969 when the NRF had just been formed, he told the press that the aim of the Foundation, was "to restore… the beautiful colonial architecture of *Newport*." [702]

At that same time, Doris herself said this: "As a resident of Newport for many years I have always taken pride in this unique and beautiful place, not only for its beauty but also for its historical heritage. Because of my interest, I have formed The Newport Restoration Foundation to preserve and restore the eighteenth century buildings for future generations." [703]

But when it came to Doris Duke and her philanthropy, the truth -- as Churchill once remarked -- was often "attended by a bodyguard of lies" [704] and when I focused on those 70 restored properties, I found that 24, representing more than one third of the entire NRF inventory, had been moved from their original locations. [705] Many weren't from Newport at all.

Of the 24, nine structures were moved within Newport from the sites on which they were built in colonial times. Others were dismantled from multiple locations in Rhode Island, Massachusetts, Connecticut and New Jersey, trucked to Newport and then *rebuilt*. One, known as The Farm House at 72 Spring Street actually came from Doris's own New Jersey estate and the centerpiece of Prescott Farms in Portsmouth, The Robert Sherman Windmill, was moved four times before arriving at the site of The Barefoot General's abduction.

Six Newport Restoration houses that form a ring around Queen Anne Square never existed in their current locations. Two of them, the Beria Brown House at 41 Mill Street and the West-Hathaway House at 15 Mill came from "off island." The Swansea House at 3 Cozzens Court came from Swansea, Mass and the two houses that anchor the corner of Thames Street up a short block -- the Thorton-Wilder House at 53-55, originated in Johnston,

The Robert Sherman Windmill at Prescott Farms. (Tom Perrotti photo)

RI; and the Hathaway-Macomber House at 57 was disassembled on its original site in Freetown, Massachusetts and relocated to Newport. The source for all of that is the NRF's own website. [706]

"From a purely historical perspective, it was the difference between restoring an actual colonial town and creating a theme park," said Tom Perrotti, whose late grandfather, M. Thomas Perrotti, was chairman of Newport's Redevelopment Agency for decades. [707] There's a park named for him today along the city's waterfront not far from Queen Anne Square. [708]

"So many people talk about all the good that Doris Duke did for Newport with that Restoration Foundation," said Newport Housing Authority Executive Pauline Perkins-Moyé in an interview for this book. "But it came at a price. It took nearly a decade after your housing series shook things up on West Broadway, but those wonderful people like the Rev. Ballard got a taste of what *we* experienced when we tried to get Doris Duke to help our community by keeping that Lyman house on Kingston Avenue. With Miss Doris it always seemed to be her way or the highway and there's a lesson in that for these troubled times. Whether we are dirt poor or upper-class, we are all in the same boat when it comes to 'The One Percent.' So we have to stick together. After all, what race do we belong to anyway, but the human race?" [709]

CHAPTER TWENTY-SEVEN

THE DUKE CURSE

In the world of sports, it is held that strange things happen to basket-ball teams that beat Duke University in the NCAA tournament. [710] In 2013 the Duke Basketball Report cited 46 separate instances of extreme bad luck, dating back to 1984, from multiple player injuries to a string of coach resignations and DUI/drug arrests that depleted the benches of Duke's rivals. While that reporting pushed coincidence into the realm of conspiracy theory, a number of Newporters began to sense that certain people who came into close contact with Doris *herself* were somehow marked.

Indeed, if she left a wake of bad karma behind her, it may have derived from two of the principal sources of her income: Duke Power (now Duke Energy) and The American Tobacco Company, one of the original 12 members of The Dow Jones Industrial Average. [711]

Founded in 1904 by Doris's father James Buchanan "Buck" Duke, and his brother Benjamin Newton Duke, the successor company to Duke Power, Duke Energy is a sprawling electrical power and gas distributor with 29,000 employees supplying energy to 7.7 million retail electrical customers in six states and 1.6 million consumers of natural gas in five states. [712] The Fortune 500 listed its market value in the last fiscal year at $59.36 billion with profits of $3.75 billion. [713] Over the decades, Duke Power and Duke Energy have been cited for multiple environmental and civil rights violations.

In 2006 researchers from the University of Massachusetts identified Duke Energy as the 46th largest corporate producer of air pollution in the U.S., releasing up to 36 million pounds of toxic chemicals per year. [714] In 2015, according to *The Associated Press*, Federal authorities launched a criminal investigation surrounding Duke Energy's coal ash spill into a North Carolina River – the 3rd largest in U.S. history. It reportedly spewed enough toxic sludge to fill 73 Olympic-sized swimming pools [715] In 2019 that same U. Mass group ranked Duke Energy No. 11 on its "Toxic 100 Water Polluters Index." [716]

Prior to passage of the 1964 Civil Rights Act, The U.S. Supreme Court, in <u>Griggs vs. Duke Power</u>, found that the company had a policy of openly discriminating on the basis of race in hiring and assigning workers at its Dan River plant [717] Even after passage of the landmark legislation, the High Court determined that Duke Power continued to racially discriminate by creating education requirements for job placement that didn't directly relate to the work being done. [718]

Perhaps the most infamous episode in Duke Power's modern history involved the strike by coal miners at the Brookside Mine and Prep Plant in Harlan County, Kentucky during their struggle to join The United Mine Workers. In June 1973, the miners at Brookside voted to join the UMW in an election run by The National Labor Relations Board, but negotiations with Duke Power's Eastover subsidiary broke down. The miners commenced a strike which lasted 13 months. It was chronicled in *Harlan County, USA*, the 1976 Academy Award-winning documentary, shot by Hart Perry and directed by Barbara Kopple. [719] Writing for *The Atlantic* two years earlier, Fred Harris documented the working and living conditions that the miners and their families faced in the county dominated by Duke Energy, known as "Bloody Harlan:"

> The median family income is $4600 a year. Only 23 percent of those in the county over the age of twenty-five have complet-ed high school. Forty percent of the county's dwellings lack

some or all of plumbing, water, or toilet facilities. Thirty percent of the families lack automobiles. More than twenty-four babies out of a thousand die before they are one year old, and the expenditure per child in the public schools is one-half the national average. The unemployment rate in the county is 7 percent; that doesn't count those who have long since given up looking for the scarce or nonexistent jobs. [720]

But whatever villainy lay in the energy portion of Doris Duke's portfolio, it paled in comparison to the legacy of death that resulted from the initial source of her wealth: her father's creation and marketing of cigarettes through The American Tobacco Company.

As reported by the BBC in 2012, the single product most responsible for Doris' wealth -- the modern cigarette as we know it -- was "the greatest artifact of death in the 20th century, killing more than 100 million people." [721]

For centuries, cigarettes had been hand-rolled, but Buck Duke first struck it rich by creating the packed white cylindrical design popular since the early 1900's. It turned out to be a remarkably efficient cancer delivery system, high in tar, nicotine and fillers. He bought a machine that could produce 10,000 cigarettes a day. He then snapped up his rivals, P.J. Lorillard and R.J. Reynolds, but The Feds filed an antitrust suit forcing him to break up some of American Tobacco's holdings.

Still, as early as the 1920's, Buck understood the dangers of smoking and refused to let his wife Nanaline or their daughter Doris touch tobacco. Until that time, women rarely smoked; put off by the indelicate process of hand rolling. But Buck saw them as a lucrative market, so he openly advertised to women, while falsely touting

Lucky Strike ads emphasizing health & aimed at women.

the "health" benefits of his principal brand, Lucky Strike.

Who can ever forget the iconic pitch lines, "LSMFT: Lucky Strike Means Fine Tobacco" or "It's toasted," a slogan attributed to the fictional character of Don Draper in the pilot episode of "Mad Men." [722]

So was there an actual "Duke Curse?" Consider the record. Among the many Duke-family tragedies, her half-brother Walker Inman died suddenly, under mysterious circumstances at the age of 60. An autopsy was performed but the results were never released, and the body was cremated. [723]

Doris's godson, Pony Duke wrote that at the age of 17, Walker "celebrated" Doris's birth in 1912 by retreating to his room and instructing "the servants to bring him his usual cocktail every 20 minutes until he passed out." *His* son Walker II, who lived with Doris at Rough Point in his early teens, overdosed on meth in 2010 at the age of 56 [724] after depleting much of his inheritance on a reported $90,000-a-month lifestyle. [725]

Following in Doris's tradition of epic litigation, his twin children, Georgia and Walker III, (aka Patterson) spent years in a legal battle over his estate. [726] In 2013 *Rolling Stone* reported that they'd grown up "horribly neglected and abused," locked up in a basement strewn with feces and subjected to scalding baths. [727] But no premature death seemed to haunt Doris more than that of her only child with whom she was pregnant in the summer of 1940. [728]

THE LOSS OF BABY ARDEN

Since the billionairess and her husband, James Cromwell, hadn't had relations in many months, Pony Duke speculated that the father might have been one of Doris's two recent lovers: British MP Alec Cunningham-Reid or ex-Olympic champion and surfing legend Duke Kahanamoku who had introduced her to the long board. [729] In fact, reportedly terrified that she might give birth to a mixed-race child, there was speculation at the time that Doris might have actually sought to induce a miscarriage by entering the turbulent surf off Diamond Head late in her pregnancy. [730]

As Pony Duke later put it in his biography, "The crowd on the beach became alarmed. Duke Kahanamoku stood... and watched in silence. She was bruised and cut when she finally left the water. Doris and Duke drove back to Shangri-La. By the time they reached the mansion, there was blood seeping through her bathing suit. Doris screamed in pain." Later, at Queen's Hospital, she gave birth to a three-pound baby girl she named Arden.

Duke Kahanamoku

Less than 24 hours later on July 11th, 1940, the child was dead.

Pony recounted that Doris asked to see little Arden so that she could hold her one last time. "The anxious nurses waiting outside the door," he wrote, "first heard a low crying that slowly crescendoed into an animal-like wail."

After being informed by doctors that she would never again give birth, Doris set off on a decades-long pursuit of mystic religions. In 1988 at the age of 75, she adopted Chandi Heffner, a 35 year-old former Hare Krishna devotee she believed to be the reincarnation of Arden. [731]

In a profile of Chandi in *Vanity Fair*, Doris's friend Nancy Cooke de Herrera, told Bob Colacello, "Doris had gone surfing. There was a rumor that she did it deliberately." [732] Even esteemed historian Michael Beschloss, writing a tribute to Kahanamoku in *The New York Times*, gave credence to the story that the legendary surfer was Arden's father. "Several biographers have argued that the baby was almost certainly Kahanamoku's," he wrote. "Three weeks after the birth, his timing perhaps provoked by dread of a public scandal, Kahanamoku married Nadine Alexander, a Cleveland-born dance teacher at the Royal Hawaiian Hotel." [733]

BRUTAL TO HER STAFF

As to her Karmic bank account, the tall tobacco heiress was deep in the red when it came to how she treated the dozens of workers in each of her estates. The staffs at Duke Farms, Rough Point, Falcon Lair and

Shangri-La were victims of regular mistreatment. For decades, not a single one earned medical or pension benefits. According to Patrick Mahn, her former business manager, they were often berated and subject to firing at will. [734]

Further, Doris was notoriously stingy. If a servant broke a single glass, they had to pay for it. Seven weeks before the death of Eduardo Tirella, she exercised enough influence over local authorities in New Jersey to get criminal charges filed against Michael Cilento, a chef at Duke Farms whom she accused of stealing two Limoges china plates allegedly worth $500. [735] Cilento, who denied taking the plates found in his quarters, told police that his three-year-old son had removed them from the pantry. Yet Doris persisted in the prosecution in which the chef faced three to five years in prison. His bail was $5,000, ten times the value of the plates.

Peter Byrne, a former RAF pilot during World War II, who had a five-month affair with Doris in Hawaii in 1967, recounted another incident with her staff that he'd witnessed.

"There was one time when a delivery truck came in the front of Shangri-La and one of the statues that she had there was broken. Doris was absolutely furious. So she lined up all of the servants in the front yard. There were like 20. Gardeners, maids and cooks. She said, 'I want to know who broke this statue.' They wouldn't say anything. So she said, 'You'd better tell me or else.' They all stood silent. So she pointed to five of them (counting) 'One, two, three, four, five. You're fired.' She sacked them all on the spot. These were people who'd served her loyally; many for years. They had families with children. She was very vindicative." [736]

When her chief designer, Eduardo Tirella, turned those abandoned greenhouses into a world-class botanical display, acting as both architect and general contractor, Doris's business manager at the time, the late Pete Cooley, insisted on paying him an hourly rate of $7.00. [737] In most coverage of the Gardens, their design is attributed entirely to Doris herself [738] but the extensive records from her files at the Rubenstein Library document how, for years, Eduardo oversaw every detail of the layout and execution of the floral display, enclosed under the once moribund greenhouse roofs.

One of the many garden designs Eduardo Tirella executed for Doris Duke on her 2700 acre estate in New Jersey. He also designed parts of multiple residential spaces for her including at her Park Avenue apartment, Falcon Lair in LA, Shangri-la in Hawaii and Rough Point

David Rimmer, the manager of The Duke Gardens Foundation, who dealt with Eduardo for years on every detail of his design, told me that after his death, he was actually instructed by Cooley to reach out to Eduardo's grieving family and retrieve the unused portion of the round-trip airline ticket Doris had bought him for his final trip to Newport.

"COOLEY DIDN'T WANT ME THERE"

On the night of Eduardo's homicide, it was Rimmer who got the call from Howard McFarlane, Doris's caretaker up at Rough Point, who broke the news that there had been "an accident."

"So I called Pete Cooley in New York and told him what had happened." Rimmer said. Assuming he'd be needed up in Rhode Island, Rimmer, who had just flown back that day from Falcon Lair in LA, went immediately to Newark Airport and caught a late flight to Boston, taking a small plane down to Newport Air Park. "Cooley had been dodging my calls, up to that point" he said. "So I called Rough Point and got Miss Duke's personal maid Elsa on the phone. She told me that she understood how concerned I was, but Cooley didn't want me there. They had instructions not to let me in." [739]

Apparently Rimmer, who'd grown close to Eduardo, didn't fit into the post-death scenario that Cooley was concocting with Doris's attorney Wesley Fach. As we now know, the two of them later conspired with police chief Joseph Radice to bury the truth.

"So there was nothing I could do," Rimmer told me, "except turn around. I stayed the night in a local motel and flew back (to New Jersey) the next day."

Doris's stinginess was legendary and like most members of the Newport Summer colony she never tipped. In fact, Richard Tanner, who regularly flew her from Newport to New York and New Jersey in twin engine Aero Commanders, recalled that the only billionaire who ever showed him the courtesy of a tip for his steady hand in the cockpit was Henry Ford II. [740]

As far back as 1945 Doris insisted that cabbies were due *only* what was on the meter. Stephanie Mansfield wrote that at one point a London hack driver chased Duke after she'd refused to tip him. [741] She also recounted how, at Thanksgiving, when her New Jersey farm manger wanted to buy fresh turkeys for the staff, Doris insisted on frozen birds that were 30 cents a pound cheaper. [742]

Doris's papers from The Rubenstein Library at Duke University revealed a particularly heartless instruction she gave to Cooley after she received a letter on May 13th, 1965 from a Mrs. Emma G. Stoudt, a 52-year-old worker at the VA Supply Depot, near Duke Farms in South Somerville, New Jersey. She'd been driving to work in her 1955 station wagon when suddenly "a mother deer and baby appeared on the road." They were part of a herd of several thousand that Doris had cultivated on the property. [743] Swerving to avoid them, Mrs. Stoudt wrote that she lost control of her vehicle.

"I hit a tree on the north side of the road. I hit the windshield with my head and smashed it. — I needed five stitches. I hit the dashboard with my jaw. I am bruised and sore all over."

Making it clear that she was "not looking for anything for herself," and that she was "grateful to be alive, and thankful (her) neck was not broken," Mrs. Stoudt appealed to Doris to "contribute something toward" her car, which was totaled. She ended the letter by noting that "My husband and I both have to work to pay off our home. This loss has hit us hard. I wish you could find it in your heart to help us out."

At bottom of the letter Pete Cooley wrote, "IGNORE – instructions of D.D. 5.19.65." [744]

HOWARD McFARLANE'S HEART ATTACK

Perhaps the cruelest expression of Doris's stinginess occurred after her Rough Point caretaker Howard McFarlane (Linda's father) had a heart attack in 1968. He was living with his family on the third floor of Rough Point when it occurred.

But rather than move him to first floor accommodations or a more suitable location off the estate, Doris insisted that he would have to travel between floors in a dumbwaiter. As Linda later recounted in her book, she and her mother and brother had to yank on the pullies to bring him up and down as he sat crammed on a chair in the tiny lift. [745]

The only mercy Doris showed was allowing the family to move down to the 2nd floor, but the McFarlanes, mother, daughter and son still had to do the heavy lifting. Doris finally relented and let them move to Duke Farms in New Jersey where they could live on the first floor, but sadly, Howard died three weeks later.

Apart from the maid who got washed out to sea, never to be heard from again, and Eduardo Tirella's violent end, unexpected death found its way to another of Doris's properties. David Rimmer himself, who loyally served her for years, experienced personal tragedy in 1958 when his young wife Barbara was thrown from a horse at Duke Farms as she prepared for a routine morning ride. When the horse fell back onto her, she was instantly killed.

"It seemed that so many people in Doris's service ended up meeting terrible fates," said Eduardo's niece Donna Lohmeyer." "It was almost as if they were cursed."

Few were more negatively impacted than the family of Dr. Phillip McAllister, the Assistant Medical Examiner who'd gone rogue and protected Doris on the night of Tirella's death, participating knowingly in the cover-up that permitted her to escape justice.

McALLISTER'S DESCENT

As noted, Dr. McAllister was my family doctor growing up. He made regular house calls and was an excellent surgeon, operating on me for an injury I got running track in high school. His son Phil, aka "Junior," was in my class at De La Salle. The doctor's wife Emmy was close to my mother Albina. Dr. McAllister was an Irish immigrant who served with distinction in the U.S. Army Medical Corps in World War II. Emmy emigrated from Germany.[746] In the early 50's he became President of The Newport Medical Society and had a thriving practice. [747] Politically active, he was Democratic Chairman in Middletown [748] and Emmy ran for State Senate. [749] They bought a beautiful home on Green End Avenue in Middletown and had another residence in the Virgin Islands.

But after the Tirella cover-up in 1966, Dr. McAllister's life began to fall apart.

Phil and his younger brother Brendan, once a champion surfer, were arrested multiple times for drug-related crimes. [750] Both fled to St. Thomas. Brendan OD'd there in 1973.[751] Phil overdosed in '75. Their sister Patsy died at the age of 35 in 1987.[752]

The doctor was later charged with overprescribing opiates. A close friend of mine who lived near McAllister's medical office on Pelham Street, remembers junkies regularly shooting up in Touro Park, up the street, with drugs they'd scored from him. [753]

Dr. McAllister's Medical License was soon threatened. A 1983 RI Supreme Court Decision forced him to reveal evidence of his overprescribing. [754]

By the 1990's, well into their seventies, Dr. McAllister and Emmy ended up living in low income senior public housing on Newport's Chapel Terrace. [755] All five members of that once thriving family are now buried in St. Mary's Cemetery in Portsmouth, north of Newport.

CHAPTER TWENTY-EIGHT

THE UNPLEASANTNESS AT PLAISANCE

If one were to prick any of the delicate fingers of Mary Ridgely Carter Beck, the few droplets of blood that emerged would have been as blue as any American aristocrat's. Her lineage dated back to George Calvert, 1st Baron Baltimore, responsible for founding the settlement known today as Maryland [756] and Henry Lee III, known as "Light Horse," [757] the ninth governor of Virginia who was the father of Robert E. Lee. [758] With her husband James "Jimmy" Beck, President of The English Speaking Union in Newport, [759] she threw lavish parties at Plaisance, their 6,500 square foot French Provincial-style estate on Ledge Road, just around Cliff Walk from Rough Point. [760]

In 1958 she was named Newport's Woman of The Year. [761] For the 1963 premier of *Cleopatra,* the most expensive film epic of the era, starring Elizabeth Taylor, Richard Burton and Rex Harrison, she and her husband hosted an extravaganza for legendary Hollywood mogul Spyros Skouras who ran 20th Century Fox. [762] The Duke and Duchess of Windsor were the godparents of their son Ridgely. [763]

But there was a strange, utterly incongruous reality that went on behind the doors of Plaisance, known to only a few of the Becks' closest friends and to almost no one beyond those who served them. It seems that Mrs. Beck, the society doyenne, secretly cultivated rats – dozens of them. [764] She did this during two periods in the 1960's, creating a vermin problem that spilled over onto Cliff Walk and threatened to engulf the tony residences along

The Beck Family, Jimmy, Ridgley, and Mary (Jerry Taylor photo)

Ledge Road. [765] It was a strange real-life manifestation of the popular horror film *Willard,* and its sequel *Ben.*

I'd heard rumors of it as a child, but never believed them until a retired police officer I interviewed for the Duke case happened to mention it and I chased down the story. [766] But before I get into the details, consider The Becks' position of influence and respect within the Newport Summer Colony.

On July 17th, 1954 Louis and Elaine Lorillard, Doris Duke's neighbors, staged the first Jazz Festival, at The Newport Casino, further down Bellevue Avenue. [767] Produced by Boston impresario George Wein, it starred Billy Holiday, Ella Fitzgerald, Gene Krupa, Oscar Peterson and George Shearing in two days of performances attended by 13,000 fans [768] The event was so successful that it spawned The Newport Folk Festival in 1959, featuring Pete Seeger, Odetta, The Kingston Trio, and an 18-year-old discovery named Joan Baez. [769] Bob Dylan first appeared at the 1963 festival and made rock history there two years later when he went electric. [770] The two festivals became iconic summer events in Newport and continue to draw thousands each summer to Fort Adams where they're now staged.

But three years after the Lorillards and Wein first brought thousands into Newport's historic tennis venue, Mary Beck created a more intimate musical series of her own, geared entirely to her socialite friends.

Starting in 1957 she ran "The Carnival of Music" at an amphitheater near King Park on the Newport waterfront, inviting stars like Hollywood's Rhonda Fleming to sing to hundreds of fellow Summer Colonists.[771]

That same year, Mrs. Beck was responsible for the arrival in Newport of the 90-foot barkentine Mayflower II, a replica of the vessel that had brought The Pilgrims to Plymouth in 1620. The tiny vessel entered Newport harbor on June 28th, 1957 after Mrs. Beck had issued a formal invitation for the square rigger which made a storm tossed trans-Atlantic crossing. [772]

She not only headed the welcoming committee but treated the Australian Captain and British crew to a luncheon at Ida Lewis Yacht Club before hosting a "supper party" that evening at Plaisance. [773] When it came to their social standing among "The Avenue Crowd," the Becks were highly respected, due in part, to Jimmy's pedigree.

WORKING FOR THE "FILM CZAR"

Born to a prominent Philadelphia family and a 1914 Graduate of Princeton, his own father, James M. Senior, was Solicitor General of The United States in the Calvin Coolidge administration. An accomplished pianist, Jimmy went to England in 1927, where he became an executive for the RCA Victor Recording company. The following year he married Clarissa Madeline Georgina Felicite "Claire"Tennant, the daughter of Edward Priaulx Tennant, 1st Baron Glenconner, who had recently divorced Major Lionel Hallam Tennyson, 3rd Baron Tennyson, the grandson of the celebrated poet. Jimmy and Claire had twin children: James Montgomery Beck III and Virginia, born in 1929. The couple divorced a decade later. [774]

But his social connections led Beck to a powerful position in the film industry. From 1929 to 1937 he was the U.K. representative of Will H. Hays, President of The Motion Picture Producers and Distributors of America. [775] Hays was known as "The First Film Czar." [776] As head of the MPPDA he created the dreaded "Hays code," otherwise known as "The Magna Carta;" a list of content that was forbidden on screen. [777]

For the next 25 years Hays became one of the most powerful and feared men in Hollywood. Some of that patina rubbed off on the much more genteel and dapper James Montgomery Beck, who along with his wife became a highly sought-after dinner guest and party host.

One event in 1962 was indicative of the Becks' standing in Newport's social strata. It was given in honor of Robert Wilson Goelet, heir to one of the wealthiest land-owning families in New York City, who helped fund Queen Anne Square.

At one time his family's holdings included 55 acres on the island of Manhattan "stretching along the East Side from Union Square to 48th Street." [778] In 1947 Goelet offered Ochre Point, his spectacular Beaux-Arts-style Newport estate to the United Nations for the site of its new headquarters. Later, after New York City was chosen, he donated the Newport mansion and its grounds, built in 1890, to The Roman Catholic Diocese of Rhode Island for the establishment of Salve Regina College (now a university).[779] He then bought Champs Soleil, a Bellevue Avenue French-Norman style chateau on 5 acres, where, among many events he threw a buffet dinner dance for 400 to celebrate the U.S. victory in the 1964 America's Cup series.

Two years earlier, at Plaisance, Mr. and Mrs. James Beck gave a helicopter party for Goelet's grandchildren and their son Ridgely. The chopper, which landed on the Becks' lawn, took the children of some of Newport's most prominent families aloft for brief rides over the coast, two at a time. Among then, Dallas, Julie and Toby Pell, children of the Senator and his wife Nuala, who lived at Pelican Lodge across Ledge Road and Victoria Leiter, daughter of Mrs. Robert "Oatsie" Charles, a close friend of Doris Duke, who lived next door to Plaisance in a cottage on the property of Land's End, the onetime estate of Edith Wharton. [780]

Three years later, the Becks capped off the summer season with a disco-themed party for Ridgely, then 14, and "100 juniors". [781]

THE BEST KEPT SECRET ON LEDGE ROAD

In discussing Coogan's lot and whether the wealthy Irish owner of Whitehall had abandoned it after being brutally snubbed by Newport society, historian Paul F. Miller, called the saga a "pervasive legend," [782] That's how I felt after hearing the story of Mrs. Beck keeping rats, around the time I started serving drinks to Jimmy Beck at The Newport Reading Room.

The year was 1962. As was the custom at our house, beginning in the late 1950's "Uncle Bert" and "Aunt Dorothy" Holmwood would celebrate the holidays with my parents in the company of a jovial Irishman named Phil Singleton who was a guard at Manufacturer's Hanover Bank in Manhattan. On certain years when Dorothy Farrington Rice, the second wife and widow of Dr. Rice would visit Newport for Christmas, Dorothy and Bert would accompany her.

So that year, a day or so after the 25th, Bert made his famous Manhattans as we exchanged presents, sung carols and Phil told the same Irish jokes we'd laugh at every season. That's when Dorothy told us of the job, she had taken that summer as a lady's maid to Mrs. Beck.

"It didn't last very long," she said. "Not after how she treated the dogs and that business with the rats." Bert grinned, moving about the room, filling glasses from a silver cocktail shaker.

We listened, stunned as Dorothy continued.

"Mrs. Beck had these two enormous dogs," she said. "But they were skin and bones. She never seemed to feed them. So one night Bric Market delivered about a dozen steaks for a dinner she was throwing." Dorothy then held her fingers two inches apart. "Steaks this thick. They were all laid out on the counter as the cook and his wife seasoned them. And those poor animals were in the kitchen just salivating. So, I waited 'til the cooks' backs were turned and pushed two of those steaks off the counter. The dogs grabbed them and gobbled them up on the spot."

Dorothy's blue eyes twinkled as she told the story. "After all, how could you let a pair of beautiful dogs like that starve, when you were feeding rats?"

At that point my parents eyed each other. My sister, then 12, looked at me, as astonished as I was. "What do you mean rats?" my mother asked.

"Big ones," she said. "Black as coal. This long, from nose to tail." She held her hands ten inches apart. "They used to come in through holes by the kitchen door and the cooks would feed them. God can strike me down dead if I'm lying."

"But why would she do that?" I asked. I had already begun to observe some eccentricities from Members of The Reading Room, but I couldn't picture Jimmy Beck, always splendid in ascots, linen trousers and Saville Row sports jackets, countenancing such behavior.

"I don't know," said Dorothy, "These people have always danced to their own drummer."

"Soon after that," said Bert, "she gave her notice. Dot had no trouble finding a more worthy employer."

He leaned over and gave his beloved wife a kiss on the cheek, then raised the shaker.

"Now who needs a refill?"

HOW THE STORY CAME BACK TO ME

After that Christmas I filed the "rat" story among the many legends I'd heard over the years about the goings-on behind the tall gates of Newport's mansions. Each summer on early evenings my family would get in the car and take "spins" around Ocean Drive after stopping at Harlow's, a local ice cream counter adjacent to the Aquidneck Island Creamery.

My mother, who had heard the stories from her mother and other servants on the estates like Bert and Dorothy, would talk about the legendary jewel thefts from Bois Doré, the French Chateau-style estate near Salve Regina that had been the home of Campbell Soup heir Elinor Winifred Dorrance Hill. [783] As we drove by that estate on Narragansett Avenue and paused to gaze at the beautiful gold inlaid doors, she'd joke to my sister and me, "That's where the Campbell Soup Kids live."

When we passed Seafair the once ominous-looking estate on Ocean Drive, now owned by Jay Leno, [784] my mother would tell of how a Roman Catholic priest had perished there during the Hurricane of '38 when, as she put it, "a tidal wave swept through the place." Seafair, had been built in 1936 for Verner Z. Reed Jr., Vice President of Chase Manhattan Bank, and beyond the '38 story, three servants *did* drown there during a hurricane in 1945 as the family and staff of William van Alen, who had rented the mansion for the summer, sought to escape. [785]

But those stories of Newport's history had never fully resonated with me until I began to dig into the Tirella death. Now the rat story came back to me.

It happened as I interviewed Norman Mather, a distinguished retired Detective who worked the crash site as a young patrolman in 1966. He went on to be named Newport's Policeman of The Year in 1971 and after retiring from the PD, became Dean of Students at Salve Regina.

We'll report on his account of Eduardo's homicide in Chapter Thirty-Three, but it was his detailed memory of Mrs. Beck that caused me to revisit the legend of the rats on Ledge Road. Over multiple interviews, this is what he told me:

"I was fortunate to grow up in Hunter House, one of the first colonial homes to be restored by The Newport Preservation Society. [786] My parents came from England and my mother was the tour guide there. We lived on the top floor. Through Mr. Holbert Smales, who became the first Executive Secretary for the Society, I got my first job as houseboy at The Whitehouse estate. It was called Eastbourne Lodge, a large red brick mansion built around 1890 that sat on four acres on Rhode Island Avenue near Kay Street. Mr. Whitehouse, whose father was a diplomat, had, himself been the Ambassador to Laos and Thailand. They had a young son, Sheldon, named for his grandfather, who would go on to become the current U.S. Senator from Rhode Island.

"The Whitehouses were incredibly kind people. When I started as a houseboy at the age of 15, they had a staff of seven. I did small jobs like sweeping the front of the house and making sure the car was washed each Sunday before services at Trinity Church. I was there two years and Mrs. Whitehouse actually offered to pay for my college education. They entertained once or twice a week and among their frequent dinners guests were the Becks, who always brought their son Ridgely. He was a nice kid, but a bit of a loner. He always dined by himself in the kitchen -- that was one thing I remember that stood out, since most couples came to the dinners alone."

When Det. Mather mentioned the Becks, I thought back to Dorothy Holmwood's tale. So, without being too specific, I asked him. "Did you ever hear any rumors about certain, let's just say, *unusual* goings on at the Becks' place on Ledge Road?"

Right away Norman shot back, "You mean how she kept rats?"

"Was that *true?* I'd heard it way back when, but always thought it was a wives' tale."

"Peter," he said, "I not only *heard* about it; I *saw* it."

CHAPTER TWENTY-NINE

CITY ORDERS EXTERMINATION

Retired Detective Inspector Norman Mather went on: "See, my second job was as a delivery boy for Bric Market, one of the two main provisioners who serviced the estates." [787]

"OK..." I said, "So what happened?"

"Once a week, among the meat and other food the Becks had ordered for themselves, I delivered the following: a case of Carnation condensed milk. 24 cans. Also 12 loaves of Harvest Oatmeal Bread, six gallons of white milk and a case of Purina Dog Chow, which contained 48 cans. The cooks at Beck's house would mix it all up -- the milk, the bread and the dog food and they would put it in the kitchen in bowls. The rats would actually come through the kitchen door. They had holes carved out at the bottom where the rats could get through..."

"You're kidding."

"It's the truth. And the rats would come in and eat that concoction and then they would leave. Whenever I stopped at Beck's house, the cooks, a husband and wife team, would make me homemade cookies. I don't mean to sound unkind. It was a nice gesture, but when I left, I'd throw the cookies out the window of the truck. The smell in the kitchen because of the rats... You had to close your nose when you walked in there. The rest of the house wasn't too bad."

"Did none of the people who came to parties at Plaisance, know about this?"

"No. In fact, Senator Pell began to see a large accumulation of rats in the neighborhood. So he put up signs asking neighbors to secure the lids on their trash cans, thinking that rats were getting into the garbage. He had no clue that the Becks were feeding them."

"So how did the word get out?

"One night the Becks were having some construction done and the holes in the kitchen door got covered with plywood. They were throwing a dinner for the Lieutenant Governor of Rhode Island and a couple of rats came in the front door. Sure enough, one of them ran across the table in front of everybody. After that, they shut the place down for a while."

This is the story that appeared in *The Newport Daily News* on May 21st, 1965:

City Orders Extermination Of Rats Infesting Cliff Area

Acting on complaints, the Health Department yesterday opened a campaign against a heavy infestation of rats in the Cliff Walk area just south of Bailey's Beach.

Dr. Philomen P. Ciarla, superintendent of health, said today he ordered Mr. and Mrs. James M. Beck of Ledge Road to call in professional exterminators "to take care of the situation." He said he had given them until today to reply, but up to this noon he had heard nothing from the Becks. He said if they did not remedy the situation, the Health Department will.

Dr. Ciarla said he visited the Beck estate this morning and saw food dishes on the lawn and rat holes, but he saw no rats.

Neighbors who have complained of the situation said they

had seen many rats on the Cliff Walk side of the Beck estate and on the lawn of the adjoining estate belonging to Mrs Dolan Sellar. The estate on the other side of the Becks' is that of U. S. Sen. and Mrs. Claiborne Pell.

One stroller along the Cliff Walk said he had seen as many as "three dozen" rats at one time Wednesday evening.

A Daily News staffman and two residents of the Bailey's Beach area went to the slope in front of Mrs. Sellar's home early last night and saw about 20 rats on the two lawns and others scuttling among the rocks on the shore.

The Health Department said a similar situation three years ago led to a summer-long rebuilding of the Beck residence by the trustees controlling that estate.

Two neighbors who had lived near Ledge Road confirmed the story along with a member of one of Newport's most prominent landscaping families [788] whose grandfather serviced Seaweed, the nearby Horace Trumbauer-designed estate of Mrs. Rita Dolan Sellar, whose family first lit the streets of Philadelphia with gas. [789] Mrs. Sellar was also the grandmother of Sandra Thornton, a marine biologist who would later marry Sheldon Whitehouse, Rhode Island's junior senator. [790]

The first neighbor to confirm the rat story was Harle Tinney, who, at the time, lived at Belcourt, just north of Rough Point. She not only *knew* the Becks, but Jimmy's son James III, lived for several years with the Tinney family, working as a tour guide.

I asked her how many members of the Summer Colony were aware of the Becks' connection to the rat problem before it became public.

"Very few," she said. "All of the estates in the neighborhood, including Rough Point, were besieged by rats at the time, but like Senator Pell, we were kept in the dark about the source.

"Believe it or not it wasn't the first time it happened. Before that dinner in 1965, they'd closed Plaisance in '62 and the fire department took barrels and barrels of rats out of the place." [791]

I was baffled why someone of Mrs. Beck's refinement would cultivate rats. Harle told me that it had to do with her deep love for her son.

"Ridgely was her darling and could do no wrong," she said. "The story I heard was that when he was a little boy — he might have been five or six years old — he had a pet white rat... And he'd let it out of the cage once in a while. Well, it got out one time and it mated with some of the wharf rats on the Cliff Walk. Mary could not say anything against Ridgely, and they fed the rats to the point where the family had to move out of Plaisance."

Another onetime neighbor was Kim Canning, who, as a child, lived with her half-brothers in a house called No View at 38 Ledge Road. It had been rented by her father James, the Executive Director of The Rhode Island Turnpike and Bridge Authority, who supervised construction of the bridge linking Newport and Jamestown, later named for Senator Pell.

"Before we moved in, just a few doors up from Plaisance," she said, "my parents had to thoroughly fumigate the house because of the rat infestation. I remember one Easter when our cat had her babies in a protected space, because she was afraid the rats would get to them." [792]

I contacted Ridgely Beck who is now 72. Though he was away at prep school at the time of Eduardo Tirella's death, he called Doris Dukes' restoration work, "Phenomenal." [793]

"She did wonders for the town," he said. "All the houses she bought and fixed up."

Norman Mather had told me that as a child Ridgely spent a lot of time in a tree house on the grounds of Plaisance, which he inherited after his parents passed away: Jimmy, at the age of 80 in 1972, [794] Mary, two years later. [795] When Mather became Dean of Students at Salve Regina, he got to know Ridgely, then in his early 20's. At that time, he told me, Beck drove a sporty little Hillman convertible. "The girls there loved him, said Mather. "He was quite the ladies' man."

But in 1974 Ridgely was named executor of his mother's estate. [796] After that, according to Ronald "Ollie" Oliver, a close friend who lived at Plaisance for a time, "Ridgely grew his hair long and started driving a Porsche." [797]

By Ridgely's own account, he followed in his parents' footsteps and began throwing large parties at the estate. "It was quite a scene for many, many, many, many years," he told me. "I would have parties like every night. Year round. Late night ones. Very late."

"Ridgely was a night owl," remembered Oliver, "he loved after-hour parties. That was the thing back then. Everybody was doing coke. Dealers would show up and everybody would buy some and stay up being brilliant all night. I went to a few, but I was more of a day person."

One party at Plaisance, into which Ollie Oliver made a legendary entrance, started early one evening a year after Mary Beck's death. Ollie's arrival was so memorable that it was written up in *The Newport Daily News* under the headline "Gate-crasher gets into party by a unique vertical approach." [798] Back then, Ollie, a dare-devil skier and yachtsman who was 25, was working as maître d' at Newport's White Horse Tavern, He'd taken up sky diving, so he decided to arrive by parachute.

"I couldn't think of a more fun way to get to the party," he told *Daily News* reporter William Kutik, at the time. [799] His intent was to drop into The Waves, the estate across Ledge Road built by famed architect John Russell Pope who'd designed the Jefferson Memorial. Pelican Lodge, the Pell residence, was adjacent to it overlooking Bailey's Beach.

But in the early evening of August 21st 1975, Ollie's prospective arrival became increasingly dangerous as the night air turned cool and a 25 knot southwest wind came up. Plaisance was just a few yards from the rocks and the turbulent ocean. So if he missed his landing zone by only a few yards, Ollie might have gone into the drink, or worse.

Gate-crasher gets into party
by a unique vertical approach

By BILL KUTIK

It was the only way to beat the party's cover charge.

Like many of the other young bar and restaurant workers in town, Ronald Oliver had no intention of missing last night's party at Plaisance, Ridgely Beck's house on the Cliff Walk off Ledge Road.

But hostess Rosalind Rustigian had no intention of blowing thousands of dollars on her end-of-season bash for the locals and was charging everybody $10 a head to get in. Besides, the 23-year-old Providence native is going to

and anyone who knows him will tell you he's a very resourceful guy. Since February, when sky-diving became his passion, Ollie has logged 66 jumps, including one last July 5 onto the grounds of Bonnie Crest on Harrison Avenue.

So he decided to combine business with pleasure (or pleasure with pleasure) and make his 67th jump onto the grounds of The Waves, next door to the party. Roz agreed to waive the entry fee.

"Actually, I just couldn't think of a more fun way to get to the party," Ollie said.

crowded the fourth-floor Sky Bar to watch the plane weave in and out of the mist.

On the third pass at 2,500 feet, Ollie jumped and for a breath-holding eight seconds or so free fell toward the water. Then the chute popped open, and one guest gasped, "God, it's full of holes."

But those were just the cut-out control panels, and the jump went routinely until about 800 feet. Then Ollie, all 115 pounds of him, got hit by a stiff gust, that carried him across Ledge Road into a neighboring yard. Photographers and onlookers

OLIVER on his way to party.

Newport Mercury August 22nd, 1975

"We were in a single engine plane that had taken off from Taunton, Mass," he told me. "We made one pass over the party and dropped an orange wind streamer. It got carried three quarters of the way across the Sakonnet River" on the other side of the island."

Now, as the plane made its final approach, the entire staff at The Clarke Cooke House on the waterfront, where Ollie spun records at The Candy Store disco, went up to the 4th floor to watch.

"Typically, you'd go out at 3,000 feet and pop the shoot at 2,500 feet," he said, "But that night I held on until I was down to 800 feet so I could be sure I was going to hit Ridgely's. My girlfriend at the time was freaking out because she saw me falling and falling. But I was just doing that to keep from getting blown across Ledge Road and into the water. Then, just a few hundred feet above the ground, a gust of wind hit, and I landed in the bushes of a neighboring yard."

Moments later as the jubilant crowd at the party surrounded him, neighbor Oatsie Charles presented Ollie with a bottle of champagne.

"That was quite a party," said Ridgely.

He went on to spend his summers in Europe as he rented out Plaisance to the high rollers who started coming to Newport to recapture the halcyon days when "The Baileys Beach crowd" ruled that part of town.

In 2003, *The New York Times* featured him, in a piece. Back then he was fighting a 40 percent increase in the tax assessment on Plaisance. "I certainly have an incentive to rent this year," Ridgely told the *Times* reporter. Without disclosing just how *much* he was charging, the story noted that "the going rate for a house like his is $40,000 to $60,000 a month." [800]

Eight years later Ridgely listed Plaisance for sale. The asking price was $11 million, [801] but he wasn't able to sell it until 2014 when it went for $5 million. Now living in much smaller quarters on John Street off Bellevue, I asked him about the story of his white rat leading to all the others.

"No, it wasn't my pet, that I recall," he told me. "Anyway, that problem got taken care of." [802] That's all he would say on that matter.

One close friend of Ridgely's, who asked not to be identified, believed that the 1971 horror classic *Willard* had been inspired by Ridgely's story. But, in fact, the film starring Bruce Davison in the title role, was adapted from the short novel *Ratman's Notebooks,* by Northern Irish author Stephen Gilbert. [803] Moreover, the plot line was the antithesis of what occurred on Ledge Road. In the film, Willard's mother learns that he's been feeding rats and orders him to destroy them, which, in defiance, he refuses to do.

That film became the 12th highest grossing release of 1971 [804] and resulted, a year later in a sequel, *Ben.* [805] Michael Jackson sung the title song, which won a Golden Globe and was nominated for an Academy Award. [806]

Still, in looking back on this bizarre story, I found it unbelievable that the Becks could survive socially in Newport after their scandalous cultivation of vermin became public, not just once but twice. So I asked Harle Tinney how a woman as refined as Mary Beck, with her lineage dating back to The 1st Baron Baltimore, could have acquiesced to it all?

"The explanation is very simple, she said. "Mary loved Ridgely. The sun rose and set with Ridgely. From the time he was born until she died, Ridgely could do no harm. So if he collected rats, that was fine with her."

CHAPTER THIRTY

RENAISSANCE MAN

The deeper I got into untangling the forensics of the homicide itself, the more interested I became in understanding the victim, Eduardo Tirella: who he was; what drove him; and why he'd continued working for Doris, given the trajectory of his career and his capabilities as a designer across multiple disciplines from fashion to feature film. I understood *why* he went to work for her in the first place. After all, she had an unlimited checkbook that allowed him to travel the world assembling priceless artworks and honing his skill set. But once he'd completed Duke Gardens in 1964, why did he *stay on*, particularly after his life in L.A. and Big Sur was becoming so full?

The first time I focused on his name was in the summer of 2018 after CNN had replayed Trump's 2016 press conference in which he'd made that boast about being able to "shoot somebody" in "the middle of Fifth Avenue." At the time, I Googled, "Doris Duke" + victim + "Newport, RI" but all of the newspaper coverage reflected the official "accident" line.

By then, I'd already spoken to several of the Newport cops who had worked the crash scene and they'd uniformly told me that they'd suspected foul play. But back in 1966 the great newspapers and wire services of the world had accepted the conclusion of the Newport PD and after that there was little else on Eduardo for decades. Even his six-year-long design of the 11 interconnected Gardens of The World at Duke Farms was dismantled by 2008. [807]

I spent weeks trying to locate any of his eight siblings who might still be alive, but all of them had died. That's when I found the obituary of his sister Anita which led me to his niece Donna. She greeted me warmly and said that virtually every day since Eduardo's death she'd prayed that the truth might come out.

It was through Donna Lohmeyer, over the last two years, that I came to appreciate the depth and breadth of the extraordinary man killed so violently and abruptly outside Rough Point.

UNDER THE WILDCAT

Eduardo Giuseppe Tirella was born on June 8th, 1924 in Dover, New Jersey, the 12th child of Severino (Sam) and Etilia Falgione Tirella, who had emigrated from Italy near Naples. [808] He was actually the second one of their children to be named Eduardo. They had lost another son at the age of 11 to pneumonia.

"In fact," Donna told me, "of the 12 kids, only 9 lived to maturity. But Eddie was closest to my mother, who was two years older. The other four sisters and three brothers were much older than the two of them. Since Eddie was the baby of the family, his mother shared a special bond with him and when he died, she passed away six weeks later -- many said of a broken heart." [809]

Sam Tirella prospered over the years, owning several meat markets, but he died when Eddie was 13, "So our uncle Al took over the family business and in 1942 he bought the Wildcat Roller Coaster at Bertrand Island, a small family amusement park on Lake Hopatcong in Mt. Arlington, New Jersey. Eddie's mother, my grandmother Etilia, owned and operated the cotton candy stand across from the coaster. During summers, all of the kids and grandkids worked at the park and Eddie, who was an aspiring singer, spent hours at The Villa (then called the

June Rose Ballroom) where another young Italian singer named Dino Martini -- soon to be known as Dean Martin -- performed. My family had a bungalow under the coaster where we stayed. In fact, my playpen was on the front porch. The cars of the coaster passed within feet and I'd wave to them going by.

"At Dover High, Eddie was very popular. He became a cheerleader and was active in theater. As they got older, he and my mother would hang out at The Wigwam dance club where Glenn Miller and Count Basie played. Uncle Eddie always had stars in his eyes, in the best sense of that phrase. He became an accomplished piano player and singer in his own right and soon dreamed of Broadway and Hollywood; aspirations that he achieved to some degree, but his entry into those worlds came through his amazing design sense and that began with fashion -- notably hats."

Eddie started working in the millinery depart-ment of Saks Fifth Ave-nue in New York City, designing hats for stars like Mae West and Lena Horne. "We believe that's where he and Edmund Kara met," said Donna, "since Edmund designed dresses for Lena. Soon Eddie parlayed his friend-ship with Mae into a two year theatrical run of 'Di-amond Lil' that started on Broadway. He not only sang in the show but de-

Eduardo after the War, when he was a young hat designer at Saks.

signed her costumes. Eventually he and Edmund moved to Los Angeles where they shared a house on Stanley Hills Place off Laurel Canyon. He wasn't concerned about being openly gay on the West Coast, but he was closeted with the family in New Jersey."

FROM HATS TO CAFES TO HOUSES

By 1951 Eduardo Tirella had established himself as one of the pre-eminent millinery designers in Beverly Hills. He was cited in January of that year by *L.A. Times* gossip columnist Hedda Hopper for his design of a hat for actress Ann Sheridan, described as "the woman with the smartest head on her shoulders." It happened at an Ambassador Hotel charity event attended by 850 women. [810]

In October he was featured, along with Oleg Cassini, as one of "Saks' famous designers" in "Inside S.F.A.," a store magazine. [811] That same month Eduardo's design of an elaborate "Marie Antoinette-like headdress" for musical star Constance Moore, was featured in *Photoplay Magazine*. [812]

The Marie Antionette head dress for Constance Moore

While hat design was his "day job," Eduardo never abandoned his dream of making it as a singer. By early 1953 he was billing himself as "Eddie Tirella." In a review of a new show at L.A.'s Café Gala, a rival to the celebrated Coconut Grove, *Hollywood Reporter* critic Jac Wilson praised Eddie's "romantic ballads and novelty songs" calling him "a high spot in the talent lineup." [813]

He was also part of a review at the legendary Cabaret Concert Theater in Silver Lake, a popular venue for a number of gay and straight performers, located at 4212 Sunset Boulevard in an old studio where D.W. Griffith had shot silent films. [814]

By the late Fifties Eddie had moved from fashion to interior and landscape design. After a year at UCLA, he'd begun renovating houses. In 1958 *The L.A. Times* did a feature titled, "Rescued By Remodeling," on his transformation of a simple frame bungalow into a showplace, "restyled with Oriental colors, textures and landscape with the flavor of the far east." [815]

Writing to Eddie's sister Anita that same month, Broadway producer Charlie Wood, who was about to mount a play with Tallulah Bankhead, visited the tiny house, which he described as "a Japanese dreamland." "Surely," he wrote, "Eddie has advanced his reputation as one of the up and coming designers in southern California." [816]

Within months, Eduardo was introduced to Peggy Lee, who asked him to use those same skills to transform her modest ranch house in Beverly Hills into an Italian-themed garden hideaway. When the finished job was showcased on CBS's *Person To Person* in 1960, the legendary singer told host Charles Collingwood, "it was done by an Italian. Ed Tirella, a friend of mine." [817]

Soon Eddie was designing custom furniture for the stars, including a four poster bed in a tent-like enclosure for James Coburn. Gossip columnist Louella Parsons, another hat client of Eddie's from the early 50's, devoted half a 1964 column to the $5,000 bed which utilized 15 different fabrics imported from Venice. It was "a surprise," she wrote, "from Coburn's wife Beverly." The bed was waiting for the actor after his return from a two month shoot in Mexico for the film "Major Dundee" in which he co-starred with Charlton Heston. [818] In 2021 dollars that custom bed would have cost $42,000. [819]

"Eduardo Tirella and Edmund Kara each had exquisite taste," said film financier Steve Ransohoff, whose father Marty hired both of them that same year for his production of *The Sandpiper*, starring Elizabeth Taylor and Richard Burton. It was Ransohoff who first discovered Sharon Tate and introduced her to Eddie and the circle of stars up at Big Sur who hung out at Nepenthe, the storied restaurant high above the coast. One of them was Kim Novak.

Kim Novak, Martin Ransohoff and Eduardo Tirella at Big Sur.

"My mother remembered just how kind Eduardo was to my twin brother Kurt and me back then," Steve told me in an interview for this book. "We were about eight years-old and our Dad wanted to take us to one of his film premiers, but we didn't have suits. When Eduardo heard that, he came over to the house in L.A. right away. He brought two suits from Saks where he'd worked, then measured us — making the chalk marks — and after the suits had been tailored, he brought them back just in time for us to make the premier." [820]

Around that same time Eduardo became enamored with Kaffe Fassett, a handsome young painter who was the son of Nepenthe's founders. When I tracked him down in London where he lives today, he shared a number of memories of Eddie as a designer and gregarious friend.

"During one of our first conversations," said Kaffe, who's now 83, "Eduardo told me that when he would decorate for people, the first thing he'd do would be to take them to the new house and sit them down. He'd make a bouquet of flowers and put it on a table, light candles and talk about the colors that the rooms could be. It all started with a bouquet of flowers. When I heard that, my mind just burst with imagination, thinking about how I would do a mural of nasturtium leaves. Eduardo always got my mind working, He was very inspiring to me as a young painter." [821]

As to Eddie's skills at transforming modest spaces, Kaffe related a story from around 1964 when he was living in an old mess hall at Anderson Creek, south of Big Sur.

"It was in the same complex where writer Henry Miller had lived," he said. "A series of old buildings that been used to house convicts working on the coast highway years before. I rented this huge space for $25 a month, which was fabulous, It was on the coast with the sea beating below and lots of flowers everywhere. When Eduardo came to visit me there, he said, 'You haven't done anything with your outdoors. It's just wild.'"

"I told him that I didn't have time to build a garden. And he said, 'Do you have the afternoon off?' I said, 'Yes,' And he said, 'Come on.' So we went to the beach and loaded a truck up with driftwood and stones and he built me a garden *literally* that same day. It was extraordinary. What Eduardo did with that garden exemplified his energy and imagination and that was very exciting to me."

FLOWERS AGAIN

Another story Kaffe told me underscored the infectious joie de vivre that Eddie inspired in other people; in this case, the woman who had founded Deetjen's Big Sur Inn, a kind of storybook wooden village of rooms constructed in the early 1930's by Helmuth Deetjen, a Norwegian immigrant and his wife Helen. They'd built much of it from material reclaimed from Monterey's Cannery Row. [822]

By the mid-Sixties Eduardo and Edmund had rented a two-story house in Mule Canyon from the Fassett family. Edmund lived there full time and carved works from redwood trees in a studio on the first floor.

Eddie commuted up from L.A. on weekends in his Morgan roadster.

"But before he and Edmund rented that place," said Kaffe, "Eduardo would stay at Deetjen's and he became fascinated by the old woman who built the Inn. At one point, in advanced age, she was holed up in her bedroom, seemingly very ill and near death. At least that's what she told everyone. So one day Eduardo said to me, 'Let's go down to the beach.' When we got there, he picked Sage and wild grasses and wildflowers and he assembled them into a beautiful bouquet. We drove to the Inn and knocked on Mrs. Deetjen's bedroom door to say hello. She was lying inside and moaning, saying, 'I don't want to die. I don't want to die...' Suddenly Eduardo grabbed the bouquet from my hands and threw open her door. He bounded over to the edge of the bed and shoved the flowers in her face, exclaiming, "You think that you're DYING? Well smell this! You're not dying, YOU'RE LIVING!' And the old woman came to, just like that!" Kaffe snapped his fingers.

"She just sat up and she started laughing... That was Eduardo Tirella, a force of positivity if there ever was one. He brought beauty to everyone who was fortunate enough to come into his life."

Pola Zanay, another artist back then, who would ride up to Bug Sur with Eddie on weekends, remembered that he was also a vegan chef, given to preparing elaborate feasts for his friends.

"Halloween was a major event at Nepenthe, where they had an annual Masked Ball," she told me. "The October before he died, Eduardo asked if I would help him decorate. He had purchased a huge pumpkin and he had a gigantic pot that he could put the pumpkin into. He filled it up with vegetables and water and cooked it in this pot. He asked me to help him decorate a really, really long table in front of the cabin and we decorated it with flowers and fall leaves. It was beautiful." [823]

Flowers were an essential element in another Eduardo story that Donna Lohmeyer told me. It happened in June of 1960, just before her 8th grade graduation. Eddie was back home in New Jersey and Donna, who had long blonde hair, was greatly anticipating her end-of-year dance.

"I needed a trim," she told me, "and a nice German neighbor of ours had a daughter who had just started beauty school. She began cutting my hair, first on one side, then the other and then she tried to even-out the first side and before I knew it, I looked like Friar Tuck. [824] But uncle Eddie rescued me. He went into our yard and picked sprigs of orange blossoms. He teased the top of my hair into half curls and tucked a white blossom into each one, turning a pumpkin into a princess in a matter of moments. All I lacked on my way to that dance were glass slippers. But that's who he was. He got so much joy out of making the lives of people around him more beautiful. It was that quality that Doris coveted so much. She knew his Hollywood career was taking off and sensed he wanted to leave her. I had a sense of it too, at the time. After all, Doris Duke had dominated New Jersey for decades. My family didn't realize it, but the two of them were on a collision course."

PART FOUR

CHAPTER THIRTY-ONE

TAYLOR, BURTON, NOVAK & TATE

On the October day in 1964 when *The Sandpiper* started shooting in Big Sur, producer Marty Ransohoff, then 37 and on a hot streak, put two other films into production. [825] After co-founding Filmways, a company that had made a fortune on rural sitcoms in the early Sixties, he'd been responsible for a string of successful features beginning with the comedy *Boys Night Out*, starring James Garner and Kim Novak, who lived in Carmel Highlands and introduced him to Big Sur. [826]

In 1962 Marty bought land and built a house there. Before long he became friends, through Novak, with Edmund Kara and his partner Eduardo Tirella. [827] A year later, on the set of one of his TV series, *Petticoat Junction*, the producer spotted a pretty 20-year-old actress named Sharon Tate whom he put under contract. [828]

She got her first feature acting role in *Eye of The Devil,* a Gothic horror film produced by Ransohoff starring David Niven. By then Marty had become so impressed by Eduardo's design skills that he hired him for the production. Eddie soon introduced Sharon to Edmund, and she made frequent trips up the coast where she stayed at Deetjen's and spent hours at the house in Mule Canyon, taking Polaroids of his work.

Eduardo with Sharon at Big Sur. Sharon with Edmund.

"We used to go up to Big Sur with my dad," remembered Steve Ransohoff. "My brother Kurt and I would watch Edmund carve at the house up the street from Nepenthe. Sharon would come by and take us on hikes to the Elf Forest behind Deetjens. We'd go down to the beach with Edmund and Eduardo hunting for Abalone off the rocks. There was a driftwood beach we'd go to with Edmund where he'd get wood to carve. It was a kind of magical time, for us." [829]

The filming of *Eye of The Devil* proved a challenge for Ransohoff who lost his first two directors and settled on a third, while having to replace Sam Peckinpah on *The Cincinnati Kid*, starring Steve McQueen, after the hard-fisted director of *The Wild Bunch,* insisted on a darker, more realistic tone for the poker-themed film. [830]

Eduardo, Niven and Sharon (in a wig) on the *Eye of The Devil* set.

"Big Sur became an oasis for Marty," said Romney Steele, the granddaughter of Bill and Lolly Fassett, who opened Nepenthe in 1949. An
accomplished chef in her own right, Romney authored, *My Nepenthe*, a
compelling memoir in which she described how the site of the restaurant
became the fixation of two other Hollywood icons, Orson Welles and
his then wife Rita Hayworth:

> Returning from San Francisco during a War Bond Drive they
> decided to head back to L.A. on the new scenic route,
> Highway One. Looking for a spot to picnic, they ventured
> up a meandering dirt road that took them to a cabin on a
> hill overlooking the south coast. Entranced by the view,
> they went looking for a realtor to sell them the cabin. As
> the story goes, they gathered up the money between them,
> put $156 down to hold the purchase, measured the kitchen
> for a new stove and the windows for curtains, and then went
> on their way, never again to return. Within a year Welles and
> Hayworth divorced and later sold the cabin and property to
> my grandparents. [831]

Martin Ransohoff was so taken with Big Sur that he decided to use it as
the backdrop for his next major production. He wrote a 38 page outline
for *The Sandpiper* over a weekend, later engaging Dalton Trumbo to write
the script, sharing screenplay credit with Michael Wilson. The plot revolved around a Bohemian painter and single mother who lived in what
was described as "a shack," above the Coast. When her son is sent to an
Episcopal school for troubled boys, she meets a buttoned down minister
who quickly falls in love with her, only to face the moral dilemma of
leaving his loyal wife and ending his religious career.

After offering the lead to Kim Novak who passed, Ransohoff flew
to London where he presented the starring roles to Elizabeth Taylor and
Richard Burton. They had just made *The Yellow Rolls Royce*, following their
scandalous tour de force on-screen and off in *Cleopatra*.

The principal target of the world's paparazzi at the time, the couple
signed-on after Ransohoff guaranteed a $1 million payday for Taylor
and half that for Burton, who for tax reasons, could only commit to
shooting 29 days of the film in the U.S. [832] Then, after director William

Wyler got delayed, Ransohoff hired Oscar winner Vincent Minnelli and production commenced with Eva Marie Saint, another Academy Award winner, cast to play Burton's wife.

In an interview for her book in 2008, Ransohoff told Romney Steele that "Eduardo pushed me for the Nepenthe element in the film." By then, Marty was so impressed with Tirella that he was quoted as saying, "Anything he touches can turn into something beautiful." [833] He hired him to design the interiors for Taylor's "shack" and engaged Edmund Kara to carve the nude bust of Liz for in the film. They each received upfront credits and Eduardo appeared in several scenes, including a folk dancing sequence shot on Nepenthe's Terrace.

Eduardo, third from left, being filmed with a line of folk dancers for *The Sandpiper.*

Ransohoff then cast his protegé Sharon in a secondary role, but as he later confessed, when he brought her to the set, Taylor, jealous of Tate's beauty, chided him playfully, "How dare you bring that girl here while *mother* is on the stage." [834]

Playful or not, all of Tate's scenes ended up on the cutting room floor, though she attended the premier. By then, Ransohoff had advanced Sharon's career immensely by casting her in *The Fearless Vampire Killers*, a horror/black comedy, directed by the man who would become her future husband, Roman Polanski. Immediately following *The Sandpiper* she co-starred in *Don't Makes Waves*, Ransohoff's take on the craze for Malibu surfer films. In that film Eduardo was billed as "technical advisor" and played another cameo. [835] Over the next two years, his friendship with Sharon deepened as she spent more and more time up at Big Sur.

According to a biography of Elizabeth Taylor by Darwin Porter and Danforth Prince, which relied on interviews with her long time gay assistant Richard Hanley, [836] Burton, who was said to be bisexual, became smitten with Eduardo. One weekend during production, after Eddie had booked a singing job in San Francisco, Porter and Prince wrote that Burton accompanied him there, while Liz was rumored to have stayed behind in Monterey to spend time with the novelist and screenwriter Peter Viertel. Then married to Deborah Kerr, Viertel's many screen credits included *The African Queen*. According to Hanley (per Porter and Prince) the Burton-Tirella San Francisco trip "caused some jealous tension between Burton and Minnelli," who was also reported to be bi-sexual [837] and rumored to have "wanted Tirella for himself." [838]

Whether any of that was true, it was Eduardo's personal magnetism, along with his design skills that endeared him to so many people including Kaffe Fassett who worked on the dance sequences for *The Sandpiper*. At one point after shooting wrapped at Big Sur, the production moved to the Boulogne Studios in Paris where a reproduction of Nepenthe's terrace was built.

"When we worked together in Paris I stayed in a charming hotel with Eduardo," Kaffe told me in an interview for this book. [839] "I had some wild adventures alongside him, going cruising. We were very close. Though there was nothing sexual between us, I loved and admired him, and he was hugely supportive of my career as a painter. Eduardo was also a dreamer. He told me how, when he was young, he would drive by Doris Duke's property in New Jersey every few days and say to himself, 'One day I'm going to go into that place and see what it's all about. Now here I am creating The Gardens of The World with Doris Duke.'"

Kaffe's perspective on Eduardo was crucial for me in researching this book because he was the only surviving friend and contemporary of him, I could find, who understood what it was like to be a gay man in the 1960's. More importantly, as he related to me and recounted in his book, *Dreaming In Color*, Kaffe spent a memorable weekend with Eddie and Doris at Rough Point:

> At one point, Doris sent her private plane to fetch me and take me to meet them at her other family estate on the ocean in Newport, Rhode Island. It was a stormy night, but my flight got through. Eduardo and Doris were held up in New York and would come in the next day. When Doris and Eduardo finally arrived, the house came alive—dogs, music, conversation.
>
> Doris allowed me free run of the house to paint anything I wanted, so I set up my easel in a corner of the enormous kitchen and did a study of brown and white dishes and fruit. She was very appalled by that. She said, "You have all the treasures of Europe and the Orient here and you're picking bowls of fruit on a marble table in the kitchen?" [840]

Kaffe told me that when Eduardo traveled with Doris collecting art treasures, he would call her "Mrs. Green" so that "If they went into an antique shop, nobody would know that she was the richest woman in the world." [841]

"One thing that was sad to me," he said, was that Doris so wanted to be a jazz singer. That was her great longing, and of course, Eduardo was this incredible jazz man. He was always playing music and singing, and they'd go into clubs and sing, but when she sang, to me, it was in this wispy, sad little voice. So threadbare. She was so very big and tall and handsome; you'd think that she'd have a deep throaty voice like Marlene Dietrich. But her's was the voice of a child."

With respect to Big Sur, Kaffe said that Eduardo had "opened his eyes" to it. "One day he took me back into the canyon behind where he and Edmund lived. He looked at this tiny little waterfall, and the little ferns growing around it and he said, 'This is complete beauty. You couldn't create art any better than this.' And I stood there rather naïve. I had grown up in this place. To me it was ordinary, but he made me see it as magic.'"

Eduardo Tirella in 1966, months before he died, still scouting art treasures in Europe for Doris Duke.

LEARNING OF HIS DEATH

There seemed to be something spiritual in the way that Kaffe learned Eduardo was gone.

"I had a very, very strange mystical thing happen," he told me. "In 1966 I was walking down a street in London. I had a new boyfriend at the time, and I said to him, 'You have to meet my friend Eduardo. He's just the most amazing man.' Literally just before that, one of the songs he'd sing came into my mind. 'You're Nearer Than My Head Is To My Pillow.' [3] Just then, my boyfriend said he needed to pop into a shop and a few moments later he came out with a newspaper in his hand. He said, 'There's an article that says Tirella. Wasn't that his name?' And he opened the paper to a headline. He looked at me and said, 'He's just been killed.' I couldn't believe it, because Eduardo was one of the most alive people I've ever known."

---

3   A song Judy Garland sang and recorded at her Carnegie Hall concert.

Four days after he died, Eduardo was laid to rest in the family plot at St. Mary's Cemetery in his hometown of Dover, New Jersey. The burial following a solemn high Requiem Mass at Sacred Heart Church was attended by hundreds of his friends and extended family. Taylor and Burton sent flowers. Martin Ransohoff and Kim Novak each sent chrysanthemums. [842]

For her thoughts on Eddie, I reached out to the legendary star of *Vertigo* and so many other memorable films. She sent me this reply:

"I loved him very much and miss his sweet voice in the songs he'd sing at parties and in the forest behind his house in Big Sur. So pure and filled with kindness and love for all creatures great and small. He did not deserve his ending!" [843]

Not long after the funeral, Peggy Lee sent this note to Anita, Eddie's sister:

"Words are never adequate, but somehow I felt I must try and tell you how much I share your love for Eddie. He will always live in our hearts. It would give you comfort if you could hear the beautiful things that are said about him almost every day by his friends to whom he has given so much. I have a particularly warm spot in my heart for you, because he had expressed his love for you so many times." [844]

As to the funeral itself, the headline in *The New York Daily News* under a page-wide photo of the gravesite read, "Doris Absent From Jersey Funeral Of Her Long-Time Friend, Eduardo." [845]

The heiress who was responsible for his death *did* send an arrangement of roses and the staff from Duke Farms drove up with flowers. But David Rimmer, the estate manager there, who'd been earlier barred from Rough Point by Duke's business manager Pete Cooley, told me that his offer to participate in the funeral was spurned.

"One of Eduardo's brothers had asked me to be a pall bearer and I was happy to do it because Eduardo and I had been so close, but when I asked Miss Duke she said, 'See Pete Cooley about it,' and when I called him repeatedly, he just hung up on me, so I didn't do it and I always felt bad about it. There was just no way Cooley wanted me involved. [846]

DORIS REPORTEDLY CONFESSES

As I reviewed the evidence of Sharon Tate's close friendship with Eduardo and the kind way that she'd treated Marty Ransohoff's eight-year-old sons, I was drawn back to the incident which began this book. It involved Sharon's sister Patti, then eleven, who had an abrupt encounter with Doris Duke's caretaker at Falcon Lair, months before Sharon was killed.

The nervous way that she'd entered the old Valentino estate to pick up Patti was indicative of Sharon's state of mind back then, two and a half years after Eddie's close circle of friends came to believe that Doris had killed him with intent.

Of course no one could say for sure what was in the billionaire's mind when she got behind the wheel of the Dodge Polara, but a month or so after my investigation of the death was published in *Vanity Fair*, I got an intriguing email. The subject matter read only "Doris Duke" and the message was cryptic. "If you care to give me a call… something of interest for you on Doris… I was (her) lover for five months – after the (man) she killed."

The email was written by Peter Byrne, an Irishman who had enlisted in the Royal Air Force during World War II and flown dozens of missions as a reconnaissance pilot. He later became a big game hunter and adventurer with multiple expeditions to the Himalayas. In 1967 he was running safaris to Africa and India.

When I contacted him in August of 2020, he was 90 years old, but seemed to have the energy and mental acuity of a 50 year old. He was happy to discuss his time in Hawaii with Doris Duke.

"I met her in June of 1967," he told me, "at a party in Honolulu, thrown by a friend of mine there named George Frelinghuysen." [847]

As reported in a piece from *The Honolulu Advertiser* on May 30th, 1967, Frelinghuysen was a "millionaire art collector… dubbed 'the host with the most,' who had arrived in Hawaii and moved into the presidential suite (plus an adjoining suite) at the Kahala Hilton Hotel." There he was expected to host a series of parties in the coming weeks. [848]

"Doris was there one night, and we met," Byrne told me. "I went home to her place at Diamond Head and stayed the night. I was hunting in those days. I had my own Safari company in India and Nepal, and I worked for 7 months of each year. Then, moving into the Monsoon Season starting in May, I took 5 months off."

Byrne said that for all that time he and Doris were virtually inseparable. "We lived in Los Angeles at Falcon Lair and in New Jersey and at her apartment in New York as well as Honolulu. But when it came to October, I wasn't feeling good about being with her. She made me nervous. She was very vindicative. She was very powerful, and she could be very, very mean. So right about then at the end of October, I said, 'I've got to go back to hunting. I've got bookings, and she said, 'If you walk out that door you're never coming back.' And to myself , I said, 'Great. Wonderful.'

"I left her at the end of October and saw her again a couple of times. Years later I was in New York and she called me. She had a nephew, Walker Inman. She wanted to get him out of her hair for a month and she said, 'I hear that you're going down to climb Kilimanjaro' and I said, 'Yes.' She said, 'Will you take him with you?' And I did. He wasn't a bad kid. Sadly, he later killed himself with an overdose of drugs. Anyway, (Doris and I) never lived together again."

At that point in the conversation I asked him if she'd ever spoken about Eduardo Tirella. Without skipping a beat, Byrne said, "I know that she killed him, because she told me."

All I could say was, "Wow." After the deal she'd made with the Newport police, I hadn't expected that Doris would make a confession, but the former RAF pilot was adamant.

"I'll tell you her exact words, which are in my mind to this day," he said. "We started talking about him and what happened with the car. As we talked, she was very cautious, but her exact words were, 'He got what he deserved. *Nobody* two times me.' Those were her exact words."

I had to take that for what it was: the account of a man who had reached out to me "over the transom," but his well-documented bona fides and his relationship to Frelinghuysen and Hawaii at the same time Doris Duke was there had checked out.

Based on what I'd learned from many of Eduardo's friends, I believed that Doris Duke had coveted his *professional* relationship with her as chief designer. But what if her jealously went deeper? What if she had harbored *sexual* feelings for the handsome designer who was twelve years younger? And if so, who did she think he was "two-timing" her with? She not only knew he was close to Edmund Kara, but she'd hired the two of them [849] to do the design work on The Self Realization Fellowship, a spiritual center she was funding high in the hills above Los Angeles. [850]

Then I thought of that weekend she'd spent at Rough Point with Eduardo and Kaffe Fassett. Though the two gay men were just friends, could Doris, whom Byrne called "a nymphomaniac," have suddenly become jealous because she *imagined* that there was actually something between *them* and she wanted Eduardo for herself?

In 2007, writing in *The L.A. Times,* Dr. David Buss, a Ph.D. and psychologist, concluded that "jealousy is possibly the most destructive emotion housed in the human brain. It's the leading cause of spousal murder worldwide (and) those who experience jealousy (themselves) suffer too. They feel anxious, depressed, angry, humiliated, out of control, sometimes suicidal."[851]

Every one of those qualities seemed to describe Doris Duke.

She'd killed Eduardo literally minutes *after* he'd announced he was leaving, following seven years as her "constant companion." That happened within months of that violent incident at Falcon Lair, where she reportedly got her jaw broken by Joe Castro, whom she'd stabbed in a jealous rage three years before that. Castro had told his L.A. lawyer Edward Brown that he'd twice saved Doris from suicide. In the months before the Falcon Lair incident she'd been depressed about the death of her second husband, Porfirio Rubirosa. Doris was notorious for her heavy use of drugs and alcohol. Could all of that explain the central element in any murder case: *motive?* And if she *did* confess to Peter Byrne was it because she harbored some sense of guilt?

It all seemed in keeping with what I learned after I located the first police officer who'd arrived outside Rough Point moments after Doris Duke had crushed Eduardo Tirella to death.

CHAPTER THIRTY-TWO

THE CASE
FOR MURDER

In Rhode Island's criminal law of homicide, the degree of culpability — and therefore punishment — hinges on the issue of intent. Apart from "murder one" -- typically reserved for the killing of law enforcement officers or other special circumstances [852] — second degree murder is a function of "malice aforethought" as it has been for centuries. [853] Traffic deaths are usually associated with "manslaughter," [854] because they involve "accidents" which are, by definition, unintended. Keep in mind that in 1971 Doris Duke was found civilly negligent in Eduardo's death. So there was clearly enough evidence to charge her under the Rhode Island Motor Vehicle statute with, "Driving so as to endanger, resulting in death." [855] That didn't happen. But even if she'd been so charged back in 1966, her lawyers could have argued that the homicide was unforeseen and *that* might have mitigated any punishment — unless she'd been drinking.

At the time, her pro tem physician, Dr. McAllister, had insisted, "There was absolutely no evidence of alcohol in the blood of either Miss Duke or Tirella" [856] and caretaker Harold McFarlane, whom Registry investigator Perrotti *did* interview, told him that "Miss Duke seldom drank alcoholic beverages." [857]

But common-law husband Joe Castro told his L.A. attorney that Doris had used "alcohol and drugs to excess, starting in the mid 1950's." [858] Leon Amar, a Spanish-Moroccan decorator, who became her lover in the late '60's told Stephanie Mansfield that "Doris drank a lot. When she drank, she became violent... She threw a bottle of wine at me once and nearly killed me." [859] Mansfield also reported that Doris was known to drink heavily, even in the afternoon. [860]

In the AVIS case lawyers representing Duke's interests were so audacious, they actually asserted that, "The death of Edward Tirella was proximately caused by his own act or neglect." [861]

But the lab report on *his* blood showed that he'd tested negative for alcohol or barbiturates. [862] Could the same be said for Doris? We'll never know. That's because, in contrast to what Dr. McAllister reported, Chief Radice admitted, "We could not administer sobriety tests because of her injuries." [863] Normally, if "the fix," hadn't been in, the question of whether Doris was under the influence would have been central to manslaughter charges.

WHAT ABOUT MURDER?

Intentional homicide wasn't even under consideration back then, but what about it? Under Rhode Island law, all records of "accidental" deaths have to be retained permanently by the investigating authorities. [864] But like so many other official records in this story, the file on the homicide of Eduardo Tirella was reported missing from Newport Police archives for decades. [865]

I later obtained a copy from a confidential source, but even before I opened it, I'd uncovered evidence that the truth behind Tirella's death was actually proven *within hours* after crash. It was documented by the Newport Police Department's chief accident investigator whose findings went far beyond manslaughter. In fact, he concluded that Doris Duke had acted with intent.

To consider that, let's review what is undisputed. We know that Eduardo got out of the car and walked to the gates. [866] From Doris's October 9th statement we know that he had just enough time to unwrap the unlocked chain from around the gates when the station wagon "leaped forward." [867] The damage to the gates shows that they were struck virtually head-on at a point when they were still closed.

The Rough Point gates closed inward the morning after the crash as one of Doris Duke's German Shepherds roams in the background.
(Jerry Taylor photo)

With the help of Donna Lohmeyer I got Tirella's official autopsy report which had been buried for more than five decades in the basement of the RI Medical Examiner's office, misfiled under the name "TIRELLA, Edmund G." Published here for the first time, it proves that his injuries were entirely inconsistent with Chief Joseph Radice's official theory of the crash.

Doris Duke had told the police and Radice had assured the press that "Tirella… was crushed against the irons gates." [868] But the autopsy report, filed by Dr. James J. Flanagan, shows that except for a fracture of his right hip, all other injuries to Eduardo's body were *above* the waist. He sustained zero damage to his legs. [869]

Eduardo Tirella's autopsy report filed under the name Tirella, Edmund G.

The Dodge Polara was six and a half feet wide. [870] It was idling 15 feet from the gates -- more than enough room to open them without Doris having to put the vehicle in reverse. Then, by Doris's own account, it "leaped forward" at a "fast" speed from "a dead stop." [871]

All of the damage to the gates was *below* Tirella's waist. So, if Doris Duke *had* crushed him against those gates as she'd told Chief Radice, why were there no injuries to his lower body?

The answer began to emerge when I got an unpublished photo taken by the actual news photographer who'd covered the event. A heavily cropped version of it had already been published on that Facebook Group, "If you Grew Up in Newport." It was posted by a woman named Jane Maguire whom I soon learned was married to John Quigley. [872] John's stepfather Ed had been a freelance photographer at the time of Tirella's death. In fact, it was his compelling coverage of the homicide scene that led to a permanent job on *The Newport Daily News*. [873]

When I started working at the paper, eight months later, Ed Quigley was one of the two staff photographers along with Ron LaChance. It was Quigley who later took the photo of Stephen Robertson's "perp walk" the night he surrendered to Newport Police at Headquarters.

So I reached out to John and Jane who went down into their basement on Long Island and found a series of Ed's negatives and photos. What they sent me, published first in the July/August issue of *Vanity Fair* and now in this book, took the investigation to a whole new level. The image below is a much wider angle of the post-crash photo, with compelling new details.

Ed Quigley's shot from inside the gates at Rough Point shortly after the crash. Sgt. Fred Newton can be seen working the scene at lower right.

First, there are several witnesses to the left of the damaged gates. One of them was Paul Faerber, who grew up to be a Newport Fire Captain. It was Paul who went up into the attic of Fire Headquarters and located the logbook recording the response times of the Newport and Middletown "rescue wagons" that late afternoon.

Near a bicycle, you can see two of the balusters that snapped off the gates as they were blown out over the two-by-five-inch metal *stop*. Located in the lower foreground of the shot, you can see that it was riveted into the concrete to keep the freely-swinging gates inward. The owner of that Stingray bike was Steve Mey (not pictured) then a nine year old paperboy who delivered *The Newport Daily News* along the "Avenue route."

He had just dropped off a paper with Arthur Maloney, the night watchman at Marble House down the street, when he returned to his route and peddled south toward Rough Point. [874] By the time he got to Rock Cliff, the Harold Vanderbilt estate, Mey told me, "I heard this loud noise and stopped. I couldn't have been more than a long block away and I saw this white station wagon smashed against a tree across from the Duke place. So I immediately headed back to Arthur's, burst in and told him what had happened. He ran upstairs to call it in, so I got back on my bike, cut across the Marble House lawn and came out through the gates onto Bellevue. By the time I got to Rough Point where the gates were bent and pushed out, I heard sirens."

Joseph G. Silvia, the blacksmith who'd repaired those gates, told me that, "They were exceptionally heavy. Wrought iron. It would have taken quite a bit of force for them to go up and over that stop." [875]

THE MAN WHO CRACKED THE CASE

The photo at left reveals something else significant: the man in the fedora hat at the lower right of the frame who was inspecting the gates. His name was Fred Newton Jr. A detective sergeant at the time, he was promoted to lieutenant the next year. I actually found a *Daily News* profile of him that I'd written on the methods he used in training all of the Newport PD's recruits. [876]

Newport Daily News, Friday, December 1, 1967   7

The New Breed: Eight Rookies Train

By PETER A. LANCE

The era of the round faced, neighborhood policeman is over. With crime a multi - billion dollar business, a corruptive s c i e n c e, today's policeman must be the composite of a barrister, court justice, psychologist, medic, ballistics expert and super - sleuth.

At Marlborough Street headquarters, eight rookies are hearing that being a policeman means more than just directing traffic or chasing pranksters.

Since Nov.' 13, when they were sworn in at City Hall, the new patrolmen have undergone extensive textbook and field training. At the conclusion of their six - week basic instruction course, they will have logged more than 120 hours in the classroom and on the beat.

"Police work today is a far cry from what it was in the twenties and thirties," said Lt. Frederick Newton, supervisor of the training program. "A policeman has to know more, and he has to be able to use his knowledge in a technologically advanced society.

"When the new men were sworn in, the chief told them that when he started on the department 30 years ago they gave him a badge, a gun and a nightstick, and sent him out on his beat. Times have changed. Today when a man starts out we make sure he knows his business."

The six week orientation period is grueling and expensive. Each of the recruits paid $140 for a "basic issue" uniform consisting of a shirt, trousers

visiting lecturers, expects in various criminology fields l i k e Robert Harmon, state narcotics inspector, who will speak to the men on drug abuse.

"I never realized there was so much to being a policeman," said one of the rookies at a riot gun drill recently on Goat Island.

"You know it's funny, people seem to act differently towards you when they find out you are joining the force," said recruit Charles Dwyer of 3 Tyler St. "A few of the old friends act coldly towards you, but t h e great majority of them respect you."

The seven other men at the session snugly dressed in nylon overcoats agreed.

Like several of the other recruits, firearms are not a novelty to Dwyer. In the Marines he received the marksmanship medal and was a prize winning boxer.

Recruit Eugene J. Sullivan of 28 Fair St. was discharged recently from the Air Force where he spent four years in the military police. "Recruit William N. Clapper Jr. (of 9 Barney Court) is certainly no stranger to firearms," Lt. Newton said. "He's been hunting since he was 14 years old."

"Each day one of the recruits is chosen corporal to inspect his teammates and act as squad leader of the day's activities," Lt. Newton said. "I think the responsibility is healthy for the men and it brings them closer together as a team."

Morning inspection for the young officers is at 8:15 a.m. Then ahead the recruits

though not ' compulsory, has been very good," he said.

A map of the city looms like an enormous pie on the wall in Lt. Newton's office, divided into e i g h t segments called 'tracts' which are subdivided into the 17 beats manned daily by the department's 84 men. The nine new recruits, who will begin manning these beats early next year, will be considerably better equipped than the Keystone constables of yesteryear to see that the pie urban remains intact.

"In addition Lt. John Hopkins is working towards his bachelor's degree at the URI extension in Providence, and Capt. Jeremiah Sullivan recently completed 12 weeks of study at the FBI National Academy for Police Work in Washington."

Twenty- four members of the Auxiliary Police Force are attending weekly volunteer lectures given at headquarters by Lt. Newton. "The attendance,

IN THE CLASSROOM — Lt. Frederick W. Newton Jr., instruction supervisor and statistical analyst of the Police Department, conducts a lecture on recent Supreme Court decisions affecting police work. Eight new recruits and a ninth who will join them after Christmas will raise the manpower level of the department to 84 men.

Sgt. Newton was known as a straight shooter and a professional who always conducted himself by the book. Decades ago, I'd lost touch with Fred, whose nickname was "Fig," and he'd died at the age of 70 in 1999. But six years after that fateful crash, he'd risen in the department to become Assistant Police Chief and by 1980 he had the top job, Chief of Police.[877] My sense was that if anyone had discovered what really happened at Rough Point it was Fred Newton and I finally learned what *he'd* learned after I located the first officer to respond.

"HE ROLLED UP ON THE HOOD"

Edward Angel had been a rookie patrolman assigned to "The Avenue beat." He'd just gone on duty that night at 5:00 pm and within minutes, the radio crackled in his unit with word of an accident. He hit the roof lights and sped to the scene. This is what he told me he found on arrival:

"There was a woman inside the vehicle. She was extremely upset. I looked down and found someone underneath the car all rolled up. I was inexperienced and young, so I guess I blurted out, 'He's under the car.' That sent her into shock.

"She jumped out and thank God, there was a young Navy nurse there — Judith Thom - and I asked if she could help her." [878] I was just focused on whoever was under the vehicle; whether he was still alive."

Later, after the two Rescue wagons arrived and Newport's truck extricated the body, Angel, who had been on the job less than a year at that point, pulled out a pad and pen, and started to make a sketch of the scene.

"I walked into Bellevue, looked down and I saw some skin and blood," he said. "I drew a diagram of what I thought had been the point of impact between the subject and the vehicle -- where I thought he'd been run over."

Not sure, at that point, who Tirella was or his relation to the woman he now realized was Doris Duke, patrolman Angel's first thought was that she might have hit *a pedestrian* crossing the Avenue after she'd gone through the gates.

"I submitted my findings," he recalled, "and the next day, before I was to go back on duty, I got called in by Sergeant Newton, who'd been my training officer. He took me back up to the scene and explained to me how the gates, which normally opened inward, had been pushed out. He showed me markings on the gates that suggested somebody had been forced up on the hood of the car. Then he walked me back into Bellevue, explaining that the blood and the skin that I'd found was from when the body rolled off and fell in front of the car. At that point it was rolled over..." [879]

I'd been conducting the interview with retired officer Angel over the phone and I wasn't sure I'd heard him correctly.

"Are you telling me that Fred Newton thought that Eduardo Tirella went up on the hood of the wagon *before* it hit the gate?" Angel was quick to respond. "That's what he told me. That was his theory of the crash, and that at some point after the gates blew open, she hesitated and tapped the brakes and he rolled off. At that point he was run over by the vehicle and dragged to the point where he was still underneath it when it hit the tree."

The shocking visual image of what he told me prompted a number of questions: When he went up on the hood, was Eduardo *facing* Doris on the other side of the windshield? If his body hadn't rolled off, could he have survived the crash?

The significance of Edward Angel's account was groundbreaking. Based on what he told me regarding Sgt. Newton's calculations, Doris Duke had committed an act of intentional murder. In fact, leading up to it, she had engaged in four affirmative/voluntary acts prior to the Dodge Polara "leaping forward" from "a dead stop."

First, she'd slid over behind the wheel. Next, she'd released the parking brake by hand. She'd then moved the wheel-mounted shift lever from "park" to "drive" and finally, she'd hit the accelerator. The wagon surged forward and struck Tirella who went up on the hood.

But instead of "crushing" him against the gates, as Chief Radice had claimed, Eduardo remained on the hood, alive, as the Dodge blew through the gates with enough force that it bent them and knocked out five of the 34 balusters. It was only *after* Doris hesitated, tapping the brakes, that the victim rolled off onto Millionaire's Row and she made a conscious decision to keep going.

The parallel tire-wide gouge marks "an inch-and-a-half to two-inches deep," which Robert Aughey had photographed 30 feet back, support that sequence of events, as do the tire marks that Lewis Perrotti found along the gravel inside the gate.

The 1966 Dodge Polara was 18 feet long.[880] The rear tires were three feet from the back bumper, so the math would have been right: the front bumper 15 feet from the gate – the tires gouges in the gravel 15 feet back from there. Edward Friedman, attorney for the Tirella family, had made an uncontested statement at trial that, "Tirella was dragged and was pinned beneath the car when it stopped."[881] It now seemed clear that he was dragged from the very location where Edward Angel had first noticed the blood and the skin. I went back and re-examined Eduardo's Death Certificate, reproduced in Chapter One, and found evidence of precisely the same thing. It read, "Decedent struck by auto while opening iron gates and then dragged under the vehicle."

Ed Quigley's photo of the underside of the Dodge Polara wagon with what appears to be blood at lower right.

In the newly discovered shot showing Sgt. Newton, no residue of blood or skin is visible anywhere near the gate stop. But another photo by Ed Quigley taken from *under* the Dodge after Tirella's body had been removed, suggests that Doris had dragged him across Bellevue to the tree.

In that shot above, just below the left rear tire you can see a length of pipe from the post-and-rail fence on the Quatrel estate and to the right of that, just below it, a small pool of what looks like blood. The rear differential also appears to be blood stained.

Curiously, it was the negative of that very photo that went missing from *The Newport Daily News* archives at the Historical Society. And yet, John Quigley's wife Jane found the print (above) made in 1966.

What's more, when I interviewed him, Robert Aughey Jr., Tirella's nephew, recalled that the morning after the crash he noticed a sticky substance near where his uncle's body had come to rest.

"I remember kneeling down and putting my fingers in it," he told me. "Lifting them up, they were red with blood." [882]

Looking back at Eduardo's Death Certificate there's nothing in it to support Chief Radice's public statement that he'd been "crushed" against the gates. In fact, the graphic description of his injuries support a finding that he'd been crushed under the wheels of the wagon:

"Fractures of skull, ribs (rt) side of chest; Fractured right humerus, hip and 6 and 7 dorsal vertebrae; Subarachnoid hemorrhages; Transection of dorsal cord. Rupture of rt. lung and bilateral hemothorax. Multiple tears of spleen and liver. Multiple abrasions and contusions of body surface." [883]

The forensic evidence to support Sgt. Newton's "up on the hood" analysis is clear and convincing and a number of long retired police officers from the Newport, PD who worked the case, now agree.

CHAPTER THIRTY-THREE

"IT MOVED
LIKE A ROCKET"

I reached out to retired Newport Police detective Al Conti, who had spent the last 20 years of a 28 year career in plain clothes. He was a veteran of many investigations on and off Bellevue Avenue, including multiple jewel thefts from Bois Doré which he solved. At one point he also recovered a valuable painting stolen from the home of Nuala Pell, wife of the Senator. I asked him about Fred Newton's theory of the crash as recounted by officer Angel.

"If it was me that night," said Conti, "and I'm facing the car, my first instinct would be to jump up on the hood. What happened to Mr. Tirella was outrageous, no matter what the cause, but to think that he might have seen his own death coming is an awful prospect to consider." [884]

As to the cover-up of the case by the Newport, PD I tracked down Norman Mather, the 20-year veteran of the Department who retired in 1984 as an Inspector and earlier recounted the story of Mrs. Beck. On the night of Eduardo's death he got to the crash scene not long after Patrolman Angel had arrived and Doris Duke had just emerged from her run into Rough Point. At that moment, he told me, she was in the middle of Bellevue Avenue, crying.

"So I said, 'Miss Duke, my name is Patrolman Mather. Were you in the car?' And she kept on crying. She wouldn't answer me." Just then, Mather said, "Chief Radice arrived in his black Chrysler. It had the seal of the City of Newport on the door, but it was otherwise unmarked. So the Chief got out, walked over to me and said, 'Mather, I'll take over. You go back to the station and type it out.'" [885] The retired Inspector then had a vivid recollection of Radice escorting Doris Duke "arm-in-arm" into Rough Point as Sergeant Don Bergeron arrived and took immediate command of the scene.

An unpublished photo of the Dodge wagon 45 minutes after Doris Duke burst through the gates of Rough Point. The police officer pointing at right was Sgt. Don Bergeron. (Ed Quigley photo).

Later, back at Newport Police headquarters, Mather put an official accident report form (in triplicate) into a typewriter and proceeded to follow the Chief's orders. "Suddenly," he said. "Sgt. Bergeron rushed in and pulled out my original and my copies with the carbon paper. He crumpled them up. So I said, 'What are you doing?' And he said, 'This matter is being taken care of by *Chief Radice*. You don't have to do any more.' And with that, my report got thrown into a trash can."

Mather speculated that after the Chief walked into Rough Point with Doris something had changed. "Did he make a deal with her? I don't know. But the next day I went up to Radice's office on the second floor and I asked him, 'Hey Chief, what's going on?' He looked up at me and said, "Mather, I'm the Chief. What I say goes. Now get out of my office.'"

Another Patrolman who arrived on the scene that night was Bill Watterson. In the small world of Newport, Bill, now retired after 30 years, is the first cousin of Brad Watterson, another classmate of mine from De La Salle who later lived around the corner from Dr. Phillip McAllister's office.

"When I got there, said Watterson, "Clem Brown from Pelham Garage, who rented the wagon to Doris, had his tow truck lifting it up. I had the sedan version of that Dodge Polara and it was very powerful. It moved like a rocket. So when she hit those gates, she had to be really going, to do that kind of damage."

After the Middletown Rescue wagon took Doris to Newport Hospital, Watterson went to the hospital's Emergency Room expecting to find her there. "But she wasn't in the E.R.," he remembered. "She was in the old waiting room on the Friendship Street side of the hospital —what was then the main entrance."

Watterson told me that Doris was "in the lobby, off to the side, on the phone." He didn't know who she was talking to, but when she hung up, he was able to question her briefly.

"She was holding what looked like a rag up to her mouth," he said. "She might have had a bloody lip, but she had no other physical injuries beyond superficial cuts or bruises; what I used to call 'steering wheel injuries.' She said, 'I don't have my license with me,' but I got her date of birth and a brief story of what happened."

"Doris said that (after Tirella got out) she'd slid over behind the wheel and when she did, she put it in gear. It then jolted forward." Soon after that, Watterson remembered, "The nurses were trying to get her to go. I don't know if she was waiting for phone calls or calling her lawyer, but I went back up to the scene up on Bellevue."

Watterson's account of briefly questioning Doris dovetails with the interrogatories from the AVIS case that I found in The National Archives. In them she said she'd "discussed the accident with police" on the night of Tirella's death.[886] That explained the similar account reported by *The Newport Daily News* the next day at a time when Doris was being hidden from state investigators.

Bill Watterson retired in 1995 as a veteran detective in the Bureau of Criminal Investigation. I asked him pointedly if he believed there had been a cover-up by Chief Radice in the Tirella homicide. He responded without hesitation: "There's no if, and, or but about it. In the old police Department under Radice if you were a patrolman you were a peon. Old Joe called the plays, and *nobody* was in a position to buck him if they wanted to keep their badge."

THE MISSING REPORT

Throughout my investigation, which started with a blank page and a hunch, the most important single document that eluded me was the official report of The Newport Police Department. When former *Washington Post* reporter Stephanie Mansfield was researching her definitive Duke biography *The Richest Girl In The World* in 1990, she wrote to Eduardo's sister Anita and noted that she was unable to "locate the file" on his death at the Newport PD. [887]

Newspaper coverage of the 1971 Tirella wrongful death trial detailed how that police report included transcripts of Miss Duke's two "interviews" with Newport Police after the crash. Both were entered into evidence, but the trial transcript had disappeared from state judicial archives.

Since the Newport police cleared Doris on the basis of those interviews, that elusive file would have been the best evidence of a police cover-up. But even without it, I reached the conclusion that Tirella was murdered by the possessive heiress and that the police brass had suppressed the evidence, allowing her to escape criminal charges.

My findings were based on hundreds of pieces of empirical evidence I'd uncovered and analyzed surrounding the crash and its aftermath. The process involved dozens of interviews with police officers, fact witnesses, the Rough Point staff, friends of Duke and Tirella, the discovery of the previously hidden autopsy report and the crash scene photos that confirmed Sgt. Fred Newton's analysis within hours of the death.

As related to me by retired Patrolman Angel, Sgt. Newton determined that Eduardo had gone "up on the hood" of the Dodge Polara.

Then, after blasting through the wrought iron gates, Doris braked for a moment, causing Tirella to roll off, whereupon she drove forward with intent—dragging him to his death.

That's what I learned, even *without* the official report. In Chapter Eighteen I discussed my obsession with finding it. Then, after searching for more than a year, I got it.

Except for withholding Sgt. Newton's "hood" analysis, which would have surely demanded Miss Duke's immediate arrest, I was gratified to learn that 95% of the findings in that official file were in sync with my own. It not only included the Newport PD's two "transcripts" reproduced in Chapter Seven, but there was also an eight-page summary by Lewis Perrotti, the state Registry of Motor Vehicles investigator, who had been prevented from interviewing the killer.

The official file, parts of which are contained in the Appendix on pages 323-325 included Sgt. Newton's detailed report, complete with diagrams that dovetail with my independent findings. It included the report of Patrolman Angel, who told me that he'd found skin and blood fragments on Bellevue Avenue. The file recounted his interviews with Judith Thom and her father Lewis, the first civilian witnesses on the scene. They'd told Officer Angel that minutes after the crash, Doris admitted that *"she had run over Ed"* In fact, his interviews with the Thoms, directly contradict the three-page Q&A described as the "interrogation" of Doris Duke by Captain Paul Sullivan four days later.

MINIMIZING TIRELLA'S INJURIES

One of the first things that struck me in the report was that in a section entitled INJURED, Doris Duke was listed first, as experiencing "Shock" and "Lacerations of the face." (Appendix page 323) But below that, while noting "Edwardo" Tirella had died, the extent of his injuries was left blank. The black redaction obscures his L.A. street address: 2048 Stanley Hills Place in Laurel Canyon.

Newport PD report detailing Doris Duke's injuries vs. no stated injuries for Eduardo.

Contrast that with the copy of his Death Certificate obtained independently from the Rhode Island Medical Examiner.

Eduardo Tirella's death certificate documenting his fatal injuries, consistent with his body being dragged across Bellevue Avenue under the Dodge Polara wagon.

In gruesome detail it describes the horrific extent of his injuries.

As reported, in Chapter Seven, the "bedroom interview" with Doris Duke was conducted on October 9th, 1966, two days after the crash, by Lt. Frank Walsh and Det. George Watts, following Doris's return home (Saturday). Until then she'd been kept incommunicado at Newport Hospital by Dr. McAllister.

It's worth remembering that this brief session took place Sunday in the presence of Doris's business manager Pete Cooley who had pointedly insisted that Doris's estates manager, David Rimmer be *excluded* from Rough Point during that weekend.

Registry investigators Perrotti and Al Massarone (prevented from talking to Doris before then) caught the tail end of the brief session as Duke sat in bed. It was on the basis of the limited questions and her anemic response that Chief Joseph Radice closed the case the next day, declaring it an "unfortunate accident," but after state Attorney General Nugent chastised him, the chief quickly backtracked, insisting that the probe was still open. That's when Doris's Rhode Island lawyer Aram Arabian suggested that the police "write something up" and if he approved, she would sign it.

Then, in contravention of any conventional law enforcement norm, in which the police serve as the objective finders of fact, the Newport PD produced that contrived 3 page "transcript" of a Q&A that never took place. As detailed in Chapter Seven the most remarkable thing about that account -- supposedly typed by a stenographer during a live "interrogation" of Duke at Rough Point on October 11th -- is that the police got her date of birth wrong in answer to the first question, which she then had to correct and initial on the typed copy.

In examining that "transcript," retired NYPD homicide Det. James Moss was shocked by the lengths that the Newport Police Department went to in order to exonerate the killer. "On page two," Det. Moss said, "they actually asked and answered a variation of the same question twice."

> Q. Is there any possibility, Miss Duke, that your foot could
>   have engaged the accelerator pedal?
> A. Not to my knowledge.

"Apparently they wanted to give her a further excuse for confusing the gas pedal with the brake. So they asked and answered that question again in a slightly different way."

> Q. Is there a possibility that your foot slipped off the
>   brake pedal onto the accelerator pedal?
> A. That could have happened, *but I have no recollection of it.*

"But this time, when the police answered for her, 'That could have happened,' her lawyers apparently objected, because she ended up writing in, 'but I have no recollection of it,' then initialing it, 'D.D.'"

"That was her attorneys' way of protecting her," said Det. Moss, "since the 'could have happened' admission might have exposed her to charges of criminal negligence. But Doris Duke was *never* subjected to an 'interrogation' in real time as the Q&A states. If she had been, her lawyers would have prevented her from answering that way."

After examining the newly discovered police report in depth, Det. Moss reached this conclusion:

"This had to be the biggest homicide investigation in Newport history at the time and one would think that the Chief would have conducted it 100% by the book, especially with the Rhode Island Attorney General looking over his shoulder. But no. In fact, in the entire three-page Q&A, the police never used the word 'homicide.' I have never seen an 'investigation' more favorable to the only person of interest—the killer—who was also the only living witness to the death. I don't fault any of the junior members of the department, including Sgt. Newton and patrolmen Angel, Watterson, Mather and Ring. They were clearly prevented by the Chief from telling the full truth at the time and they've come forward now to set the record straight. But I can say this, without a doubt: if that report had included Sgt. Newton's actual conclusion that Tirella had gone up on the hood of the wagon, rolled off and Doris Duke had driven over him, she would have been in handcuffs. So, as Mr. Perrotti from the Registry of Motor Vehicles concluded, 'the fix was in.'"

FORENSIC ANALYSIS

I submitted the evidence uncovered in this investigation to Harm Jansen, a senior staff engineer with Collision and Injury Dynamics, one of the nation's top forensic consulting firms, located in El Segundo, California. [888]

He drilled down specifically on Sgt. Fred Newton's theory of the crash and agreed that Eduardo Tirella had gone up on the hood of the Dodge Polara wagon just before Doris Duke drove it through the gates.

"There is no evidence he was pinned against the gates," says Jansen. "We know he was on the hood. We also know he got run over-mid street. To me it's clear. This was a multi-sequence event in which the driver made a number of affirmative decisions in the course of the incident. The analysis of his injuries, limited to upper body, the head-on damage to the lower sections of the gates, the account of the first officer on the scene and the contemporaneous investigation by the senior police accident investigator, Sergeant Newton, lead me to conclude that the event did *not* occur as described by Doris Duke." [889]

CHAPTER THIRTY-FOUR

THE COVER-UP
CONTINUES

Three months after Eddie's death, Sheila Graham included this in her syndicated column: "The Doris Duke-Eduardo Tirella auto tragedy had a counterpart at the beginning of the Bette Davis/Joan Crawford horror picture, *What Ever Happened to Baby Jane?* [890] Not having screened the 1962 Robert Aldrich picture since seeing it in high school, I found it and watched the opening. In it, Joan Crawford's character crushes her sister "Jane," played by Bette, against the wrought iron gates of their mansion which is identified in the film as "the old Valentino place," Falcon Lair, the very Beverly Hills estate where Eduardo Tirella had redesigned the kitchen for Doris Duke. That classic work of psycho-noir was in theaters *four years* before the homicide at Rough Point. I wondered, was it just another bit of irony in a story pregnant with it, or could the film have planted a seed in Dee Dee's mind?

The simplest explanation for all of this is that Duke's murder of Tirella began as a spur-of-the-moment act, fueled by anger and alcohol that simply veered out of control.

The crash scene in *What Ever Happened To Baby Jane* **at the gates of what is identified in the film as "the old Valentino place."**

But one thing is clear: once Eduardo went up on the hood of that wagon and rolled off, even if she'd had a flickering moment of doubt that caused her to tap the brakes outside the gates, Doris then decided to *commit*, confident that her lawyers and damage control specialists would keep her out of prison.

The first week in April 2019, after never mentioning Eduardo in the nearly 20 years since the Rough Point museum had been open, [891] a new exhibit appeared at the end of the tour. A source close to The Restoration Foundation told me that it was planned as an attempt to "get ahead" of what I might report [892] after I'd reached out publicly to members of the Newport Facebook Group. [893] In a video announcing the exhibit, Rough Point's curator said that, "a lot of locals... have heard a local myth, so we wanted to put all the facts out so that people would know exactly what happened and that it was just an unfortunate accident." [894]

Apart from embracing Chief Radice's explanation for the homicide, the exhibit contained multiple misstatements of fact enshrined on a wall at the Rough Point museum; including the false claim that, "After several days in court, Duke settled with the Tirella family" and Radice's assertion that "Tirella and Doris were on their way to dinner that evening."

Typically, the exhibits at the end of the guided tour of the museum rotate every season. But as of early November of 2020, two weeks before Rough Point was to close for the season, a visit to the estate by a friend of mine who lives in Newport, revealed that the NRF's exhibit (below) which embraces the false "accident" theory of the crash, remains intact.

The Accident at the Rough Point Gate

On the evening of October 7, 1966, Doris's friend and interior designer, Eduardo Tirella, was struck and killed while opening the front gate at Rough Point. Doris was driving the car. While we can never know exactly what happened, it is undeniably a tragic event.

We do know that Tirella and Doris were on their way to dinner that evening. She was driving a rented car and unfamiliar with the transmission. Eyewitnesses said Doris was incoherent and clearly in shock following the incident.

Many rumors and half-truths surround this tragedy. Some say Tirella was Duke's lover and he had wronged her, so she killed him- except that Tirella had romantic relationships with men. Some locals claim Doris paid off the Newport Police chief (who retired six months later) and her $25,000 donation to the Cliff Walk restoration was hush money for the accident.

Perhaps the most persistent tale is that Doris Duke founded the Newport Restoration Foundation as a way of apologizing to the city. While Doris Duke did found NRF two years after the accident, she had been in talks with other preservationists about possible historic preservation projects as early as 1965, based on correspondence in the Doris Duke Archives at Duke University.

In 1971, the Tirella family brought a civil suit against Doris Duke for damages and lost wages from Eduardo's death. After several days in court, Duke settled the case with the Tirella family.

Tirella Crash Exhibit. While containing multiple false statements, it covered a wall at the end of the Rough Point tour for the 2019 and 2020 seasons.

THE DISAPPEARING GATES

By any measure, in the context of this story, the massive wrought iron gates that guard the entry to Rough Point are evidence of how Eduardo Tirella died. Until quite recently they remained as they had been in the fall of 1966.

This is a shot taken by John Quigley, stepson of *Daily News* photographer Ed Quigley, on March 15th, 2019. At that time they were fully intact.

March 15th, 2019 (John Quigley)

But months later in November of 2019 the gates were severely damaged by a catering truck attempting to enter the grounds. They were then removed from the pillars which had been cracked just above the bronze plaques with the estate's name and address: 680 Bellevue Avenue.

Rough Point in early 2020 after the gates were removed. The force of the collision with the truck cracked the pillars just above the brass plaques. (John Quigley)

Arguably, The Newport Restoration Foundation, had three months before the outbreak of the COVID-19 crisis to repair them and one might have expected that they would, since May 1st, 2020 was set to mark the twentieth anniversary of the estate's opening to the public as a home museum. [895]

Yet in June, the pillars were reduced to less than half their size and across the once elaborate entrance to the estate the NRF had installed the kind of metal fence one might find dividing pastures at Duke Farms.

**By June 2020, the gates were replaced by this small green fence.
(Tom Perrotti photo)**

As this book nears publication in December 2020, the old gates are still down and there is further evidence that The NRF seems bent on hiding those reminders of Tirella's death. As the photo below demonstrates, *the gates themselves* have been relegated to a corner of the estate where they lie covered by boards and a tarp.

The gates, photographed in early November, 2020.

THE SILVER SWAN

Meanwhile, efforts to rehabilitate the image of Doris Duke continue. In January, 2020 Charles A. Burns, a tour guide at Rough Point who has been a guest speaker at Sotheby's Institute, [896] wrote a laudatory piece for *The New York Social Diary* entitled, "Guardian Spirit: Newport Legacy of Doris Duke," in which he admittedly sought to "dispel what are indeed misleading stereotypes" of the heiress. [897]

On April 7th, 2020, after a research, writing and editing process that took seven years, [898] *The Silver Swan*, author Sallie Bingham's long awaited Duke biography was published by Farrar, Strauss and Giroux, a division of Macmillan Publishers. [899] A member of the legendary Louisville family that published *The Courier Journal*, [900] Bingham devoted only 15 paragraphs in her 336 page book to the death of Eduardo Tirella, whom she repeatedly referred to as "Edward."

Virtually every sentence in her analysis of the crash contained a material misstatement of fact. Further, she cited David Rimmer, manager of Duke Farms, as a principal source for how the "accident," occurred, when, as reported here, he was pointedly excluded from Rough Point after he arrived in Newport late on the night of the homicide and returned to New Jersey the next day.

In researching *The Silver Swan*, Bingham never spoke directly to Rimmer, relying instead, on transcripts of interviews he gave in 2003 and 2004. Consider how her book, from a legendary publishing house, continues to distort the truth behind Tirella's death. Below are Bingham's verbatim paragraphs with my responses based on the research for this book:

> **FROM THE SILVER SWAN:** "David explained that the car that had killed Edward was an Avis rental that Edward had arranged because the only car kept at Rough Point was 'an old clunker.' As always, Edward drove when he and Doris wanted to leave Rough Point for dinner in Newport. David explained that the rental car's engine tended to accelerate due to some unspecified problem with the automatic choke. David believed this was what had caused the accident."

RESPONSE: Rimmer told me that he was "speculating" when he thought that the rented Dodge Polara wagon contained an automatic choke. His reasoning was that if the vehicle was started in cold weather, the choke might have caused it to accelerate. "When I gave those interviews," he said, "I wasn't aware that it was 5:00 o'clock in the afternoon," I assumed Eduardo and Doris had come out in the morning, so that was an opinion that proved to be wrong. Besides, I wasn't even *in* Newport at the time of the crash."

Bingham also relied on a news story quoting Chief Radice who falsely reported that they were on their way to dinner on the night of Tirella's death, rather than heading out to pick up The Reliquary of St. Ursula, which she refers to elsewhere in the book as "the bust of an unknown queen, bought cheaply at a Newport junk shop."

FROM THE SILVER SWAN: "Immediately after the accident, there were stories in the press, and since the Tirella family continued to push for a settlement of $1.1 million to compensate for the income they claimed Edward would have made during his lifetime, a court trial seemed inevitable. In fact, a jury was chosen to ascertain whether Doris had been guilty of negligence in Edward's death, but before it could meet, the case was dismissed, the prosecutor declaring that the cause of death was an accident. After another year of legal struggles, the Tirellas agreed to accept $200,000 as compensation, but the clouds of rumor around the incident never fully dissipated."

RESPONSE: As documented in this book with files from Doris's own papers at The Rubenstein Library, after the heiress repeatedly *refused* to settle with Tirella's family for as little as $200,000, they were forced to file a wrongful death action in December, 1967 in Rhode Island Superior Court. The case was delayed by Duke's attorneys for years but finally came to trial during 10 days in June of 1971, covered nationally by the *AP* and *UPI,* during which Miss Duke was found *liable* for Eduardo's death. The case was never "dismissed," as Bingham reports. But during the damage phase, Duke's attorney Aram Arabian, attacked Eduardo's reputation so aggressively that the jury's damage award was only $75,000.

The Rubenstein files contain multiple letters discussing settlement requests from Tirella's family starting at $600,000 and going down to $200,000 which were rejected by Duke's attorneys. Those files which Bingham asserts she relied on, also contain multiple letters to

Duke's lawyer and business manager on the commencement of trial and the selection of the jury, which was not only empaneled, but heard evidence for 10 days. Further, Bingham confuses civil litigation with a criminal case. In this instance there was no "prosecutor," and the case was not "dismissed," though the Tirellas failed to overturn the paltry damage award on appeal.

FROM THE SILVER SWAN: "Since she walled herself off from the press, refusing interviews that would have given her a chance to explain what had happened, the easy animosity and fascination that often color our perceptions of rich women controlled the story of Edward's death."

RESPONSE: Bingham is correct that Doris "walled herself off from the press," but she fails to note that she did so after effectively compromising Dr. McAllister, the Medical Examiner who sequestered her in Newport Hospital on "the night of." As the newly found Registry of Motor Vehicles report reveals, even after she got home on Saturday investigators Perrotti and Massarone tried to interview her and were then thwarted by her lawyers.

The Registry report also notes that on Sunday, October 9[th,] it was Dr. McAllister who gave the final O.K. for Doris to be questioned. That happened in her bedroom with Wesley Fach and Pete Cooley, hanging on each one of the few words she uttered as Lt. Frank Walsh -- soon to become Radice's successor — asked those four questions.

THE MISSING RELIQUARY

When Adam Fithers photographed the interior of Rough Point on the 52nd anniversary of Tirella's death, the artifact that Eduardo and Doris were leaving the estate to appraise -- the Reliquary of St Ursula — was where it had been for years, on a chest of drawers between two gold candlesticks, at the bottom of the grand staircase. In *The Silver Swan*, while wrongfully characterizing it as "the bust of an unknown queen" Sallie Bingham rightfully noted that Doris had put it there "in a place of honor."

The very presence of that Reliquary conflicts with the story perpetuated by the NRF in its 2019-2020 exhibit: that on the night Doris Duke killed Eduardo, they were, "on their way to dinner."

The St. Ursula Reliquary on October 7th, 2018. (Adam Fithers photo)

In May of 2020, for reasons unknown, the Reliquary was removed by the NRF from where it had rested for years across from the foot of Rough Point's main staircase. As of early November 2020 it was no longer on display.

The removal of the gates and that artifact from public view, suggest a continuing effort by The Newport Restoration Foundation to rewrite the Doris Duke narrative and sanitize the circumstances surrounding Tirella's death.

THE POWER OF MONEY

Given the importance of the Reliquary to this story and the apparent sensitivity of the NRF to its presence at Rough Point, I asked nationally-recognized antiquities appraiser Dr. Elizabeth Stewart for her thoughts on the symbolic value of that artifact to the owners of great estates like Doris Duke.

"St. Ursula was one of the most popular international saints in Medieval Europe," she wrote in a brief monograph. [901] "According to legend she was a young Breton princess, the daughter of a Roman-British king in the 4th Century A.D. who had betrothed her to a pagan prince. As the legend has it, to delay her nuptials, she gathered 11,000 fellow virgins, trained them as soldiers, and set sail from the coast of France destined for Rome where she hoped to meet the Pope.

"After docking in Germany, the legend says that she and her virgin army made it by land to Cologne where they were captured by Huns and martyred after they refused to give up their bodies or renounce their faith. Today the Church of St. Ursula is purported be on the site of their mass grave. The church's walls are filled with thousands of bones said to have been unearthed there. Because she was a pilgrim who died with her faith intact, Ursula soon became the most famous Saint in Europe, beloved by The Knights Templars at the time of the Crusades. So enduring was her fame, that Christopher Columbus himself claimed what were later called "The Virgin Islands" in her name and in 1610 Caravaggio immortalized her in his legendary painting, "Martirio di Sant'Orsola." [902]

According to Dr. Stewart, similar reliquaries, believed to contain the bones of saints, became revered among robber barons of the Gilded Age like J.P. Morgan.

"Today there's another St. Ursula Reliquary in The Metropolitan Museum," she wrote, "along with 23 related reliquary busts.

"The art form symbolized the power of money to buy a piece of The Divine. Since you've cited that reliquary in the context of Eduardo Tirella's death, it's not surprising that those whose job it is to preserve the Doris Duke legend, might be uncomfortable with its continuing display at Rough Point."

A REMINDER OF "THAT HORRIBLE NIGHT"

More than half a century after the murder— despite the ongoing efforts by Duke's Restoration Foundation to rewrite history in her favor— I wondered how the death of her longtime friend, decorator and curator had affected the woman for whom a vast fortune seemed to buy so little happiness.

Donna Lohmeyer told me that for months after Eddie's death, late at night, Doris would call her mother (his sister) and weep with her on the phone over his loss. [903] "Mom said that Doris told her she kept a picture of him in a silver frame next to her bed in every one of her estates."

But if she did, such a photo was no longer visible in her bedroom at Rough Point on the 52nd anniversary of his death. And if she'd had any lingering remorse, it soon seemed to pass. Within weeks of Tirella's funeral, Doris finally took possession of the St. Ursula reliquary. Eventually she put it on that chest of drawers in her main hall at the foot of the stairs where it stood until recently. Every night after that, when she went up to bed and every morning when she came down, that artifact was there to remind her of "that horrible night." Still, Doris Duke was a woman with enough money and power to view the world entirely through her own distorted lens and like a classic narcissist she managed to turn even that last work of art, which she'd asked Eduardo to endorse, into her own image.

After she died and Rough Point became a "home museum," existing today in perpetuity just as she'd left it, the old staff remembered how she'd referred to The Reliquary not as the image of Saint Ursula, but as *Saint Cecilia*, patron saint of music, whose feast day was November 22nd. [904]

That happened to be Doris Duke's own birthday.

CHAPTER THIRTY-FIVE

THE REDEMPTION OF STEPHEN ROBERTSON

In Chapter Four of this book, having begun to tell the story of The Quality Lunch Murders, I had to know how it ended. I'd sensed from the coverage that there were vast pieces missing. As terrible as the double murder was, Stephen Robertson was beloved in Newport; particularly by senior officials in the police department like Capt. Paul Sullivan who had been on the board of The Boys Club.

Any other suspect who had killed two sailors in a city where the economy was dominated by the Navy, then eluded the authorities in what developed into a 32 state All Points search, only to return and walk into Headquarters blocks from the crime scene, might have been locked down in an interrogation room. Based on what I knew of the Newport police mindset *back then,* a confession might have been "induced" long before the suspect was read his Miranda Rights.

That was the sense I got in 1967 when I covered a seminar on recent Supreme Court decisions regarding search, seizure and interrogation. Sponsored by the Rhode Island A.G.'s office, it took place six weeks before Steve's arrest. Of the 100 policeman in attendance, all of the officers

I spoke to were critical of those reforms, particularly when it came to questioning suspects and few would have given a pre-arrest detainee in Steve's position as much leeway. [905]

But, despite the hyper-violent nature of the crime, his flight from justice and the way he had inadvertently embarrassed the cops by giving up right under their noses, Magoo was treated with kid gloves, arrested after he'd shown them the murder weapon and arraigned quietly. [906]

Then, with multiple eyewitnesses to the slaying and his apparent confession, he'd gone to trial, asserting the insanity defense.

At that point, his lawyers had the near impossible burden of proving him eligible for commitment under "The M'Naghten Rule" established in the mid 19th century in the British House of Lords, but still the law in Rhode Island. That rule required proof that at the time of killing those sailors, Robertson was "laboring under such a defect of reason, from disease of mind, to not know the nature and quality of the act, or if he did, that he did not know what he was doing was wrong." [907]

For Steve, whose I.Q. was in the genius category, to have the presence of mind to calmly exit the luncheonette after taking two lives in front of multiple witnesses, then elude the police in four states only to slip past a dragnet and surrender, the insanity defense was a real legal reach.

Since he'd already confessed, it was likely that a guilty plea, saving the state the expense of a trial and the families of the two victims years of extended emotional grief, would have been the honorable move.

A YOUNG MAN OF PRINCIPAL

Having worked with Magoo as a counselor at Boys Club Camp, I'd always known him to be highly principled -- worthy of an appointment to the U.S. Military Academy. I'd since learned that as a West Point cadet he'd made it through "Beast Barracks," the ultimate test of those deserving of a commission, but that he'd withdrawn from the Point *on his own,* after he came to believe that his time management skills might fail him in service to his country.

So I had to know why he'd agreed to go to trial when a guilty plea would have surely resulted in the minimum possible sentence. The trial coverage in *The Daily News* was spotty and though the rumor was that in prison he had become an advocate for prisoners' rights, the *Providence Journal's* online archives were effectively non-existent.

He'd been paroled decades ago and the last time I'd seen him was at his pretrial hearing. Various sources had told me that they'd spotted him late at night at various Dunkin' Donuts locations around Aquidneck Island. But despite my best efforts I couldn't nail down his whereabouts. No one seemed to have a phone number for him or an email address.

Then in April of 2020, a Google-alert I'd set up for Steve revealed that his brother Phil had died. The wake had been held at O'Neill's Funeral Home on Spring Street, where I'd spent many a night with my mother on my knees saying the rosary for a departed friend or relative. O'Neill's was one of the three principal mortuaries in Newport, along with Hambly's and Memorial, which my family had patronized ever since my grandmother Julia was waked there. She'd get a calendar every year from Charles Edenbach who ran the parlor on Broadway and out of loyalty, her modest will decreed that she'd be laid to rest there.

Meanwhile, the head of the O'Neill family was Patrick O'Neill Hayes, the late lawyer and State Senator. Pat, as everybody knew him, has shown up at several important junctures of this story. Not only did he represent the second highest bidder in the 1968 auction of Annandale Farm, but he was part of a group of investors that bought Idle Hour, the Muriel Vanderbilt estate the year before. He'd been a partner in the esteemed law firm of Corcoran, Peckham and Hayes and his son Michael, always a clothes horse at De La Salle, founded a luxury clothing store in the Casino Block on Bellevue that has successfully catered to The Avenue Crowd for 37 years.

William W. Corcoran, a senior partner in Pat's old firm, still goes to work each day in a suit and tie at the age of 91. He was on the Board of The Boys Club, and in 1967 when Stephen Robertson got his "one phone call" from police headquarters on the night of his surrender, he called Bill.

Along with the involvement of Capt. Paul Sullivan in Steve's arrest, that was another expression of the many intersecting threads in this story.

So, thinking that I might track down Steve through "O'Neill's" I dialed the funeral home on Spring Street in search of Charlie Hayes, Pat's nephew. I'd seen him the previous June on a trip to Newport when a family member had suddenly passed away. Then, in the early summer of 2020, when I called the funeral home Charlie answered right away.

"Peter, what can I do for you?"

"I've been trying to find Magoo and I saw that you just waked his bro—" I didn't even get the words out when Charlie said, "You want his number?"

"Yes, absolutely. Thanks."

"Anything for a De La Salle Boy. By the way, I have to tell you. Steve paid me within 48 hours for all of Phil's funeral expenses – casket, wake, burial. Everything. Usually it takes months."

"Well, everybody always said he was a straight—" I caught myself before I used an utterly inappropriate metaphor. "Thanks Charlie."

I hung up and dialed, wondering what Steve would sound like after all these years. I hadn't set eyes on him since October of '67 when Capt. Sullivan had slipped me that enigmatic hint about the Duke case. But I got his voice mail. So I waited a day and called again. No response.

Then a few nights later my iPhone rang with his name on the home screen, since I'd entered it into my address book. I anxiously picked up and the first words out of his mouth after 53 years were, "Peter *Anthony* Lance. How the hell are ya?"

Christ, he'd remembered my middle name which maybe half a dozen people in Newport knew and most of them were dead.

FLIGHT, REMORSE & REDEMPTION

Over the next nine days, in a series of interviews, Stephen Magoo Robertson gave me every twist and turn in the remarkable story of his escape from Newport, north through Massachusetts and eventually to New York before he came to grips with what he'd done and returned to face what was coming to him.

Later, talking to Joseph Filipkowski, the Furlough Coordinator at the state prison where Steve served half of his initial life sentence, I came to understand how Robertson had become a kind of "jailhouse lawyer" and champion for inmate rights, eventually working to reform Rhode Island's penal system.

But first I had to get his side of the story on what happened just after 1 AM at The Quality Lunch on Broadway nearly a year to the day after Eduardo Tirella's death.

"So Steve, take me back. The Quality Lunch was a place open late and guys would go there after they'd been to the bars to get a little something to eat. You were driving a Mustang?"

"Right. It was black. I bought it new because I was working two jobs at the time: at Raytheon in Production Control and part time at the Park Holm Boys Club where I was a Unit Director. When the club closed that night, I went down to the All American Club on Thames Street to play Shuffleboard. It's now O'Brien's Pub. I actually played in a league back then. I was there a couple of hours and had two to three beers at most – Stubbies, they called them. About half of what you'd get in a bottle. If you drank one, your blood alcohol level would be under a .01.

"Anyway, I left there just after midnight, drove to The Quality Lunch and ordered coffee and a steak sandwich. John Sarras and Gus Gianiotis were working that night and Willie Amato was sitting just down the counter." [908]

From that point Steve's recollection of events was remarkably consistent with what Gus, through his wife, Julia, had told me when I interviewed them hours after the shooting back in '67. He then gave me his account of what happened next.

"There were three guys at the counter. All in civvies. Sailors as I later found out. One was celebrating a birthday. Willie was sitting next to them and they started arguing. I could see they were intimidating him, so I said to them, in the politest possible way, 'Look. He's an old man. He's had a few drinks. Why don't you just cut him some slack?' That's when the lead guy cut in and said 'That's none of your damn business. We're gonna take him out and work him over a bit. And when we finish with him, we're gonna start with you.'

"I don't like to see old people mistreated or picked on, particularly when they can't defend themselves. I never liked bullies. I always challenged them. And that's when I walked out."

Steve told me that his Mustang was parked a block north near City Hall. He walked up to it and pulled a .30-30 lever-action rifle out of the trunk.

"Getting back quickly to assist Mr. Amato was a priority for me," he said. "So on the way back, I carried the weapon, as I'd been trained at West Point, double-timing at Port Arms until I got to the door."

By that point, John Sarras, the owner of the coffee shop had ejected Amato and one of the sailors out onto Broadway and locked the front door when Steve came in through the rear on Spring Street.

"My principal reason for going back was to provide some cover for the old man," he remembered. "To make sure he was safe. But as soon as the two sailors saw me threats were made. Loud threats. One of the staff remembered me saying 'I'll take care of this,' and I fired. Just then, I looked out and saw Willie on Broadway. He was safe but it turned out to be at tremendous cost. Two people were dead unnecessarily."

I asked him what happened next.

"With that kind of gunfire downtown, did you hear any sirens?"

"When I got back to my car, I heard none. The last ferry to Jamestown was at 11:00 pm so I drove north on Route 138, the East Main Road, because I figured that at the Mount Hope Bridge, one of the only two ways off the island at that time of night, I might get stopped. I crossed The Tiverton Bridge and took Fish Road up to Route 24 toward Boston."

"How did you find your way to New York? That odyssey must have been pretty terrifying."

"Yeah. I soon realized that this wasn't some movie. This was real. As I drove along, I remember saying to myself, 'I can't believe this just happened.' But it did. So I just kept on driving, trying to clear my head."

At that point in flight, Stephen Robertson, now a murderer, was using his highly gifted intelligence to runs the odds on escape rather than considering the moral weight of his actions. He reasoned that if he got too close to Route 128, the beltway around Boston, he might encounter a roadblock.

"I had the radio on and a few reports were coming out, so I decided to drive North, take Route 2 West across Massachusetts, rather than going across Route 9 toward Worcester. By the time I got to where Route 2 crosses 122 south I pulled off the road and dozed for two or three hours.

"When I woke up, I heard news that the All-Points Bulletin was now a 32 state alert, so I made my way down towards Pittsfield, Mass., where I got onto Route 20 West toward The New York State Thruway. It was probably 6:30 or so in the morning, just beginning to get light."

It was then that Stephen Magoo Robertson, the one-time Boys Club "Boy of The Year," and graduate of a Catholic high school where he'd been on The Diocesan Honor Society, finally came to grips with what he'd done. [909]

"So, instead of heading North on 87 I headed south, eventually getting on Route 95 North back to Newport. And then – you couldn't make this up – when I got to Rhode Island I came into a roadblock. So I said to myself, 'I'll just surrender.' But for whatever reason they stopped the car in front of me. They eyed me and then let me go and stopped the car behind me. I could never explain that to this day, but that allowed me to head home through Kingston, over the old Saunderstown Bridge to Jamestown, where I got on the ferry and I stayed in my car.

"My brother later told me that there had been news reports all day about armed officers with shotguns, two to a car. He was worried, thinking that if I'd been stopped, I'd have shot it out. But that was the last thing on my mind at that point. When the ferry hit Newport, they waived me off. Keep in mind that my black Mustang with the plate number had been identified hours earlier, but I didn't see a single police officer, so I drove directly to Headquarters on Marlborough Street and parked in the police lot. I bounded up the steps and walked into the lobby where I saw Sergeant Tilly, who I'd played basketball with, and said, 'I believe you're looking for me.'

PRISON THAT NIGHT

"The first question Sgt. Tilly asked me was 'You don't have any weapons on you, do you Steve?' And I said, 'No.' He just took my word for it and never searched me. Then he called upstairs and Capt. Sullivan almost broke his neck rushing downstairs. He looked at me wide-eyed and out of breath, then said, 'We have the right to search your car Steve.' And I said, 'Sure.' So they handcuffed me, took me outside and recovered the rifle from my trunk. That's when the Captain said, 'I have to inform you that at this point you are under arrest.'

The Newport Police were incredibly deferential to Steve, a local kid they'd all grown up with who had shown so much promise. They arranged for him to be arraigned inside Headquarters that night by Judge Arthur J. Sullivan and then, led out, cuffed from the front, in that perp walk covered in Chapter Four. At that point he was loaded into the rear of a State Police vehicle and delivered to the dreaded Adult Correctional Institution in Cranston, known as "The ACI."

Stephen Robertson in cuffs following his arraignment at Newport Police Headquarters on October 6th, 1967. He's being escorted by Sheriff Joseph G. Silvia (left) Deputy Sheriff William F. Blake and an unidentified Rhode Island State Trooper on his way to the ACI in Cranston. (Ed Quigley Photo).

Built in 1878, by the mid 1960's it was considered one of the toughest state prisons in America. The inmate population was heavily controlled by "the Mob." As noted in Chapter Ten, New England's Cosa Nostra was run out of Providence, not Boston, and Raymond Patriarca, aka "The Old Man," was the boss. The LCN, as the FBI would call them, controlled the entire North Wing. For a mental picture, think of that great razor-blade-cutting-garlic scene in *Goodfellas*.

The principal killer for Patriarca who dominated the prison was Gerry Ouimette. He was of French Canadian ancestry, which meant he could never become a "made guy" since he wasn't Italian. But he'd been fiercely loyal to Patriarca all the same. Gerry's brother John was the alleged mastermind of the 1975 Bonded Vault robbery at Hudson Fur Storage in Cranston, not far from the ACI. That was reportedly where Patriarca and his soldiers held some $32 million in cash, jewels and gold bullion. [910]

Revisionist history has it that the audacious robbery was an inside job with "The Old Man," hitting the place himself, using the Ouimettes, so he could keep the Feds from seizing his ill gotten gains and pocket other swag stolen by members of his borgata (family) that he'd come to see as unworthy. [911]

When I asked Steve about how he felt being locked up in that prison for the first time in his life, he didn't say much. In fact, he was so humble about the groundbreaking efforts he'd made over the years, working from the inside on behalf of inmates, that I had to consult the man who knew him best in his final years at the ACI.

Joseph Filipkowski, now retired, had run the first prisoner furlough program in Rhode Island, which Steve Robertson had worked to create. He told me how, faced with the prospect of being controlled inside by the wiseguys, Magoo had actually threatened Gerry Ouimette with a baseball bat and lived to tell about it.

"Ouimette was one of the most ruthless and feared gangland figures in Rhode Island," said Filipkowski. "At that point he knew Steve had nothing to lose. I mean, he was a civilian who'd just shot a couple of sailors in cold blood. So Gerry actually backed down. That gave Steve a lot of prison cred and he used it not just to survive, but to thrive on the inside." [912]

Filipkowski described Steve as "meticulous" and "a man of impeccable honesty."

"When I started the furlough program in 1975," he said, "Steve was part of my caseload. He'd served nearly eight years at that point and was in minimum security. I was so impressed with him that I said, 'Steve, I want you to work in the office.' It was just him, my secretary, and myself. I never met an inmate in my entire career who was such a hard worker and so honest. He was the living embodiment of 'penal reform.' In fact, he was paroled the first time he was eligible."

Though he had pulled two life sentences to run concurrently over 20 years, Steve first worked on changing the parole laws which had, until then, forbidden "Lifers" from applying for release before they'd "done their twenty." He testified before the Rhode Island State Assembly and The Senate and got the eligibility minimum cut in half. He then worked to set up the furlough program, and after his release in 1976, he started working for the Post Office in Providence. [913]

"Before you knew it," said Filipkowski, "he was President of the Postal Union."

Soon, the man who had made it through Beast Barracks at West Point had more ambitious plans. Steve decided to run for the State Senate from a district in Providence. But when a number of signatures on his qualifying papers were denied by the Secretary of State, Steve set his sights on challenging him. In the 1980 statewide election, although he didn't win, he actually carried Newport County with 31,000 votes. Then, from what I had learned, he quietly retired into relative anonymity.

But before he did, Magoo made one final visit to The Quality Lunch. Late one night, during one of our interviews, Steve opened up about it.

"You know how they say, 'People return to the scene of the crime?' Well I had absolutely no reason ever to go back to that diner. But I later realized that, that night, when it happened, it was so hectic, I forgot to pay. So about two and a half weeks after my release I drove down to Newport and waited until the place was empty. It was just John Sarras himself in the place, so I went in.

"I said, 'John are you surprised to see me?'"

"He calmly said, 'How are you Steve? Are you doing well?'"

"I said, 'I'm just starting off. But John, you know what I noticed? When I left that night with all the commotion, I never paid you. So I'm going to insist on paying you for my meal,' which I did. I actually paid him for the bill and gave him a tip. He shook my hand as I walked out." [914]

THE FATE THAT MIGHT HAVE BEEN

Perhaps the saddest and most touching part of our interviews was when Steve told me that after he'd been arraigned, when he was facing trial, he had wanted to plead guilty and "do the right thing," but the criminal lawyer he was assigned — none other than the unscrupulous Aram Arabian -- had convinced his parents that invoking the insanity defense would be his best shot at avoiding prison.

It was a legally-baseless move that allowed Arabian to rack up his legal fees and prosecutor James S. O'Brien to soak up the headlines during Robertson's trial. With his conviction assured it was a slam dunk. O'Brien was the same former City Solicitor my slum housing exposé had proven negligent in enforcing the Housing Code. As far as I was concerned, he and Arabian were a pair of corrupt bookends to Stephen Robertson's fate.

In the ultimate irony of this saga, Goo told me that his first choice for criminal counsel was none other than Matt Faerber, who happened to be out of the country at the time. Matt was the larger-than-life lawyer who had successfully defended Timmy and Julia Sullivan.

Everybody called him "Judge" because he'd served on the Bench of The Probate Court in the early Fifties. [915] He drove a black convertible with red leather upholstery and traveled the world defending soldiers, sailors and military officers whom he believed had been falsely accused.

His win-loss record was second to none.

Matt lived a block away from my family growing up. His first wife Kay, whom he divorced and married again, had loaned my mother her wedding dress. Matt Jr. was my close friend as a boy and *his* cousin, Paul grew up to become the Fire Captain who found the logbook detailing the Duke-Tirella crash. As a nine-year old, with his father Eugene "Jeeps" Faerber, Matt's brother, Paul had raced up to Bellevue Avenue after they heard the call on a police radio. In fact, we were so close to the Faerber clan, that, after my mother retired from The Courthouse, she went to work as a para-legal in the law offices of Matthew Faerber in one of the three Victorian houses he'd purchased adjacent to the Elms: East Court, Middle Court and West Court. Matt lived there with his second wife, a marvelous Irishwoman named Sadie, whom he'd met at The Plaza Hotel.

There was little doubt in my mind that if Matt had been available to take Goo's case, he would have encouraged him to plead guilty and avoid a trial. When I mentioned that to Steve, his voice trailed off, considering how his future might have been so different.

But fate is fate and if he hadn't gone to the ACI, he might not have redeemed himself and done so much for prisoner's rights.

-30-

ACKNOWLEDGMENTS

This book has provided me with the rarest of gifts -- a chance to go back to my hometown and attempt to clarify a story that my own newspaper got wrong at the time -- a story that has haunted many a Newporter. But that process of investigating and writing, which now spans two years, has proven to be so much more. It's been an exercise in self-analysis and memory focus. Was what I recalled as a child and young man really the way Newport *was,* or had I succumbed to my own mythology of what I *remembered* it to be? Answering those questions was the challenge I faced as I sought to find what Carl Bernstein, my former colleague from ABC News, calls "the best available version of the truth."

My obsession with the homicide at Rough Point was such that in 2004 when my father Joe died at the age of 90, I spoke to Bill Parvo, who had worked at Rough Point from time to time doing intricate painting jobs for Doris Duke. I hadn't seen him in years and just prior to my father's wake I asked him about the so-called "accident." At that time, Bill had a specific memory of the Rough Point gates. "They were really, really heavy," he recalled. "When you pulled one of them open you really had to put your back behind it."

I asked him if he had any knowledge of the crash and he said, "I'd heard that she drove through those gates with such power that she knocked off the escutcheon plate at the top." I was unfamiliar with that term, so Bill explained that there was an eight to ten-inch-long piece of metal welded onto the cross bar at the top of the gates to keep them from swinging outward. It was designed to do the same job as the metal "stop" riveted into the ground down below. Only neither element had been able to keep that two-ton Dodge wagon from forcing the gates open.

I hadn't given Bill Parvo's recollection much thought until I got the missing police report. Sure enough on the second page of his account, Sgt. Fred Newton described finding, "a piece of metal that was used as a gate stop normally attached to the center span at the top of the gates." He was confirming officially the story that Bill Parvo had heard only as a rumor after the crash. Bill was one of hundreds of Newporters with some association to Rough Point who had wondered, over the years, what really happened on Bellevue Avenue late on that afternoon in October of Sixty Six.

Now as I finish this book, I take some comfort in knowing that my obsession with getting to "the best available version of the truth," has been shared by others. There are many people like Bill who deserve my thanks for their contributions great and small; not the least of which were the Sherman brothers, Ned and Albert, whose newspaper gave me my introduction to "the game."

If this book is proof of anything, it's the enduring importance of local journalism – particularly the daily print coverage of events in a small community. *The Newport Daily News* not only offered me a chance to cut my teeth in this profession, but its past issues on *newspapers.com* allowed me to confirm my reporting after more than 50 years. As denigrated as reporters have been in The Age of Trump, facts will always be facts and well archived print newspapers represent a kind of daily "paper ballot" of history; forever there to be recounted and scrutinized.

Once I dove into the investigation in 2018, that archive helped me immensely, along with the fragile, yellowed clippings of my stories that my mother had lovingly preserved in scrapbooks.

But more important than any other aspect of the factual investigation, was the willingness of surviving members of the Newport Police Department, the Fire Department and other state and local agencies to share their personal knowledge of events.

I began with that dedicated Facebook Group, "If you Grew Up In Newport, RI, Share Some Memories," and branched out from there. With respect to the more than 10,500 members of that group, special thanks should go to its founder, Kelly Payne Stewart and to Larry Bettencourt who has kept the Duke-Tirella story alive for years with regular postings.

DISTANT RELATIVES

Tom Perrotti, is one of my oldest friends. Back in 1964 along with Fred Brown we had a Kingston Trio-inspired folk group called The Viking Town Trio. That's right. At the time we believed, like so many Newporters did, that The Norseman built The Tower. Tom's family ran a series of drugstores, starting with Perrotti's Park Pharmacy, down the street from where I lived. My aunt Julia worked there behind the perfume counter and one of her closest friends was Koula Sarras, wife of John, the co-owner of The Quality Lunch.

Among the many connections I was able to make in this endeavor, none brought as much joy to me as learning that Louis A. Perrotti, the 87-year old Registry of Motor Vehicles investigator, was a distant cousin that Tom had never met.

"When I'd drive down to Newport from Providence," Mr. Perrotti told me, "I'd go into the pharmacy on Broadway and grab a handful of match books (which bore the company name) and when I got back to Providence, I'd give them out and proudly say, 'These are my people that run this beautiful drug store.'"

THE POLICE

In what turned into a kind of human chain investigation, Tom Perrotti suggested that I talk to Al Conti, the veteran detective I'd met once or twice back during my tenure at *The Daily News* but didn't know well. Al was not only a seasoned investigator, who had recovered millions in jewels and paintings stolen from various Newport estates, but he'd had a flourishing career as an actor, having appeared in a half dozen feature films shot in Newport.

Al put me in touch with a number of current officers and spent hours helping me search for the "Holy Grail" of this investigation: the missing police report. He then introduced me to former Patrolman Edward (Eddie) Angel, the single most important living source to the events that happened outside the gates of Rough Point on that fateful late afternoon in 1966.

When it came to the central focus of the book: the crime itself, no one was more valuable in his analysis of the Newport PD's handling of it than retired NYPD detective James Moss, who not only examined most of the forensic evidence I'd uncovered, but actually came to Newport and assisted me in pursuing the investigation on the street.

Brad Watterson my De La Salle classmate, who won nine letters in football, basketball and track, shared his memory of Dr. McAllister and put me in touch with his cousin Bill, the first patrolman to speak to Doris Duke, post-crash at Newport Hospital.

Once I found officer Angel, the two people who played the most crucial role in helping me solve the mystery were Jane Maguire and her husband John Quigley, whose stepfather Ed had mentored me when he became a staff photographer for *The Daily News* in 1966. A reporter can't assemble the pieces of a puzzle like this without *the pieces* and by going down into their basement and searching through years of Ed's printed photos and negatives, the Quigleys handed me The Rosetta Stone with the shot that showed Sgt. Fred Newton working the gates.

EDUARDO'S NIECE

As noted in the narrative, the most important person who gave me insights into Eduardo was his niece Donna. She had been the closest to him of all the Tirella grandchildren. It's impossible for me to measure her contributions to this book, not just in terms of her editorial input on Eddie's life and the photos she provided to help illustrate it, but in the research assistance she provided writ large.

When it comes to Donna Lohmeyer and her daughter Dara, the phrase, "I can't thank them enough" is far too inadequate.

Special thanks go to John Pelosi—the esteemed New York attorney who got me to the finish line on the first three of my HarperCollins books—for reading this one with such care. On the west coast, Les Abell, the incredibly skilled lawyer who represents me, is living proof that patience and a great sense of humor are essential qualities for any great attorney.

My longtime Santa Barbara friend Lynn Cederquist proof read many early drafts and deserves great credit for her diligence. The hardcover, trade paperback and Kindle editions of "Homicide At Rough Point, are laid out so visually thanks to the mastery of designer Tom Morine, while the Audible edition, which I've narrated, was produced by Dennis Kao who also got me through the marathon 19-hour edition of my last HarperCollins book, *Deal With The Devil*.

VANITY FAIR

None of this would have been possible without the enduring friendship and skill of my manager Richard Arlook of The Arlook Group who got an early draft of the story to Krista Smith, then the West Coast editor of Vanity Fair. She generously read it in the midst of her last cover story and recommended it to VF's creative editor David Friend who's spent decades making writers like me look good.

David, in turn, took the piece to Radhika Jones, VF's amazing editor-in chief, whose father, Robert L. Jones, was a significant force behind the Newport Jazz & Folk Festivals. As such, Radhika, spent many summers in Newport as a child. She green lit the final 8,000 word draft that David edited and it was laid out over 14 spectacular pages in the July/August 2020 issue.

MY FAMILY

My most immense debt in all of this goes to my family; in particular my cousin Sheila and her husband Harlen Tyler whose dedication and kindness allowed Joe Lance to thrive and remain in good health in our house on Ashurst place in the years after my mother Albina passed away.

My sister Mary, who went on to become an award winning documentary filmmaker, shared with me two of the greatest parents any kids could hope for. They weren't just loving, but incredibly supportive and politically "woke" decades before that was even a thing. We talked politics: local, state and federal around the dinner table each night and Bina went to bed with a small transistor radio listening to Jerry Williams' news-based talk radio program on WBZ in Boston.

Each morning before school we tuned into the radio newscasts of Jerry Nevins on WADK and Jerry Taylor on WEAN — the man who took the photos of the twisted Rough Point gates. During every political convention and space shot we were riveted to the TV. In the course of our many "spins" around the Ocean Drive or our visits to Uncle Burt and Aunt Dorothy, a respect for Newport's history seeped into my sister and me as if we were touring an enormous museum.

SEN. CLAIBORNE PELL

I want to offer a special thanks to a man who inspired me throughout my life growing up in Newport. Claiborne Pell, served six terms as Rhode Island's senior senator and he's cited in multiple parts of this book. A Princeton graduate, he distinguished himself during World War II in the U.S. Coast Guard where, starting as a sailor, he rose to the rank of Lieutenant, as the ships he served on, escorted U.S. troops across the dangerous North Atlantic. Post war, given his fluency in Italian, he became a civil affairs officer in Sicily. The son of a diplomat and Congressman, his family gave their Bellevue Avenue mansion to The Catholic Church, where it became St. Catherine Academy.

One of the Senator's greatest achievements was in sponsoring the 1972 education reform bill that created what became known as "Pell Grants," providing financial aid to tens of thousands of U.S. students. He not only worked to establish Newport as JFK's "Summer White House," but the bridge spanning Narragansett Bay is deservedly named for him. Through Matt Faerber I met the senator one Sunday at Pelican Lodge where he gave me the most important career advice I ever received. He said, "Never be afraid to chase your dreams."

THE U.S. NAVY

Although I've done my best to underscore the importance of the U.S. Naval Base to Newport's economy, it's important to try and describe the impact the sailors and officers of that service branch made on the people of Newport. From my father Joe to Harlen Tyler to the parents of hundreds of the kids I grew up with, they first came to The City By The Sea in uniform. Many retired and stayed. Even more rotated out to other duty locations. As such, because of CRUDESLANT and the U.S. Naval War College, I was fortunate to go to school with children who had lived all over this country; many of them at bases around the world. Their unique sense of duty to country and the discipline their parents had instilled in them helped me appreciate what was possible beyond the shores of Aquidneck Island.

The Navy had other residuals benefits. It wasn't by chance that Rogers High School dominated New England athletics for decades. And why? Because the coaches there were able to recruit some of the most talented athletes in the nation. We were lucky enough to get a few of them at De La Salle, which is why we held our own every few years during the annual Thanksgiving Day football game at Freebody Park.

Phil Graham, the former publisher of *The Washington Post*, is credited with describing journalism as "the first rough draft of history" so when it comes to Newport, I hope that you will consider this book an updated draft of the city's continuing story.

My investigation began with the question: "Did Doris Duke get away with murder" and for me, answering that has become a wonderful journey of self-discovery; one that allowed me to revisit the lucky consequence of being a Newporter. In what other city of its size, would the world's greatest jazz and folk musicians, yachtsmen and tennis players gather each season to compete for international headlines? What town of 47,000 (when the ships were in) would play host to two consecutive U.S. Presidents? Where else could a working-class kid grow up with such exposure to natural beauty, historical significance and exceptional people? Gardner Dunton of *The Journal* and Jim Edward of *The Daily News* inspired me. My parents, Bina and Joe, gave me the hunger to question, but Newport gave me the capacity to dream.

The gates at Rough Point before their removal in 2019, photographed by Adam Fithers on the 52nd anniversary of Eduardo's death. At that point the escutcheon plate was welded firmly to the cross piece at the top and the stop was riveted into the concrete at the bottom. The crash site across Bellevue where Doris Duke dragged Tirella's body is now overgrown and covered by a fence. The tree the two-ton wagon smashed into – scarred for years from the impact of the crash – is almost invisible. It's as if the physical evidence of the killing, like the gates and the memory of Eduardo himself, have been erased… Until now.

ABOUT THE AUTHOR

Peter Lance, a graduate of Northeastern University, Columbia University's Graduate School of Journalism and Fordham University's School of Law, won five Emmys for his work as a producer and correspondent for WNET and ABC News. In addition to The Sevellon Brown Award he won The Robert F. Kennedy Journalism Award, The Scripps Howard Prize and The National Headliner Award. Mid-career he worked as a writer, producer or showrunner on multiple network television series including *Crime Story, Miami Vice, Wiseguy,* and *JAG.* Between 2003 and 2013 HarperCollins published four of his investigative books, *1000 Years for Revenge, Cover-up, Triple Cross* and *Deal With The Devil.* Lance's first novel, *First Degree Burn,* sold out of its print run of 55,000 in 1997 when first published by Berkley; earning a page-one story in the WSJ and a starred review in Publisher's Weekly. In 2014 he wrote the forward to a new edition of *Murder, Inc.,* the true crime classic by Burton Turkus and Sid Feder first published in 1951. *Homicide At Rough Point* emerged from his investigation chronicled in the July/August 2020 edition of *Vanity Fair.* His website is **peterlance.com** email: **pl@peterlance.com**

APPENDICES

Page 1 of The Newport PD official report into Eduardo Tirella's Death.

CITY OF NEWPORT - POLICE DEPT.

CLASSIFICATION	CODE	LOCATION OF INCIDENT	PAGE No.	TIME REPORTED		DATE			COMPLAINT No.
		Bellevue Ave Opp. Doris Duke Est.	2	A.M. 5:00		10	7	66	4848
COMPLAINANT phone Call					PHONE				NBR CASE NO. 4090

If juvenile, get full name, age, d.o.b, address, parent's names, school, grade, initial disposition, time ordered back:

NATURE OF INCIDENT:

Officer Angel Reports:

STATEMENT OF JAMES HANLEY ▓▓▓▓▓

" I was driving South on Bellevue ave . I noticed a car that had crashed into a tree. I did not see the accident take place. I got out of my car to assist a woman whom I noticed was bleeding from the mouth As I approached her she said her friend had left. She then started walking around looking for her friend. I then left to call the police. Another passerby stayed with the women who was bleeding from the mouth."

STATEMENT OF LOUIS THOM ▓▓▓▓▓ at Milwaukee Wis.

" I stopped to help the woman who was bleeding from the mouth. She kept yelling for someone named Ed. She then went up the driveway and into the house and shortly therafter came out saying she had run over him."

STATEMENT OF MRS. JUDITH THOM ▓▓▓▓▓

" I got out of the car to help her. She went into the house (referring to the Doris Duke Estate) I followed her . She appeared to be in a state of shock. She walked rapidly through the house looking for someone named Ed. Then she came down the stairs saying she had run over Ed. and she had to go find him. She then walked back to the scene. I tried to comfort her."

NOTE:

None of the above actually saw the accident take place.

Officer Angel Reports:

When I arrived at the scene I saw a woman whom I later found out t be Doris Duke, sitting on the front seat of ▓▓▓▓▓ that had been involved in an accident,. She was being comforted by a young wave. I asked her if she was alright, and if there was anyone else injured. She replied "A friend I can't find my friend. I then looked under the car and saw a man lying on the ground under the car. I went to my radio and asked that a wrecker be sent to the scene immediately and to rush the rescue wagon. I then tried in vain along with Mr Hanley to lift the car by means of our bumper jacks. The rescue wagóns, Middletown & Newport , arrived and they tried to lift the car with their jacks. They were working on the car when the wrecker arrived (Pelham St Garage). The car was then lifted off the victem and he was taken to Newport Hosp. in the Newport Rescue wagon . Doris Duke was taken to the Newport Hosp. by the Middletown Rescue wagon for treatment of Shock and a laceration of the mouth. I then proceeded to take statments from witnesses, and to take measurments.

Officer Costello Reports:

There was a peice of glass found in the driveway to the estate Specimens of glass from the headlight and Parking lights of the vehicle involved were taken and placed in the evidence locker in seperate packages. Photograps were taken at the scene also.

Note: I rechecked with James Hanley as to the position of The women he saw bleeding from the mouth. He stated behind the steering Wheel and the door was just slightly opened.

Reporting Officer		O. O. B:		Dup.		Rec'd Recovered		Compl.		Closed		Night		By, O. In C.
Angel														· C.S.C.

Report of Officer Edward Angel

CITY OF NEWPORT POLICE DEPT.   HOW RECEIVED   ☐COMP ☐SIGHT ☐DISP. ☐ARREST

CLASSIFICATION	CODE	LOCATION OF INCIDENT		TIME REPORTED		DATE		COMPLAINT NO.

Location of Incident:)Opp. Doris Duke Estate — Bellevue Ave

TIME REPORTED 5:07 PM   DATE 10 7 66   COMPLAINT NO. D4848 409C

COMPLAINANT: Phone call Fire Dept.

OF M. V. VEH. GET BELOW DATA

OWNER NAME & ADDRESS: Avis Rent A Car   Sheraton Biltmore Prov RI

MAKE OF VEHICLE	ROAD CONDITION	WEATHER	ATTITUDE OPEN
66 Dodge	Dry	Clear	Good

Accident: Vehicle (Auto) - Vs + Ped.

     The station received a call from the Fire Dept at 5:07 PM requeting a car be sent to the end of Bellevue ave to assist at an auto accident. Car # 4 was sent.

     The injured parties were removed from the scene and I then proceeded with the investigation. (See my report page #2). The vehicle involved had come to rest at the base of a tree on the West side of Bellevue ave on the Chartier Real Estate property. Tire marks and the position of the vehicle indicated the ca# (   ) had entered Bellevue ave from the enterence way to the Doris Duke Estate Rough Point. The Gate to the Estate had been badley damaged and there were parts of the gate spread over the road. The vehicle involved had travelled across Bellevue ave mounted the sidewalk, ripped through an iron rail fence, and was resting at the base of a tree. There was extensive damage to the front end of the Vehicle   Point of impact appeared to be approx. 12 ft west of the gate to the Estate. The victem was then dragged across Bellevue ave and was lying under the vehicle   when I arrived. The vehicle involved was a 1966 Dodge (Automatic Transmission). Tagged and placed in the evidence locker were the bars from the iron fence that were knocked out of the gate from the impact.

     The vehicle was towed to the pelham st garage and impounded and a pocket book belonging to Miss Duke was tagged and placed in the evidence locker. It was inventoried by Officers Angel & Watterson, see attached inventory.

Lewis Perrotti of Reg investigator

REPORTING OFFICER	ARRESTING OFFICER				
Angel *Angel*		SC INF ☐ / TO JUV ☐	BICYCLE ☐ / OTHER ☐		C.S.C.

Report of Officer Edward Angel cont'd.

ANNOTATIONS

INTRODUCTION

1   Alisa Statman with Brie Tate, *Restless Souls: The Sharon Tate Family's Account of Stardom, The Manson Murders, and a Crusade for Justice* (New York Dey Street-It Books 2013) pp, 1-3.

2   Hadley Meares, "Prisoners of Fame: Falcon Lair, Rudolph Valentino, Doris Duke and The Cult of Celebrity Death" *KCET* January 14th, 2016.

3   Danny Mangin, "Doris Duke's Rough Point," *The New York Times*, 2006.

4   EJ Dickson, "9 Best Books About Charles Manson and the Family Murders," *Rolling Stone*, August 1st, 2019

PREFACE

5   Cleveland Amory, *The Last Resorts* (Harper and Brothers New York 1948) p. 171-173.

6   Thornton Wilder, *Theophilus North* (Harper & Row New York 1973). p. 14-16.

7   The Gilded Age list of the top 400 members of New York society as compiled by Social arbiter Ward McAllister, the confident and friend of society's "grand dame" at the time, Caroline Schermerhorn Astor. The popular conception was that 400 was the number of crème de la crème that could fit into Mrs. Astor's ballroom at 350 Fifth Avenue which made way, decades later, for The Empire State Building.

CHAPTER ONE

8   Roger Catlin, "The Billionaire And Her Butler," *The Hartford Courant*, February 9th, 2008.

9   Ken Franckling, "Fear and loathing on 'Millionaire's Row," *United Press International,* September 28th, 1986.

10   Pony Duke and Jason Thomas, *Too Rich: The Family Secrets of Doris Duke* (New York: HarperCollins, 1996) p. 175.

11   "Duke Estate Death Ruled an Accident," *The New York Times,* October 12th, 1966.

12   Romano et al. vs Doris Duke, Rhode Island Supreme Court. Case No. 1603-A. Plaintiff's Brief on Appeal pp.10-11, citing trial transcript pp. 429 + 644.

13   Author's interview with Patrick Mahn, Doris Duke's former business manager, July 27th, 2018.

14   Author's interview with Donna Lohmeyer, Eduardo Tirella's niece, September 21st, 2018.

15   Stephanie Mansfield, *The Richest Girl in The World* (New York, G.P. Putnam's Sons 1992) p. 219.

16   R. Edward Brown, sworn deposition in Brown vs. Hill, Farrer & Burrell et. al. Rubenstein Library, Box 375 Folder 1. p. 39.

17   Author's interview with Glen Cheda, friend of Edmund Kara, October 11th, 2018.

18   Author's interview with Johnny Nutt, Rough Point gardener, July 27th, 2018.

19   Author's interview with Harle Tinney, friend of John Perkins Brown, October 4th, 2018.

20   Romano et. al. vs. Avis U.S. Dist. Court, Case. No. 3870. Defendant's Answers Interrogatories, June 30th, 1968. No. 31.

21   Author's interview with former Newport Police Dept. Patrolman (Ret.) Edward Angel, October 26th, 2018.

22   Phillip C. McAllister, Report of County Medical Examiner, Tirella, Edmund G. October 7th, 1966 Pronounced: 5:30 pm; "Doris Duke Kills Friend in Crash," *The Newport Daily News*, October 8th, 1966. "Tirella died instantaneously of brain injuries."

23   "Death of Miss Duke's Friend Ruled 'Unfortunate Accident.'" *The Newport Daily News,* October 10th, 1966.

24   Romano et. al. vs. Avis U.S. Dist. Court, Case. No. 3870. Defendant's Answers Interrogatories. June 30th, 1968. No. 27.

25   "Duke Estate Death Ruled an Accident," *The New York Times,* October 12th, 1966.

26   "Ken Rowe, "Radice: 42 Years A Cop," *The Newport Daily News,* May 16th, 1967.

27   "Walsh Named Chief of Newport Police," *The Newport Daily News*, May 29th, 1967.

28   "3 Policemen Retire Here," Sgt. George Watts, *The Newport Daily News*, August 27th, 1976.

29   "Cliff Walk Fence Faces City Probe," *The Newport Daily News*, February 17th, 1958. "The Privileges Of The Shore," Editorial, *The Newport Daily News* December 29th, 1961: "Barring passage by means of a chain link fence along the Cliff Walk at 'Rough Point,' the Doris Duke estate might give the City a final reason for going to the courts to determine just what rights, under the state constitution, the people have not only along the Cliffs, but to all parts of the shore." The editorial cites Section 17 of Article 1 of the R.I. Constitution of 1842 which governs public access to the shores around the state.

30   T. Curtis Forbes, "Doris Duke Gives $25,000 to Restore Cliff Walk," *The Newport Daily News,* October 15th, 1966.

31   U.S. Inflation Calculator

32   Author's interview with Lewis A. Perrotti, Field Investigator, RI Registry of Motor Vehicles. October 27th, 2018; author's interview with Linda McFarlane Knierim, daughter of Rough Point caretaker. September 23rd, 2018; "Doris Duke Doctor Bars Press Quiz Temporarily," *Long Beach Press Telegram* October 9th, 1966.

33   T. Curtis Forbes, "1968: A Year of Progress in Urban Renewal," *The Newport Daily News*, December 31st, 1968; "Doris Duke Tells Aim Here: Has Pride in Newport." *The Newport Daily News*, September 23rd, 1969. According to The Newport Restoration Foundation website: "Heiress and philanthropist Doris Duke founded NRF in 1968 to rescue and preserve the earliest architectural heritage of Newport, which was threatened at the time by long-time neglect and various urban renewal efforts. In her lifetime, Duke bought and restored 70 18th- and early 19th-century houses, most of which are still owned today by NRF and leased as private residences to tenant/stewards."

34   "If You Grew Up In Newport, RI Share Some Memories." Facebook group.

35   Author's interview with Donna Lohmeyer, Eduardo Tirella's niece, September 21st, 2018.

36   Letter from R. Sar Mischiara to Liberty Mutual July 25th, 1967 RE: TIRELLA et. al vs. Avis AD202-56742, A113-39259: "Getting down to real 'brass tacks,' we both agree that $200,000.00 is a fair, just and reasonable amount in settlement."

37   Ibid. Mansfield. p. 237.

38   "Jury Picked In Doris Duke Accident Case," *The Providence Journal,* June 16th, 1971.

39   Alan M. Dershowtiz, *Reversal of Fortune: Inside the von Bülow Case.* (New York: Random House 1985) von Bülow was acquitted on both counts of assault with intent to murder in the second trial.

40   "Doris Duke In Court On Death," *United Press International,* June 18th, 1971.

41   "Jury Sees Movie Excerpts Tied to Tirella's Advice," *The Providence Journal,* June 25th, 1971. "Statements made in pretrial proceedings that his gross earnings rose from $13,650 in 1962 to $43,674.40 in 1965."

42   Ibid. U.S. Inflation Calculator

43   Romano et. al. vs Doris Duke, Rhode Island Supreme Court. Case No. 1603-A. Plaintiff's Brief on Appeal p. 9 citing trial transcript pp. 346 + 348.

44   Ibid.

45   Eduardo Tirella correspondence with David Rimmer, Duke Gardens Foundation January 31st, 1962 to March 10th, 1964. Rubenstein Library Box 5 Folder 26; "significant glass house collection: The Gardens were closed in 2008:

46   Tom Valentine Patrick Mahn, *Daddy's Duchess An Unauthorized Biography of Doris Duke.* (Lyle Stuart, Secaucus 1987) p. 146.

47   Author's interview with Pola Zanay, October 12th, 2018.

48   Stephen Heffner, "Doris Duke, Now Only An Elusive Shadow," *The Providence Sunday Journal* November 29th, 1987.

49   Thomas F. Kelleher, Justice, Rhode Island Supreme Court. Decision on Appeal. 304 A.2d 47 (1973) Romano et. al. vs. Doris Duke Supreme Court of Rhode Island. May 4th, 1973.

50   David Green letter to Anita Tirella Aughey re: Disbursements from Romano et. al vs. Duke. July 17th, 1973 per attorney Edward I. Friedman. Total distribution to eight heirs: $44,866.44.

51   Ibid. Zanay interview.

52   "About The Meadowbrook," *The Meadowbrook Project.*

53   Edward Tirella. Honorable Discharge August 10th, 1945.

54   "850 Women Attend 'The Thing for Spring' Given by Saks For Charity Event," *The Los Angeles Times,* January 27th, 1951. "Inside SFA," Beverly Hills, California. Sales insert.

55   Maggie Bartel and Alton Slagle, "Fate Folded Golden Hands," *New York Daily News,* October 10th, 1966.

56   *Person to Person* Airdate October 20th, 1960. Episode Eight.

57   "Doris Duke Cooks," *Vogue,* November 1st, 1966; "Doris Isle Home in Vogue," *Honolulu Advertiser* October 28th, 1966.

58   "Doris Duke Sued For Divorce," *Los Angeles Herald Examiner*, January 11th, 1964.

59   Walter Ryce, *"Sculptures by the reclusive Edmund Kara see light of day again,"* The Monterey County Weekly," June 16th, 2016.

60   Harvey Kubernick, *Canyon of Dreams: The Magic And The Music of Laurel Canyon* (New York, Sterling Publishing Co. 2009) pp. 6-8.

61   <u>Romano et al. vs Doris Duke</u>, Rhode Island Supreme Court. Case No. 1603-A. Plaintiff's Brief on Appeal p. 11 citing trial transcript pp. 476 + 623-633.

62   Ibid. p. 8. <u>Romano et al. vs Doris Duke</u>, Rhode Island Supreme Court. Case No. 1603-A. Plaintiff's Brief on Appeal p. 11 citing trial transcript p. 429; Sharon Tate's filmography:

63   Edward Tirella credits imdb.com

64   Ibid. Thomas F. Kelleher. <u>Romano et al. vs Doris Duke</u>. Supreme Court of Rhode Island. May 4th, 1973.

CHAPTER TWO

65   "Frederick William Vanderbilt Dead," *United Press International*, June 30th, 1938.

66   The Breakers, Marble House, Rock Cliff, Rough Point, Beaulieu and Sandy Point Farm in Portsmouth.

67   Guided Tour of Rough Point, conducted by Charles A Burns, October 7th, 2018.

68   "Doris Duke Feted At Newport Dance," *The New York Times*, August 24th, 1930.

69   Eric Pace, "Doris Duke, 80, Heiress Whose Great Wealth Couldn't Buy Happiness, Is Dead, *The New York Times,* October 29th, 1993; "James B. Duke Wills Bulk of $100,000,000 To Widow And Child." *The New York Times,* October 24th, 1925.

70   Paul Lieberman and John J. Goldman, "A Tale of Money and Mystery," *The Los Angeles Times,* April 10th, 1995.

71   Ibid.,"Doris Duke, Heiress Whose Great Wealth Couldn't Buy Happiness, Is Dead." *The New York Times,* October 29th, 1993: "And in 1966 there was the accidental death of Eduardo Tirella, an interior decorator who was a close friend, when the car she was driving slammed him against a gate on Rough Point, the Newport estate."

72   Ibid. Lieberman and Goldman.

73   Author's interviews with Patrick Mahn, July 27th and August 4th, 2019

74   Dinitia Smith, "The Death And Delirious Life of Doris Duke. *New York Magazine,* December 6th, 1993. Quoting Patrick Mahn.

75   Bob Colacello, "Doris Duke's Final Mystery," *Vanity Fair,* March 1994.

76   See END NOTE: 473 CHAPTER EIGHTEEN.

77   Ibid. Tom Valentine Patrick Mahn, *Daddy's Duchess An Unauthorized Biography of Doris Duke.* (Secaucus, Lyle Stuart 1987)

78   Ibid. Pony Duke and Jason Thomas, *Too Rich: The Family Secrets of Doris Duke* (New York, HarperCollins 1996) p. ix. p. 242.

79   "James Buchanan Duke: Father of The Modern Cigarette. *BBC News*, November 13th, 2012.

80   Ibid. Lieberman and Goldman.

81   Elizabeth Mehren, "The Duchess Who Posted Bail: Tobacco Heiress Doris Duke Shares a Love of Art, Music, Good Life With Friend Imelda Marcos. *The Los Angeles Times,* November 7th, 1987.

82   Ibid. Valentine and Mahn p. 138.

83   Wesley Fach, attorney for Doris Duke Memoranda 11.18 and 11.29.66 re: effort to use contacts at *The World Journal Tribune* to get columnist Jack O'Brien to retract his piece of November 18th, 1966 citing Duke's butcher knife attack on Joe Castro. Rubenstein Library Box 3 Folder 7 p. 9.

84   "Doris Duke Car Hits, Kills Decorator Guest," *New York Daily News*, October 8th, 1966; R. Edward Brown, sworn deposition in Brown vs. Hill, Farrer & Burrell et. al. Rubenstein Library, Box 375 Folder 1. p. 39.

85   Ibid. Daddy's Duchess p. 138.

86   Author's email correspondence with Rene Arazamendez, Manager, Research Getty Images, May 7th, 2020.

87   Author's email correspondence with Andrew Smith, Rhode Island Judicial Archives, July 31st to August 1st, 2018.

88   Stephanie Mansfield correspondence to Anita Aughey March 30th, 1990.

89   Author's search of The Newport Daily News photo archives at The Newport Historical Society October 2nd, 2018.

90   Sallie Bingham, *The Silver Swan: In Search of Doris Duke.* (New York: Fararr, Straus and Giroux 2020). pp. 182-185.

91   Peter Lance, "Seabees Swarm Over Aged Ship Being Lifted From Harbor Bottom," *The Newport Daily News*, June 14th, 1967. Author's first professional byline.

92   Peter Lance *ABC News* credits imdb.com

93   Peter Lance biography *HarperCollins.com*

94   RealClear Politics, citing *CNN* video of President Donald J. Trump's speech in Sioux City, IA, January 23rd, 2016.

95   Peter Lance, "The Spy Who Came In For The Heat," *Playboy*, August, 2010.

96   Ibid. Facebook Group: "If You Grew Up in Newport, RI."

97   Peter Lance, "The New Breed: Eight Rookies Train," *The Newport Daily News*, December 1st, 1967.

98   "Lawyers Chase O.J. Simpson Over $70 Million Wrongful Death Judgement. *The Associated Press*, January 30th, 2018.

99   Memo from Edward F. Burke, Special Counsel to Attorney General J. Joseph Nugent "Report of Investigation," Eduardo G. Tirella, November 4th, 1966.

100   David Green letter to Anita Tirella Aughey, July 17th, 1973. In the letter he details the legal fees and disbursements for the representation of Tirella's heirs in <u>Romano et. al. vs. Doris Duke</u>." Attorney Green, whose law offices were at 535 Fifth Avenue, New York, 17, N.Y., lists $2,000.00 as the "Legal Fee of Joseph Nugent." According to inflation-calculator.com that fee was the equivalent of $11,549.05 in 2020 dollars.

101   Author's interview with Denise Clement, February 4th, 2019.

CHAPTER THREE

102   Charles H. Dow, *Newport: the City by the Sea: Four Epochs in Her History. An Age of Shadowy Tradition. An Era of Commercial Success and Social Splendor. A Generation of Decadence. A Half Century of Unparalleled Development* (John P. Sanborn Publisher, Newport 1880).

103   Andrea McHugh, "The Classic Coast, the Triangle Trade and Slave History," *Discovery Newport* September 26th, 2019.

104 "The Day Rhode Island Hanged 26 Pirates," New England Historical Society.

105 Emil E. Jamail, "Kennedy's To Occupy Estate Here In 1964," *The New port Daily News*. October 30th, 1963.

106 "Mrs. Onassis Is Vice President, Restoration Foundation Reveals," *The Newport Daily News*, September 25th, 1969.

107 Emery Batts, *Saints And Sectaries: Ann Hutchinson and the Antinomian Controversy in the Massachusetts Bay Colony* (The University of North Carolina Press. Chapel Hill 1962).

108   Mark W. Gordon, "Rediscovering Jewish Infrastructure: 2018 Update on United States 18th and 19th Century Synagogues," American Jewish Historical Society.

109 Andy Smith, "Newport's Touro Synagogue celebrates its 250th anniversary," *The Providence Journal,* August 18th, 2013.

110 The Oldest Newspaper in Each New England State. New England Historical Society.com *The Newport Mercury*, founded in 1759, was identified as the nation's oldest newspaper during one of the *New Hampshire Gazette*'s lulls. It didn't *quite* disappear, having been published by *The Newport Daily News* as a weekly with reprinted daily stories for out-of-town subscribers. In 2018 it became *Mercury Magazine.*

111 Timeline of Newport, Rhode Island. *Wikipedia*

112 The 1968 Presidential Election *270towin.com* Richard M. Nixon, the Republican candidate won 301 electoral votes, Hubert Humphrey, the Democratic candidate won 191 and George Wallace, the American Independent Candidate won 46.

113 The 1972 Presidential Election *Wikipedia*. Richard M. Nixon, the Republican Candidate won 520 electoral votes. George S. McGovern won 17 electoral votes, carrying only The State of Massachusetts with 1,112,078 popular votes or 54.20%. The State of Rhode Island gave McGovern, his second highest vote percentage against Nixon in the 50 states at 46.81. Only Washington, D.C. which McGovern also carried, gave him a higher percentage than Nixon at 78.10%.

114 John W. Finney, "274 Military Bases Target of Federal Economy Plan," By John W. Finney, *The New York Times,* April 17th, 1973.

115 Ibid. Mansfield p. 292.

116 *BlackPearlNewport.com*

117   The Black Pearl was the founding ship of The American Sail Training Association and the signature vessel of Tall Ships America, founded by the Black Pearl's former owner Barclay Warburton III, who sailed his little brig across the Atlantic to the U.K. in 1972.

118   Timothy M. Phelps, "Op-Ed: I broke the Anita Hill story. Here's what we need to learn from her treatment," *The Los Angeles Times*, September 18th, 2018. After a distinguished career as a reporter and editor for *The Baltimore Sun* and *The New York Times* he retired from *The Los Angeles Times* in 2015.

119   Timothy M. Phelps, bio, *The Los Angeles Times*.

CHAPTER FOUR

120   Peter A. Lance," "World Press Covered Cup Races," *The Newport Daily News*, September 21st, 1967.

121   Author's interview with Julia and Gus Gianiotis, October 6th, 1967.

122   Author's interview with William Amato, October 6th, 1967.

123   Author's encounter with Ed Quigley, October 6th, 1967.

124   Peter Lance. Story on Quality Lunch Shooting. New England Wire. *The Associated Press*, October 6th, 1967.

125   Peter Lance. Follow: Story on Quality Lunch Shooting. New England Wire. *The Associated Press*, October 6th, 1967.

CHAPTER FIVE

126   Cleveland Amory, *The Last Resorts* (Harper and Brothers New York 1948) p. 247.

127   President Franklin D. Roosevelt's New Deal programs forced an increase in taxes to generate needed funds. The Revenue Act of 1935 introduced the Wealth Tax, a new progressive tax that took up to 75 percent of the highest incomes. Many wealthy people used loopholes in the tax code. The Revenue Act of 1937 cracked down on tax evasion by revising tax laws and regulations." Revenue Act of 1935. *Wikipedia*.

128   Ibid. Facebook Group: "If You Grew Up in Newport, RI." May 5th, 2018

129   Linda McFarlane Knierim, *A Summer Cottage Through A Child's Eye. A Caretaker's Daughter. Rough Point Newport, Rhode Island.*" (2016 CreatSpace). p. 90.

130   Ibid.

131   Ibid.

132   Author's interview with Rocky Cleffi September 25th, 2018.

133   Alton Slagle, "Doris Duke's Doctor's Bar Death Probe," *New York Daily News,* October 9th, 1966.

134   Alton Slagle, "Behind Iron Gate: Wealth, Tragedy," *New York Daily News*, October 10th, 1966.

135   "Police Await Doris Duke's Recovery to Question Her," *United Press International*, October 9th, 1966.

136   Author's interview with Lewis A. Perrotti, Field Investigator, RI Registry of Motor Vehicles. October 27th, 2018.

137   "Heiress Not Charged in Auto Death," *The Associated Press,* October 10th, 1966.

138   Lt. Frank H. Walsh, Report of interview, "October 9, 1966 About 12:30 pm" Official report of The Newport Police Department p. 1.

139   Alton Slagle, "R.I. Law Chief Asks Full Report on Doris," *New York Daily News,* October 11th, 1966.

140   Ibid.

CHAPTER SIX

141   Author's interview with confidential source, October 8th, 2018.

142   "Doris Duke Kills Friend in Crash," *The Newport Daily News*, October 8th 1966

143   "Statements Offered in Doris Duke Trial," *The Providence Journal* June 22nd, 1971.

144   Romano et. al. vs. Avis U.S. Dist. Court, Case. No. 3870. Defendant's Answers Interrogatories. June 30th, 1968. Doris Duke's response to interrogatory answer No., 27.

145   Author's Interview with Detective William Watterson, Newport Police Department (ret.) June 25th, 2019.

146   Ibid. Romano et. al. vs. Avis Interrogatory answer No. 31.

147   Author's interview with Judith Thom Wartgo, September 21st, 2018.

148   Official report of The Newport Police Department. p 4.

149   Ibid. Slagle October 9th, 1966.

150   Ibid. Wartgo interview.

151   Stephanie Mansfield, *The Richest Girl in The World* (New York, G.P. Putnam's Sons 1992)

152   Author's interview with Robert Aughey Jr. September 25th, 2018.

153 Author's interview with Det. James Moss (NYPD Ret.) October 4th, 2018.

154 Ibid.

CHAPTER SEVEN

155 Author's interview with William O'Connell October 18th, 2018.

156 Ibid. <u>Romano et. al. vs. Avis</u> Interrogatory answer No. 27

157 Ibid. Moss interview.

158 Lewis A. Perrotti, Investigators and Examiner's Report: Homicide of Eduardo Guiseppe Tirella. Rhode Island Registry of Motor Vehicles. October 19th, 1966. P. 3

159 "Doris Tells of Fatal Crash And Project Is Cut Short," *New York Daily News* October 12th, 1966.

160 "Duke Estate Death Ruled An Accident," *The New York Times*/United Press International, October 12th, 1966.

161 "Tirella's Death Called Unfortunate Accident" *The Providence Journal*, October 11th, 1966.

162 "Doris Duke Pays Record Price of $102,000 for Goddard Piece" *The Newport Daily News*. May 27th, 1971.

163 "Doris Duke Joins Black Church in N.J. *UPI* June 30th, 1971; Notes on People, *The New York Times* July 1st, 1971.

164 "Doris Duke In Choir of Predominantly-Black Church," *The Providence Journal,* July 1st, 1971.

165 "Doris Duke In Court On Death," *United Press International,* June 18th, 1971.

CHAPTER EIGHT

166 William Claiborne, "Rhode Island 4 Years Later: Pullout Still Hurts, " *The Washington Post*, March 27th, 1977.

167 "Mrs. H. Oelrichs, Social Leader, Dies," *The New York Times,* November 23rd, 1926.

168 "The Great Gatsby," *AFI Catalogue of Feature Films. The First 100 Years* (1974).

169 F. Scott Fitzgerald, *The Great Gatsby* (Wisehouse Classics Stockholm 2016). p. 10

170   Passenger log, RMS Celtic. Liverpool, England to New York City Arrival October 19th, 1926.

171   Passenger log, RMS Mauretania, Cherbourg, France to New York City Arrival September 2d, 1927.

172   Albert E. Holmwood and Dorothy F. Sutherland, New York State Marriage Index, 1881-1967.

173   "A Nod to Ham Rice," *Harvard Magazine,* March, 1999.

174   "Alexander Hamilton Rice," *Harvard '98 Second Report.* p. 158.

175   Eric I. Rutkow and Ira M. Rutgow, "George Crile, Harvey Cushing and The Ambulance Americaine: military medical preparedness in World War I," *PubMed.gov.*

176   "Dr. Alexander H. Rice, 80, Explorer Geographer, Dies," *The Newport Daily News*, March 13th, 1956.

177   Frederick Sumner Mean (Editor) *Harvard's Military Record in the World War,* (Harvard University Press Cambridge, MA, 1921)

178   Rick Archbold and Dana McCauley, *Last Dinner on The Titanic* (Hyperion New York 1997).

179   "Mrs. A.H. Rice Dies in Paris Store," *The New York Times,* July 13th, 1937.

180   "William Bentinck-Smith *"...a Memorial to My Dear Son" Some Reflections on 65 Years of the Harry Elkins Widener Memorial Library.* (Harvard College Library, Cambridge 1980). 27 pages; "Mrs. G.D. Widener Opens New Villa," *The New York Times*, August 21st, 1915.

181   "Mark J. Plotkin, "Alexander Hamilton Rice: Brief life of an American explorer: 1875-1956," *Harvard Magazine.*

182   Edward Tenner, "Harvard, Bring Back Geography," *Harvard Magazine,* May-June 1988.

183   "E.J. Berwind Dies, Coal Operator," *The New York Times,* August 19th, 1936.

184   *Bloomberg News,* November 10th, 1966.

185   Ibid. *The New York Times*, August 21st, 1915.

186   "Explorer Rice Weds Mrs. G.D. Widener – Law Requiring Five Days Delay After Securing License Waived by a Court Order – Plans for Secrecy Fail – Bishop Lawrence Officiates at Ceremony in Emmanuel Church Vestry Witnessed by 12 Persons," *The New York Times*, October 7th, 1915.

187   "Former Mrs. Widener Shares Perils in South America," *The New York Tribune* May 1st, 1920.

188 "2 More Mansions on 5th Ave. To Die," *The New York Times* August 9th, 1957. *The Times* reported that the Trumbauer-designed Rice townhouse at 901 Fifth Avenue and a five story home adjacent, built in 1926 for another Newport summer colonist, Florence Adele Vanderbilt Twombly, granddaughters of Cornelius Vanderbilt, were sold to make way for a modern 19 story residential apartment building to sit on the corner of Fifth Avenue and East 71st Street adjacent to the Frick Museum.

189 Society column, *New York Daily News,* March 18th, 1934.

190 Ibid. *The Newport Daily News*, March 13th, 1956.

191 Cleveland Amory, *The Last Resorts* (Harper and Brothers New York 1948) p. 169.

192 William Norwich, "STYLE:" Show Me the Monkey," *The New York Times,* February 23rd, 2003.

193 Ibid, *The New York Times,* July 13th, 1937.

194 "Mrs. A.H. Rice, 79, On Museum Boards," *The New York Times*, December 5th, 1969.

195 "John P. Upham Ends Life," The *Associated Press/The New York Times*, June 10th, 1934.

196 Ibid, *The Newport Daily News*, March 13th, 1956.

197 Christopher Gray, "Whatever happened to the Fourth Footman?" *The New York Times,* September 13th, 2012.

198 Terry H. Schwadson, "Newport 'Downstairs,'" *UpCountry Magazine,* July, 1976.

199 "60 Room Miramar Given to RI Episcopal Diocese By George Widener, Sister," *The Newport Daily News*, May 11th, 1957.

200 Ibid. The complex was known as "The Miramar Cottages."

201 U.S. Census. 1940 showing that the Holmwoods resided in Palm Beach, Florida in 1935 and East. 74th Street In New York City by 1940.

202 "Auction of Jewels Sets World Mark," *The Associated Press/The Phoenix Gazette*, May 5th, 1965. The story noted that "Jeweler Harry Winston paid $348,000 for a handful of baubles, a few of which he had originally sold to Mrs. Rice. A ruby ring with a pigeon-blood stone of nearly 10 carats was bid by Van Cleef & Arpels of New York for $85,000. The same jeweler had sold the ring to Mrs. Rice six years ago for about $100,000."

203 Author's interview with Eileen Brown, October 10th, 2020.

204   Philadelphia's Union League Club was founded in 1862. *UnionLeague. org;* The Oglethorpe Club in Savannah opened in 1870. *Oglethorpe club.org;* Cleveland Amory, *The Last Resorts* (Harper and Brothers New York 1948).

CHAPTER NINE

205   Author's Interview with Richard Tracy October 12th, 2020.

206   George P. Wetmore Papers *Rhode Island Historical Society.*

207   "Constitution, By-Laws, Officers and Stockholders of The Newport Reading Room," Incorporated 1854. 1907.

208   Ibid.

209   Albert Stevens Crockett, *When James Gordon Bennett was Caliph of Bagdad* (Funk & Wagnalls, New York 1926).

210   Archives of The Redwood Library.

211   Author's interview with Dan Konchar, May 15th, 2020.

212   Jack Forster, "The House That Plant Built – 101 Years of Cartier Man sion History," *Hodinkee.com* September 19th, 2016.

213   David W. Dunlap, "Cartier Spruces Up To Show Off Its Jewels in Style," *The New York Times,* April 26th, 2000.

214   Clarendon Court 626 Bellevue Avenue, *HouseHistree.*

215   Enid Nemy, "Marthy 'Sunny' von Bulow, at 76; heiress fell into coma 28 years ago." *The New York Times*, December 7th, 2008. *State v. von Bulow, 475 A.2d 995* (R.I. 1984).

216   "Reversal of Fortune," *The Internet Movie Database.* 1990.

217   Bruce Weber, "Eileen G. Slocum, 92, Dies' Society Doyenne and Republican Stalwart," *The New York Times*, August 1st, 2008.

218   Deborah Davis, *Party of The Century, The Fabulous Story of Truman Capote and His Black And White Ball* (John Wiley & Sons Hoboken, 2006).

219   Deborah Davis *Gilded: How Newport Became America's Richest Resort* (John Wiley & Sons, Hoboken, 2009) p. 24.

220   "Herman Huffer Dies In France," *The Newport Daily News,* September 11th, 1964.

221   "Comte Armand Marc de Saint Héerem Montmorin, *Encyclopedia Britannica*, 1911 edition.

222   "Huffer's Sloop Wins Pt. Judith Race," *The Newport Daily News*, September 9th, 1957.

223 "Fire Sweeps Shipyard At Jamestown. *The Newport Daily News*, December 5th, 1957.

224 "5.5's Begin Races Friday to Pick U.S. Entry In This Fall's Olympics." *The Newport Daily News*, June 24th, 1964.

225 "Miss Marguerite Slocum Makes Debut in Newport," *The New York Times*, August 19th, 1962.

226 Autor's interview with Richard Tracy, October 12th, 2020.

227 "In Social Circles: Dr. Charles S. Dotterer Wins Newport Country Club's President Cup Tournament," *The Newport Daily News*, September 17th, 1953.

228 "Dr. Charles Dotterer Heads Hospital Staff," *The Newport Daily News,* January 26th, 1950.

229 156 Broadway, Newport, RI 02840. *Noreys.com.*

230 "City Pays Tribute To Navy On 'Day,'" *The Newport Daily News,* October 29th, 1965.

231 Michael Feldberg, "Judah Touro: American Jewish Philanthropist," *The American Jewish Historical Society.*

232 "Touro Park and Old Stone Mill, *The Cultural Landscape Foundation.*

233 "The Whirlaway Wedding of Mary Cushing and Peter Beard In Newport," *Vogue,* October 1st, 1967.

234 Author's interview with confidential source August 11th, 1967. StarMessages Moon Phase for August 11th, 1967.

235 "Minnie Cushing and Peter Beard Wed in Newport," *The New York Times,* August 13th, 1967.

CHAPTER TEN

236 Sue Reed, "If You Grew Up in Newport, RI," Facebook Group. Larry Bettencourt post January 3rd, 2013.

237 Al Stoos, "If You Grew Up in Newport, RI," Facebook Group. Larry Bettencourt post October 2nd, 2018.

238 U.S. Federal Census. 1940. Newport, RI. Roll: m-t0627-03760. p. 2B. Enumeration District: 3-30; column 13.

239 Ken Rowe, "Radice: 42 Years A Cop," *The Newport Daily News* May 16th, 1967.

240 Author's interview with Captain Paul Faerber, Newport Fire Dept. (Ret.) February, 16th, 2019.

241 Harriet Gee, "Judge Tours Doris Duke's Mansion. Court Held at Shan-gri-la. *Honolulu Star Bulletin,* April 28th, 1967; "Youth Loses Suits Against Doris Duke," *Honolulu Star Bulletin*, May 2nd 1967; Ibid Lieber-man and Goldman: There were four visitors waiting when the ambu-lance pulled through the gates of Falcon Lair on Sept. 20, 1993--her favorite dogs from Duke Farms, 150-pound akitas and German shep-herds. Author's interview with Chris Mey, October 26th, 2020.

242 "Duke Dogs Hit by Police Order," *The Newport Daily News*, May 22nd, 1964.

243 "Cliff Walk Fence Faces City Probe," *The Newport Daily News,* Febru-ary 17th, 1958.

244 Barbara Marsh, "Only A Mountain Goat Could Stroll on Part of Cliff Walk.," *The Newport Daily News*. June 4th, 1966.

245   Ibid. Pony Duke and Jason Thomas, *Too Rich* p. 144.

246 Author's interview with Woody Ring (Newport PD Ret.) October 4th, 2018.

247 2145 Pierce Street, Hollywood, FL, Unit 433. Warranty Deed #100839799, BK 31285 p. 1582. Recorded in Broward County Febru-ary 16th, 2001.

248 Author's interview with Andrew Flynn, July 5th, 2018.

249 Author's interview with Elayne Paranzino October 4th 2018. Elayne Paranzino email to author November 11th, 2018.

250 R.I. Census. Enumeration District/Census Tract 333. Ibid. U.S. Federal Census column 31.

251 City Directory of Newport, RI For The Year July 1945 to July 1946, Eastern Publishing Company. Newport, RI. P. 176.

252 Florida Department of Health. Marriage Indexes. 1822-1875 and 1927-2001. March 18th, 1970.

253 Ibid. Andrew Flynn

254 "Auto-Train Crash Claims Life of Newport Resident," *The Newport Daily News*. February 2nd, 1955.

255 Ibid. Flynn.

256 Burial records: Joseph A. Radice. St. Columba Catholic Cemetery, Mid dletown, RI. May 14th, 1899 to July 21st, 1997.

257 2145 Pierce Street, Hollywood, FL, Unit 433. Warranty Deed #100839799, BK 31285 p. 1582. Recorded in Broward County Febru-ary 16th, 2001.

258 Elayne Paranzino email to author November 11th, 2018.

259   Ibid. Andrew Flynn.

260   Author's interview with Elayne Paranzino March 7th, 2019.

261   2145 Pierce Street, Hollywood, FL, Unit 432. Warranty Deed # 71-26046. Rec #4430 page 152. Unit 433 Warranty Deed #100839799, BK 31285 p. 1582. Recorded in Broward County February 16th, 2001.

262   2145 Pierce Street, Hollywood, FL, Unit 428. Warranty Deed # 90011865 Recorded in Broward County January 10th, 1990.

263   "Two Denials, Guilty Plea, Appeal Follow State Police Bookie Raid," *The Newport Daily News,* October 24th, 1951.

264   Brittanica.com, The use of credit cards.

265   "Goffe Building Razed In Spectacular Fire," *The Newport Daily News*, November 11th, 1949.

266   "3 Policeman Retire Here," *The Newport Daily News.* August 27th, 1976.

267   "Walsh Named Chief of Newport Police," *The Newport Daily News,* May 29th, 1967.

268   "Paul J. Sullivan to head March of Dimes Campaign," *The Newport Daily News*, November 5th, 1966.

269   Author's interview with Tim Sullivan September 27th, 2018

.270 "Tirella's Death Called Unfortunate Accident," *The Providence Journal,* October 11th, 1966.

CHAPTER ELEVEN

271   Deborah Davis *Gilded: How Newport Became America's Richest Resort* (John Wiley & Sons, Hoboken, 2009) p. 25.

272   Bonnie Poisson, "There's A Stunning Chinese Tea House in RI," *Only In Your State* , January 19th, 2018.

273   "The Swiss Village, a railroad magnate's replica village has become home to a genetic seed bank for rare breeds of livestock," Atlas Obscura.

274   Henry James, *The American Scene* (Harper & Brothers, New York 1907).

275   "Who's Who: James Watson Gerard," biography, *firstworldwar.com*

276   The Sixty-Four Men Who Run America, *Financial Chronicle*, August 30th, 1930.

277   "Gen. C. Vanderbilt Dies On His Yacht. Great-Grandson and Name-sake of Commodore Succumbs in Miami to Brain Hemorrhage. He Won Distinction As Soldier, Inventor, Engineer, Yachtsman," *The Associated Press/New York Times,* March 2nd, 1942.

278   T.J. Stiles, *The First Tycoon: The Epic Life of Cornelius Vanderbilt* (Vintage Books, New York 2009)

279   Cleveland Amory, *The Last Resorts* (Harper and Brothers, New York 1948) p. 14.

280   "Newport County Tax Records. Vision Government Solutions. As of August 2nd, 2014.

281   Richard Morris Hunt's biography *The Harvard Graduate's Magazine* Vol. I, 1982-1893.

282   Ibid. Amory.

283   Ibid Mansfield. p. 244.

284   "Hunter House," *The Preservation Society of Newport County.*

285   Paul Goldberger, "Restored Homes Are Bringing a New Look to Old Newport, RI." *The New York Times*, August 25th, 1976.

286   Peter Lance, "Vanderbilt Scuttled Lipton's Hopes," *The Newport Daily News,* September 9th, 1967.

287   "Harold Vanderbilt, Yachtsman, Is Dead." *The New York Times,* July 5th, 1970.

288   "Motive Unclear In Suicide Leap," *The Associated Press,* June 26th, 1961.

289   "Lusitania Sunk By A Submarines, Probably 1,260 Dead; Twice Torpedoed Off Irish Coast; Sinks in 15 Minutes; Capt. Turner Saved; 'Frohman and Vanderbilt Missing' Washington Believes That A Grave Crisis Is At Hand," *The New York Times,* May 8th, 1915.

290   Olivia Skinner, "Tragic Chapters In The Lives of The Vanderbilts," *The St. Louis Post Dispatch,* September 1st, 1961.

291   "George Vanderbilt Is Killed in Plunge From Hotel on Coast, *The New York Times*, June 25th, 1961.

292   Ibid.

293   Ibid. *Post-Dispatch.*

294   Howard Kroplick, "The Five Vanderbilt Cup Trophies (1904-2007)" March 16th, 2016.

295   "George Vanderbilt III Is Divorced In The Isles," *Honolulu Star Bulletin*, March 22nd, 1961.

296 Ibid. "Motive Unclear" *The Associated Press.*

297 Ibid.

298 Ibid. "George Vanderbilt Killed In Plunge," *The New York Times.*

299 "Vanderbilt Wrote Will Day Before Suicide," *The Associated Press/ Long Beach Independent,* August 24th, 1961.

300 "Estate Lawyers Sue A Vanderbilt For A Fee," *New York Daily News,* June 1st, 1967.

CHAPTER TWELVE

301 Official report of The Newport Police Department p. 4

302 Ibid.

303 "Oliver Jennings, Capitalist Dead. Director of Many Companies, 71." *The New York Times,* October 14th, 1936.

304 "Board of Review to Weigh Mailands Apartment Plea," *The Newport Daily News,* January 12th, 1955.

305 "Oliver Gould Jennings Villa Sold," *The Newport Mercury* March 7th, 1952.

306 "Evicted Heiress 'Holding Fort." *Fort Lauderdale News,* April 24th, 1979.

307 "Landlord Fails to Evict Mrs. Vanderbilt," *United Press International/ The Berkshire Eagle,* October 28th, 1978.

308 "Headliners. Unlikely Casting," *The New York Times,* December 31st, 1978.

309 Ibid. "Evicted Heiress," *Fort Lauderdale News.*

310 Amy Hotz, "Keeping Up With The Joneses," *The Wilmington (North Carolina) Star News,* February 25th, 2007.

311 "Louise Mitchell Vanderbilt," Obituary, *The Honolulu Advertiser* April 30th, 1995.

312 Author's interview with Harry B. Casey, Newport County Sheriff (ret.) September 29th, 2020.

313 "Mrs. Muriel Vanderbilt Adams, Society Leader, Dies in Florida," *The New York Times,* February 4th, 1972.

314 Ibid.

315 "Police Chief Gives Thanks," *The Newport Daily News,* July 5th, 1966.

316 "Foiled Extortionist of Vanderbilt Sought," *The Boston Globe,* October 19th, 1966.

317   "Man Avoids Police Trap In Extortion, *The Newport Daily News*, October 15th, 1966.

318   "Extortion Case Lead Is Hinted by Radice," *The Newport Daily News,* October 17th, 1966.

319   Ibid. Middletown police chief Donald Homen was quoted earlier by *The Newport Daily News* as saying he was very upset about the incident in which Newport detectives unsuccessfully attempted to capture the extortionist in Middletown without informing the Middletown police in advance.

320   "Press Blast Police Chief Radice On Handling of Public Information," *The Newport Daily News,* November 3rd, 1966. "Police Chief Joseph A. Radice last night was rapped by newsmen for what was referred to as 'the public-be-damned way in which he released information on the Duke case' and his' bungling of the extortion plot attempted on Mrs. Muriel Vanderbilt Adams.'"

321   Author's interview with Det. Al Conti (Newport PD Ret.) January 20th, 2019.

322   Ibid. *The Boston Globe,* "Chief Joseph A. Radice and Detective Capt. Paul Sullivan 'have gone to Massachusetts,' an officer at police headquarters said."

323   "Police Reveal New Lead In Adams Extortion Plot," *The Newport Daily News,* December 28th, 1966. Radice said "we are quite positive he's the right one." The chief added "He is in Newport right now, to the best of our knowledge" Radice said detectives "Are still working on it," He declined to reveal further details of the investigation saying, "It's a ticklish subject."

324   "Mrs. Muriel Adams Ends Residence Here," *The Newport Daily News, May 11th, 1967.* "Mrs. Muriel Vanderbilt Adams has placed her estate 'Idle Hour Farm' on Hazard Road on the market and has ended her legal residence in Newport. The first steps toward closing and 52 Acre estate were taken several weeks ago when Mrs. Adams had her horses shipped to Florida and much of her furniture made ready for shipment. The remainder of the furniture and furnishings will be sold."

325   "Attorneys Corcoran, Hayes, Buy Muriel Adams Estate," *The Newport Daily News*, June 14th, 1967.

326   Ken Rowe, "Radice: 42 Years A Cop," *The Newport Daily News,* May 16th, 1967.

CHAPTER THIRTEEN

327 Loretta Grantham, "I would have paid a fortune for one real friend," *The Palm Beach Post,* February 23rd, 1999.

328 Shawn Levy, *The Last Playboy: The High Life of Porfirio Rubirosa* (New York, HarperCollins 2014). p. 127.

329 Peter Foges, "Porfirio Rubirosa: The Most Interesting Man In The World." *Thrillist.com* May 15th, 2014.

330 Harry Olesker, "Doris Duke Worth $200 Million," *The Syracuse Herald,* December 5th, 1966.

331 Ibid Levy, pp. 143; 154.

332 Gary Cohen, "The Legend of Rubirosa," *Vanity Fair,* May 18th, 2009.

333 Ibid Levy, p. 214.

334 Mac Randall, "Joe Castro: Lush Life: A Musical Journey," *Jazz Times,* April 25th, 2019.

335 Bret Sjerven, "Lush Life A Musical Chronology of Joseph Armand Castro 1927-1966," Timeline: Chapter Six.

336 Ibid. Mansfield p. 199.

337 "Doris Duke Sued For $150,000." *The New York Times,* January 25th, 1964.

338 Ibid. Duke and Thomas. p. 156.

339 "Doris Duke Sued for $150,000," *United Press International,* January 24th, 1964.

340 Joseph Armand Castro vs. Doris Duke L.A. County Superior Court January 10th, 1964. Complaint alleging: "Defendant wrongfully unlawfully and violently assaulted plaintiff with a butcher knife and attempted to kill the plaintiff by thrusting the same into his body and defendant thereupon violently and with great force, cut and pierced plaintiff's arm with said knife, causing plaintiff great physical pain, anguish and suffering and great mental anguish and humiliation and causing a large permanent scar to be left on that arm of the plaintiff all to the plaintiff's damage in the sum of $150,000."

341 "Divorce Suit Discloses Doris Duke's Marriage," *The Los Angeles Times,* January 11th, 1964.

342 "Doris Duke Sued For Divorce," *Los Angeles Herald Examiner,* January 11th, 1964.

343 "Doris Duke Being Sued," *The Newport Daily News,* January 11th, 1964.

344 J. Harold Hughes Memo: "Personal Family And Legal Considerations Involved in Pending Litigation." Rubenstein Library Box 166 Folder 6 pp. 150-1512.

345 "Doris Duke Suit Quashed," *The Associated Press*, January 25th, 1964.

346 Letter to Doris Duke from M.B. Jackson, February 4th, 1964. Ruben stein Library Box 166 Folder 6.

347 Ibid. p. 2.

348 Ibid. p. 8.

349 Ibid. pp. 9-10.

350 "Heiress' Chef Indicted Over 2 Missing Plates," *The Central (N.J.) Home News,* August, 13th, 1966.

351 Anthony J. Rummo, "Doris Duke is witness for the state," *The (New Brunswick, NJ) Home News*, June 22nd, 1976.

352 J. Harold Hughes, "Confidential Memo from Attorney to Client," February 18th, 1964. Rubenstein Library Box 166 Folder 6.

353 Ibid. Valentine and Mahn *Daddy's Duchess* p. 138 re: Castro friend John Pease: "Lawyer Hughes, an Ex-FBI agent, had done his job well. The Pease telephone had been wiretapped. A flyer had been circulated in Honolulu labeling Pease a racketeer. Dee Dee's lawyers and hired guns had kidnapped Castro, taking him back to Shangri-La and convinced him that Johnny was really a gangster and would 'chop off his fingers or kill him' if he ever got the chance."

354 Joseph Armand Castro vs. Doris Duke Castro, L.A. County Superior Court Declaration of R. Edward Brown In Opposition to Motion to Substitute Attorneys. p. 2. Rubenstein Library Box 166 Folder 6.

355 Ibid. Sjerven liner notes for the CD collection, *Lush Life.* "Duke was represented by attorney Morton B. 'Tony' Jackson in Los Angeles, who later hired Peter Brooke, and by attorney J. Harold Hughes in Honolulu. Beside the three suits, Duke had another problem: the threat of Castro publishing a book about Duke's private life. Jackson hired writer Brooke to pose as a potential buyer to short circuit the sale of an exposé that Castro (et. al) was trying to sell."

356 Invoice: Hill, Farrar & Burrill February 29th, 1964 Disbursement by Private Investigators Herm Schlieske showing $338.05 in airfare "Honolulu – Brooke." Rubenstein Library Box 166 Folder 7. p. 19.

357 <u>Doris Duke vs. Joseph Armand Castro</u>. Complaint March 31st, 1964 alleging: "that defendant Castro has entered into negotiations with certain persons or entities with those ends in view, and for the 'sale' or delivery of such personal material for publication or commercial distribution and dissemination, for his own monetary gain or profit."

358 Invoice: Herm C. Schlieske Private Investigations Statement of Charges February 15th, 1964: "$62.35 phone 'bug' Bella Drive; $50.00 install 'bug' at Bella Drive." Rubenstein Library Box 166 Folder 6. Falcon Lair address: 1436 Bella Drive.

359 Ibid. Sjerven, September 1st, 1964: The first session for the newly minted Clover Records. Ibid, *Lush Life*. One single C-331 from the album at Gold Star Recording Studios was recorded by Larry Levine.

360 R. Edward Brown, sworn deposition in <u>Brown vs. Hill, Farrer & Burrell et. al</u>. Rubenstein Library, Box 375 Folder 1. p. 54.

361 <u>Edward R. Brown vs. Hill, Farrer & Burrell, et. al</u>, L.A. County Superior Court. Sworn Deposition, June 24th, 1965.

362 Ibid. p. 91.

363 Ronald Schwartz, *Neo-Film Noir: The New Film Noir Style from Psycho to Collateral*, (Scarecrow Press Lanham, MD. 2005) p. 72; William Hare, *LA Noir: Nine Dark Visions of the City of Angels*, (McFarland & Company 2008) p. 213.

364 Grant Peters, "Doris Duke And Her African Prince, *Confidential,* May, 1955. pp 12-15; 54-55.

365 Ibid. Mansfield. p. 221.

366 Ibid Brown depo. p. 49.

367 Ibid.

368 "Porfirio Rubirosa Is Killed As Auto Crashes in Paris," *The New York Times*, July 5th, 1965.

369 Ibid. Mansfield. p. 234.

370 Romney Steele, *My Nepenthe Bohemian Tales of Food, Family And Big Sur*. (Kansas City Andrews McMeel 2015) p. 225.

371 Edmund Kara correspondence with Doris Duke, October 1966. Rubenstein Library Box 294 Folder 14.

372 Loretta Haddad Castro obituary, *findgrave.com*

373 Ibid Mansfield p. 235.

374   Ibid. Sjerven: Peter Brooke was hired as an "assistant" to Joe Castro to help in the creation, promotion, and sale of two recordings (four sides) for one year. Ibid Mansfield: "Castro never knew that Brooke had been on Doris' payroll. 'It was,' said Brooke 'one of the best kept secrets. Joe was totally fooled.'" p. 229.

375   Ibid Mansfield.

CHAPTER FOURTEEN

376   Peter Lance "Who Really Discovered America?" Research Paper submitted to The English Department. De La Salle Academy, April 25th, 1965.

377   Peter Lance "Who Really Erected The Newport Round Stone Tower?" Essay submitted to The English Department. De La Salle Academy, March 12th, 1964.

378   Paul Du Chaillu, *The Viking Age. Volume 1,* (Charles Scribner and Sons, New York 1889) pp. 15-17.

379   C.F. Keary, *The Vikings in Western Christendom* (G.P. Putnam Sons London 1891) pp. 46-79.

380   Edward G. Bourne & Julius E. Olson, *The Northmen, Columbus and Cabot* (Charles Scribner And Sons New York 1906) pp. 57-60.

381   Sofus Larson, *The Discovery of America 20 Years Before Columbus* (Hachette Ltd. London 1924) pp. 78-80.

382   Helg Ingstad, "Vineland Ruins Prove Vikings Found New World," *National Geographic* Vol. CXXVI, November 1964. pp. 708-734.

383   Ibid.

384   Edward Peterson, *History of Rhode Island* (John S. Taylor New York 1853) pp. 171-172.

385   Tracy Breton, "Tower Built By Vikings? Bubbles Burst A Theory," *The New York Times,* September 28th, 1993.

386   John Hale, Jan Heinemeier, Lynne Lancaster, Alf Lindroos and Asa Ringbom, "Dating Ancient Mortar," *American Scientist* 2003.

387   James Alan Egan, Elizabethan America, The John Dee Tower of 1583. Renaissance Horologium In Newport, Rhode Island, (Cosmopolite Press, Newport, RI, 2011).

388   "Meet Rogers High School Athletic Hall of Fame Class of 2020," *The Newport Daily News*, January 31st, 2020.

389   "High Point of America's Bicentennial Year," *The Newport Mercury,* July 12th, 1976.

390 Phillip Ainsworth Means, *The Newport Tower* (Henry Holt New York 1942).

391 Carl Christian Rafn, *Antiqvitates Americana* Sive Scriptores Septen trionales Rerum Ante Columbianarum In America 1937. Kenneth L. Feder, Encyclopedia of Dubious Archeology: From Atlantis To the Walam Olum, (Greenwood Santa Barbara 2010). p. 80.

392 W.S. Blackett, *Lost Histories of America* (Trubner & Company London 1883) pp. 102-105.

393 Gavin Menzies, *1421: The Year China Discovered the World,* (William Morrow New York 2008).

394 Andrew Sinclair, *The Sword and The Grail: Of The Grail and Templars and a True Discovery of America* (Crown New York, 1992). Joe Baker, "Towering Debate," *The Newport Daily News,* December 20th, 2012; *Newport Naked* Winter 2013/2014.

395 Edmund Burke Delabarre, *Recent History of Dighton Rock*, (John Wilson and Son Cambridge, 1919).

396 L.A. Vigneras, "Gaspar Corte-Real," *Dictionary of Canadian Biography* (University of Toronto Press 1966).

397 "Dighton Rock and Miguel Corte-Real," *Native Heritage Project*, March 28th, 2015.

398 Will of Governor Benedict Arnold of Newport, Rhode Island; retrieved May 27th, 2010.

399 Author's interview with James Alan Egan, October 4th, 2018.

400 William Penhallow, "Archaeoastronomy: The Newport Tower," *Abstract Baltic Astronomy,* Vol. 6 71-72 1997. Also cited in The New England Antiquities Research Association Journal p. 44. 1994.

401 Julian Roberts, editor: "Renaissance Man: The Reconstructed Libraries of Euopean Scholars 1450-1700. Series One: The Books and Manuscripts of John Dee, 1527-1608" Bodleian Library, Oxford. (Adam Matthew Publications Ltd. Marlborough 2005)

402 Ibid. Elizabethan America p. 54

403 Ken MacMillan, "Discourse on History, Geography, and Law: John Dee and the Limits of The British Empire, 1576-80," Journals, *University of Toronto Press.* April 1st, 2016.

404 Ibid. Elizabethan America p. 58.

405　Christian McBurney, "Verrazzano Visits the Narragansett Indians in 1524," *The Online Review of Rhode Island History*. Note, a new bridge connecting Jamestown, Rhode Island to the mainland, built to replace the old Jamestown-Saunderstown Bridge, opened in 1992 was named The Jamestown-Verrazzano Bridge in honor of the Italian explorer who sailed under the flag of France.

406　Egan bases his principal documentation for the two vessel Brigham expedition in 1582 on the research of David Beers Quinn, who in his 1974 book, *England and the Discovery of America*, cites Richard Hakluyt's *Diverse Voyages Touching on The Discovery of America*, printed in 1582. Egan describes this connection in his book, *The John Dee Tower of 1583, A Renaissance Building In Newport, RI*. (Cosmopolite Press Newport, RI 2010). Hakluyt's list of expeditions starts in 1178 and includes Columbus, Cabot, Vasco de Gama, Cartier, and more. It's a mix of mostly Spanish, Portuguese, French and English explorers. Quin notes that the list is 'largely compiled from Ramusio,' who was an earlier Italian geographer and travel writer (1485-1557).'" The list which Egan sources to "Hakluyt Society, The Original Writings and Correspondences of the two Richard Hakluyt's (1935) Second Series No. 76. p. 172, " cites the following voyage in 1582: "H. Gilbert, Ed Heyes and Anthonie Brigham, Englishmen."

407　Ibid. p.61.

408　David Beers Quinn, Gilbert, Sir Humphry. *Dictionary of Canadian Biog raphy* (University of Toronto Press 1979).

409　Ibid.

CHAPTER FIFTEEN

410　"Slumlord Crackdown Threatened In 10 Days," *The Newport Daily News*, August 11th, 1967.

411　James C. Garman, "From the School-Lands to Kerry Hill: Two Centuries of Urban Development at the Northern End of Newport, RI," *Salve Regina University Digital Commons* 2009.

412　Ibid.

413　Myra B. Young Armstead , *Lord, Please Don't Take Me in August: African Americans in Newport and Saratoga Springs, 1870-1930* (University of Illinois Press Champaign, 1999).

414　Paul Davis, "During Newport's Gilded Age, blacks thrived too." *The Providence Journal*, March 8th, 2015.

415　"Joseph T. Ray Dies At His Home. Was 96." *The Newport Mercury*, May 7th, 1943.

416 Peter Lance, "Newport's Back Yard Part One: Slum Homes Lack Bath, Stove," *The Newport Daily News*, August 28th, 1968.

CHAPTER SIXTEEN

417 Ibid. The other three Parts were headlined "Housing Code Enforce ment Lagging," *The Newport Daily News*, August 28th, 1968, ""Laxity May Cost City U.S. Cash," *The Newport Daily News*, August 29th, 1968 and "970 From 2,993 Leaves 2,023," *The Newport Daily News*, August 31st, 1968.

418 Guide to the Church Community Housing Corporation Materials in the Adé Bethune Papers. The Church Community Corporation was incorporated in Newport, Rhode Island on November 18, 1969. The name was changed to the Church Community Housing Corporation (CCHC) in 1985. Its founders include Phil and Alma Stocklin, Sister Francis Xavier, Canon F. Lockett Ballard, Frank Boyle, Peter Grimes, and Lyle Matthews. CCHC started operations in July 1970 and the offi-cers of the first Board of Directors were Hershel M. Carter, President; Rev. Canon Lockett F. Ballard, Vice President; Alma K. Stocklin, Secre-tary, and Adé Bethune, Treasurer. CCHC was established as a non-prof-it organization whose aim was to help low and moderate-income citi-zens of Aquidneck Island, and later, all of Newport County, to live in safe and affordable housing. It has used the help of local, state, and federal programs and private and foundational support to carry out projects of homeownership, house rehabilitation, neighborhood revi-talization, low income rental housing, emergency and transitional housing, special needs housing, housing for the elderly, and home-owner/buyer education.

419 24 Burnside Avenue. Chain of Title Newport, RI. Purchase of property from Church Community Housing Corporation by Pauline A. Perkins for $15,700.00 September 6th, 1972.

420 Ibid. "Newport's Back Yard," Part One, August 28th, 1968.

421 Author's interview with Pauline Perkins-Moyé, September 20th, 2020.

422 Peggie Elgin, "Housing Code Enforced," *The Newport Daily News*, Jan-uary 8th, 1969.

423 "Alexander G. Teitz, Administrative Law Judge," *The Washington Post*, February 14th, 1992.

424 93 Kingston Avenue Chain of Title Newport, RI. From Will of Max Teitz to Alexander Teitz. Property value $2,700.00.

425 "Repairs Costly, Owner Closes House. *The Newport Daily News,* No-vember 29th, 1968.

426 "Landlord's Home Picketed," *The Newport Daily News,* November 29th, 1968.

427 Warranty Deed, June 4th, 1969 Alexander G. Teitz conveys the property at 93 Kingston Avenue to Marguerite F. Chinn in consideration of the sum of ten dollars ($10.00). The sale price was $6,000 according to an email from Caitlin A. Duffy Senior Clerk Newport Tax Assessor's Office on November 25th, 2020.

428 "Welfare Mother To Move Brood Into Tonomy Hill Next Friday," *The Newport Daily News*, December 14th, 1968.

429 Ibid.

430 Leonard J. Scalzi, 71," *The Boston Globe* June 12th, 1985.

431 "Miss Butler, Children, "Guests' of Hotel, Despite Fuss Over Bill," *The Newport Daily News*. December 13th, 1968.

432 Ibid.

433 "16 Finished Gerontology Course, "*The Newport Daily News*," June 15th, 1974.

434 "Landlord Quotes Agreement With Tenant," *The Newport Daily News*. August 29th, 1968.

435 47 Poplar Street, Chain of Title Newport, RI. Purchase of property by Nicholas Merlo for $2,048 on January 15th, 1920, sale by (his wife) Mary Merlo on February 20th, 1929 for $2,648. Purchase by The Newport Restoration Foundation in 1992 for $130,000.

436 Ibid.

437 "Daily News Winner of Top N.E. Award," *The Newport Daily News,* May 16th, 1969.

438 "Globe Honored For Story on Deputies Fees," *The Associated Press/ The Boston Globe,* May 16th, 1969.

439 Editor & Publisher, May 31st, 1969. p. 32: A photo of the plaque presentation, made at the annual meeting of the New England Associated Press Executives Association in Boston, appeared in E&P, the newspaper industry trade magazine

440 Peggy Elgin, "After Six Years, Housing Code Enforced," *The Newport Daily News,* January 8th, 1969.

441 James A. Johnson, "Making This World A Better Place For All," *The Newport Daily News,* March 25th, 2015.

442 Paul Goldberger, "Restored Homes Are Bringing a New Look to Old Newport, RI." *The New York Times*, August 25th, 1976.

CHAPTER SEVENTEEN

443 State of Rhode Island Office of Chief Medical Examiner Autopsy Report T-281-667. October 8th, 1966.

444 Phillip C. McAllister, Report of County Medical Examiner, Tirella, Edmund G. October 7th, 1966 Pronounced: 5:30 pm

445 Newport Fire Department Logbook. October 7th, 1966 5:07 pm

446 Ibid. 5:16 pm

447 "Doris Duke Friend Killed: Car Strikes N.J. Man in Newport," *The Providence Journal* October 8th, 1966.

448 Ed Quigley Photograph. October 7th, 1966.

449 Author's interview with Newport Fire Department Captain Paul Faerber, October 12th, 2018.

450 Ibid Logbook.

451 Author's interview with Janet Chartier October 4th, 2018.

452 Author's Interview with Detective William Watterson, Newport Police Department (Ret.) June 25th, 2019.

453 Author's interview with Donna Lohmeyer, June 19th, 2019.

454 Edwardo Tirella Application for U.S. Passport. December 13th, 1961. Rubenstein Library Box 350 Folder 4 p. 1.

455 Joseph A. Radice. Memorandum to Robert M. Aughey October 11th, 1966.

456 "Frank Sinatra signs with Columbia Records," *worldhistoryproject.org*, June 1st, 1943,

457 Edward M. Tirella. Honorable Discharge. U.S. Army August 10th, 1945. Army separation document.

458 Ibid. Disability for Discharge Section I AR 615-361

459 Ibid. Lohmeyer.

460 **Pete Cooley's letter to Eduardo Tirella February 15th 1963.** "We feel it was perhaps a mistake to bring you into this project. It apparently requires the services of an architect. Since you've already made some preliminary drawings etc. for which you have been paid $700 which is equal to 100 hours of the Junior Consulting Engineer's time, it is our feeling that if the architect Miss D. finally chooses uses your preliminary drawings some arrangements should be made whereby the architect credits Miss Duke by the amount already paid you for these drawings."

Eduardo Tirella's reply February 21ˢᵗ, 1963: I am a designer and <u>not</u> a Junior Consulting Engineer. I design interiors gardens and anything that requires artistic ability. It is customary for a designer of my capacity to receive the equivalent of 15% of the total cost of the job he's involved with. He, in turn, pays the architect and local architects charge around 8%. I am not interested in working on an hourly basis. I'm interested in doing beautiful work and taking the necessary time in doing so." Rubenstein Library Box 7 Folder 5 pp. 2-3.

461   Ibid. Cheda interview. October 11ᵗʰ, 2018.

462   Ibid. Kubernick, *Canyon of Dreams*. pp. 6-8.

463   Ibid. Zanay interview. October 12ᵗʰ, 2018.

464   Ibid. Duke and Thomas, *"Too Rich."* pp. 173-175.

465   Ibid. Cheda.

466   Ibid. Zanay.

467   "Death Called Accident For Heiress," *United Press International,* October 10ᵗʰ, 1966.

468   Author's interview with Linda McFarlane Knierim September 23ʳᵈ, 2018.

469   Ibid. Mansfield p. 243.

470   Penelope Green, "Ghosts Be Gone," *The New York Times*, September 18ᵗʰ, 2013.

471   Author's interview with Harle Tinney. October 3ʳᵈ, 2018.

472   Ibid.

CHAPTER EIGHTEEN

473   The following is brief description of nearly half of the more than 40 cases in Doris Duke's litigation history as documented in thousands of pages at The Rubenstein Library at Duke University:

1941-1945 Duke-Cromwell vs. Hillsborough Township Correspondence, legal memorandum, testimonials, and news clippings relating to Doris Duke Cromwell's lawsuit with the Township of Hillsborough, N.J. against $13,834,924 in taxes levied on her intangible assets. Includes official Complaint and legal briefs, 1941–1945;

1959 -71 Duke Gardens Foundation vs. Universal Restoration, Inc. Releases + Judgment in dispute Box 353 Folder 15;

1967-1969 Duke vs. La Banq Continentale: Bank correspondence and newspaper article relating to Doris Duke's bank account with La Banque Continentale, 1967–1969. This is a *Los Angeles Times* article.

1970-1973: Duke vs. John Perkins Brown. There is also a replevin-action brought by the Foundation against John P. Brown. This action was commenced in April 1970, but no final hearing or disposition appears of record. RUBENSTEIN BOX 7 FOLDER 4 p. 1.

1973-1974 Correspondence relating to John P. Brown's insistence that Doris Duke or NRF owes him money, **1973-1974** Conditions Governing Access: Access restricted Box 3 Folder 12.

1972 Daryl Ford vs. Doris Duke Execution for the matter.

1972 William J. McGair and Christopher T. Del Sesto. Includes a General Release in the matter of <u>Daryl Ford v. Doris Duke</u>, 1972 Box 353 Folder 4.

11.28.73 Duke vs. Whittaker Associates: Doris Duke's hiring of Whittaker Associates to investigate a robbery at Duke Farms (November 28th, 1973) and **Indictment** of Mr. Whittaker for practicing in the State of N.J. without a license, 1973-1978. Correspondence, memoranda, and notes, re: variety of personal issues. Topics include burglary of Doris Duke's room at Duke Farms (November 28th, 1973), the use of firearms by staff, the possible relocation of the DBO from N.Y.C. to N.J.,

1973-1976 Duke vs. Tashjian (Animal Medical Center) – related suit: Correspondence relating to Doris Duke's hiring of The Wackenhut Corp. for investigative services. Also included in the file are copies of a legal Complaint, "Doris Duke against Robert Tashjian," 1974. During the late 1960s and early 1970s, the Animal Medical Center (AMC) had a research center on the Duke Farms estate to study the aging in large animals. Doris Duke not only provided grants to the Animal Medical Center (via the Doris Duke Foundation), but also leased pastures and barns on the property of Duke Farms for a cattle center. The relationship with the AMC ended in 1974. Box 249 Folder 6 another lawsuit.

1987-1989 Duke vs. Citibank: Correspondence and legal materials relating to lawsuit, <u>Duke v. Citibank</u>, 1987 Box 170 Folder 4. <u>Doris Duke v. Citibank, N.A.</u>, Memorandum of Law in support of motion to amend complaint to add a cause of action for removal of Trustee, 1987.

1971-1975 Duke vs, Newport, RI: Certified copy of Judgment reducing the assessed value of real estate at Rough Point from $430,720.00 to $330,720.00 effective with Assessment made on December 31, 1971. Judgment made in the State of Rhode Island, Newport Superior Court, May 29ᵗʰh, 1975 Box 353 Folder 3.

1976 Harry W. Cox vs. Doris Duke Release in the lawsuit of Harry W. Cox v. Doris Duke, 1976 Apr Box 353 Folder 5.

1976 May E. McFarland v. Doris Duke, the Doris Duke Foundation, and all other Foundations controlled by Doris Duke. Settlement was for $41, 666.67, 1976 Sep Box 353 Folder 6.

1977 Richard Loveless v. Doris Duke, Duke Farms Police Department, The Animal Medical Center, and Officer Phillip Anderson. Release for lawsuit Box 353 Folder 7.

1979-1984 Bob Guccione (Penthouse Films) and Renzo Rosselini over the film Caligula Box 360 Folder 27; Box 360 Folder 28; Box 361 Folder 4 Box 361 Folder 5.

1980 Robert and Betty Doreen Flood v. Doris Duke Release in the lawsuit. Box 353 Folder 8.

1982 Peltack and Fink v. Duke Farms Release in the case Box 353 Folder 9; Box 353 Folder 10.

1949-62 Bartlett Correspondence and related legal documents, in cluding the Promissory Note, relating to Doris Duke's loan of $14,000 to the Bartlett family and the foreclosure of their house, 1949–1962 Box 93 Folder 7.

1967-68 ABE POEPOE: Promissory Note and related legal actions taken for a loan taken and defaulted on by Abe Poepoe was for $7,490.91, 1967-1968, 1975 Box 336 Folder 26.

1968-1972 Paris Theodore and Seventrees LTD. Loan, Paris Theo dore and Seventrees, LTD. Includes shares of stock in Seventrees, LTD. Also includes Agreement and Judgment in case of Doris Duke v. Paris Theodore, 1968, 1972 Box 336 Folder 28.

474   "Duke Dogs Hit By Police Order," *The Newport Daily News*, May 22ⁿᵈ, 1964; Harry Gee, "Judge Tours Doris Duke's Mansion. Court Held at Shangri-La" *Honolulu Star Bulletin*, April 28ᵗʰ, 1967; "Youth Loses Suit Against Doris Duke," *Honolulu Star Bulletin*, May 2ⁿᵈ, 1967

475   Author's interview with confidential source, October 26ᵗʰ 2020.

476   Dwight D. Eisenhower, "Statement by the President Upon Signing The Hawaii Statehood Bill," *The American Presidency Project,* March 18ᵗʰ, 1959. Hawaii became the 50ᵗʰ State in The Union on. August 21ˢᵗ, 1959.

477 <u>Romano et. al. vs. Avis</u> U.S. Dist. Court, Case. No. 3870. Defendant's Answers Interrogatories. June 30th, 1968. Doris Duke's response to interrogatory No., 2.

478 Bob Bonham, "Hillsborough Seeks to Prove Mrs. Cromwell Legal Resident," *The Central New Jersey Home News*, July 13th, 1941.

479 "Doris Duke Tax Fight Threatens to Involves All Somerset Taxpayers," *The Courier News, Bridgewater, NJ*, November 14th, 1941,

480 Drew Pearson, "'World's Richest Girl' Sets Price When Navy Asks For Yacht," *The Washington Merry-Go-Round* June 22nd, 1942.

481 "9 Big Firms Flee Jersey City's Levy," *The Camden, NJ Morning Post,* September 24th, 1942.

482 Ibid.

483 "Dorus Duke Cromwell Wins Huge Tax Suit, *The Associated Press,* May 10th, 1945.

484 Memo to John F. Day, Treasurer, The Doris Duke Trust from Pete Cooley. Subject: "Please find notarized statement of Doris Duke dated January 9th. Sworn affidavit of Doris Duke, January 9th, 1968. "I am over the age of twenty-one years and reside at Duke Farms, Somerville, New Jersey 08876." Rubenstein Library Box 7 Folder 5. pp. 18-19.

485 "Foundation is sued for $1.5 Million" *The Newport Daily News* January 21st, 1970.

486 Ibid.

487 <u>United States v. Helmsley</u>, 941 F.2d 71, 91-2-U.S. Tax Case (CCH) Paragraph 50 455 (2d. Cir. 1991) Cert denied 502 U.S. 1091 (1992).

488 "The Queen of Mean," *Court TV*, September 4th, 2007.

489 Leona Helmsley Federal Bureau of Prisons, Retrieved January 8th, 2010.

490 Enid Nemy, "Leona Helmsely, Hotel Queen, Dies at 87," *The New York Times*, August 21st, 2007. "Leona Helmsley, the self-styled hotel queen, whose prison term for income tax evasion and fraud was greeted with uncommon approval by a public who had grown to regard her as a 1980s symbol of arrogance and greed, died today at her summer home in Greenwich, Conn, She was 87. The cause of death was heart failure, her longtime spokesman, Howard J. Rubenstein, said."

491 "Suits Awarded Against Miss Duke Are 55,000." *The Newport Daily News,* November 10th, 1972.

492   Wesley N. Fach, "Memo For File, Accident Recovery For Damage to Gates," November 11th, 1966. Rubenstein Library Box 3 Folder 7. p.15.

493   Donna Lohmeyer, correspondence with Bradley Booth, Chief of Legal Services, State of Rhode Island Division of Motor Vehicles, February 11th, to July 12th, 2019 re: Access to Public Records Request, filed by Ms. Lohmeyer January 25th, 2019, pursuant to R.I. General Laws Section 38-2-1

494   Stephanie Mansfield correspondence to Anita Aughey March 30th, 1990.

495   Donna Lohmeyer Public Records Request filed with the Newport Police on October 10th, 2018. Email response from Gwen George, Records Office, Newport Police Department October 25th, 2018.

496   Carl Bernstein and Bob Woodward, *All The President's Men* (Simon and Shuster New York 1974). p 92.

497   Gwen George, Statement to City Manager Joseph Nicholson January 9th, 2019: As per our conversation earlier today these are the circumstances as best as I can recall regarding the "Duke Folder" Several months ago retired Detective Conti called asking how someone could get a copy of an accident report that happened in the 1960's. I informed him that our microfilm files only go back as far as the 1970's. He then informed me that he was looking for the Doris Duke accident. I told him that I had seen that folder when I was prepping old folders for microfilm many years ago and someone took it upstairs, where I assumed it was being put with other old folders of historic value. I informed him that I didn't have access to those folders and I believe I referred him to Captain Costa. I then received a call from a Peter Lance looking for the folder and he said that I had received a request from someone (I believe a niece) requesting a copy of the accident and I informed her that our records did not go back to the 1960's and it was my understanding that records before 1973 were sent to the archives and some were given to the historical society. To my recollection I never remember another request (just Det. Conti) for the Duke folder and I would inform anyone that was looking for any records prior to 1973 that they were not available from the records office with a request for public records.

498   Author's interview with Joseph Gallagher IV, June 21st, 2019.

CHAPTER NINETEEN

499 Author's interview with Patsy Gallagher Snyder, November 27th, 2020.

500 "The Irish in Newport," *RedwoodLibrary.org,* March 17th, 2017; "Irish Roots Run Deep In Newport," *The Providence Journal* July 20th, 2013.

501 "British Occupation of Newport." *RedwoodLibrary.org,* December 8th, 2012.

502 "A History of Irish Workers at Fort Adams," *Newport Buzz,* November 6th, 2017.

503 State of Rhode Island Division of Parks & Recreation: Fort Adams State Park (1965)

504 Fort Adams, Rhode Island, Oral history. Legends of America.com Photo By Jack Boucher.

505 Author's interview with William Dunn, September 8th, 2020.

506 "Edward C. Sullivan Named Chief," *The Newport Daily News*, January 17th, 1941.

507 "Chief Sullivan Fatally Stricken At His Home. In Department 43 Years." *The Newport Mercury*, May 23rd, 1952.

508 "The Navy And Narragansett Bay," History: Commander, Navy Region Mid-Atlantic.

509 Ibid William Dunn interview.

510 Sean Flynn, "A School, A Community," *The Newport Daily News*, June 3rd, 2018. The Dr. Michael H. Sullivan School served northern Newport, and the student body had a relatively low socioeconomic level as its attendance boundary included various low-income apartment complexes. Maria Mare-Schulz became the principal in 1997. According to Mare-Schulz, in 1997 6% of the student body spoke Portuguese and/or Spanish while about 26-28% did so in 2012. In June 2011 Sullivan moved into the former Triplett school as the original Sullivan building was demolished to make way for the new Pell School. From 2011 until its 2013 closure the school was known as Sullvan-at-Triplett School. *Wikipedia.com*

511 "The Crusader," Yearbook of the Class of 1966, De La Salle Academy. Brian John Sullivan, John Peter Sullivan, Michael Cornelius Sullivan, and Walter Daniel Sullivan. p. 27.

512 M. Catherine Callahan, "Sullivan nicknames: The list is a long one," *The Newport Daily News,* March 17th-18th 2007.

513 Don Markstein, "Rich Uncle Pennybags," *Don Marksteins Toonopedia.*

514   Janny Venema, *Kiliaen van Rensselaer (1586-1643) Designing A New World*, (State University of New York Press Albany 2011).

515   Letter of Peter Schaghen, representation of the State General in the Assembly of The Nineteen of the West India Company. 1926. New Netherland Institute. Translation: "Received 7 November 1626: High and Mighty Lords. Yesterday the ship, The Arms of Amsterdam, arrived here. It sailed from New Netherland out of the River Mauritius on the 23rd of September. They report that our people are in good spirit and live in peace. The women also have borne some children there. They have purchased the Island Manhattes from the Indians for the value of 60 guilders."

516   Maury Paul, "Heiress Who Dreaded Thought of Poverty Dies in Plunge," *The San Francisco Herald Examiner,* September 17th, 1931; U.S. Artists American Fine Art Show and Sale October 4th, 2011: Sales included John Singer Sargent's 1921 charcoal on paper portrait of Peyton J. van Rensselaer.

517   Mabel Gertrude Mason 1909 Marriage in Stockbridge, Massachusetts to Peyton J. van Rensselaer, *Index to Massachusetts Marriages, 1906-1910.*

518   Ibid. Paul.

519   Daniel Swinburn House (c. 1862) U.S. Department of The Interior.

520   "His Nurse Now Is Bridge of van Rensselaer," *The Barret (Vermont) Times,* November 23rd, 1911. This profile of Peyton's wealthier brother Cortland, ended with this report, "His brother Peyton, who married a Miss Mason of Boston, sailed recently to Italy to spend the winter."

521   "P.J. van Rensselaer Dies On Liner Here," *The New York Times*, August 13th, 1931.

522   "Newport Society Woman Leaps to Death In New York," *The Associated Press/The New York Times,* July 24th, 1925.

523   Ibid. Paul.

524   "Dr. Thomas Bennett, Summer Resident, Dead. Owner of Wildacre Here," *The Newport Daily News,* May 13th, 1932, noting that he had sold "the smaller cottage to Lilian Newlin."

525   F.L. Olmsted is Dead: End Comes to Great Landscape Architect at Waverly, Mass. Designer of Central and Prospect Parks and Other famous Garden Spots in American Cities. *The New York Times*, August 29th, 1903.

526   "Miss Newlin Weds P.J. van Rensselaer," *The New York Times,* April 10th, 1931.

527 "Death of J. van Rensselaer," *The Newport Mercury*, August 14th, 1931, referring to, "The Playhouse, Mrs. van Rensselaer's new summer residence on Ocean Avenue."

528 Ibid. *The New York Times,* August 13th, 1931.

529 "P.J. van Rensselaer Will," *The New York Times,* November 24th, 1931.

530 "Palm Beach Scene Of A Large Party," *The New York Times*, December 27th, 1938.

531 "Florida Colonists in Large Tea Party," *The New York Times*, February 7th, 1944.

532 Seaverge (c.1855). The Gerry-Hartford estate. *The Preservation Society of Newport County.* Newport Mansions 1857-1855. A large mid-nineteenth-century timber-framed cottage built for John Paine of New York... The estate subsequently became the summer home of Elbridge T. Gerry of New York, the celebrated yachtsman, then in 1927 of Mrs. Edward V. Hartford. The Harold B. Tinneys acquired Seaverge in 1955 and lived there until 1956 when they purchased nearby Belcourt for $25,000. Seaverge was sold and in 1957 demolished for subdivision.

533 "Commodore Elbridge T. Gerry, A Sketch," *The Tammany Times,* Volumes 8-9.

534 Elmer C. Griffith, Ph.D., *The Rise And Development of The Gerrymander*, (Scott, Foresman and Company Chicago 1907). pp. 72-73. The word gerrymander (originally written "Gerry-Mander") was used for the first time in *The Boston Gazette* newspaper on March 26th, 1812. Appearing with the term and helping spread and sustain its popularity, was a political cartoon which depicted a state senate district in Essex County as a strange animal with claws, wings, and a dragon-type head, satirizing the district on shape *Wikipedia*.

CHAPTER TWENTY

535 James G. Edward, "Timmy The Woodhooker Wouldn't Like It, But His House is Finally Sold. *The Newport Daily News,* September 11th, 1970.

536 Ibid.

537 "Timmy 'The Woodhooker' Riles Newport Neighbors, " *The Associated Press* July 31st, 1946.

538 "Noreen Stoner Wed in St. James." *The New York Times,* January 12th 1941; "Noreen S. Drexel Obituary, *The Newport Daily News*, November 7th, 2012,

539 Ibid. *The Associated Press, July* 31st, 1946.

540   Society, *The Philadelphia Inquirer*, August 24th, 1947.

541   "'Snobbishness,' Timmy Replies To Neighbors' Clean-Up Pleas," *The Baltimore Sun,* July 31st, 1946.

542   "Newport Elite Riled Over Junk in Timmy's Bellevue Ave. Yard," *The Boston Globe*, July 31st, 1946.

543   Ibid. *The Philadelphia Inquirer*, August 24th, 1947.

544   Ibid. James G. Edward, September 11th, 1970.

545   Ibid.

546   "Scrap In Newport. Socialite Sues To Ban Junk," *The Associated Press/ The Philadelphia Inquirer,* June 27th, 1949.

547   Ibid.

548   Ibid.

549   "Newport Fights A Middle Class Millionaire Hut," *New York Daily News*, July 9th, 1952.

550   Ibid.

551   "Apartment Hotel Proposed For Lower Bellevue Avenue." *The Newport Mercury,* July 11th, 1952.

552   Nancy Randolph, "I'll Save Newport: Mrs. van R," *New York Daily News,* September 16th, 1952.

553   Author's Interview with Harle Tinney, October 2nd, 2020.

554   "Quatrel," Hull Cove Design. Portfolio.

555   Certificate of Death, Lillian Newlin van Rensselaer, Allegheny County, File No. 10969.

556   "Mrs. Peyton J. van Rensselaer Is Dead; After Long Court Fight With Junk Dealer," *The Associated Press/The New York Times,* February 10th, 1956.

CHAPTER TWENTY-ONE

557   Ibid. McFarlane Knierim, *A Summer Cottage*. pp 85-86

.558   Author's interview with McFarlane Knierim.

559   Ibid.

560   Ibid. McFarlane Knierim, *A Summer Cottage*. p. 60.

561   Author's interview with Johnny Nutt, July 27th, 2018.

562   Ibid.

563 Owner's Manual 1966 Dodge Polara automatic. p. 11 (Parking Brake Release) p. 20. (Warning Signal).

564 Romano et. al. vs. Avis U.S. Dist. Court, Case. No. 3870. Defendant's Answers Interrogatories, June 30th, 1968. No. 31.

565 "Doris Duke In Court On Death," *United Press International,* June 18th 1971.

566 Official report of The Newport Police Department. pp. 10-12; Statements Offered in Doris Duke Trial," *The Providence Journal,* June 22nd, 1971.

567 Author's interview with Det. James Moss (NYPD Ret.), October 4th, 2018.

568 Author's interview with Lewis A. Perrotti, Field Investigator, RI Registry of Motor Vehicles, October 27th, 2018.

569 "Brakes Found 'Normal' in Duke Car. *The Providence Journal* June 24th, 1971.

570 Ibid.

571 Ibid. Perrotti interview.

572 Ibid. Perrotti report. p. 3

573 Official report of The Newport Police Department, p. 1.

574 Lewis A. Perrotti, Investigators and Examiner's Report: Homicide of Eduardo Guiseppe Tirella. Rhode Island Registry of Motor Vehicles, October 19th, 1966. p. 7.

575 Author's interview with retired Det. William Watterson, June 25th, 2019.

576 "Police Say Death Was Accidental," *United Press International,* October 12th, 1966.

577 Official report of The Newport Police Department, p. 1.

578 Donna Lohmeyer, correspondence with Bradley Booth, Chief of Legal Services, State of Rhode Island Division of Motor Vehicles, February 11th, to July 12th, 2019 re: Access to Public Records Request, filed by Ms. Lohmeyer January 25th, 2019, pursuant to R.I. General Laws Section 38-2-1

CHAPTER TWENTY-TWO

579 "Mrs. Coogan Dies, Large Landholder," *The New York Times,* December 19th, 1947.

580 "The mysterious staircase near 158th Street," *Ephemeral New York,* October 4th, 2010.

581 "Coogan's Get Whitehall: King Estate in Newport Disposed of at Mortgage Sale for $42,100." *The New York Tribune,* June 30th, 1903 p. 6.

582 Sam Roberts, "400 Years and 400 Names: Museum Tweaks City A-List," *The New York Times,* September 8th, 2009.

583 "Ward McAllister's Triumph; His Work As A 'Society Reporter' Excites Much Gossip. Other Newspaper Men Received at the Patriarchs' Ball with Chilliness For Mr. McAllister Did Not Wish Them to Obtain Descriptions of the Women's Dresses -- His Story of the Ball a Prose Poem Some of the Choicest Gems from His Pen." *The New York Times,* December 15th, 1893.

584 Deborah Davis, *Gilded How Newport Became America's Richest Resort,* (John Wiley & Sons, Hoboken 2009) p. 99.

585 "Whitehall Gutted By Fire," *The Newport Mercury,* March 11th, 1911.

586 "Owner's son to raze ruined Coogan estate." *The Newport Mercury,* February 7th, 1946.

587 Jim Coogan, ""A Little Secret In The Family Tree," *Cape Cod Times,* March 23rd, 2005 updated January 6th, 2011.

588 "New Hetty Green," *Time,* September 21th, 1941.

589 Newportmansions.org/lost Newport/1886-1895.

590 Paul F. Miller, "Newport Mansions, 1886 to 1985," The Preservation Society of Newport County.

591 Paul Miller, *Lost Newport: Vanished Cottages of the Resort Era* (Applewood Books, Carlisle, MA 2010).

592 "Disposition of Coogan Property Awaited," *The Newport Mercury,* December 26th, 1947.

593 Ibid. *Lost Newport.*

594 Cleveland Amory, *The Last Resorts* (Harper and Brothers New York 1948) pp. 232-233.

595 Ibid. *The Newport Mercury,* March 11th, 1911.

596 Author's interview with Harle Tinney, July 10th, 2020.

597 "Wealthy New York Woman Succumbs," *The Associated Press,* December 19th, 1947.

598 "Coogan Land Sale Agreement Made," *The Newport Daily News,* January 17th, 1953.

599 Leonard Falkner, "Captor of The Barefoot General," *American Heritage,* August 1960 Vol. 11 Issue 5.

600 Leonard Falkner, "Militiamen Kidnap General In Nightshirt," *The Indianapolis Star,* October 6th, 1963.

601 "NRF Property Spotlight: Prescott Farm," *Newport Restoration Foundation,* April 19th, 2019.

CHAPTER TWENTY-THREE

602 Hugh Sidey, *John F. Kennedy: Portrait of a President.* (Andre Deutch New York 1964).

603 JFK Library. President John F. Kennedy and First Lady Jacqueline Kennedy Watch First America's Cup RaceKN-C23943 15 September 1962 President John F. Kennedy and First Lady Jacqueline Kennedy watch the first race of the 1962 America's Cup from aboard the USS Joseph P. Kennedy, Jr. Nuala Pell, wife of Senator Claiborne Pell (Rhode Island), stands at right. Newport, Rhode Island. Public Domain Robert Knudsen. White House Photographs. John F. Kennedy Presidential Library and Museum, Boston

604 Author's conversation with Joseph F. Tremblay, October 1st, 1961.

605 Author's conversation with Julia Silvia Whitlock, August 26th, 1962.

606 JFK Library. Photo taken by White House Photographer. KN-C18960. President John F. Kennedy and First Lady Jacqueline Kennedy Attend Mass at St. Mary's Church Accession Number KN-C18960 Date of Material October 1st, 1961.

Description President Kennedy and First Lady Jacqueline Kennedy leave St. Mary's Church after attending Mass in Newport, Rhode Island. A crowd observes. Public Domain

607 JFK Library. President John F. Kennedy Sails Aboard Yacht Manitou KN-C23425 August 26th, 1962 President John F. Kennedy sits aboard the United States Coast Guard boat Manitou in Narragansett Bay, Newport, Rhode Island. The President sailed on the yacht during his vacation at Hammersmith Farm in Newport. Public Domain Credit Line Robert Knudsen. White House Photographs. John F. Kennedy Presidential Library and Museum, Boston; S/Y Manitou is a 62-foot-long (18.9 m) performance cruising yacht designed and built for racing on the Great Lakes and specifically to win the Chicago-Mackinac Race, It notably served as a presidential yeach for U.S. President John F. Kennedy and was known as the "Floating White House." *Wikipedia.*

608   Ryan Belmore, "Photos: President John F. Kennedy Sailing In Newport on August 26th, 1962," *WhatsUpNewport*.

609   Emil E. Jemail, "Kennedys to Occupy Estate Here In 1964," *The Newport Daily News*, October 30th, 1963.

610   Peter Lance, "Annandale Farm And Broadlawns Sold To Swiss Bank For $390,000," *The Newport Daily News,* July 24th, 1968.

611   Ibid.

612   Don Bauder, "Did President Nixon help finance part of San Diego?" San Diego Reader, July 18th, 2012.

613   Anthony Summers, *The Arrogance of Power* (Viking New York 2000) Chapter 20.

CHAPTER TWENTY-FOUR

614   Nancy L. Ross, "Jackie, Doris Resort to Remodeling Scheme," *The Washington Post,* syndicated in *The Los Angeles Times,* September 24th, 1969.

615   John W. Finney, "274 Military Bases Target of Federal Economy Plan." *The New York Times,* April 17th, 1973.

616   Linda McFarlane Knierim, *A Summer Cottage Through A Child's Eye. A Caretaker's Daughter. Rough Point Newport, Rhode Island."* (2016 CreatSpace). pp. 129-130.

617   "Low Rental Shortage Laid to Restorations," *The Newport Daily News,* August 12th, 1969.

618   "East-West Committee Pushes Access Plans," *The Newport Daily News,* February 19th, 1969. John Perkins Brown, NRF Executive Director says the Foundation, "has plans for the West Broadway Area."

619   "Foundation Switches Restoration Director," *The Newport Daily News,* September 6th, 1969. John Perkins Brown is out. Francis A. Comstock appointed.

620   "Doris Duke Tells Aim Here," *The Newport Daily News*, February 23rd, 1969.

621   William Kutik, "Tenants form a permanent organization after Miss Duke rebuffs them," *The Newport Daily News,* February 25th, 1977.

622   Holly Collins, "The Preservation Society of Newport County 1945-1965. A History. September 8th, 2006.

623   Ibid. "Low Rental Shortages Laid to Restorations."

624   Author's Interview with Paulin Perkins Moyé September 22nd, 2020.

625 "Foundation Reaffirms Better Newport Is Aim," *The Newport Daily News*, August 14th, 1969.

626 "Housing Ills To Be Aired," *The Newport Daily News,* August 28th, 1969.

627 "City's $5,000 Ante to Speed Repairs For Slum Housing," *The Newport Daily News,* September 11th, 1969.

628 "Foundation Switches Executive Director," *The Newport Daily News,* September 9th, 1969.

629 Author's interview with Harle Tinney, October 18th, 2020.

630 Ibid.

631 Author's interview with Donna Lohmeyer, October 18th, 2020.

632 Enid Nemy "In A Way, Their Newport Landlord Is Doris Duke," *The New York Times*, October 25th, 1970.

633 Ibid.

634 Ibid. "Doris Duke Tells Aim Here."

635 "Mrs. Onassis is Vice President, Restoration Foundation Reveals." *The Newport Daily News,* September 25th, 1969.

636 Ibid.

637 "Foundation is sued for $1.5 Million," *The Newport Daily News*, January 21st, 1970; "Restoration Work Will Halt: Contractor Lays off 40.," *The Newport Daily News*, November 10th, 1969.

638 "Head of Appeal Board Chides Housing Sit-ins," *The Newport Daily News*, November 8th, 1969.

639 "Jackie and Doris Resort To Remodeling Scheme," *The Los Angeles Times/The Washington Post,* September 19th, 1969.

640 "Restoration Foundation Acts To Supply Low-Rent Houses." *The Newport Daily News*, October 10th, 1969.

641 Ibid. Nemy October 25th, 1970.

642 Ibid.

CHAPTER TWENTY-FIVE

643 "Suits Awarded Against Miss Duke Are $55,000." *The Newport Daily News,* November 10th, 1972.

644 "Foundation Has Rise In Assets," *The Newport Daily News,* May 15th, 1972.

645 "Development Group Fights Housing Move," *The Newport Daily News*, January 25th, 1974.

646 Daniel Lyman House 11 Third Street, Circa 1774, *The Newport Restoration Foundation.*

647 28 Kingston Avenue Chain of Title Newport, RI. Purchase of property from Estate of Florence E Jenkins by Afro American Business Leaders, September 17th, 1971.

648 "Renewal Airing Set," *The Newport Daily News*, January 28th 1974.

649 "Development Group Fights Moving House," *The Newport Mercury*, January 25th, 1974.

650 Website of The Newport Restoration Foundation as of October 19th, 2020.

651 Ibid. "Renewal Airing Set."

652 Ibid. "Development Group Fights Moving House."

653 "Adé Bethune: The Power of One Person. Notes for a show of the artist's work. *The Catherine G. Murray Gallery,* September 8th, 2014.

654 "About Adé Bethune," Biography St. Catherine University.

655 Author's interview with Pauline Perkins-Moyé October 22nd, 2020.

656 Doris Duke Thanked By R.I. Senate," *The Newport Daily News, April 20th, 1974.*

657 Ibid.

658 Ibid. 28 Kingston Chain of Title.

659 "Old Mary Street YMCA Is Sold," *The Newport Daily News,* April 30th, 1974.

660 Ibid.

661 "Judge Halts Demolition of Mary Street YMCA," *The Newport Mercury*, December 27th, 1974.

662 "Where Generations Exercised. Wreckers Demolish YMCA gym, " *The Newport Daily News,* February 4th, 1975.

663 41 Mary Street chain of title.

664 Ibid.

665 On its website, The Five Star Alliance describes Vanderbilt Grace as a "classic luxury hotel." *Fivestaralliance.com.*

666 "Doris Duke Gets Rebate," *The Newport Daily News*, June 24th, 1975.

667 A History of Queen Anne Square And The Newport Restoration Foundation," *The Meeting Room. An Installation by Maya Lin.* May 29th, 2013.

668 Tom Valentine Patrick Mahn, *Daddy's Duchess An Unauthorized Biography of Doris Duke.* (Secaucus, Lyle Stuart 1987) pp 148-151.

CHAPTER TWENTY-SIX

669 "Our History: A Historic Building. A Timeless Story.," TrinityNewport. org. Mundy also designed The Colony House in Newport in 1739 (the alternate site of Rhode Island's legislature) and Malbone Castle and Estate (1739-1740) Newport oldest mansion, which was the home of Col. Godfrey Malbone of Virginia and Connecticut (1695-1768) a merchant and slave trader who became one of Newport's wealthiest residents. George Washington, an old friend from Virginia dined at Malbone Castle in 1756. As legend has it, while a fire consumed much of the mansion ten years later, Malbone continued to dine outside, asserting, "By God, if I must lose my house, I shall not lose my dinner."

670 John B. Hattendorf, *Semper Eadem: A History of Trinity Church in Newport: 1698-2000* (2018); pp. 128 + 262.

671 John Kinfer, "Tall Ships Reach Newport As Fog Lifts for Welcome," *The New York Times,* June 27th, 1976.

672 "Newport Art Museum To Honor The Benson Family at its Beaux Arts Ball," *What's Up Newport,* April 12th, 2016.

673 "About Us," *johnstevensshop.com.*

674 Maria Wieting, "'Acts of Mercy' series features art of Adé Bethune," *The Catholic Spirit,* December 13th, 2015.

675 William M. Kutik, "Elizabeth II, Philip arrive on Saturday," *The Newport Daily News,* July 9th, 1976.

676 Jane Nippert, "Queen will visit Newport," *The Newport Daily News,* January 21st, 1976.

677 T. Curtis Forbes, "Thousands welcome Queen, Prince Philip to Newport." *The Newport Daily News,* July 12th, 1976.

678 Ibid. Stephanie Mansfield, *The Richest Girl in The World* p. 290.

679 Kenneth Best and Sam Freedman, "Reclusive Doris surfaces in Somerville court," *The (Bridgewater, NJ) Courier News,* June 22nd, 1976.

680 "Jury Rules heiress owes investigator cash," *United Press International,* March 31st, 1977.

681 Anthony J. Rummo, "Doris Duke is witness for the state," *The (New Brunswick, NJ) Home News,* June 22nd, 1976.

682 "Duke-Whittaker Suit Settled," *United Press International,* March 31st, 1977.

683   Sam Meddis, "Detective Loses Plea," *The (Bridgewater NJ) Courier News,* January 10th, 1976.

684   Ibid. Rummo, *Home News,* June 22nd, 1976.

685   Kevin Best, "Duke: Detective Ineffective," *The (Bridgewater NJ) Courier News,* June 23rd, 1976.

686   Ibid.

687   Anthony J. Rummo, "Doris Duke denies she pushed case," *The (New Brunswick, NJ) Home News.* June 23rd, 1976.

688   Ibid.

689   Whittaker v. Duke 473 F. Supp. 908 (SDNY 1979) April 17th, 1979.

690   Ibid. Best, *The (Bridgewater NJ) Courier News,* June 23rd, 1976.

691   27.1 Degrees F. *The Old Farmers Almanac, Weather History For Newport, RI,* February 4th, 1977.

692   William M. Kutick" "Doris Duke Stirs Wrath of Tenants," *The Newport Daily News,* February 4th, 1977.

693   Ibid.

694   "Storm window flap past deadline; nobody talks," *The Newport Daily News,* February 25th, 1977.

695   William M. Kutik, "Tenants form a permanent organization after Miss Duke rebuffs them," *The Newport Daily News,* February 25th, 1977.

696   Ibid.

697   "Doris Duke Tenants Strike Back," *The Newport Daily News,* February 28th, 1977.

698   Ibid.

699   "Tenants give up battle," *The Newport Daily News,* March 11th, 1977.

700   William M. Kutik, "Duke Tenants hit by rent increases," *The Newport Daily News,* April 2nd, 1977.

701   Author's interview with Ford Ballard, November 26th, 2018.

702   "Doris Duke Tells Aim Here," *The Newport Daily News,* February 23rd, 1969.

703   Ibid.

704   Remarks before the Nazi War Criminals Interagency Working Group (IWG), *The National Archives.* "In World War II, Winston Churchill made his now famous statement: 'In wartime, truth is so precious that she should always be attended by a bodyguard of lies.'"

705 Author's Analysis of the points of origin of the inventory of 70 restored colonial-era structures from the website of The Newport Restoration Foundation. October 24th, 2020. Source: *newportrestoration. org/preservation/properties/*.

706 newportrestoration.org/preservation/properties.

707 Author's interview with Tom Perrotti October 30th, 2020.

708 "City Names Park For War Hero," *The Newport Daily News* September 27th, 1973.

709 Author's interview with Pauline Perkins-Moyé October 22nd, 2020.

CHAPTER TWENTY-SEVEN

710 "The Duke Curse Strikes Again," *DBR Archives* January 6th, 2013.

711 United States v. American Tobacco Co. 221 U.S. 106 (1911).

712 Duke Energy Company Profile, *The Fortune 500*. #123 as of May 18th, 2020.

713 Ibid.

714 Toxic 100 Study, *The Political Economy Research Institute*, released May 11th, 2006.

715 Mitch Weiss and Michael Biesecker, "U.S. Investigates NC coal ash spill," *The Associated Press*. February 13th, 2014. The Way Back Machine

716 Toxic 100 Study, peri.umass.edu/toxic-100-water-polluters-index-current.

717 Griggs v. Duke Power Co. 401, U.S. 424 1971.

718 Ibid.

719 Gary Arnold, "'Harlan County': Ardent, Absorbing. *The Washington Post,* March 23rd 1977.

720 Fred Harris, "Burning Up People to Make Electricity," *The Atlantic*, July, 1974.

721 "James Buchanan Duke: Father of The Modern Cigarette" *BBC News*, November 13th, 2012.

722 Sarah Vogelsong, "It's Toasted," *sarahvogelsong.com* January 29th, 2018.

723 Mysterious Death of Doris Duke Kin Under Probe," *The Newport Daily News*, March 18th, 1955.

724   Julia Marsh, "Heir-raising tale: Billion-dollar Duke twins survived abuse hell." New York Post, August 2nd, 2013.

725   Chloe Sorvino, "The Duke Fortune: Depleted By Lavish, Addiction-Fueled Spending?" *Forbes*, July 10th, 2014.

726   Julia Marsh and Lia Eustachewich, "Doris Duke twins lose bid to sue over 'junkie dad' who blew their billions." *New York Post,* November 29th, 2016.

727   Sabrina Rubin Erdely, "The Poorest Rich Kids in the World," *Rolling Stone,* August 12th, 2013.

728   Stephanie Mansfield, *The Richest Girl in The World* p. 271.

729   Too Rich. Kindle location 2223

730   Ibid.

731   "Heiress Doris Duke, 80." *The Associated Press. The Ashbury Park Press*, October 29th, 1993.

732   Bob Colacello, "Doris Duke's Final Mystery. *Vanity Fair,* March, 1994.

733   Michael Beschloss, "Duke of Hawaii: A Swimmer & Surfer Who Straddled Two Cultures," *The New York Times*, August, 22nd 2014.

734   Author's interview with Patrick Mahn, Doris Duke's former business manager, July 27th, 2018.

735   "Heiress' Chef Indicted Over 2 Missing Plates," *The Central New Jersey Home News,* August, 13th, 1966.

736   Author's interview with Peter Byrne, August 20th, 2020.

737   Pete Cooley correspondence to Eduardo Tirella February 15th 1963. " Rubenstein Library Box 7 Folder 5 pp. 2-3.

738   Joan K. Barbato, "Tour the world in these gardens," *The Daily Record,* Morristown, New Jersey December 30th, 1994; Wikipedia reports that the Gardens were "created by Doris Duke herself."

739   Author's interview with David Rimmer, August 26th, 2020.

740   Author's interview with Richard Tanner, August 9th, 2020

741   Ibid Mansfield p. 178-179

742   Ibid. p. 264.

743   Ibid. *Daddy's Duchess*, p. 183.

744   Mrs. Emma G. Stoudt, letter to Doris Duke, May 13th, 1965 Rubenstein Library, Box 7 Folder 6. Page 100.

745   Ibid. *A Summer Cottage Through A Child's Eye* p. 82.

746 "Sketches of Candidates," *The Newport Daily News,* October 28th, 1960.

747 "Medical Association Installs," *The Newport Daily News,* April 3rd, 1974.

748 "McAllister New Chairman of Middletown Democrats," *The Newport Daily News,* October 17th, 1960.

749 "Dutra, Mrs. McAllister's Total 372," *The Newport Daily News,* September 30th, 1960.

750 "Grand Jury Indicts 34," *The Newport Daily News*, September 17th, 1968. Brendan McAllister indicted for unlawful sale of marijuana. Cites his father's medical office at 30 West Pelham Street as his home address; "Newport Man Denies Charges," *The Newport Daily News* January 2nd, 1970. Brendan McAllister pleaded innocent to behaving in a disorderly manner; "Two Young women Injured By Crash At Pelham Street. Car driven by Brendan McAllister, 20 of 1367 Green End Avenue, Middletown;" "Bail Set For 2 Men," *The Newport Daily News, 1970.* Two local men were arraigned on drug charges. Phillip McAllister 22 of 1367 Green End Avenue, pleaded innocent to a number of counts. His bail was set at $1,000 for possession of a hypodermic needle and syringe, $1,000 for possession of amphetamine and methedrine and $450 for possession of a switchblade knife.

751 "Brendan McAllister, 23, Dies In Virgin Islands." *The Newport Daily News*, August 18th, 1973.

752 Patricia A. McAllister, Born, 1952, Died 1987, Burial at Trinity Cemetary.

753 Author's interview with Brad Watterson, August 23rd, 2018.

754 In Re: Board of Medical Review Investigation 463 A 2d. 1373 (R.I. 1983) Supreme Court of Rhode Island.

755 Marie L. Emmy McAllister," 19 Chapel Terrace Apt. 324. *The Newport White Pages,* June 28th, 1990.

CHAPTER TWENTY-EIGHT

756 William Hand Browne, *George Calvert and Cecilius Calvert Barons Baltimore of Baltimore* (Dodd, Mead And Company New York, 1890).

757 Ricardo A. Herrera, "The Zealous Activity of Capt. Lee: Light Horse Harry and Petite Guerre," *Journal of Military History*, January, 2015.

758 "Services for Mrs. Beck," *The Newport Daily News,* April 18th, 1974.

759 "James Montgomery Beck '14," *Alumni Weekly*, Princeton, University Vol. 73 p. 136.

760 "Social Circles: Helicopter Party," *The Newport Daily News*, August 27th, 1962.

761 "C. of C. Unit Honors Mrs. James M. Beck," *The Newport Daily News,* May 28th, 1958.

762 Author's interview with Harley Tinney, June 14th, 2020.

763 "Mrs. James Beck, Founded Newport Music Carnival," *The New York Times*, April 18th, 1974.

764 Author's Interview with Norman Mather May 7th, 2020. Story told to the Author by Dorothy Holmwood, December 25th, 1962.

765 City Orders Extermination of Rats Infesting Cliff Area," *The Newport Daily News*, May 21st, 1965.

766 Ibid. Mather.

767 "Elaine Lorillard, 93, a Founder of The Newport Jazz Festival, Is Dead," *The New York Times*, November 28th, 2007.

768 "James Reed, "Founder Pitches In to Again Lead Newport Fests," *The Boston Globe,* March 4th, 2009.

769 Markus Jaeger, *Popular Is Not Enough: The Political Voice of Joan Baez* (Ibidem Press Stuttgart 2014).

770 Robert Shelton, *No Direction Home: The Life and Music of Bob Dylan*. (Da Capo Press Boston 2003). p. 302.

771 "Late Blooming Ticket Sales Assure Big Success For Carnival of Music," *The Newport Daily News,* August 2nd, 1957.

772 "Mayflower's Colorful Entry Captures Heart of Newport," *The Newport Daily News,* June 28th, 1957.

773 "Mayflowers Early Arrival Snafus Newport Reception – But All Ends Well," *The Newport Daily News,* June 28th, 1957.

774 The Hon. Clarissa Madeline Georgiana Felicite "Clare" Tennant Tennyson was the daughter of Edward Priaulx Tennant, 1st Baron Glenconner and Pamela Adelaide Genevieve Wyndham. She married, firstly, Captain William Adrian Vincent Bethell, son of William Bethell and Hon. Mairi Myrtle Willoughby, on August 18th, 1915. She and Captain William Adrian Vincent Bethell were divorced in 1918. She married, secondly, Major Lionel Hallam Tennyson, 3rd Baron Tennyson, son of Hallam Tennyson, 2nd Baron Tennyson and Audrey Georgiana Florence Boyle, on March 27th, 1918. She and Major Lionel Hallam Tennyson, 3rd Baron Tennyson were divorced in 1928. She married, thirdly, James Montgomery Beck, son of Hon. James Montgomery Beck, on July 24th, 1928. She and James Montgomery Beck were divorced in 1939 She died on September 3rd, 1960 at age 64. *The Peerage.com*

775 "James Montgomery Beck: 14," Obituary *Princeton Class of 1914* Vol. 73. p. 136.

776 "Will Hays; First Film Czar, Dies; Former G.O.P. Leader was 74," *The New York Times,* March 8th,1954.

777 A resolution incorporating the Don'ts and Be-Carefuls is now officially adopted by the MPPDA. A similar resolution (also included) was previously passed by the AMPP on June 8th, 1927, *MPPDA Digital Archive* Record # 365.

778 "Robert Goelet, Financier, Dead," *The New York Times,* February 7th, 1966.

779 Ibid.

780 "Helicopter Party," *The Newport Daily News,* August 27th, 1962.

781 Social Circles "White Elephant Ball Tops Holiday Entertaining Here," *The Newport Daily News*, September 4th, 1965.

782 Paul F. Miller, "Newport Mansions, 1886 to 1985," The Preservation Society of Newport County.

783 "Elinor D. Ingersoll," 68; Soup Company Director. *The New York Times*, January 10th, 1977.

784 "Look Inside Seafair; Jay Leno's Newport, RI, Ocean Drive Estate," *NewportBuzz,* December 7th, 2017.

785 "Seafair, a.k.a. 'The Hurricane Hut," *TheGildedAgeBlogspot* December 30th, 2013.

786 Author's interview with Norman Mather, Newport Police Dept. (ret) May 7th, 2020.

CHAPTER TWENTY-NINE

787 Ibid.

788 Author's interview with Eileen Brown, granddaughter of T.J. Brown, October 10th, 2020.

789 "Rita Dolan Sellar" Obituary, *The Hartfort Courant, December* 30th, 2006.

790 "Newport chateau sells for $7.75 million," *The Newport Daily News,* October 16th, 2008.

791 Author's interview with Harley Tinney, October 2nd, 2020.

792 Author's interview with Kim Canning, June 13th, 2020.

793 Author's interview with Ridgely Beck, June 20th 2020.

794 "J.M. Beck, Clubman, Dies At 80," *The Newport Daily News,* December 8th, 1972.

795 "Mrs. James Beck, Founded Newport Music Carnival," *The New York Times*, April 18th, 1974.

796 "Carter, Virginia, estate," *The Newport Daily News,* March 27th, 1974. "

797 Author's Interview with Ronald Oliver, August 5th, 2020.

798 William M. Kutik, "Gate-crasher gets into party by a unique vertical approach," *The Newport Daily News*, August 22nd, 1975."

799 Ibid.

800 Walecia Konrad," HAVENS; A Summer Job for Your Home," *The New York Times*, June 27th, 2003.

801 Newport Manor Sold for $5 million," *The Providence* Journal, October 14th, 2014.

802 Ibid. Ridgely Beck interview.

803 Stephen Gilbert, *Ratman's Notebooks*, (Viking, New York 1969).

804 "The Numbers, Top Grossing Movies of 1971." This database shows that "Williard," released on New Year's Day, grossed $14,545,941. 8,815,721 tickets were sold.

805 Vincent Canby, "Film: In 'Ben,' A Boy Befriends a Rat." *The New York Times*, June 24th, 1972.

806 Top 100 Hits of 1972, *Billboard Magazine*. Michael Jackson's rendition of "Ben," placed 20 out of the Top 100.

CHAPTER THIRTY

807 Anne Raver, "Transformation Includes Sacrifice," *The New York Times,* May 8th, 2008.

808 Edwardo Giuseppe Tirella. Birth Certificate. Rubenstein Library Box 350 Folder 4 p.1.

809 Author's interview with Donna Lohmeyer, November 5th, 2020.

810 "850 Women Attend, 'The Thing For Spring," *The Los Angeles Times*, January 27th, 1951.

811 "Labeling The Labels," *Inside S.F.A.* October, 1951.

812 "Flickerville Glamour Gals model ribbon creations at gala benefit," *Photoplay*, October 10th, 1951.

813 Jac Wilson, "Night Club Reviews," *The Hollywood Reporter*, January 12th, 1953.

814   Advertisement: The Don Sheffey Show at The Cabaret Concert Theater.

815   Barbara Lenox, "Rescued by Remodeling," *The Los Angeles Times,* January 26th, 1968.

816   Charles Woods, letter to Anita Tirella Aughey, January 29th, 1958.

817   Person to Person (*CBS*) Airdate October 20th, 1960. Episode Eight.

818   "Louella Parsons," "Hollywood Chit Chat, " *The Newark Star Ledger,* May 2nd, 1964.

819   U.S. Inflation Calculator

820   Author's interview with Steve Ransohoff, August 5th, 2020.

821   Author's interview with Kaffe Fassett, August 11th, 2020.

822   Deetjen's History, *Deetjen's Big Sur Inn.*

823   Author's interview with Pola Zanay, November 19th, 2018.

824   Author's interview with Donna Lohmeyer, November 8th, 2020.

CHAPTER THIRTY-ONE

825   Romney Steele, interview with Martin Ransohoff, March 13th, 2008.

826   Neil Genzlinger, "Martin Ransohoff, Producer of TV and Films, Dies at 90," *The New York Times,* December 17th, 2017.

827   Ibid. Steve Ransohoff, August 5th, 2020.

828   Vincent Bugliosi, *Helter-Skelter: The True Story of The Manson Murders* (W.W. Norton New York 1994). pp 26-27.

829   Ibid. Steve Ransohoff.

830   Ronald Bergan, "Martin Ransohoff Obituary," *The Guardian,* December 27th, 2017.

831   Romney Steele, *My Nepenthe: Bohemian Tales of Food, Family and Big Sur* (Andrews McMeel Publishing 1st Edition London 2009)

832   Ibid. Romney Steele, Martin Ransohoff interview.

833   Darwin Porter & Danforth Prince, *Elizabeth Taylor: There Is Nothing Like A Dame,* (Blood Moon Productions Ltd. 2012)

834   Ibid.

835   *Don't Make Waves,* Full Cast & Crew. The Internet Movie Data Base. 1967.

836   Ibid. Porter & Danforth. Richard Hanley, an Aide Of The Burtons, Dies at 61," *The New York Times,* January 3rd, 1971.

837 Michael Musto, "Was Vincent Minnelli A Gay?" *The Village Voice*, February 26th, 2010.

838 Ibid. Porter and Prince.

839 Author's interview with Kaffe Fassett August 20th, 2020.

840 Kaffe Fassett, *Dreaming In Color* (Stewart, Tabori & Change New York 2012).

841 Ibid, Author's interview.

842 Mary Bilinkas, "Tirella Buried in Family Plot Here, "*The Dover (New Jersey) Daily Advance,* October 11th, 1966.

843 Marilyn Kim (Novak) Mallory, email to the Author, August 16th, 2020.

844 Note from Peggy Lee to Anita Tirella Aughey, December 4th, 1966.

845 "Doris, Absent From Jersey Funeral Of Her Long-Time Friend, Eduardo," *New York Daily News*, October 12th, 1966.

846 Author's interview with David Rimmer, August 26th, 2020.

847 Author's interview with Peter Byrne, August 20th, 2020.

848 Riv Tobin, "New Host On The Honolulu scene." *The Honolulu Advertiser*, May 30th, 1967.

849 Memo and Invoice sent to Doris Duke from Edmund Kara. August 10th, 1966 re: his services for carving custom-made doors for the Self-Realization Fellowship. Rubenstein Library, Box 294 Folder 14. p. 3.

850 Hadley Mears, "From Hip Hotel to Holy Home: The Self Realization Fellowship on Mt. Washington," *KCET*, August 9th, 2013.

851 David M. Buss, "Jealousy, the necessary evil," *The Los Angeles Times,* February 14th, 2007.

CHAPTER THIRTY-TWO

852 The unlawful killing of a human being with malice aforethought is murder. Every murder perpetrated by poison, lying in wait, or any other kind of willful, deliberate, malicious, and premeditated killing... or committed against any law enforcement officer in the performance of his or her duty or committed against an assistant attorney general or special assistant attorney general in the performance of his or her duty, or perpetrated from a premeditated design unlawfully and maliciously to effect the death of any human being other than him or her who is killed, is murder in the first degree. Justia.com RI General Laws. Title 11 Criminal Offenses. Chapter 11-23 – Homicide Section 1-23.1 – Murder.

853 Any other murder is murder in the second degree. The degree of murder may be charged in the indictment or information, and the jury may find the degree of murder, whether the murder is charged in the indictment or information or not, or may find the defendant guilty of a lesser offense than that charged in the indictment or information, in accordance with the provisions of § 12-17-14.

854 (a) Every person who shall commit manslaughter shall be imprisoned not exceeding thirty (30) years.

855 (a) When the death of any person ensues as a proximate result of an injury received by the operation of any vehicle in reckless disregard of the safety of others, including violations of § 31-27-22, the person so operating the vehicle shall be guilty of "driving so as to endanger, resulting in death.". Justia.com codes Rhode Island Title 31, Chapters 31-27.

856 Alton Slagle, "Behind Iron Gate: Wealth Tragedy," *New York Daily News,* October 10th, 1966.

857 Ibid. *The Providence Journal* June 24th, 1971. Lewis A. Perrotti, "Investigator's and Examiner's Report" State of Rhode Island Providence Plantations Registry of Motor Vehicles, October 19th, 1966. p. 7.

858 Ibid. R. Edward Brown, sworn deposition. Rubenstein Library, Box 375 Folder 1. pp 88-89.

859 Ibid. Mansfield p. 266.

860 Ibid. Mansfield. p. 211.

861 Romano et. al vs. Avis June 2nd, 1968. Defendant's 6th Affirmative Defense.

862 State of Rhode Island Office of Chief Medical Examiner Laboratory Report T-281-667. October 11th, 1966.

863 Alton Slagle. "R.I. Law Chief Asks Full Report on Doris," *New York Daily News,* October 11th, 1966.

864 Office of The RI Secretary of State. Records Retention Schedule LG6.

865 Ibid. Mansfield correspondence to Aughey March 30th, 1990.

866 Romano et. al. vs. Avis U.S. Dist. Court, Case. No. 3870. Defendant's Answers Interrogatories. June 30th, 1968. Doris Duke's response to interrogatory No., 31: she replied as follows: "Edward Tirella drove the automobile up to 12 or 15 feet from the north gate. I was sitting in the passenger's seat. He got out to open the gate which was locked. I moved over to the driver's seat. I put my left foot on the brake and moved the gear shift lever from "park" to "drive." The car immediately moved forward through the gates and across Bellevue Avenue where it struck a fence and stopped."

867   Doris Duke Statement to Lt. Frank H. Walsh and Det. George Watts: October 9th, 1966: "'We were going out of the estate. Mr. Tirella was the operator. We did what we have done a hundred times before. The gate was locked. He was at the lock. The car was about 15 feet from the gate. I was getting ready to drive through the gate. The car just leaped forward and I was on top of him. He was in the middle of the gate, at the lock, at the time.'"

868   "Death Was Accidental, Doris Duke Tells Cops," *The Associated Press*, October 10th, 1966.

869   State of Rhode Island Office of Chief Medical Examiner Autopsy Report T-281-667, October 8th 1966.

870   1966 Dodge Polara Station Wagon 383 V-8 2-bbl. Torque Flite (aut. 3). Model since mid-year 1965 for North America U.S. car specifications & performance data review.

871   Statements Offered in Doris Duke Trial," *The Providence Journal,* June 22nd, 1971.

872   "If You Grew Up In Newport, RI, Share Some Memories," Facebook Group. Post by Jane Maguire May 6th, 2018.

873   Author's interview with John Quigley, June 15th, 2020.

874   Author's interview with Steve Mey, November 1st, 2020.

875   Author's interview with Joseph G. Silvia, December 10th, 2018.

876   Peter Lance, "The New Breed: Eight Rookies Train," *The Newport Daily News*, December 1st, 1967. The piece quotes Lt. Fred Newton: "Police work today is a far cry from what it was in the twenties and thirties,' said Lt. Frederick Newton, supervisor of the training program. 'A policeman has to know more, and he has to be able to use his knowledge in a technologically advanced society.'"

877   "Police Official Wins Advance," *Newport Daily News,* October 11th, 1972 (Newton named Assistant Chief); "Police Chief Upheld on Cop's Suspension, *Newport Daily News* March 27th, 1980. (Police Chief Frederick W. Newton).

878   Author's interview with Patrolman Edward E. Angel (Newport PD Ret.) October 26th, 2018.

879   Ibid.

880   Ibid. 1966 Dodge Polara Station Wagon 383 V-8 2-bbl. Specs,

881   "Doris Duke In Court On Death," *United Press International,* June 18th 1971.

882   Author's interview with Robert Aughey Jr. September 25th, 2018.

883 State of Rhode Island Office of Chief Medical Examiner Autopsy Report T-281-667. October 8th, 1966.

CHAPTER THIRTY-THREE

884 Author's interview with Det. Al Conti (Newport PD Ret.) January 20th, 2019.

885 Author's Interview with Inspector Norman Mather, June 25th, 2019.

886 Romano et. al. vs. Avis U.S. Dist. Court, Case. No. 3870. Defendant's Answers Interrogatories. June 30th, 1968. Doris Duke's response to interrogatory answer No., 27.

887 Stephanie Mansfield corresp to Anita Aughey March 30th, 1990.

888 Collision And Injury Dynamics.com

889 Author's interview with Henricus "Harm" Jansen March 7th, 2019.

CHAPTER THIRTY-FOUR-

890 Sheila Graham. Syndicated column January 16th, 1967.

891 Rough Point History Newport Restoration Foundation.

892 Author's interview with confidential source, December 6th, 2018.

893 Author's post on "If You Grew Up In Newport, RI," Facebook Group. October 10th, 2018. "I thank you and all of the wonderful people on this site; particularly Larry Bettencourt who regularly posts threads about this incident. I'm doing a book on Newport and it will include a major chapter on the death of Eduardo Tirella which took place 52 years ago last Sunday. Like all of you Newporters I want to find the REAL TRUTH behind what happened.

So far, I've uncovered some astonishing evidence and I've been able to talk to a number of people who observed the incident immediately after the fact. I've also spoken to some surviving veterans of the Newport Police Dept. and others who were related to the detectives who worked the case. One of my goals is to tell the real truth behind who Eduardo Tirella was. As I've learned after connecting with his family in NJ, he was a truly remarkable Renaissance man who had a highly successful Hollywood career and for nearly a decade designed the interiors of all of Miss Duke's homes in Hawaii, L.A. NYC, New Jersey and Rough Point in Newport. Tragically he was about to leave her to resume his life in Los Angeles-- literally intending to remove his paintings and other effects from Rough Point on the afternoon he was killed. As some have speculated Eduardo was gay and was not Doris Duke's lover but he was her "constant companion" for years and personally curated many of the great works of art you can see today if you take a tour of that amazing "summer cottage" @ 680 Bellevue Avenue. One little known fact about "Eddie" as his family called him, was that he was a war hero -- a veteran of The Battle of the Bulge where he won The Bronze Star and two Purple Hearts for his service to Gen. Patton. See a photo of that decoration attached. I ask any of you who are truly interested in the facts behind his death to email me @ pl@peterlance.com. Anyone who knows me understands that I ALWAYS keep my sources confidential. Anyway, I look forward to hearing from you.

894   "'Beyond Fortune: The Life and Legacy of Doris Duke" opens at Rough Point," Newport RI.com April 2nd, 2019 YouTube.

895   In a Facebook post on March 17th, 2020, the NRF reported that, "As of today, NRF is announcing that Rough Point Museum will be postponing its opening day to May 1st, 2020. We are monitoring the current situation closely and will continue to follow guidelines recommended by the State of Rhode Island and the CDC."

896   Charles A. Burns biography, Sotheby's Institute of Art.

897   Charles A. Burns, "Guardian Spirit: Newport Legacy of Doris Duke," *New York Social Diary*, January 22nd, 2020.

898   On May 23rd, 2013, Publisher's Marketplace announced the sale of the book at auction: *DORIS DUKE* by Sallie Bingham. Memoirist, fiction writer Sallie Bingham's *DORIS DUKE: The Invention of the New Woman*, drawing on extensive unexamined primary sources and offering a dramatically new portrait of the defiantly original tobacco heiress who was a war correspondent, surfer, early champion of Islamic art and land conservation, and perhaps the greatest modern woman philanthropist.

899   Sallie Bingham, *The Silver Swan: In Search of Doris Duke* (Farrar, Strauss and Giroux New York 2020).

900   David Leon Chandler with Mary Voelz Chandler *The Binghams of Louisville: The Dark History Behind One of America's Great Fortunes* (Crown, New York 1989).

901   Elizabeth Stewart, "Monograph on The Reliquary of St. Ursula at Rough Point," August 22nd, 2020.

902   Ibid.

903   Author's interview with Donna Lohmeyer, February 2nd, 2019.

904 Newport Restoration Foundation Curatorial note: indicate this reliquary (from the 1450s) is probably from St Ursula, but past staff stories tell us that Doris Duke used to call her St. Cecilia. St Cecilia is the patron of music and her feast date is the same as Doris Duke's birthday, November 22nd.

CHAPTER THIRTY-FIVE

905 Peter Lance, "Court Rules Irritate County's Police," *The Newport Daily News*, August 22nd, 1967.

906 Author's interview with Stephen Robertson May 23rd, 2020.

907 State vs. Johnson, Supreme Court of Rhode Island February 9th, 1979.

908 Ibid. Stephen Robertson interview.

909 The Crusader, Yearbook of De La Salle Academy, Class of 1965. p. 24.

910 Amanda Milkovits," "John Ouimette, mastermind of Bonded Vault heist, has died," *The Providence Journal*, March 27th, 2017.

911 Tim White, Randall Richard and Wayne Worcester, *The Last Good Heist: The Inside Story of The Biggest Single Payday in the Criminal History of the Northeast,* (Globe Pequot Guilford, CT 2016) .

912 Author's interview with Joseph A. Filipkowsi, May 29th, 2020.

913 Ibid.

914 Author's interview with Stephen Robertson, May 14th, 2020.

915 "6,000 Claim Against Clarke Estate Disallowed," *The Newport Daily News*, May 3rd, 1951.

INDEX

E

F

Z

CPSIA information can be obtained
at www.ICGtesting.com
Printed in the USA
LVHW101428191122
733599LV00019B/188/J

9 780996 285599